the Confederacy

Diaries, Memoirs and Letters of the Civil War

Jon—
Happy 45th!
Christine

We have attempted to reproduce this collection of letters, diaries and memoirs as closely to the original presentation as possible. In their own words, these men and women told of their experiences in the midst of or shortly after the Civil War. We have not corrected any grammatical or spelling errors and, with the exception of editing for length of inclusion and replacing derogatory terms with spaces, we have endeavored to preserve their accounts as originally written.

ISBN 978-1-882077-26-7

Editing by Amy Gary
Book Research by Michele Gay
Jacket and text design by TaylorDesign

Printed in China

Contents

A Rebel War Clerk's Diary

January 1st through May 12th, 1863

At The Confederate States Capital.

By J. B. Jones
Clerk In The War Department Of The Confederate States Government;
Author Of "Wild Western Scenes," Etc. Etc.

January 1st, 1863.—This first day of the year dawned in gloom, but the sun, like the sun of Austerlitz, soon beamed forth in great splendor upon a people radiant with smiles and exalted to the empyrean.

A letter from Gen. H. Marshall informed the government that Gen. Floyd had seized slaves in Kentucky and refused to restore them to their owners, and that if the government did not promptly redress the wrong, the Kentuckians would at once "take the law into their own hands."

We had a rumor (not yet contradicted) that the enemy, or traitors, had burned the railroad bridge between Bristol and Knoxville, cutting our communication with the West.

Then it was said (and it was true) that Gen. Lee had sent his artillery back some 30 miles this side of the Rappahannock, preparatory to going into winter quarters. But this was no occasion for gloom. Lee always knows what is best to be done.

Next there was a rumor (not yet confirmed, but credited) that Stuart had made another of his wonderful reconnoissances, capturing prisoners and destroying much of the enemy's stores beyond the Rappahannock.

Then came a dispatch from Bragg which put us almost "beside" ourselves with joy, and caused even enemies to pause and shake hands in the street. Yesterday he attacked Rosecrans's army near Murfreesborough, and gained a great victory. He says he drove him from all his positions, except on the extreme left, and after ten hours' fighting, occupied the whole of the field except (those exceptions!) the point named. We had, as trophies, thirty-one guns, two generals, 4000 prisoners, and 200 wagons. This is a Western dispatch, it is true, but it has Bragg's name to it, and he does not willingly exaggerate. Although I, for one, shall await the next dispatches with anxiety, there can be no question about the victory on the last day of the bloody year 1862. Bragg says the loss was heavy on both sides.

I noticed that one of the brass pieces sent down by Lee to go to North Carolina had been struck by a ball just over the muzzle, and left a glancing mark toward the touch-hole. That ball, probably, killed one of our gunners.

January 2d.—A dispatch from Gov. Harris gives some additional particulars of the battle near Murfreesborough, Tenn. He says the enemy was driven back six miles, losing four generals killed and three captured, and that we destroyed $2,000,000 commissary and other stores. But still we have no account of what was done yesterday on the "extreme left."

Gen. Stuart has been near Alexandria, and his prisoners are coming in by every train. He captured and destroyed many stores, and, up to the last intelligence, without loss on his side. He is believed, now, to be in Maryland, having crossed the Potomac near Leesburg.

The mayor of our city, Jos. Mayo, meeting two friends last night, whom he recognized but who did not recognize him, playfully seized one of them, a judge, and, garroter fashion, demanded his money or his life. The judge's friend fell upon the mayor with a stick and beat him dreadfully before the joke was discovered.

The President was at Mobile on the 30th December, having visited both Murfreesborough and Vicksburg, but not witnessing either of the battles.

We are in great exaltation again! Dispatches from Gen. Bragg, received last night, relieve us with the information that the stronghold of the enemy, which he failed to carry on the day of battle, was abandoned the next day; that Forrest and Morgan were operating successfully far in the rear of the invader, and that Gen. Wheeler had made a circuit of the hostile army after the battle, burning several hundred of their wagons, capturing an ordnance train, and making more prisoners. Bragg says the enemy's telegraphic and railroad communications with his rear have been demolished, and that he will follow up the defeated foe. I think we will get Nashville now.

January 3d.—To-day we have a dispatch from Vicksburg stating that the enemy had re-embarked, leaving their intrenching instruments, etc., apparently abandoning the purpose of assaulting the city. This is certainly good news.

Gen. Stuart did not cross the Potomac, as reported in the Northern press, but, doubtless, the report produced a prodigious panic among the Yankees. But when Stuart was within eight miles of Alexandria, he telegraphed the government at Washington that if they did not send forward larger supplies of stores to Burnside's army, he (Stuart) would not find it worth while to intercept them.

Capt. Semmes, of the Alabama, has taken another prize—the steamer Ariel—but no gold being on board, and having 800 passengers, he released it, under bonds to pay us a quarter million dollars at the end of the war.

A large meeting has been held in New York, passing resolutions in favor of peace. They propose that New Jersey send a delegation hither to induce us to meet the United States in convention at Louisville, to adopt definitive terms of peace, on the basis of the old Union, or, that being impracticable, separation. Too late!

January 4th.—We have nothing additional from Murfreesborough, but it is ascertained that the bridges burned by the enemy on the Virginia and Tennessee Railroad cannot be repaired in a month.

It really does seem that some potent and malign influence, resident at the capital, some high functionary, by some species of occultation, controlling the action of the government, a Talleyrand in the pay of both governments, and balancing or equalizing disasters between them to magnify his importance and increase his reward, has been controlling many events since the beginning of this war, and is still engaged in the diabolical work. It now appears that several regiments were withdrawn from the vicinity of Bristol, whose presence there was necessary for the protection of the railroad and the bridges. They were brought hither after Lee's defeat of Burnside, for the protection of the capital! The President was away, and Mr. Seddon was now in the War Office. But Gen. Cooper is old in office, and should have known better; and Gen. G. W. Smith certainly must have known better. Just suppose we had been beaten at Murfreesborough, and our communications cut, west and east and south! There would have been no escape.

It had even been proposed to take a large portion of Lee's men from him, so that he must be inevitably defeated on the Rappahannock, but Lee's resignation would have shocked the people unbearably. Great injury was done him by abstracting some 20,000 of his men by discharges, transfers, and details. Nothing but his generalship and the heroism of his men saved us from ruin. The disasters of Donelson, Newbern, Nashville, Memphis, Roanoke, New Orleans, Norfolk, etc. may be traced to the same source. But all new governments have been afflicted by a few evil-disposed leaders.

Our people in arms have upheld the State; they have successfully resisted the open assaults of the invader, and frustrated the occult machinations of the traitors in our midst. We have great generals, but what were they without great men to obey them? Generals have fallen, and divisions and brigades have fought on without them. Regiments have lost their field officers and continued the fight, and companies have maintained their position after all their commissioned officers were stricken down. The history which shall give the credit of their achievements to others will be a vile calumny. Our cause would have been ruined if it had not been for the bravery and heroism of the people—the privates in our armies.

There is a rumor this morning that the enemy are advancing toward Petersburg from Suffolk. If this be so, some spy, under the protection of martial law, has informed the Yankees of our defenseless condition at that place, being alarmed at the success of our brave and patriotic men in the West.

January 5th.—We learn from Gen. Bragg that the enemy did not retire far on the 2d inst., but remain still in the vicinity of Murfreesborough. He says, however, that our cavalry are still circling the Yankees, taking prisoners and destroying stores. During the day an absurd rumor was invented, to the effect that Bragg had been beaten. We are anxious to learn the precise particulars of the battle. It is to be feared that too many of Bragg's men were ordered to reinforce Pemberton. If that blunder should prove disastrous, the authorities here will have a hornet's nest about their ears. The President arrived yesterday, and his patriotic and cheering speech at Jackson, Miss., appeared in all the papers this morning.

We hear of no fighting at Suffolk. But we have dispatches from North Carolina, stating that a storm assailed the enemy's fleet off Hatteras, sinking the Monitor with all on board, and so crippling the Galena that her guns were thrown overboard! This is good news—if it be confirmed.

A letter from Major Boyle, in command at Gordonsville, gives information that the smugglers and extortioners are trading tobacco (contraband) with the enemy at Alexandria. He arrested B. Nussbaum, E. Wheeler, and S. Backrack, and sent them with their wagons and goods to Gen. Winder, Richmond. But instead of being dealt with according to law, he learns that Backrack is back again, and on his way to this city with another wagon load of goods from Yankee-land, and will be here to-day or to-morrow. I sent the letter to the Secretary, and hope it will not be intercepted on its way to him from the front office. The Secretary never sees half the letters addressed him, or knows of one-half the attempts of persons to obtain interviews. The Assistant Secretary's duty is to dispose of the less important communications, but to exhibit his decisions.

January 6th.—To-day we are all down again. Bragg has retreated from Murfreesborough. It is said he saved his prisoners, captured cannon, etc., but it is not said what became of his own wounded. The Northern papers say they captured 500 prisoners in the battle, which they claim as a victory. I do not know how to reconcile Bragg's first dispatches, and particularly the one saying he had the whole field, and would follow the enemy, with this last one announcing his withdrawal and retirement from the field.

Eight thousand men were taken from Bragg a few days before the battle. It was not done at the suggestion of Gen. Johnston; for I have seen an extract of a letter from Gen. J. to a Senator (Wigfall), deprecating the detachment of troops from Bragg, and expressing grave apprehensions of the probable consequences.

A letter was received from R. R. Collier, Petersburg, to-day, in favor of civil liberty, and against the despotism of martial law.

Senator Clark, of Missouri, informed me to-day that my nephew, R. H. Musser, has been made a colonel (under Hindman or Holmes), and has a fine regiment in the trans-Mississippi Department.

Lewis E. Harvie, president of the railroad, sends a communication to the Secretary (I hope it will reach him) inclosing a request from Gen. Winder to permit liquors to be transported on his road to Clover Hill. Mr. Harvie objects to it, and asks instructions from the Secretary. He says Clover Hill is the point from which the smuggling is done, and that to place it there, is equivalent to bringing it into the city.

January 7th.—To-day I was requested to aid, temporarily, in putting in operation a new bureau, created by the military authorities, not by law, entitled the Bureau of Conscription. From conscription all future recruits must be derived. I found Gen. Rains, the chief, a most affable officer; and Lieut.-Col. Lay, his next officer, was an acquaintance. I shall not now, perhaps, see so much of the interior of this moving picture of Revolution; my son, however, will note important letters. It is said that Sumner's corps (of Burnside's army) has landed in North Carolina, to take Wilmington. We shall have news soon.

We are sending troops rapidly from Virginia to North Carolina.

The Northern papers say the following dispatch was sent to Washington by our raiding Stuart: "Gen. Meigs will in future please furnish better mules; those you have furnished recently are very inferior." He signed his own name.

A large body of slaves passed through the city to-day, singing happily. They had been working on the fortifications north of the city, and go to work on them south of it. They have no faith in the efficacy of Lincoln's Emancipation.

But it is different in Norfolk; 4000 enfranchised slaves marched in procession through the town the other day in a sort of frantic jubilee. They will bewail their error; and so will the Abolitionists. They will consume the enemy's commissary stores; and if they be armed, we shall get their arms.

Lee and Beauregard were telegraphed to-day in relation to the movement on Wilmington; and the President had the cabinet with him many hours.

Gen. Rains is quite certain that the fall of New Orleans was the result of treachery.

By the emancipation, Gen. Wise's county, Princess Ann, is excepted—and so are Accomac and Northampton Counties; but I have no slaves. All I ask of the invaders is to spare my timber, and I will take care of the land—and I ask it, knowing the request will never be known by them until the war is over.

January 8th.—Gen. French writes that the enemy at Suffolk and Newbern amounted to 45,000; and this force now threatens Weldon and Wilmington, and we have not more than 14,000 to oppose them. With generalship that should suffice.

All the Virginia conscripts are ordered to Gen. Wise, under Major-Gen. Elzey. The conscripts from other States are to be taken to Gen. Lee. If the winter should allow a continuance of active operations, and the enemy should continue to press us, we might be driven nearly to the wall. We must help ourselves all we can, and, besides, invoke the aid of Almighty God!

We have nothing fresh from Bragg—nothing from Vicksburg—and that is bad news.

I like Gen. Rains. He comes in and sits with me every day. Col. Lay is the active business man of the bureau. The general is engaged in some experiments to increase the efficiency of small arms.

He is very affable and communicative. He says he never witnessed more sanguinary fighting than at the battle of the Seven Pines, where his brigade retrieved the fortunes of the day; for at one time it was lost. He was also at Yorktown and Williamsburg; and he cannot yet cease condemning the giving up of the Peninsula, Norfolk, etc. Gen. Johnston did that, backed by Randolph and Mallory.

We have all been mistaken in the number of troops sent to the rescue of North Carolina; but four or five regiments, perhaps 3000 men, have gone thither from Virginia. A letter from Gen. Lee, dated the 5th inst., says he has not half as many men as Burnside, and cannot spare any. He thinks North Carolina, herself, will be able to expel the Federals, who probably meditate only a marauding expedition. And he supposes Bragg's splendid victory (what did he suppose the next day?) may arrest the inroads of the enemy everywhere for a season. At this moment I do not believe we have 200,000 men in the field against 800,000! But what of that, after seeing Lee beat 150,000 with only 20,000 in action! True, it was an ambuscade.

January 9th.—The Northern papers say the Federals have taken Vicksburg; but we are incredulous. Yet we have no reliable intelligence from thence; and it may be so. It would be a terrible blow, involving, for a time, perhaps, the loss of the Mississippi River.

But we have cheering news from Galveston, Texas. Several of our improvised gun-boats attacked the enemy's war vessels in the harbor, and after a sanguinary contest, hand to hand, our men captured the Harriet Lane, a fine United States ship of war, iron clad. She was boarded and taken. Another of the enemy's ships, it is said, was blown up by its officers, rather than surrender, and many perished. If this be Magruder's work, it will make him famous.

Our public offices are crowded with applicants for clerkships, mostly wounded men, or otherwise unfit for field duty.

How can we live here? Boarding is $60 per month, and I have six to support! They ask $1800 rent for a dwelling—and I have no furniture to put in one. Gen. Rains and

I looked at one to-day, thinking to take it jointly. But neither of us is able to furnish it. Perhaps we shall take it, nevertheless.

January 10th.—We have news from the West, which is believed to be reliable, stating that Bragg captured 6000 prisoners altogether in his late battles; took 30 cannon, 800 stand of arms, and destroyed 1500 wagons and many stores. The estimated loss of the enemy in killed and wounded is put down at 12,000. Our loss in killed and wounded not more than half that number.

To-day we have official intelligence confirming the brilliant achievement at Galveston; and it was Magruder's work. He has men under him fitted for desperate enterprises; and he has always had a penchant for desperate work. So we shall expect to hear of more gallant exploits in that section. He took 600 prisoners.

We have news also from Vicksburg, and the city was not taken; on the contrary, the enemy had sailed away. I trust this is reliable; but the Northern papers persist in saying that Vicksburg has fallen, and that the event took place on the 3d inst.

Six hundred women and children—refugees—arrived at Petersburg yesterday from the North. They permit them to come now, when famine and pestilence are likely to be added to the other horrors of war! We are doomed to suffer this winter!

January 11th.—The message of Gov. Seymour, of New York, if I am not mistaken in its import and purposes, will have a distracting effect on the subjugation programme of the government at Washington. I shall look for riots, and perhaps rebellions and civil wars in the North.

Mr. Stanley, ycleped Governor of North Carolina, has written a letter (dated 31st December) to Gen. French, complaining that our soldiery have been guilty of taking slaves from their humane and loyal masters in Washington County, against their will; and demanding a restoration of them to their kind and beneficent owners, to whom they are anxious to return. Gen. French replies that he will do so very cheerfully, provided the United States authorities will return the slaves they have taken from masters loyal to the Confederate States. These may amount to 100,000. And he might have added that on the next day all—4,000,000—were to be emancipated, so far as the authority of the United States could accomplish it.

The enemy's gun-boats (two) came up the York River last week, and destroyed an oyster boat. Beyond the deprivation of oysters, pigs, and poultry, we care little for these incursions.

Confederate battery with Federal transports in the background

January 12th.—The news of the successful defense of Vicksburg is confirmed by an official dispatch, to the effect that the enemy had departed up the Mississippi River. By the late Northern papers, we find they confess to a loss of 4000 men in the several attacks upon the town! Our estimate of their loss did not exceed that many hundred. They lost two generals, Morgan and another. We did not lose a hundred men, according to our accounts. The Herald (N. Y.) calls it "another Fredericksburg affair."

The estimate of the enemy's loss, at Murfreesborough, from 12,000 to 20,000, in killed, wounded, and prisoners, and ours at from four to nine thousand. Bragg says he will fight again near the same place, and his men are in high spirits.

Our men fight to kill now, since the emancipation doom has been pronounced. But we have had a hard rain and nightly frosts, which will put an end to campaigning during the remainder of the winter. The fighting will be on the water, or near it.

The legislature is in session, and resolutions inimical to the passport system have already been introduced. But where are State Rights now?

Congress meets to-morrow.

January 13th.—The generals in North Carolina are importunate for reinforcements. They represent the enemy as in great force, and that Weldon, Goldsborough, Raleigh, and Wilmington are in extreme peril. Lee cannot send any, or, if he does, Richmond will be threatened again, and possibly taken.

How shall we live? Boarding ranges from $60 to $100 per month. Our landlord says he will try to get boarding in the country, and if he succeeds, probably we may keep the house we now occupy, furnished, at a rent of $1200, for a mere robin's nest of four rooms! But I hope to get the house at the corner of First and Casey, in conjunction with Gen. Rains, for $1800. It has a dozen rooms.

January 14th.—Gen. Beauregard, some of whose forces have been taken from him and sent to the defense of Wilmington, is apprehensive that they may be lost, in the event of the enemy making a combined naval and land attack, and then Charleston and Savannah would be in great peril. Gens. Smith and Whiting call lustily for aid, and say they have not adequate means of defense.

Some 4000 more negroes have been called for to work on the fortifications near Richmond. I believe 10,000 are at work now.

A letter "by order" of the Secretary of War to Col. Godwin, in King and Queen County, written by Judge Campbell, says that blockaders are allowed to run through, provided they be not suspicious parties. The government takes what it wants at seventy-five per cent. and releases the rest. The parties are liable to have their goods confiscated by the Secretary of the Treasury, who, however, the letter proceeds to say, has never molested any one in the illicit trade—smuggling.

In Congress, yesterday, Mr. Foote called for a committee to investigate the commissary's contract with Haxhall, Crenshaw & Co., and was particularly severe on Major Ruffin, in the commissary's office, whom he understood was a partner in the flour concern.

Mr. Foote introduced a series of resolutions to-day, tempting the Northern States to make peace with us separately, excluding the New England States, and promising commercial advantages, etc. But we must treat as independent States, pledging a league with those that abandon the United States Government—offensive and defensive—and guaranteeing the navigation of the Mississippi River to the Northwestern States. They were referred to the Committee on Foreign Relations, of which he is the chairman. This is nothing.

But neither yesterday nor the day before was there a quorum of both houses; a sad spectacle in such a season of gloom. It was enlivened, however, by a communication from the Surgeon-General, proposing to send surgeons to vaccinate all the members. They declined the honor, though the small-pox is raging frightfully.

To-day a quorum was found in each house, and the President's message was sent in. I have not read it yet.

January 15th.—The President's message is highly applauded. It is well written; but I do not perceive much substance in it, besides some eloquent reproaches of England and France for the maintenance of their neutrality, which in effect is greatly more beneficial to the United States than to us. The President essays to encourage the people to continued effort and endurance—and such encouragement is highly judicious at this dark epoch of the struggle. He says truly we have larger armies, and a better supply of arms, etc., now, than we have had at any time previously.

The President says he will, unless Congress directs differently, have all Federal officers that we may capture, handed over to the States to be dealt with as John Brown was dealt with. The Emancipation Proclamation, if not revoked, may convert the war into a most barbarous conflict.

Mr. Foote, yesterday, introduced a resolution requesting the recall of our diplomatic agents; and, after a certain time, to notify the foreign consuls to leave the country, no longer recognizing them in an official capacity.

A bill was introduced making Marylanders subject to conscription.

January 16th.—Gen. Lee is in the city, doubtless to see about the pressure upon him for reinforcements in North Carolina. Gen. Smith still writes from Goldsborough for more men, with doleful forebodings if they be refused.

From Eastern Tennessee, we have bad accounts of outrages by the disloyal inhabitants, who have fled, to escape conscription, to the mountains and caves, many of them taking their families. At night they emerge from their hiding-places, and commit depredations on the secessionists.

It has been blowing a gale for two days, and there are rumors of more losses of the enemy's ships on the coast of North Carolina.

A letter was received by the government to-day from Arizona, justifying Col. Baylor for his policy of dealing with the Indians. I do not hear of any steps yet on the part of the President.

A report of the commandant at Camp Holmes, Raleigh, N. C., states that 12,000 conscripts have been received there altogether; 8000 have been sent off to regiments, 2000 detailed on government work, 500 deserted, etc.

The Enquirer to-day publishes the fact that a ship, with stores, merchandise, etc., has just arrived at Charleston; that six more are on the way thither, and that a steamer has successfully run the blockade from Wilmington with cotton. This notification may increase the vigilance of the blockading fleet. The Enquirer is also perpetually tilting with the Raleigh Standard. I doubt the policy of charging the leading journals in North Carolina with predilections for the Union. I believe the Enquirer has no settled editor now.

Mr. Foote favors the conscription of Marylanders. If such an act should be likely to pass, Gen. Winder will be beset with applications to leave the Confederacy.

January 17th.—Gen. Lee has left the city. His troops, encamped thirty miles north of Richmond, marched northward last night. So it is his determination to cross the Rappahannock? Or is it a demonstration of the enemy to prevent him from sending reinforcements to North Carolina? We shall know speedily.

North Carolina, one would think, is soon to be the scene of carnage; and it is asked what can 16,000 men do against 60,000?

The enemy began the attack on Fort Caswell yesterday; no result. But one of his blockaders went ashore in the storm, and we captured the officers and crew.

All the conscripts in the West have been ordered to Gen. Bragg.

Shall we starve? Yesterday beef was sold for 40 cts. per pound; to-day it is 60 cts. Lard is $1.00. Butter $2.00. They say the sudden rise is caused by the prisoners of Gen. Bragg, several thousand of whom have arrived here, and they are subsisted from the market. Thus they injure us every way. But, n'importe, say some; if Lincoln's Emancipation be not revoked, but few more prisoners will be taken on either side. That would be a barbarous war, without quarter.

I see that Col. J. W. Wall, of New Jersey, has been nominated, and I suppose will be elected, U. S. Senator. He was confined for months in prison at Fort Lafayette. I imagine the colonel is a bold, able man.

January 18th.—It was bitter cold last night, and everything is frozen this morning; there will be abundance of ice next summer, if we keep our ice-houses.

In these times of privation and destitution, I see many men, who were never prominent secessionists, enjoying comfortable positions, and seeking investments for their surplus funds. Surely there must be some compensation in this world or the next for the true patriots who have sacrificed everything, and still labor in subordinate positions, with faith and patient suffering. These men and their families go in rags, and upon half-rations, while the others fare most sumptuously.

We are now, in effect, in a state of siege, and none but the opulent, often those who have defrauded the government, can obtain a sufficiency of food and raiment. Calico, which could once be bought for 12½ cts. per yard, is now selling at $2.25, and a lady's dress of calico costs her about $30.00. Bonnets are not to be had. Common bleached cotton shirting brings $1.50 per yard. All other dry goods are held in the same proportion. Common tallow candles are $1.25 per pound; soap, $1.00; hams, $1.00; oppossum $3.00; turkeys $4 to $11.00; sugar, brown, $1.00; molasses $8.00 per gallon; potatoes $6.00 per bushel, etc.

These evils might be remedied by the government, for there is no great scarcity of any of the substantials and necessities of life in the country, if they were only equally distributed. The difficulty is in procuring transportation, and the government monopolizes the railroads and canals.

Our military men apprehend no serious consequences from the army of negroes in process of organization by the Abolitionists at Washington. Gen. Rains says the negro cannot fight, and will always run away. He told me an anecdote yesterday which happened under his own observation. An officer, when going into battle, charged his servant to stay at his tent and take care of his property. In the fluctuations of the battle, some of the enemy's shot fell in the vicinity of the tent, and the negro, with great white eyes, fled away with all his might. After the fight, and when the officer returned to his tent, he was vexed to learn that his slave had run away, but the boy soon returned, confronting his indignant master, who threatened to chastise him for disobedience of orders. Cæsar said: "Massa, you told me to take care of your property, and dis property" (placing his hand on his breast) "is worf fifteen hundred dollars." He escaped punishment.

Some 200,000 of the Abolition army will be disbanded in May by the expiration of their terms of enlistment, and we have every reason to believe that their places cannot be filled by new recruits. If we hold out until then, we shall be able to resist at all vital points.

January 19th.—We have rumors of fighting this morning on the Rappahannock; perhaps the enemy is making another advance upon Richmond.

There was a grand funeral to-day,—Gen. D. R. Jones's; he died of heart disease.

Gen. Bragg dispatches that Brig.-Gen. Wheeler, with his cavalry, got in the rear of Rosecrans a few days ago, and burned a railroad bridge. He then penetrated to the Cumberland River, and destroyed three large transports and bonded a fourth, which took off his paroled prisoners. After this he captured and destroyed a gun-boat and its armament sent in quest of him.

We have taken Springfield, Missouri.

Rosecrans sends our officers, taken at Murfreesborough, to Alton, Ill., to retaliate on us for the doom pronounced in our President's proclamation, and one of his generals has given notice that if we burn a railroad bridge (in our own country) all private property within a mile of it shall be destroyed. The black flag next.

We have no news from North Carolina.

Mr. Caperton was elected C. S. Senator by the Virginia Legislature on Saturday, in place of Mr. Preston, deceased.

An intercepted letter from a Mr. Sloane, Charlotte, N. C., to A. T. Stewart & Co., New York, was laid before the Secretary of War yesterday. He urged the New York merchant, who has contributed funds for our subjugation, to send merchandise to the South, now destitute, and he would act as salesman. The Secretary indorsed "conscript him," and yet the Assistant Secretary has given instructions to Col. Godwin, in the border counties, to wink at the smugglers. This is consistency! And the Assistant Secretary writes "by order of the Secretary of War!"

January 20th.—The rumor of fighting on the Rappahannock is not confirmed. But Gen. Lee writes that his beeves are so poor the soldiers won't eat the meat. He asks the government to send him salt meat.

From Northern sources we learn that Arkansas Post has fallen, and that we have lost from 5000 to 7000 men there. If this be true, our men must have been placed in a mantrap, as at Roanoke Island.

Mr. Perkins, in Congress, has informed the country that Mr. Memminger, the Secretary of the Treasury, has hitherto opposed and defeated the proposition that the government buy all the cotton. Mr. M. should never have been appointed. He is headstrong, haughty, and tyrannical when he imagines he is dealing with inferiors, and he deems himself superior to the rest of mankind. But he is no Carolinian by birth or descent.

We see accounts of public meetings in New Jersey, wherein the government at Washington is fiercely denounced, and peace demanded, regardless of consequences. Some of the speakers openly predicted that the war would spread into the North, if not terminated at once, and in that event, the emancipationists would have foes to fight elsewhere than in the South. Among the participants I recognize the names of men whom I met in convention at Trenton in 1860. They clamor for the "Union as it was, the Constitution as it is," adopting the motto of my paper, the "Southern Monitor," the office of which was sacked in Philadelphia in April, 1861. Our government will never agree to anything short of independence. President Davis will be found inflexible on that point.

There was a rumor yesterday that France had recognized us. The news of the disaster of Burnside at Fredericksburg having certainly been deemed very important in Europe. But France has not yet acted in our behalf. We all pray for the Emperor's intervention. We suffer much, and but little progress is made in conscription. Nearly all our resources are in the field. Another year of war, and ——!

January 21st.—Last night the rain fell in torrents, and to-day there is a violent storm of wind from the N. W. This may put an end, for a season, to campaigning on land, and the enemy's fleet at sea may be dispersed. Providence may thus intervene in our behalf.

It is feared that we have met with a serious blow in Arkansas, but it is not generally believed that so many (5000 to 7000 men) surrendered, as is stated in the Northern papers. Gen. Holmes is responsible for the mishap.

Conscription drags its slow length along. It is not yet adding many to the army. The Assistant Secretary of War, and several others, "by order of the Secretary of War," are granting a fearful number of exemptions daily. Congress, I hope, will modify the exemption bill immediately. It is believed enrolling officers, surgeons, and others are permitting thousands to remain at home "for a price." Even clerks in the War Department, it is said, are driving a lucrative business in "getting men off," who should be on duty, in this war of independence. Young men in the departments, except in particular cases, will not stand in good repute "when the hurly burly's done, when the battle's lost and won."

Congress is at work projecting the organization of a Supreme Court.

January 22d.—We have reliable intelligence of the sinking of the U. S. gun-boat Hatteras, in the Gulf, by the Alabama. She was iron-clad, and all the officers and crew, with the exception of five, went down.

Gen. Whiting telegraphs to-day for the use of conscripts near Wilmington, in the event of an emergency. Several ships have just come in safely from abroad, and it is said a large number are on the way.

Mr. Miles yesterday reported, from the Military Committee, a bill repealing the existing exemption law, and embracing all male residents between the ages of 18 and 45 years. The President, or Secretary of War, to have authority to grant exemptions in certain cases, if deemed expedient. This ought to give us 200,000 more men. And they will be required.

A resolution was passed demanding of the Commissary and Quartermaster-General the number of their employees capable of performing military duty. It would be well to extend the inquiry to the War Department itself.

A letter from Norfolk states that at a grand ball, in celebration of the emancipation of the negroes, Gen. Vieille opened the dance with a mulatto woman of bad character as his partner; and Mrs. V. had for her partner a negro barber.

January 23d.—The Northern papers are filled with what purports to be the intercepted correspondence of Mr. Benjamin with Messrs. Mason and Slidell. Lord John Russell is berated. The Emperor of France is charged with a design to seize Mexico as a colony, and to recognize Texas separately, making that State in effect a dependency, from which cotton may be procured as an offset to British India. He says the French Consuls in Texas are endeavoring to detach Texas from the Confederacy. If this be a genuine correspondence, it will injure the South; if it be false (if the allegations be false), it will still injure us. I have no doubt of its genuineness; and that Mr. Sanders, once the correspondent of the New York Tribune, was the bearer. If Texas leaves us, so may Louisiana—and the gigantic Houmas speculation may turn out well at last.

Mr. Curry has brought forward a copyright bill; Mr. Foster, of Alabama, has introduced a bill to abolish the passport system—leaving the matter to railroad conductors.

A dispatch from Gen. Bragg assures us that our cavalry are still capturing and destroying large amounts of Rosecrans's stores on the Cumberland River.

Col. Wall has been elected Senator from New Jersey. They say he is still pale and ill from his imprisonment, for opinion sake. I hope he will speak as boldly in the Senate as out of it.

I met Gen. Davis to-day (the President's nephew), just from Goldsborough, where his brigade is stationed. He is in fine plumage—and I hope he will prove a game-cock.

Major-Gen. French, in command at Petersburg, is a Northern man. Our native generals are brigadiers. It is amazing that all the superior officers in command near the capital should be Northern men. Can this be the influence of Gen. Cooper? It may prove disastrous!

January 24th.—Gen. Smith writes that he deems Wilmington in a condition to resist any attacks.

The exposition of Mr. Benjamin's dispatches has created profound mortification in the community.

Another transport has been taken from the enemy in the Cumberland River. No further news from Arkansas.

There is a white flag (small-pox) within seventy yards of our house. But it is probable we must give up the house soon, as the owner is desirous to return to it—being unable to get board in the country.

Gen. Rains, who has been making a certain sort of primer, met with an accident this morning; one of them exploded in his hand, injuring his thumb and finger. He was scarcely able to sign his name to official documents to-day.

Mr. Hunter has brought forward a measure for the funding of Treasury notes, the redundant circulation having contributed to produce the present fabulous prices in the market.

In the New Jersey Legislature petitions are flowing in denunciatory of Lincoln's Emancipation scheme, which would cast into the free States a large excess of profitless population.

Gabriel J. Rains, C.S.A.

January 25th.—Gen. Lee mentions, in his recent correspondence, an instance of the barbarity of some of the Yankee soldiers in the Abolition Army of the Potomac. They thrust into the Rappahannock River a poor old negro man, whom they had taken from his master, because he had the small-pox; and he would have been drowned had he not been rescued by our pickets. It is surmised that this dreadful disease prevails to an alarming extent in the Yankee army, and probably embarrasses their operations. Our men have all been vaccinated; and their recklessness of disease and death is perhaps a guarantee of exemption from affliction. Their health, generally, is better than it has ever been before.

The government at Washington has interdicted the usual exchange of newspapers, for the present. This gives rise to conjecture that Lincoln experiences grave difficulties from the adverse sentiment of his people and his armies regarding his Emancipation Proclamation. And it is likely he has met with grave losses at sea, for the invading army in North Carolina has retired back on Newbern. But the season for naval enterprises is not over, and we are prepared to expect some heavy blows before April.

The revelations in the intercepted dispatches captured with Mr. Sanders, whose father is a notorious political adventurer, may be most unfortunate. They not only show that we even were negotiating for six war steamers, but give the names of the firms in Europe that were to furnish them. The project must now be abandoned. And Louis Napoleon will be enraged at the suspicions and imputations of our Secretary of State regarding his occult policy.

Gen. Rains has invented a new primer for shell, which will explode from the slightest pressure. The shell is buried just beneath the surface of the earth, and explodes when a horse or a man treads upon it. He says he would not use such a weapon in ordinary warfare; but has no scruples in resorting to any means of defense against an army of Abolitionists, invading our country for the purpose, avowed, of extermination. He tried a few shell on the Peninsula last spring, and the explosion of only four sufficed to arrest the army of invaders, and compelled them to change their line of march.

January 26th.—The Northern papers say Hooker's grand division crossed the Rappahannock, ten miles above Falmouth, several days ago.

Burnside has issued an address to his army, promising them another battle immediately.

Gen. Lee advises the government to buy all the grain in the counties through which the canal runs. He says many farmers are hoarding their provisions, for extortionate prices.

I have no house yet. Dr. Wortham had one; and although I applied first, he let Mr. Reagan, the Postmaster-General, have it. He is a member of President Davis's cabinet—and receives $6000 salary.

There is much indignation expressed by the street talkers against Mr. Benjamin and Mr. Sanders, in the matter of the intercepted dispatches: against Mr. Benjamin for casting such imputations on Napoleon and his consular agents, and for sending his dispatches by such a messenger, in the absence of the President; against Sanders for not destroying the dispatches. Many think the information was sold to the United States Government.

Col. Wall has made a speech in Philadelphia. He said he should take his seat in the United States Senate as an advocate of peace; and he boldly denounced the Lincoln administration.

Our official report shows that our military authorities, up to this time, have burnt 100,000 bales of cotton in Arkansas. I have not learned the amount destroyed in other States—but it is large. Gen. Lee thinks the object of the expeditions of the enemy on the Southern coast is to procure cotton, etc. The slaves can do them no good, and the torch will disappoint the marauders.

Strong and belligerent resolutions have been introduced in the United States Congress against France, for her alleged purpose to obtain dominion in Mexico. It is violative of the Monroe doctrine. And Mr. Benjamin's accusation against the consuls (embracing a French design on Texas) might seem like a covert purpose to unite both the Confederate and the United States against France—and that might resemble premeditated reconstruction. But diplomatists must be busy—always at their webs. President Davis would be the last man to abandon the ship Independence.

January 27th.—It is too true that several thousand of our men were captured at Arkansas Post, and that Little Rock is now in danger.

There seems to be no probability, after all, of an immediate advance of the enemy across the Rappahannock.

But there are eight iron-clad gun-boats and ninety sail at Beaufort, North Carolina, and, it is reported, 52,000 men. Wilmington will probably be assailed.

Mr. Foote said, yesterday, if Indiana and Illinois would recede from the war, he should be in favor of aiding them with an army against Lincoln. And all the indications from the North seem to exhibit a strong sentiment among the people favoring peace. But the people are not the government, and they sink peace and reconstruction together.

Yesterday Mr. Crockett, of Kentucky, said, in the House of Representatives, that there was a party in favor of forming a Central Confederacy (of free and slave States) between the Northern and Southern extremes. Impracticable.

To-day we have news of the bombardment of Fort McAlister, near Savannah. No result known. Now we shall have tidings every few days of naval operations. Can Savannah, and Charleston, and Wilmington be successfully defended? They may, if they will emulate the example of Vicksburg. If they fall, it will stagger this government—before the peace party in the North can operate on the Government of the United States. But it would not "crush the rebellion."

January 28th.—The bombardment of Fort McAlister continued five hours yesterday, when the enemy's boats drew off. The injury to the fort can be repaired in a day. Not a man was killed or a gun dismounted. The injury done the fleet is not known. But the opinion prevails here that if the bombardment was continued to-day, the elongated shot of the enemy probably demolished the fort.

Last night and all this day it snowed incessantly—melting rapidly, however. This must retard operations by land in Virginia and probably in North Carolina.

January 29th.—It appears from the Northern press that the enemy did make three attempts last week to cross the Rappahannock; but as they advanced toward the stream, the elements successfully opposed them. It rained, it snowed, and it froze. The gun carriages and wagons sank up to the hubs, the horses to their bodies, and the men to their knees; and so all stuck fast in the mud.

Rappahannock River, Virginia. Bridge across the Rappahannock

I saw an officer to-day from the army in North Carolina. He says the prospect for a battle is good, as soon as the roads admit of marching.

We have nothing further from the bombardment near Savannah. The wires may not be working—or the fort may be taken.

Gov. Vance has sent to the department a strong protest against the appointment of Col. August as commandant of conscripts in Northern Tennessee. Col. A. is a Virginian—that is the only reason. Well, Gen. Rains, who commands all the conscripts in the Confederate States, is a North Carolinian. But the War Department has erred in putting so many strangers in command of localities, where natives might have been selected. Richmond, for instance, has never yet been in the command of a Southern general.

There are indications of a speedy peace, although we are environed by sea and by land as menacingly as ever. The Tribune (New York) has an article which betrays much desperation. It says the only way for the United States Government to raise $300,000,000, indispensably necessary for a further prosecution of the war, is to guarantee (to the capitalists) that it will be the last call for a loan, and that subjugation will be accomplished in ninety days, or never. It says the war must then be urged on furiously, and negro soldiers sent among the slaves to produce an insurrection! If this will not suffice, then let peace be made on the best possible terms. The New York World denounces the article, and is for peace at once. It says if the project (diabolical) of the Tribune fails, it may not be possible to make peace on any terms. In this I see indications of a foregone conclusion. All over the North, and especially in the Northwest, the people are clamoring for peace, and denouncing the Lincoln Emancipation Proclamation. I have no doubt, if the war continues throughout the year, we shall have the spectacle of more Northern men fighting against the United States Government than slaves fighting against the South.

Almost every day, now, ships from Europe arrive safely with merchandise: and this is a sore vexation to the Northern merchants. We are likewise getting, daily, many supplies from the North, from blockade-runners. No doubt this is winked at by the United States military authorities, and perhaps by some of the civil ones, too.

If we are not utterly crushed before May (an impracticable thing), we shall win our independence.

January 30th.—There is a rumor that Kentucky has voted to raise an army of 60,000 men to resist the execution of Lincoln's Emancipation Proclamation.

Fort Caswell, below Wilmington, has been casemated with iron; but can it withstand elongated balls weighing 480 pounds? I fear not. There are, however, submarine batteries; yet these may be avoided, for Gen. Whiting writes that the best pilot (one sent thither some time ago by the enemy) escaped to the hostile fleet since Gen. Smith visited North Carolina, which is embraced within his command. This pilot, no doubt, knows the location of all our torpedoes.

Nothing further from Savannah.

Mr. Adams, the United States Minister at London, writes to Mr. Seward, Secretary of State, dated 17th of October, 1862, that if the Federal army shall not achieve decisive successes by the month of February ensuing, it is probable the British Parliament will recognize the Confederate States. To-morrow is the last day of January.

I cut the following from yesterday's Dispatch:

"The Results of Extortion and Speculation.—The state of affairs brought about by the speculating and extortion practiced upon the public cannot be better illustrated than by the following grocery bill for one week for a small family, in which the prices before the war and those of the present are compared:

1860.		1863.	
Bacon, 10 lbs. at 12½c	$1 25	Bacon, 10 lbs. at $1	$10 00
Flour, 30 lbs. at 5c	1 50	Flour, 30 lbs. at 12½c	3 75
Sugar, 5 lbs. at 8c	40	Sugar, 5 lbs. at $1 15	5 75
Coffee, 4 lbs. at 12½c	50	Coffee, 4 lbs. at $5	20 00
Tea (green), ½ lb. at $1	50	Tea (green), ½ lb. at $16	8 00
Lard, 4 lbs. at 12½c	50	Lard, 4 lbs. at $1	4 00
Butter, 3 lbs. at 25c	75	Butter, 3 lbs. at $1 75	5 25
Meal, 1 pk. at 25c	25	Meal, 1 pk. at $1	1 00
Candles, 2 lbs. at 15c	30	Candles, 2 lbs. at $1 25	2 50
Soap, 5 lbs. at 10c	50	Soap, 5 lbs. at $1 10	5 50
Pepper and salt (about)	10	Pepper and salt (about)	2 50
Total	$6 55	Total	$68 25

"So much we owe the speculators, who have stayed at home to prey upon the necessities of their fellow-citizens."

We have just learned that a British steamer, with cannon and other valuable cargo, was captured by the enemy, two days ago, while trying to get in the harbor. Another, similarly laden, got safely in yesterday. We can afford to lose one ship out of three—that is, the owners can, and then make money.

Cotton sells at seventy-five cents per pound in the United States. So the blockade must be felt by the enemy as well as ourselves. War is a two-edged sword.

January 31st.—We have dispatches from Charleston, to-day, which reconcile us to the loss of the cargo captured by the blockading squadron early in the week. An artillery company captured a fine gun-boat in Stone River (near Charleston) yesterday evening. She had eleven guns and 200 men.

But this morning we did better still. Our little fleet of two iron-clads steamed out of Charleston harbor, and boldly attacked the blockading fleet. We crippled two of their ships, and sunk one, completely raising the blockade, for the time being. This will frustrate some of their plans, and may relieve Wilmington.

The attack on Fort McAlister was a failure. The monitor which assaulted the fort sustained so much injury, that it had to retire for repairs.

Several blockade-runners between this and Williamsburg were arrested and sent to Gen. Winder to-day by Lieut. G. D. Wise. Gen. W. sent them to Gen. Rains. Mr. Petit and Mr. James Custis (from Williamsburg) came with them to endeavor to procure their liberation. Gen. Rains sent them back to Gen. W., with a note that he had no time to attend to such matters. Such business does not pertain to his bureau. I suppose they will be released.

Major Lear, of Texas, who was at the capture of the Harriet Lane, met on the captured steamer his mortally-wounded son, the lieutenant.

A few days ago, Lieut. Buchanan was killed on a United States gun-boat by our sharpshooters. He was the son of Admiral Buchanan, in the Confederate service, now at Mobile. Thus we are reminded of the wars of the roses—father against son, and brother against brother. God speed the growth of the Peace Party, North and South; but we must have independence.

Mr. Hunter was in our office to-day, getting the release of a son of the Hon. Jackson Morton, who escaped from Washington, where he had resided, and was arrested here as a conscript. The Assistant Secretary of War ruled him entitled to exemption, although yesterday others, in the same predicament, were ruled into the service.

February 1st.—The Virginia Legislature, now in session, has a bill under discussion for the suppression of extortion. One of the members, Mr. Anderson, read the following table of the prices of

AGRICULTURAL PRODUCE.

Before the war.	Now.

White wheat, per bushel	$1 50	White wheat, per bushel	$4 50
Flour, per barrel	7 50	Flour, per barrel	22 00
Corn, per bushel	70	Corn, per bushel	3 50
Hay, per hundred	1 00	Hay, per hundred	3 50
Hides, per pound	7	Hides, per pound	40
Beef, per pound	8	Beef, per pound	50
Bacon, per pound	13	Bacon, per pound	60
Lard, per pound	15	Lard, per pound	1 00
Butter, per pound	30	Butter, per pound	1 50
Irish potatoes	1 00	Irish potatoes	5 00
Sweet potatoes	1 00	Sweet potatoes	6 00
Apple brandy	1 00	Apple brandy	15 00
Wool, per pound	30	Wool, per pound	2 00
MANUFACTURES.			
Bar iron, per pound	4	Bar iron, per pound	20
Nails, per pound	4	Nails, per pound	60
Leather, sole, per pound	25	Leather, sole, per pound	2 50
" upper, pcr pound	33	" upper, per pound	3 50
COTTON GOODS.			
Osnaburgs, per yard	10	Osnaburgs, per yard	75
Brown cotton, per yard	10	Brown cotton, per yard	75
Sheeting, per yard	15	Sheeting, per yard	1 25
WOOLEN GOODS.			
Coarse jeanes	45	Coarse jeanes	4 00
Crenshaw's gray	2 00	Crenshaw's gray	28 00

MISCELLANEOUS.

Coarse shoes	$1 50	Coarse shoes	$15 00
High-quartered shoes	3 50	High-quartered shoes	25 00
Boots	7 50	Boots	60 00
Wool hats, per dozen	7 00	Wool hats, per dozen	50 00

STOCKS.

Dividends on stocks in cotton companies, worth in May, 1861, $25 to $50 per share, now from $112 to $140.

It is doubtful whether the bill will pass, as most of the members are agriculturists.

It is said and believed that several citizens from Illinois and Indiana, now in this city, have been sent hither by influential parties, to consult our government on the best means of terminating the war; or, that failing, to propose some mode of adjustment between the Northwestern States and the Confederacy, and new combination against the Yankee States and the Federal administration.

Burnside has at last been removed; and Franklin and Sumner have resigned. Gen. Hooker now commands the Federal Army of the Potomac—if it may be still called an army. Gen. R——, who knows Hooker well, says he is deficient in talent and character; and many years ago gentlemen refused to associate with him. He resigned from the army, in California, and worked a potatoe patch, Yankee like, on speculation—and failed.

February 2d.—After the feat at Charleston, Gen. Beauregard and Commodore Ingraham invited the consuls resident to inspect the harbor, and they pronounced the blockade raised, no United States ship being seen off the coast. Then the general and the commodore issued a proclamation to the world that the port was open. If this be recognized, then the United States will have to give sixty days' notice before the port can be closed again to neutral powers; and by that time we can get supplies enough to suffice us for a year. Before night, however, some twenty blockaders were in sight of the bar. It is not a question of right, or of might, with France and England—but of inclination. Whenever they, or either of them, shall be disposed to relieve us, it can be done.

There was a fight near Suffolk yesterday, and it is reported that our troops repulsed the enemy.

The enemy's gun-boats returned to the bombardment of Fort McAlister, and met no success. They were driven off. But still, I fear the fort must succumb.

Senator Saulsbury, of Delaware, has been arrested by the Sergeant-at-Arms of the Senate, for his denunciation of Lincoln as an "imbecile." And a Philadelphia editor has been imprisoned for alleged "sympathy with secessionists." These arrests signify more battles—more blood.

February 3d.—It appears that Gen. Pryor's force, 1500 strong, was attacked by the enemy, said to be 5000 in number, on the Blackwater. After some shelling and infantry firing, Gen. P. retired some eight miles, and was not pursued. Our loss was only fifty; it is said the enemy had 500 killed and wounded; but I know not how this was ascertained.

Gold in the North now brings 58½ cents premium. Exchange sells at $1.75. Cotton at 96 cents per pound!

They are getting up a fine rumpus in the North over the imprisonment of an editor.

To-day, when conversing with Judge Perkins in relation to having a passport system established by law, he admitted the necessity, but despaired of its accomplishment. "For," said he, "nothing can be done in Congress which has not the sanction of the Executive." He meant, I thought, from his manner and tone, that the Executive branch of the government was omnipotent, having swallowed up the functions of the other co-ordinate branches. I cannot understand this, for the Executive has but little appointing patronage, the army being completely organized, having supplementary generals, and all officers, under the grade of brigadiers, being promoted as vacancies occur.

February 4th.—One of the enemy's iron-clad gun-boats has got past our batteries at Vicksburg. Gen. Pemberton says it was struck "three times." But it is through.

The enemy's presses reiterate the assertion that Gen. Longstreet is in Tennessee with his corps; and that the detachments from Gen. Lee's army amount to 75,000 men. This is evidently for the purpose to encourage Hooker's army to cross the Rappahannock. These presses must know that Gen. Lee's whole army was less than 75,000 men; that Longstreet is still with him, and that only one small brigade has been sent away to North Carolina. Well, let them come! They will be annihilated. But is it not diabolical in the New York Post, Times, etc. to urge their own people on to certain destruction? If Hooker had 300,000, he could not now come to Richmond!

We have extremely cold weather now; and, probably, the rivers in Virginia will be frozen over to-night.

February 5th.—It snowed again last night. Tuesday night the mercury was 8° below zero.

A dispatch from Gen. Beauregard says sixty sail of the enemy have left Beaufort, N. C., for Charleston. A British frigate (Cadmus) has arrived at Charleston with intelligence that the Federal fleet of gun-boats will attack the city immediately; and that the British consul is ordered away by the Minister at Washington. The attack will be by sea and land. God help Beauregard in this fearful ordeal!

February 6th.—Gen. Lee thinks Charleston will be assailed, and suggests that all the troops in North Carolina be concentrated near Wilmington, and he will undertake the defense of the rest of the State. Nevertheless, if the government deems it more important to have his troops sent to North Carolina, than to retain them for the defense of Richmond, he must acquiesce. But he thinks Hooker will attempt the passage of the Rappahannock, at an early day, if the weather will admit of it. In regard to the last attempt of Burnside to cross his army (when he stuck in the mud), Gen. Lee says it was fortunate for the Federals that they failed to get over. No doubt he was prepared for their reception.

Congress is doing nothing but voting money for themselves. The President (some of the members say) is their master, and they await his nod. These are his enemies.

February 7th.—We have a dispatch from Texas, of another success of Gen. Magruder at Sabine Pass, wherein he destroyed a large amount of the enemy's stores.

But we are calmly awaiting the blow at Charleston, or at Savannah, or wherever it may fall. We have confidence in Beauregard.

We are more anxious regarding the fate of Vicksburg. Northern man as he is, if Pemberton suffers disaster by any default, he will certainly incur the President's eternal displeasure. Mississippi must be defended, else the President himself may feel the pangs of a refugee.

"That mercy I to others show, That mercy show to me!"

February 8th.—From intelligence received yesterday evening, it is probable the Alabama, Harriet Lane, and Florida have met off the West Indies, and turned upon the U. S. steamer Brooklyn. The account says a large steamer was seen on fire, and three others were delivering broadsides into her. The United States press thought the burning steamer was the Florida.

From Charleston or Savannah we shall soon have stirring news. They may overpower our forces, but our power there will be completely exhausted before resistance ceases. There will be no more "giving up," as with New Orleans, Norfolk, etc. Yet there is a feverish anxiety regarding Vicksburg. Pemberton permitted one iron-clad gun-boat to pass, and all our boats below are now at its mercy.

The House of Representatives, at Washington, has passed the "negro soldier bill." This will prove a "Pandora's Box," and the Federals may rue the day that such a measure was adopted.

February 9th.—Gen. Lee requests that all dispatches passing between his headquarters and the War Department be in cipher. He says everything of importance communicated, he has observed, soon becomes the topic of public conversation; and thence is soon made known to the enemy.

The iron-clad gun-boat, which got past Vicksburg, has been up the Red River spreading devastation. It has taken three of our steamers, forty officers on one, and captured large amounts of stores and cotton.

Gen. Wise made a dash into Williamsburg last night, and captured the place, taking some prisoners.

Custis (my son) received a letter to-day from Miss G., Newbern, via underground railroad, inclosing another for her sweet-heart in the army. She says they are getting on tolerably well in the hands of the enemy, though the slaves have been emancipated. She says a Yankee preacher (whom she calls a white-washed negro) made a speculation. He read the Lincoln Proclamation to the negroes: and then announced that none of them had been legally married, and might be liable to prosecution. To obviate this, he proposed to marry them over, charging only a dollar for each couple. He realized several thousand dollars, and then returned to the North. This was a legitimate Yankee speculation; and no doubt the preacher will continue to be an enthusiastic advocate of a war of subjugation. As long as the Yankees can make money by it, and escape killing, the war will continue.

February 10th.—No stirring news yet. The enemy's fleet is at Port Royal, S. C. Everywhere we are menaced with overwhelming odds. Upon God, and our own right arms, we must rely, and we do rely.

To-day, in cabinet council, it is believed it was decided to call out all conscripts under forty-five years of age. The President might have done it without consulting the cabinet.

Yesterday Mrs. Goddin, the owner or wife of the owner of the house I occupy, failing to get board in the country, and we having failed to get another house, took possession of one room of the little cottage. We have temporarily the rest: parlor, dining-room, and two chambers—one of them 8 by 11—at the rate of $800 per annum. This is low, now; for ordinary dwellings, without furniture, rent for $1800. Mr. G. has an hereditary (I believe) infirmity of the mind, and is confined by his father in an asylum. Mrs. G. has four little children, the youngest only a few weeks old. She has a white nurse, who lost her only child (died of scarlet fever) six days ago; her husband being in the army. It is a sad spectacle.

To-day beef was selling in market at one dollar per pound. And yet one might walk for hours in vain, in quest of a beggar. Did such a people ever exist before?

February 11th.—There is a rumor that Major-Gen. Gustavus W. Smith has tendered his resignation.

Some idea may be formed of the scarcity of food in this city from the fact that, while my youngest daughter was in the kitchen to-day, a young rat came out of its hole and seemed to beg for something to eat; she held out some bread, which it ate from her hand, and seemed grateful. Several others soon appeared, and were as tame as kittens. Perhaps we shall have to eat them!

February 12th.—Congress has not yet restricted the class of exempts, and the work of conscription drags heavily along. All under forty-five must be called, else the maximum of the four hundred regiments cannot be kept up. It reminds me of Jack Falstaff's mode of exemption. The numerous employees of the Southern Express Co. have been let off, after transporting hither, for the use of certain functionaries, sugars, etc. from Alabama. And so in the various States, enrolling and other officers are letting thousands of conscripts slip through their hands.

February 13th.—There is a rumor in the papers that something like a revolution is occurring, or has occurred, in the West; and it is stated that the Federal troops demand the recall of the Emancipation Proclamation. They also object to serving with negro troops.

But we ought to look for news of terrific fighting at Savannah or Charleston. No doubt all the troops in the field (Federal) or on the water will be hurled against us before long, so as to effect as much injury as possible before defection can spread extensively, and before the expiration of the enlistments of some 200,000 men in May.

And what are we doing? But little. The acceptance of substitutes who desert, and the exemption of thousands who should be fighting for the country, employ hundreds of pens daily in this city. Alas, that so many dishonest men have obtained easy places! The President has been grossly imposed upon.

February 14th.—A beautiful day. Yet Gen. Lee is giving furloughs, two to each company. If the weather should be dry, perhaps Hooker will advance: a thing desired by our people, being confident of his destruction.

The papers issued extras to-day with news from the Northwest, based upon the account of a "reliable gentleman," who has just run the blockade. He says Ohio, Kentucky, Indiana, and Illinois have resolved to meet in convention, at Frankfort, Ky., for the purpose of seceding from the United States, and setting up a confederacy for themselves, or joining the Southern Confederacy. I fear the "reliable gentleman" is not to be relied upon. Yet it would be well for the Western States, a just retribution to New England, and a very great relief to us.

Gen. Lee is urging the department to have the meat at Atlanta brought to his army without delay. It is here the army will be wanted.

I saw pigs to-day, not six weeks old, selling in market at $10 a piece.

I met Col. Bledsoe to-day, on a visit to the city, who told me Fenelon never tasted meat, and lived to be ninety years old. I am no Fenelon, but I shall probably have to adopt his regimen. I would barter, however, some of his years for a good supply of food. We must have peace soon, or a famine.

February 15th.—Already, as if quite certain that the great Northwest would speedily withdraw from the Eastern United States, our people are discussing the eventualities of such a momentous occurrence. The most vehement opposition to the admission of any of the non-slaveholding States, whose people have invaded our country and shed the blood of our people, into this Confederacy, is quite manifest in this city. But Virginia, "the Old Mother," would, I think, after due hesitation, take back her erring children, Ohio, Illinois, Indiana, and perhaps one or two more, if they earnestly desired to return to her parental protection.

Some of the Cotton States might revolt at such a project, and even the cabinet might oppose the scheme of adding several powerful free States to the Confederacy; but it would not all suffice to prevent it, if they desire to join us. It is true, the constitution would have to be modified, for it is not to be supposed that slaves would be held in any of the States referred to; but then slavery would be recognized by its proper term, and ample guarantees would be agreed upon by the great free States which abandon the United States on the issue of emancipation.

Ohio, Indiana, and Illinois, added to the thirteen Confederate States, would speedily constitute us a people of sufficient military power to defy the menaces of the arms of the greatest powers of the earth; and the commercial and agricultural prosperity of the country would amaze the world.

I am of the opinion that Virginia, Maryland, Delaware, Kentucky, North Carolina, Tennessee, Arkansas, and Missouri would form a league of union with Ohio, Illinois, and Indiana, even if the rest of the Southern States were to reject the alliance. But who can foresee the future through the smoke of war, and amid the clash of bayonets? Nevertheless, division and subdivision, would relieve all of the burden of debt, for they would repudiate the greater part, if not the whole, of the indebtedness of both the present governments, which has been incurred in ravaging the country and cutting each other's throats. The cry will be: "We will not pay the price of blood—for the slaughter of our brothers!"

February 16th.—Another gun-boat has got past Vicksburg. But three British steamers have run into Charleston with valuable cargoes.

Gen. Lee is now sending troops to Charleston, and this strengthens the report that Hooker's army is leaving the Rappahannock. They are probably crumbling to pieces, under the influence of the peace party growing up in the North. Some of them, however, it is said, are sent to Fortress Monroe.

Our Bureau of Conscription ought to be called the Bureau of Exemption. It is turning out a vast number of exempts. The Southern Express Company bring sugar, partridges, turkeys, etc. to the potential functionaries, and their employees are exempted during the time they may remain in the employment of the company. It is too bad!

I have just been reperusing Frederick's great campaigns, and find much encouragement. Prussia was not so strong as the Confederate States, and yet was environed and assailed by France, Austria, Russia, and several smaller powers simultaneously. And yet Frederick maintained the contest for seven years, and finally triumphed over his enemies. The preponderance of numbers against him in the field was greater than that of the United States against us; and Lee is as able a general as Frederick. Hence we should never despair.

February 17th.—Gen. Lee is not sending troops to Charleston. He is sending them here for the defense of Richmond, which is now supposed to be the point of attack, by land and by water, and on both sides of the James River. Well, they have striven to capture this city from every point of the compass but one—the south side. Perhaps they will make an attempt from that direction; and I must confess that I have always apprehended the most danger from that quarter. But we shall beat them, come whence they may!

February 18th.—Mr. H——s, another of Gen. Winder's detectives, has gone over to the enemy. He went on a privateering cruise from Wilmington; the vessel he sailed in captured a brig, and H——s was put in command of the prize, to sail into a Confederate port. Instead of this, however, H——s sailed away for one of the West India islands, and gave up his prize to Com. Wilkes, of the United States Navy.

One or two of the regiments of Gen. Lee's army were in the city last night. The men were pale and haggard. They have but a quarter of a pound of meat per day. But meat has been ordered from Atlanta. I hope it is abundant there.

All the necessaries of life in the city are still going up higher in price. Butter, $3 per pound; beef, $1; bacon, $1.25; sausage-meat, $1; and even liver is selling at 50 cents per pound.

By degrees, quite perceptible, we are approaching the condition of famine. What effect this will produce on the community is to be seen. The army must be fed or disbanded, or else the city must be abandoned. How we, "the people," are to live is a thought of serious concern.

Gen. Lee has recommended that an appeal be made to the people to bring food to the army, to feed their sons and brothers; but the Commissary-General opposes it; probably it will not be done. No doubt the army could be half fed in this way for months. But the "red tape" men are inflexible and inscrutable. Nevertheless, the commissaries and quartermasters are getting rich.

February 19th.—The resignation of Gen. Gustavus W. Smith has been accepted by the President. It was well done—the acceptance, I mean. Who will Gen. Winder report to now? Gen. Winder has learned that I am keeping a diary, and that some space in it may be devoted to the history of martial law. He said to Capt. Warner, his commissary of prisons, that he would patronize it. The captain asked me if Gen. Winder's rule was not dwelt upon in it. I said doubtless it was; but that I had not yet revised it, and was never in the habit of perusing my own works until they were completed. Then I carefully corrected them for the press.

Major-Gen. Pickett's division marched through the city to-day for Drewry's Bluff. Gen. Lee writes that this division can beat the army corps of Hooker, supposed to be sent to the Peninsula. It has 12,000 men—an army corps 40,000. Brig.-Gen. Hood's division is near the city, on the Chickahominy. Gen. Lee warns the government to see that Gens. French and Pryor be vigilant, and to have their scouts closely watching the enemy at Suffolk. He thinks, however, the main object of the enemy is to take Charleston; and he suggests that every available man be sent thither. The rest of his army he will keep on the Rappahannock, to watch the enemy still remaining north of that river.

I sent a communication to the President to-day, proposing to reopen my register of "patriotic contributions" to the army, for they are suffering for meat. I doubt whether he will agree to it. If the war be prolonged, the appeal must be to the people to feed the army, or else it will dissolve.

February 20th.—We have exciting news from the West. The iron-shod gun-boat, Queen of the West, which run past Pemberton's batteries some time since, captured, it appears, one of our steamers in Red River, and then compelled our pilot to steer the Queen of the West farther up the river. The heroic pilot ran the boat under our masked batteries, and then succeeded in escaping by swimming. The Queen of the West was forced to surrender. This adventure has an exhilarating effect upon our spirits.

Hon. James Lyons sent to the President to-day a petition, signed by a majority of the members of Congress, to have me appointed major in the conscription service.

February 21st.—Major-Gen. Hood's division passed through the city to-day, and crossed over the river. I hope an attack will be made at Suffolk. It is too menacing a position to allow the invader to occupy it longer.

No attack on Charleston yet, and there is a rumor that the command of the expedition is disputed by Foster and Hunter. If it hangs fire, it will be sure to miss the mark.

February 22d.—This is the anniversary of the birth of Washington, and of the inauguration of President Davis, upon the installation of the permanent government of the Confederate States. It is the ugliest day I ever saw. Snow fell all night, and was falling fast all day, with a northwest wind howling furiously. The snow is now nearly a foot deep, and the weather very cold.

My communication to the President, proposing an appeal to the people to furnish the army with meat and clothing (voluntary contributions), was transmitted to the Secretary of War yesterday, without remark, other than the simple reference. The plan will not be adopted, in all probability, for the Secretary will consult the Commissary and Quartermaster-General, and they will oppose any interference with the business of their departments. Red tape will win the day, even if our cause be lost. Our soldiers must be fed and clothed according to the "rules and regulations," or suffer and perish for the want of food and clothing!

I have some curiosity to learn what the President has indorsed, or may indorse, on the paper sent him by Mr. Lyons, signed by half the members of Congress. Will he simply refer it to the Secretary? Then what will the Secretary do? My friends in Congress will likewise be curious to learn the result.

February 23d.—I saw a letter from Gen. Lee to-day, suggesting to the government on appeal to the Governors of the States to aid more directly in recruiting the armies. He says the people habitually expect too much from the troops now in the field; that because we have gained many victories, it does not follow that we shall always gain them; that the legitimate fruits of victory have hitherto been lost, for the want of numbers on our side; and, finally, that all those who fail to go to the field at such a momentous period as this, are guilty of the blood of the brave soldiers who perish in the effort to achieve independence.

This would be contrary to the "rules and regulations" as understood by the Adjutant and Inspector-General (a Northern man), and no doubt the Secretary of War and the President will reject the plan.

The petition of forty members of Congress in my behalf came from Mr. Seddon, the Secretary, to our bureau to-day. He asks the superintendent if there is a necessity for such an officer, one whose rank is equal to that of a commandant of a camp of instruction. He says important services only should require the appointment of such an officer. Well, Gen. Rains recommended it. I know not whether he can say more. I shall not get it, for Congress has but little influence, just now.

February 24th.—Gen. Longstreet is now in command of Gen. Smith's late department, besides his own corps. Richmond is safe.

Our papers contain a most astonishing speech purporting to have been delivered by Mr. Conway, in the United States Congress. Mr. C. is from Kansas, that hot-bed of Abolitionism. He is an avowed Abolitionist; and yet he advocates an immediate suspension of hostilities, or at least that the Federal armies and fleets be ordered to act on the defensive; that the independence of the Confederate States be recognized, upon the basis of a similar tariff; free-trade between the North and South; free navigation of the Mississippi, and co-operation in the maintenance of the Monroe doctrine. I like the indications apparent in this speech. Let us have a suspension of hostilities, and then we can have leisure to think of the rest. No doubt the peace party is growing rapidly in the United States; and it may be possible that the Republicans mean to beat the Democrats in the race, by going beyond them on the Southern question. The Democrats are for peace and Union; the Republicans may resolve to advocate not only peace, but secession.

February 25th.—On the 18th inst. the enemy's battery on the opposite side of the Mississippi River opened on Vicksburg. The damage was not great; but the front of the town is considered untenable.

The Conscription bill has passed the United States Senate, which will empower the President to call for 3,000,000 men. "Will they come, when he does call for them?" That is to be seen. It may be aimed at France; and a war with the Emperor might rouse the Northern people again. Some of them, however, have had enough of war.

To-day I heard of my paper addressed to the President on the subject of an appeal to the people to send food to the army. He referred it to the Commissary-General, Col. Northrop, who sent it to the War Department, with an indorsement that as he had no acquaintance with that means of maintaining an army (the patriotic contributions of the people), he could not recommend the adoption of the plan. Red tape is mightier than patriotism still. There may be a change, however, for Gen. Lee approves the plan.

February 26th.—We have good news from Vicksburg to-day. The Queen of the West, lately captured by us, and another gun-boat, attacked the Indianola, the iron-clad Federal gun-boat which got past our batteries the other day, and, after an engagement, sunk her. We captured all the officers and men.

Sunken ship near Jamestown

February 27th.—No news from any quarter to-day.

Gen. Joseph E. Johnston is discontented with his command in the West. The armies are too far asunder for co-operative action; and, when separated, too weak for decisive operations. There is no field there for him, and he desires to be relieved, and assigned to some other command.

I was surprised to receive, to-day, the following very official letter from the Secretary of War:

"Richmond, Va., Feb. 27th, 1863.
"J. B. Jones, Esq.

"Sir:—The President has referred your letter of the 19th inst. to this department.

"In reply, you are respectfully informed that it is not deemed judicious, unless in the last extremity, to resort to the means of supply suggested. The patriotic motives that dictated the suggestion are, however, appreciated and acknowledged.

"Your obedient servant,
"James A. Seddon,
"Secretary of War."

March 1st.—To-morrow we remove to new quarters. The lady's husband, owning cottage, and who was confined for seven months among lunatics, has returned, and there is not room for two families. Besides, Mrs. G. thinks she can do better taking boarders, than by letting the house. What a mistake! Beef sold yesterday for $1.25 per pound; turkeys, $15. Corn-meal $6 per bushel, and all other articles at the same rates. No salaries can board families now; and soon the expense of boarding will exceed the incomes of unmarried men. Owners and tenants, unless engaged in lucrative business, must soon vacate their houses and leave the city.

But we have found a house occupied by three widows in Clay Street. They have no children. They mean to board soon among their relatives or friends, and then we get the house; in the mean time, they have fitted up two rooms for us. We should have gone yesterday, but the weather was too bad. The terms will not exceed the rent we are now paying, and the house is larger. I espied several fruit trees in the back yard, and a space beyond, large enough for a smart vegetable garden. How delighted I shall be to cultivate it myself! Always I have visions of peas, beans, radishes, potatoes, corn, and tomatoes of my own raising! God bless the widows sent for our relief in this dire necessity!

Met Judge Reagan yesterday, just from the Council Board. I thought he seemed dejected. He said if the enemy succeeded in getting command of the Mississippi River, the Confederacy would be "cut in two;" and he intimated his preference of giving up Richmond, if it would save Texas, etc. for the Confederacy. Texas is his adopted State.

March 2d.—The enemy burnt the steamship Nashville on Saturday near Savannah. She was employed taking provisions to Fort McAlister. I think it was destroyed by an incendiary shell.

There is a rumor to-day of the burning of railroad bridges between this and Fredericksburg.

I signed an agreement to-day with Mr. Malsby to publish my new "Wild Western Scenes." He is to print 10,000 copies, which are to retail at $2; on this he pays me 12½ per cent. or 25 cents for every copy sold; $2500 if the whole are sold. He will not be able to get it out before May.

We moved into the west end of Clay Street to-day, and like the change. There are no children here except our own. The house is a brick one, and more comfortable than the frame shell we abandoned.

March 3d.—We like our new quarters—and the three Samaritan widows, without children. They lend us many articles indispensable for our comfort. It is probable they will leave us soon in the sole occupancy of the house. There is ground enough for a good many vegetables—and meat is likely to be scarce enough. Bacon is now $1.37½ cts. per pound, and flour $30 per barrel. The shadow of the gaunt form of famine is upon us! But the pestilence of small-pox is abating.

We have now fine March weather; but the floods of late have damaged the railroad bridges between this and Fredericksburg. The Secretary of War requested the editors, yesterday, to say nothing of this. We have no news from the West or from the Southeast—but we shall soon have enough.

The United States Congress has passed the Conscription Act. We shall see the effect of it in the North; I predict civil war there; and that will be our "aid and comfort."

Gen. Toombs has resigned; and it is said Pryor has been made a major-general. Thus we go up and down. The President has issued a proclamation for prayer, fasting, etc., on the twenty-seventh of this month. There will certainly be fasting—and prayer also. And God has helped us, or we should have been destroyed ere this.

March 4th.—The enemy bombarded Fort McAlister again yesterday, several gun-boats opening fire on it. It lasted all day; during which one of the iron-clads retired, perhaps injured. We had only two men wounded and one gun (8 in. columbiad) dismounted. The fort was but little injured.

Recent Northern papers assert that their gun-boats have all passed through the canal opposite Vicksburg. This is not true—yet.

Lincoln is now Dictator, his Congress having given him power to call out all the male population between the ages of twenty and thirty-five years, and authority to declare martial law whenever he pleases. The Herald shouts for Lincoln—of course. We must fight and pray, and hope for revolution and civil war in the North, which may occur any day.

Our cavalry, under Gen. Jones, has done some brilliant skirmishing recently in the vicinity of Winchester; and as soon as the March winds dry the earth a little, I suppose Hooker will recommence the "On to Richmond." We shall be weaker the next campaign, but our men are brave.

March 5th.—Yesterday the government seized the flour in the mills and warehouses; and now the price has risen from $30 to $40 per barrel. I wrote to the Commissary, in view of the dissatisfaction of the people, and to prevent disturbances, advising him to seize the 5000 barrels in the hands of the small speculators, and to allow so many pounds per month to each inhabitant, at the rate paid by government. This would be beneficent and popular, confining the grumblers to the extortioners. But he will not do it, as the Constitution only provides for impressments for the public use.

Our dinner to-day (for seven, for the servant has an equal share) consisted of twelve eggs, $1.25; a little corn bread, some rice and potatoes. How long shall we have even this variety and amount? Bad beef in market, this morning, sold at $1.25 per pound.

After bombarding Fort McAlister on the 3d inst. and all night, the enemy's fire ceased. The fort was not much injured, says the dispatch. There is a rumor to-day that the fort has been reduced—but no one believes it.

Gen. Van Dorn has had a fight in Tennessee, killing and wounding 1000 and capturing 2600 prisoners. Our loss is said to have been heavy.

Gen. Lee writes that now, since Lincoln may call out 3,000,000 men, and has $900,000,000 voted him, we must put out all our strength, if we expect to keep the field. We shall certainly have an exciting time. But there may be use for some of the Federal troops in the North! If not, I apprehend that Richmond must withstand another siege and assault. It is said they have dropped the "Constitution and the Union" in the United States, and raised the cry of the "Nation" and the "Flag." This alarms me. If they get up a new sensation, they will raise new armies.

Gold is selling at a premium of $4.25 in Confederate notes.

We bought a barrel of flour to-day (that is, my wife paid for one not yet delivered), from a dealer who was not an extortioner, for the moderate sum of $28.00. This, with what we have on hand, ought to suffice until the growing wheat matures.

For tea we had meal coffee, and corn cakes without butter. But we had a half-pint of molasses (for seven) which cost 75 cts. The gaunt specter is approaching nearer every day!

Every morning there is a large crowd of Irish and Germans besieging Gen. Winder's office for passports to go North. Is it famine they dread, or a desire to keep out of the war? Will they not be conscripted in the North? They say they can get consular protection there.

March 6th.—I have meditated on this day, as the anniversary of my birth, and the shortening lapse of time between me and eternity. I am now fifty-three years of age. Hitherto I have dismissed from my mind, if not with actual indifference, yet with far more unconcern than at present, the recurring birthdays which plunged me farther in the vale of years. But now I cannot conceal from myself, if so disposed, that I am getting to be an old man. My hair is gray—but nevertheless my form is still erect, and my step is brisk enough. My fancies, tastes, and enjoyments have not changed perceptibly; and I can and often do write without glasses. I desire to live after this war is over, if it be the will of God—if not, I hope to exist in a better world.

We have no news of interest to-day. A letter says the non-combatants, even the women and children, heedless of danger, were voluntary spectators of the bombardment of

Vicksburg the other day. The shells often exploded near them, and behind them, but the fascination was so great that they remained on the ground; even one had an arm carried away by a ball! Can such a people be subjugated?

Houses (furnished) are beginning to be offered more plentifully than ever before; their occupants and owners finding their ordinary incomes insufficient for subsistence. I suppose they mean to find in the country an escape from famine prices prevailing in the city.

There is a rumor this evening of the fall of Vicksburg; but that rumor has been whispered here several times during the last few months. No one believes it. When Vicksburg falls, many an invader will perish in its ruins.

March 7th.—The President is sick, and has not been in the Executive Office for three days. Gen. Toombs, resigned, has published a farewell address to his brigade. He does not specify of what his grievance consists; but he says he cannot longer hold his commission with honor. The President must be aware of his perilous condition. When in adversity, some of those he has trusted, discuss the bases of reconstruction; and when we are prosperous, others, in similar positions, agitate the question of reorganization—the motive of both being his ruin. But I suppose he has calculated these contingencies, and never anticipated paving a bed of roses to recline upon during the terrible, and sometimes doubtful struggle for independence.

The rumor that Vicksburg had fallen is not confirmed; on the contrary, the story that the Indianola, captured from the enemy, and reported to have been blown up, was unfounded. We have Gen. Pemberton's official assurance of this.

Col. Gorgas, Chief of Ordnance, a Pennsylvanian, sent into the department to-day, with a request that it be filed, his oath of allegiance to this government, and renunciation of that of the United States, and of his native State. This would indicate that the location of his nativity has been the subject of remark. What significance is to be attributed to this step at this late day, I know not, and care not. An error was committed in placing Northern men in high positions to the exclusion of Southern men, quite as capable of filling them.

March 8th.—Judge Meredith's opinion, that foreigners, Marylanders, and others, who have served in the army, have become domiciled, and are liable to conscription, has produced a prodigious commotion. Gen. Winder's door is beset with crowds of eager seekers of passports to leave the Confederacy; and as these people are converting their Confederate money into gold, the premium on specie has advanced.

Judge Campbell, Assistant Secretary of War, has decided that Judge Meredith's opinion is not authority; and hence his son-in-law, Lieut.-Col. Lay, who at present wields the Conscription Bureau, acts accordingly. But Gen. Rains has a contrary opinion; and he intended to see the President yesterday, who is understood to coincide with Judge Meredith. It is also alleged that Secretary Seddon concurs in this opinion; and if this be the case, an explosion is imminent—for Judge Campbell must have given instructions "by order of the Secretary," without the Secretary's knowledge or consent.

I advised the general to see the President and Secretary once a week, and not rely upon verbal instructions received through a subordinate; he said the advice was good, and he should follow it. But he is much absorbed in his subterrene batteries.

March 9th.—We have no news to-day. But the next act of this terrible drama is near at hand. The Northern papers have reports of the fall of Vicksburg and Charleston. Unfounded. They also say 22,000 men have deserted from the Army of the Potomac. This is probably true.

There is much denunciation of the recent seizure of flour; but this is counteracted by an appalling intimation in one of the papers that unless the army be subsisted, it will be withdrawn from the State, and Virginia must fall into the hands of the enemy. The loss of Virginia might be the loss of the Confederacy.

March 10th.—No war news of importance.

Just at this time there is a large number of persons passing to and from the North. They are ostensibly blockade-runners, and they do succeed in bringing from the enemy's country a large amount of goods, on which an enormous profit is realized. The Assistant Secretary of War, his son-in-law, Lt.-Col. Lay, the controlling man in the Bureau of Conscription, and, indeed, many heads of bureaus, have received commodities from Maryland, from friends running the blockade. Gen. Winder himself, and his Provost Marshal Griswold (how much that looks like a Yankee name!), and their police detectives, have reaped benefit from the same source. But this intercourse with the enemy is fraught with other matters. Communications are made by the disloyal to the enemy, and our condition—bad enough, heaven knows!—is made known, and hence the renewed efforts to subjugate us. This illicit intercourse, inaugurated under the auspices of Mr. Benjamin, and continued by subsequent Ministers of War, may be our ruin, if we are destined to destruction. Already it has unquestionably cost us thousands of lives and millions of dollars. I feel it a duty to make this record.

To-day we have a violent snow-storm—a providential armistice.

It has been ascertained that Hooker's army is still near the Rappahannock, only some 20,000 or 30,000 having been sent to the Peninsula and to Suffolk. No doubt he will advance as soon as the roads become practicable. If Hooker has 150,000 men, and advances soon, Gen. Lee cannot oppose his march; and in all probability we shall again hear the din of war, from this city, in April and May. The fortifications are strong, however, and 25,000 men may defend the city against 100,000—provided we have subsistence. The great fear is famine. But hungry men will fight desperately. Let the besiegers beware of them!

We hope to have nearly 400,000 men in the field in May, and I doubt whether the enemy will have over 500,000 veterans at the end of that month. Their new men will not be in fighting condition before July. We may cross the Potomac again.

March 11th.—Gen. Fitzhugh Lee has made a dash into Fairfax (near Washington) a day or two ago, and captured the Federal Gen. Slaughter and other officers, in their beds.

Last night one of the government warehouses in this city was burnt. It is supposed to have been the work of an incendiary traitor; perhaps in retaliation for the recent impressment of flour. Yesterday the lower house of Congress passed a resolution restricting impressments. This has a bad aspect.

The Bureau of Conscription, to-day, under the direction of Col. Lay, decided that all clerks in the departments, appointed subsequent to the eleventh of October last, are liable to be enrolled for service. Yet the colonel himself has a clerk appointed in January last.

Gold sells at $5 in Confederate States notes for one; U. S. Treasury notes are at a premium here of $2.50. Even the notes of our State banks are at 60 per cent. premium over Confederate notes. This is bad for Mr. Memminger. An abler financier would have worked out a different result.

All the patriotism is in the army; out of it the demon avarice rages supreme. Every one seems mad with speculation; and the extortioners prey upon every victim that falls within their power. Nearly all who sell are extortioners. We have at the same time, and in the same community, spectacles of the most exalted virtue and of the most degrading vice.

Col. Mattel, the former commandant of conscripts for North Carolina, who was wounded at Kinston, and yet was superseded by Col. Lay's friend, Col. August, is now to be restored, and Col. A. relieved. Upon this Col. L. has fallen sick.

Mr. Duffield, whom Col. Lay and Mr. Jacques had appointed A. A. G. over me, has not yet, for some cause, got his commission. The Secretary or some one else may have "intervened."

March 12th.—To-day we have no army news.

Mr. Richard Smith issued the first number of The Sentinel yesterday morning. Thus we have five daily morning papers, all on half sheets. The Sentinel has a biography of the President, and may aspire to be the "organ."

John Mitchel, the Irishman, who was sentenced to a penal colony for disturbances in Ireland, some years ago, is now the leading editor of the Enquirer. He came hither from the North recently. His "compatriot," Meagher, once lived in the South and advocated our "institutions." He now commands a Federal brigade. What Mitchel will do finally, who knows? My friend R. Tyler, probably, had something to do with bringing him here. As a politician, however, he must know there is no Irish element in the Confederate States. I am sorry this Irish editor has been imported.

The resignation of Gen. Toombs is making some sensation in certain circles. He was among the foremost leaders of the rebellion. He was Secretary of State, and voluntarily resigned to enter the army. I know not precisely what his grievance is, unless it be the failure of the President to promote him to a higher position, which he may have deemed himself entitled to, from his genius, antecedents, wealth, etc. But it is probable he will cause some disturbance. Duff Green, who is everywhere in stormy times, told me to-day that Gen. Toombs would be elected Governor of Georgia this fall, and said there were intimations that Georgia might make peace with the United States! This would be death to the government—and destruction to Toombs. It must be a mistake. He cannot have any such design. If he had, it would be defeated by the people of Georgia, though they sighed for peace. Peace is what all most desire—but not without independence. Some there are, in all the States, who would go back into the Union, for the sake of repose and security. But a majority would not have peace on such terms.

Still, it behooves the President to be on his guard. He has enemies in the South, who hate him much.

March 13th.—To-day a great calamity occurred in this city. In a large room of one of the government laboratories an explosion took place, killing instantly five or six persons, and wounding, it is feared fatally, some thirty others. Most of them were little indigent girls!

March 14th.—Gen. Pemberton writes that he has 3000 hogs-heads of sugar at Vicksburg, which he retains for his soldiers to subsist on when the meat fails. Meat is scarce there as well as here. Bacon now sells for $1.50 per pound in Richmond. Butter $3. I design to cultivate a little garden 20 by 50 feet; but fear I cannot get seeds. I have sought in vain for peas, beans, corn, and tomatoes seeds. Potatoes are $12 per bushel. Ordinary chickens are worth $3 a piece. My youngest daughter put her earrings on sale to-day—price $25; and I think they will bring it, for which she can purchase a pair of shoes. The area of subsistence is contracting around us; but my children are more enthusiastic for independence than ever. Daily I hear them say they would gladly embrace death rather than the rule of the Yankee. If all our people were of the same mind, our final success would be certain.

This day the leading article in the Examiner had a striking, if not an ominous conclusion. Inveighing against the despotism of the North, the editor takes occasion likewise to denounce the measure of impressment here. He says if our Congress should follow the example of the Northern Congress, and invest our President with dictatorial powers, a reconstruction of the Union might be a practicable thing; for our people would choose to belong to a strong despotism rather than a weak one—the strong one being of course the United States with 20,000,000, rather than the Confederate States with 8,000,000. There may be something in this, but we shall be injured by it; for the crowd going North will take it thither, where it will be reproduced, and stimulate the invader to renewed exertions. It is a dark hour. But God disposes. If we deserve it, we shall triumph; if not, why should we?

But we cannot fail without more great battles; and who knows what results may be evolved by them? Gen. Lee is hopeful; and so long as we keep the field, and he commands, the foe must bleed for every acre of soil they gain.

March 15th.—Another cold, disagreeable day. March so far has been as cold and terrible as a winter month.

March 16th.—Gen. Hill is moving toward Newbern, N. C., and may attack the enemy there.

The weather continues dreadful—sleeting; and movements of armies must perforce be stayed. But the season of slaughter is approaching.

There was an ominous scantiness of supply in the market this morning, and the prices beyond most persons—mine among the rest.

Col. Lay got turkeys to-day from Raleigh; on Saturday partridges, by the Express Company. Fortunate man!

March 17th.—On Saturday, the enemy's lower Mississippi fleet attacked our batteries at Port Hudson. The result reported is that only one of their gun-boats got past, and that in a damaged condition. The frigate Mississippi, one of the best war steamers of the United States, was burned, and the rest retired down the river, badly repulsed. We sustained no loss.

To-day, the Secretary of War sent in a paper indorsing Judge Meredith's opinion in regard to foreigners who have accepted service in our country, viz., that they are liable to conscription. This is in the teeth of the decision of the Assistant Secretary, Judge Campbell, Col. Lay's father-in-law, and upon which the bureau has been acting, although Gen. Rains, the Superintendent, permitted it with reluctance, upon the assurance of Col. L. that such was the will of the department. This business may produce an explosion.

I walked with Gen. Rains this afternoon in Capitol Square. He is annoyed at the action of Col. Lay in following the instructions of the Assistant Secretary of War in regard to foreigners. The decision had not the sanction of the Secretary of War, Mr. Seddon. He thinks several thousand men may have been permitted to escape military service by it. He intended to lay Judge Campbell's decision before the President, but it disappeared very mysteriously from his desk. And to-day it reappeared just as mysteriously. And, simultaneously, and quite as mysteriously, a paper appeared, signed by Mr. Seddon, Secretary of War, suggesting that the bureau act in conformity with Judge Meredith's opinion, directly in the teeth of Mr. Assistant Secretary Campbell's decision! And it was dated March 13th, full four days before. What delayed it, and who brought it, no one seemed to know. Col. Lay suggested that it be sent back, with an indorsement that the bureau had been already acting under the decision of Judge Campbell (just the reverse of the opinion), Assistant Secretary of War, "by order of the Secretary of War."

To this Gen. R. demurred, and said the bureau would conform its action to Mr. Seddon's suggestions; and he charged a clerk to preserve that paper. Col. L. grumbled awfully at Mr. Seddon's off-hand decision, without mature reflection.

Gen. Stewart (of Maryland) was at the office a short time before, and advocated Mr. Seddon's views; for he knew how many Marylanders would be embraced in the decision, as well as other foreigners.

Lieut.-Col. A. C. Jones, Assistant Adjutant-General, had, in the name of the bureau, notified Gen. Winder, this morning, that Marylanders, etc. were not liable to bear arms for the South after being in the service two years!

The general says he will have all the commandants of conscripts written to immediately; and that he will have an interview with the Secretary of War in relation to the matter.

Every man we can put in the field is demanded; and many fear we shall not have a sufficient number to oppose the overwhelming tide soon to be surging over the land. At such a crisis, and in consideration of all the circumstances attending this matter, involving the loss of so many men, one is naturally startled at Judge Campbell's conduct.

March 18th.—I sent an extract from my Diary of yesterday to the Hon. T. H. Watts, Minister of Justice. I know not whether he will appreciate its importance; but he has professed friendship for me.

The city is in some excitement to-day, for early this morning we had intelligence of the crossing of the Rappahannock by a portion of the Federal army. During the day the division of Hood defiled through the streets, at a quick pace, marching back to Lee's army. But the march of troops and the rumbling of artillery have ceased to be novel spectacles to our community. Some aged ladies ran out as they passed, calling the bronzed Texans their "children," and distributed loaves of bread and other food among them. I never saw a merrier set than these brave soldiers, who have been through the "fire and the flood" numberless times. Some of them had three or four loaves on their bayonets.

Gen. Lee himself left early this morning, on an extra train, having been "caught napping" here, the first time. The enemy crossed the river yesterday.

But during the day a dispatch was received from Gen. J. E. B. Stuart (cavalry), stating that he had attacked the enemy on this side of the river, and beaten him back, forcing him to recross with loss. The particulars of the fight were not stated; but it is believed we lost a brigadier-general, killed.

March 19th.—Snowing. It is estimated that we lost 250 men, killed, wounded, and taken, in the fight on the Rappahannock; the enemy's loss is not known, but certainly was heavy, since they were defeated, and fled back, hotly pursued.

Confederate money still depreciates, in spite of the funding act. Some of the brokers are demanding ten dollars Confederate notes for one in gold! That is bad, and it may be worse.

The enemy are advancing from Corinth, and there are not sufficient troops to resist them. Gen. Johnston says if men are taken from Bragg, his army may be destroyed; and none can be ordered from Mobile, where there are only 2500 for land defense.

March 20th.—The snow is eight inches deep this morning, and it is still falling fast.

Not a beggar is yet to be seen in this city of 100,000 inhabitants!

Hood's division, mostly Texans, whose march to the Rappahannock was countermanded when it was ascertained that the enemy had been beaten back across the river, were all the morning defiling through Main Street, in high spirits, and merrily snowballing each other. And these men slept last night out in the snow without tents! Can such soldiers be vanquished?

Yesterday Floyd's division of State troops were turned over to the Confederacy—only about 200!

We have no further particulars of the fight on the Rappahannock; we know, however, that the enemy were beaten, and that this snow-storm must prevent further operations for many days. Several Eastern Shore families, I learn, are about to return to their homes. This is no place for women and children, who have homes elsewhere. We are all on quarter-rations of meat, and but few can afford to buy clothing at the present prices.

March 21st.—The snow is nearly a foot deep this morning, as it continued to fall all night, and is falling still. It grows warmer, however.

But we now learn that the Indianola was destroyed in the Mississippi by the officers, upon the appearance of a simulated gun-boat sent down, without a crew! This was disgraceful, and some one should answer for it.

Col. Godwin writes from King and Queen County, that many of the people there are deserting to the enemy, leaving their stock, provisions, grain, etc., and he asks permission to seize their abandoned property for the use of the government. Mr. Secretary Seddon demands more specific information before that step be taken. He intimates that they may have withdrawn to avoid conscription.

March 22d.—It was thawing all night, and there is a heavy fog this morning. The snow will disappear in a few days.

A very large number of slaves, said to be nearly 40,000, have been collected by the enemy on the Peninsula and at adjacent points, for the purpose, it is supposed, of co-operating with Hooker's army in the next attempt to capture Richmond.

The snow has laid an embargo on the usual slight supplies brought to market, and all who had made no provision for such a contingency are subsisting on very short-commons. Corn-meal is selling at from $6 to $8 per bushel. Chickens $5 each. Turkeys $20. Turnip greens $8 per bushel. Bad bacon $1.50 per pound. Bread 20 cts. per loaf. Flour $38 per barrel,—and other things in proportion. There are some pale faces seen in the streets from deficiency of food; but no beggars, no complaints. We are all in rags, especially our underclothes. This for liberty!

The Northern journals say we have negro regiments on the Rappahannock and in the West. This is utterly untrue. We have no armed slaves to fight for us, nor do we fear a servile insurrection. We are at no loss, however, to interpret the meaning of such demoniac misrepresentations. It is to be seen of what value the negro regiments employed against us will be to the invader.

March 23d.—The snow has nearly disappeared, and the roads are very bad. No food is brought to the market, and such as may be found in the city is held at famine prices.

I saw a letter to-day from Bishop Lay, in Arkansas. He says affairs in that State wear a dark and gloomy aspect. He thinks the State is lost.

Gen. Beauregard writes the Hon. Mr. Miles that he has not men enough, nor heavy guns enough, for the defense of Charleston. If this were generally known, thousands would despair, being convinced that those charged with the reins of power are incompetent, unequal to the crisis, and destined to conduct them to destruction rather than independence.

March 24th.—Judge Lyons has granted an injunction, arresting the impressment of flour by the Secretary of War, and Congress is debating a bill which, if passed, will be a marked rebuke to the government.

Notwithstanding the wishes of the Secretary of War, the President, and Gen. Rains, Lt.-Col. Lay is still exempting Marylanders, and even foreigners who have bought real estate, and resided for years in this country, if they have "not taken the oath of domicile."

In Eastern Tennessee, 25,500 conscripts were enrolled, and yet only 6000 were added to the army. The rest were exempted, detailed, or deserted. Such is the working of the Conscription Act, fettered as it is by the Exemption Law, and still executed under Judge Campbell's decision. Gen. Rains has the title, but does not execute the functions of Superintendent of the Bureau of Conscription. The President has been informed of everything.

March 25th.—We have no news to-day, excepting the falling back of Rosecrans from Murfreesborough, and a raid of Morgan and capture of a train of cars. Rosecrans means, perhaps, to aid in the occupation of the Mississippi River. It will be expensive in human life.

Although our conscription is odious, yet we are collecting a thousand per week. The enemy say they will crush the rebellion in ninety days. In sixty days half their men will return to their homes, and then we may take Washington. God knows, but man does not, what will happen.

March 26th.—We have dispatches (unofficial) from the West, stating that one of the enemy's gun-boats has been sunk in attempting to pass Vicksburg, and another badly injured. Also that an engagement has occurred on the Yazoo, the enemy having several gun-boats sunk, the rest being driven back.

It snowed a little this morning, and is now clear and cold.

Mr. Seddon is vexed at the unpopularity of the recent impressments by his order. It was an odious measure, because it did not go far enough and take all, distributing enough among the people to crush the extortioners.

March 27th.—This is the day appointed by the President for fasting and prayers. Fasting in the midst of famine! May God save this people! The day will be observed throughout the Confederacy.

The news from the West, destruction of more of the enemy's gun-boats, seems authentic. So far we have sustained no disasters this spring, the usual season of success of the enemy by water.

Mr. G. W. Randolph was the counsel of the speculators whose flour was impressed, and yet this man, when Secretary of War, ordered similar impressments repeatedly. "Oh, man! dressed in a little brief authority," etc.

Mr. Foote has brought forward a bill to prevent trading with the enemy. Col. Lay even gets his pipes from the enemy's country. Let Mr. Foote smoke that!

A gentleman said, to-day, if the Yankees only knew it, they might derive all the benefits they seek by the impracticable scheme of subjugation, without the expenditure of human life, by simply redoubling the blockade of our ports, withdrawing their armies to the borders, and facilitating trade between the sections. We would not attack them in their own country, and in a month millions of their products would be pouring into the South, and cotton, tobacco, etc. would go to the North in vast quantities. I wonder the smart Yankee never thinks of this! Let both sides give passports freely, and an unlimited intercourse would be immediately established.

March 28th.—We have nothing additional or confirmatory from the West. A letter from Gen. Beauregard states that he has but 17,000 men in South Carolina, and 10,000 in Georgia, 27,000 in all. He asks more, as he will be assailed, probably, by 100,000 Federals. The President refers this important letter to the Secretary of War, simply with the indorsement, "this is an exact statement of affairs in South Carolina and Georgia."

Col. Lay predicts that we shall be beaten in thirty days, or else we shall then be in the way of beating the enemy. A safe prediction—but what is his belief? This deponent saith not. There will be fearful odds against us, and yet our men in the field fear nothing.

We are sending Napoleons up to Lee. But the weather, which has been fine for the last two days, is wet again. If Hooker makes a premature advance, he will be sure to "march back again."

An amusing letter was received from an officer in Tennessee to-day. He was taken prisoner by seven Federals when straying some distance from camp, and subsequently hearing the men express some anxiety to be at home again with their families, gave them some brandy which he happened to possess. He then suggested a plan by which they might return to their homes, viz., to become his prisoners, and being paroled by him. After consultation, they agreed to it, and released him. He then paroled them, giving them the usual certificates to exhibit to their officer, and so, taking another drink, they pursued their different ways. If this disposition prevails extensively among the Western Federals, we may look for speedy results in that quarter. Rosecrans may lose his laurels in a most unexpected manner.

March 29th.—No news. Yet a universal expectation. What is expected is not clearly defined. Those who are making money rapidly no doubt desire a prolongation of the war, irrespective of political consequences. But the people, the majority in the United States, seem to have lost their power. And their representatives in Congress are completely subordinated by the Executive, and rendered subservient to his will. President Lincoln can have any measure adopted or any measure defeated, at pleasure. Such is the irresistible power of enormous executive patronage. He may extend the sessions or terminate them, and so, all power, for the time being, reposes in the hands of the President.

A day of reckoning will come, for the people of the United States will resume the powers of which the war has temporarily dispossessed them, or else there will be disruptions, and civil war will submerge the earth in blood. The time has not arrived, or else the right men have not arisen, for the establishment of despotisms.

Everything depends upon the issues of the present campaign, and upon them it may be bootless to speculate. No one may foretell the fortunes of war—I mean where victory will ultimately perch in this frightful struggle. We are environed and invaded by not less than 600,000 men in arms, and we have not in the field more than 250,000 to oppose them. But we have the advantage of occupying the interior position, always affording superior facilities for concentration. Besides, our men must prevail in combat, or lose their property, country, freedom, everything,—at least this is their conviction. On the other hand, the enemy, in yielding the contest, may retire into their own country, and possess everything they enjoyed before the war began. Hence it may be confidently believed that in all the battles of this spring, when the numbers are nearly equal, the Confederates will be the victors, and even when the enemy have superior numbers, the armies of the South will fight with Roman desperation. The conflict will be appalling and sanguinary beyond example, provided the invader stand up to it. That much is certain. And if our armies are overthrown, we may be no nearer peace than before. The paper money would be valueless, and the large fortunes accumulated by the speculators, turning to dust and ashes on their lips, might engender a new exasperation, resulting in a regenerated patriotism and a universal determination to achieve independence or die in the attempt.

March 30th.—Gen. Bragg dispatches the government that Gen. Forrest has captured 800 prisoners in Tennessee, and several thousand of our men are making a successful raid in Kentucky.

Gen. Whiting makes urgent calls for reinforcements at Wilmington, and cannot be supplied with many.

Gen. Lee announces to the War Department that the spring campaign is now open, and his army may be in motion any day.

Col. Godwin (of King and Queen County) is here trying to prevail on the Secretary of War to put a stop to the blockade-runners, Jews, and spies, daily passing through his lines with passports from Gens. Elzey and Winder. He says the persons engaged in this illicit traffic are all extortioners and spies, and $50,000 worth of goods from the enemy's country pass daily.

Col. Lay still repudiates Judge Meredith's decision in his instructions to the Commandants of Camps of Instruction. Well, if we have a superabundance of fighting men in the field, the foreign-born denizens and Marylanders can remain at home and make money while the country that protects them is harried by the invader.

The gaunt form of wretched famine still approaches with rapid strides. Meal is now selling at $12 per bushel, and potatoes at $16. Meats have almost disappeared from the market, and none but the opulent can afford to pay $3.50 per pound for butter. Greens, however, of various kinds, are coming in; and as the season advances, we may expect a diminution of prices. It is strange that on the 30th of March, even in the "sunny South," the fruit-trees are as bare of blossoms and foliage as at mid-winter. We shall have fire until the middle of May,—six months of winter!

I am spading up my little garden, and hope to raise a few vegetables to eke out a miserable subsistence for my family. My daughter Ann reads Shakspeare to me o' nights, which saves my eyes.

March 31st.—Another stride of the grim specter, and corn-meal is selling for $17 per bushel. Coal at $20.50 per ton, and wood at $30 per cord. And at these prices one has to wait several days to get either. Common tallow candles are selling at $1 per pound. I see that some furnished houses are now advertised for rent; and I hope that all the population that can get away, and subsist elsewhere, will leave the city.

The lower house of Congress has passed a most enormous tax bill, which I apprehend cannot be enforced, if it becomes a law. It will close half the shops—but that may be beneficial, as thousands have rushed into trade and become extortioners.

I see some batteries of light artillery going toward Petersburg. This is to be used against the enemy when he advances in that direction from Suffolk. No doubt another attempt will be made to capture Richmond. But Lee knows the programme, I doubt not.

April 1st.—It is said we have taken Washington, a village in North Carolina. And it is represented that large supplies of meat, etc. can be taken from thence and the adjacent counties.

Every day we look for important intelligence from Charleston, and from the West.

Mr. Seddon, the Secretary of War, has receded from his position in regard to resident aliens.

April 2d.—This morning early a few hundred women and boys met as by concert in the Capitol Square, saying they were hungry, and must have food. The number continued to swell until there were more than a thousand. But few men were among them, and these were mostly foreign residents, with exemptions in their pockets. About nine a.m. the mob emerged from the western gates of the square, and proceeded down Ninth Street, passing the War Department, and crossing Main Street, increasing in magnitude at every step, but preserving silence and (so far) good order. Not knowing the meaning of such a procession, I asked a pale boy where they were going. A young woman, seemingly emaciated, but yet with a smile, answered that they were going to find something to eat. I could not, for the life of me, refrain from expressing the hope that they might be successful; and I remarked they were going in the right direction to find plenty in the hands of the extortioners. I did not follow, to see what they did; but I learned an hour after that they marched through Cary Street, and entered diverse stores of the speculators, which they proceeded to empty of their contents. They impressed all the carts and drays in the street, which were speedily laden with meal, flour, shoes, etc. I did not learn whither these were driven; but probably they were rescued from those in charge of them. Nevertheless, an immense amount of provisions, and other articles, were borne by the mob, which continued to increase in numbers. An eye-witness says he saw a boy come out of a store with a hat full of money (notes); and I learned that when the mob turned up into Main Street, when all the shops were by this time closed, they broke in the plate-glass windows, demanding silks, jewelry, etc. Here they were incited to pillage valuables, not necessary for subsistence, by the class of residents (aliens) exempted from military duty by Judge Campbell, Assistant Secretary of War, in contravention of Judge Meredith's decision. Thus the work of spoliation went on, until the military appeared upon the scene, summoned by Gov. Letcher, whose term of service is near its close. He had the Riot Act read (by the mayor), and then threatened to fire on the mob. He gave them five minutes' time to disperse in, threatening to use military force (the city battalion being present) if they did not comply with the demand. The timid women fell back, and a pause was put to the devastation, though but few believed he would venture to put his threat in execution. If he had done so, he would have been hung, no doubt.

About this time the President appeared, and ascending a dray, spoke to the people. He urged them to return to their homes, so that the bayonets there menacing them might be sent against the common enemy. He told them that such acts would bring famine upon them in the only form which could not be provided against, as it would deter people from bringing food to the city. He said he was willing to share his last loaf with the suffering people (his best horse had been stolen the night before), and he trusted we would all bear our privations with fortitude, and continue united against the Northern invaders, who were the authors of all our sufferings. He seemed deeply moved; and indeed it was a frightful spectacle, and perhaps an ominous one, if the government does not remove some of the quartermasters who have contributed very much to bring about the evil of scarcity. I mean those who have allowed transportation to forestallers and extortioners.

Gen. Elzey and Gen. Winder waited upon the Secretary of War in the morning, asking permission to call the troops from the camps near the city, to suppress the women and children by a summary process. But Mr. Seddon hesitated, and then declined authorizing any such absurdity. He said it was a municipal or State duty, and therefore he would not take the responsibility of interfering in the matter. Even in the moment of aspen consternation, he was still the politician.

I have not heard of any injuries sustained by the women and children. Nor have I heard how many stores the mob visited; and it must have been many.

All is quiet now (three p.m.); and I understand the government is issuing rice to the people.

April 3d.—Gen. D. H. Hill writes from North Carolina that the business of conscription is miserably mismanaged in that State. The whole business, it seems, has resolved itself into a machine for making money and putting pets in office.

No account of yesterday's riot appeared in the papers to-day, for obvious reasons. The mob visited most of the shops, and the pillage was pretty extensive.

Crowds of women, Marylanders and foreigners, were standing at the street corners to-day, still demanding food; which, it is said, the government issued to them. About midday the City Battalion was marched down Main Street to disperse the crowd.

Congress has resolved to adjourn on the 20th April. The tax bill has not passed both Houses yet.

Gen. Blanchard has been relieved of his command in Louisiana. He was another general from Massachusetts.

April 4th.—It is the belief of some that the riot was a premeditated affair, stimulated from the North, and executed through the instrumentality of emissaries. Some of the women, and others, have been arrested.

We have news of the capture of another of the enemy's gun-boats, in Berwick Bay, Louisiana, with five guns. It is said to have been done by cavalry.

A dispatch just received from Charleston states that the enemy's monitors were approaching the forts, seven in number, and that the attack was commencing. This is joyful news to our people, so confident are they that Gen. Beauregard will beat them.

April 5th.—Snow fell all night, and a depth of several inches covers the earth this morning. It will soon melt, however, as it is now raining. The Northern invaders who anticipate a pleasant sojourn during the winter and spring in this climate, have been very disagreeably disappointed in these expectations.

A surgeon was arrested yesterday for saying there was "a power behind the throne greater than the throne." Upon being asked by the mayor what power he alluded to, he answered "the people." He was released.

April 6th.—It seems that it was a mistake about the enemy's monitors approaching the forts in Charleston harbor; but the government has dispatches to the effect that important movements are going on, not very distant from Charleston, the precise nature of which is not yet permitted to transpire.

Generals Johnston and Bragg write that Gen. Pillow has secured ten times as many conscripts, under their orders, as the bureau in Richmond would have done. Judge Campbell, as Assistant Secretary of War, having arrested Gen. P.'s operations, Generals J. and B. predict that our army in Tennessee will begin, immediately, to diminish in numbers.

The rails of the York River Railroad are being removed to-day toward Danville, in view of securing a connection with the N. C. Central Road. It seems that the government thinks the enemy will again possess the York River Railroad, but it cannot be possible a retreat out of Virginia is meditated.

April 7th.—Nothing definite has transpired at Charleston, or if so, we have not received information of it yet.

From the West, we have accounts, from Northern papers, of the failure of the Yankee Yazoo expedition. That must have its effect.

Judge Campbell, Assistant Secretary of War, has decided in one instance (page 125, E. B. Conscript Bureau), that a paroled political prisoner, returning to the South, is not subject to conscription. This is in violation of an act of Congress, and general orders. It appears that grave judges are not all inflexibly just, and immaculately legal in their decisions. Col. Lay ordered the commandant of conscripts (Col. Shields) to give the man a protection, without any reason therefor.

It is now said large depots of provisions are being formed on the Rappahannock. This does not look like an indication of a retrograde movement on the part of Gen. Lee. Perhaps he will advance.

This afternoon dispatches were received from Charleston. Notwithstanding all the rumors relative to the hostile fleet being elsewhere, it is now certain that all the monitors, iron-clads, and transports have succeeded in passing the bar, and at the last accounts were in readiness to begin the attack. And Beauregard was prepared to receive it. To-morrow we shall have exciting intelligence. If we are to believe what we hear from South Carolinians, recently from Charleston (I do believe it), Charleston will not be taken. If the ground be taken, it will not be Charleston. If the forts fall, and our two rams be taken or destroyed, the defenders will still resist. Rifle-pits have been dug in the streets; and if driven from these, there are batteries beyond to sweep the streets, thus involving the enemy and the city in one common ruin.

April 8th.—We learn to-day that the enemy bombarded our forts at Charleston, yesterday, two hours and a half. But few of our men were injured, and the forts sustained no damage of consequence. On the other hand, several of the iron-clads and monitors of the enemy were badly crippled; one of the latter, supposed to be the Keokuk, was sunk. Since then the bombardment has not been renewed. But no doubt the enemy will make other efforts to reduce a city which is the particular object of their vengeance. Every one is on the qui vive for further news from Charleston. Success there will make Beauregard the most popular man in the Confederacy, Lee excepted.

Speculation is running wild in this city; and the highest civil and military officers are said to be engaged, directly or indirectly, in the disgraceful business of smuggling. Mr. Memminger cannot be ignorant of this; and yet these men are allowed to retain their places.

April 9th.—Nothing additional has occurred at Charleston, the enemy not having renewed the attack. At Vicksburg all was quiet, and the enemy abandoning their canal. Such news must have a depressing effect upon the North. They will see that their monitors and iron-clads have lost their terrors. They have lost some twenty war steamers within the last few months; and how many of their merchantmen have been destroyed on the ocean, we have no means of knowing.

British and French capitalists have taken a cotton loan of $15,000,000, which is now selling at a premium of four per cent. in those countries. Our government can, if it will, soon have a navy of Alabamas and Floridas.

But we are in danger of being sold to the enemy by the blockade-runners in this city. High officers, civil and military, are said, perhaps maliciously, to be engaged in the unlawful trade hitherto carried on by the Jews. It is said that the flag of truce boats serve as a medium of negotiations between official dignitaries here and those at Washington; and I have no doubt many of the Federal officers at Washington, for the sake of lucre, make no scruple to participate in the profits of this treasonable traffic. They can beat us at this game: cheat us in bargaining, and excel us in obtaining information as to the number and position of troops, fortifications, etc.

April 10th.—We are not informed of a renewal of the attack on Charleston. It is said our shot penetrated the turret of the Keokuk, sunk.

In New York they have been exulting over the capture of Charleston, and gold declined heavily. This report was circulated by some of the government officials, at Washington, for purposes of speculation.

Col. Lay announced, to-day, that he had authority (oral) from Gen. Cooper, A. and I. G., to accept Marylanders as substitutes. Soon after he ordered in two, in place of Louisianian sutlers, whom he accompanied subsequently—I know not whither. But this verbal authority is in the teeth of published orders.

April 11th.—Gen. Beauregard telegraphs that Gen. Walker has destroyed another Federal gun-boat in Coosa River. They are looking for a renewal of the attack on Charleston, and are ready for it.

Gen. Lee writes that he is about sending a cavalry brigade into Loudon County to bring off commissary's and quartermaster's stores. This will frighten the people in Washington City! He also writes that, unless the railroads be repaired, so as to admit of speedier transportation of supplies, he cannot maintain his present position much longer.

The President has published a proclamation, to-day, appealing to the patriotism of the people, and urging upon them to abstain from the growth of cotton and tobacco, and raise food for man and beast. Appended to this is a plan, "suggested by the Secretary of War," to obtain from the people an immediate supply of meat, etc. in the various counties and parishes. This is my plan, so politely declined by the Secretary! Well, if it will benefit the government, the government is welcome to it; and Mr. Seddon to the credit of it.

April 12th.—Gen. Van Dorn, it is reported, has captured or destroyed another gun-boat in the West.

Night before last another riot was looked for in this city by the mayor, and two battalions of Gen. Elzey's troops were ordered into the city. If the President could only see the necessity of placing this city under the command of a native Southern general, he might avoid much obloquy. The Smiths, Winders, and Elzeys, who are really foreigners, since the men from their States are not liable to conscription (vide Judge Campbell's decision), are very obnoxious to the people. Virginians can never be reconciled to the presence of a mercenary Swiss guard, and will not submit to imported masters.

Notwithstanding the Enquirer urges it, and Mr. Barksdale, of Mississippi, persistently advocates it, Congress still refuses to confer additional powers on the President. Twice, within the last week, Congress has voted down the proposition to clothe the President with power to suspend the writ of habeas corpus. Congress has likewise refused to reconsider the vote postponing the consideration of the bill to create a Court of Claims. Judge S——was here, working for it; but was doomed to disappointment.

A few nights since a full Federal band came within a hundred yards of our men, the Rappahannock only separating them, and played "Dixie." Our men cheered them lustily. Then they played "Yankee Doodle," when the Yankees cheered. After this they played "Home, sweet Home!" and all parties cheered them. There may be something significant in this. The pickets have orders not to fire on each other, when no demonstration is in progress.

Our members of Congress get salaries of $2750. A cobbler (free negro), who mends shoes for my family, told me yesterday that he earned $10 per day, or $3000 per annum.

A pair of pantaloons now costs $40; boots, $60; and so on.

We have warm weather at last, and dry. Armies will soon be in motion.

Our government and people seem now to despair of European intervention. But the President says our armies are more numerous, and better armed and disciplined than at any period during the war. Hence the contest will be maintained indefinitely for independence. With these feelings the third year of the war opens. May God have mercy on the guilty men who determine more blood shall be shed. The South would willingly cease the sanguinary strife, if the invader would retire from our territory; but just as willingly will she fight hereafter as heretofore, so long as a foeman sets foot upon her soil. It must soon be seen with what alacrity our people will rush to the battle-field!

April 13th.—The Federal monitors, gun-boats, and transports no more menace the City of Charleston! The fleet has sailed away, several of the iron-clads towed out of the harbor being badly damaged. But before leaving that part of the coast, the Yankees succeeded in intercepting and sinking the merchant steamer Leopard, having 40,000 pairs of shoes,.etc. on board for our soldiers. It is supposed they will reappear before Wilmington; our batteries there are ready for them.

Gen. Wise assailed the enemy on Saturday, at Williamsburg, captured the town, and drove the Federals into their fort—Magruder.

The President was ill and nervous on Saturday. His wife, who lost her parent at Montgomery, Ala., a month ago, and who repaired thither, is still absent.

Congress still refuses to clothe the President with dictatorial powers.

Senator Oldham, of Texas, made a furious assault on the Secretary of War, last Saturday. He says Senators, on the most urgent public business, are subjected to the necessity of writing their names on a slate, and then awaiting the pleasure of some lackey for permission to enter the Secretary's office. He was quite severe in his remarks, and moved a call on the President for certain information he desired.

The Sentinel abuses Congress for differing with the President in regard to the retention of diplomatic agents in London, etc. And the Enquirer, edited by John Mitchel, the fugitive Irishman, opens its batteries on the Sentinel. So we go.

April 14th.—We have nothing additional from Gen. Wise's expedition against Williamsburg; but it was deprecated by our people here, whose families and negroes have been left in that vicinity. They argue that we cannot hold the town, or any portion of the Peninsula in the neighborhood; and when the troops retire, the enemy will subject the women and children to more rigorous treatment, and take all the slaves.

We have news from Tennessee, which seems to indicate that Gen. Van Dorn has been beaten, losing a battery, after a sanguinary battle of several hours. Van Dorn had only cavalry—7000. This has a depressing effect. It seems that we lose all the battles of any magnitude in the West. This news may have been received by the President in advance of the public, and hence his indisposition. We shall have news now every day or so.

Albert Pike is out in a pamphlet against Gens. Holmes and Hindman. He says their operations in Arkansas have resulted in reducing our forces, in that State, from forty odd thousand to less than 17,000. It was imprudent to publish such a statement. Albert Pike is a native Yankee, but he has lived a long time in the South.

Gov. Vance is furious at the idea of conscribing magistrates, constables, etc. in North Carolina. He says it would be an annihilation of State Rights—nevertheless, being subject to militia duty by the laws of the State, they are liable under the Act of Conscription.

Well, we are getting only some 700 conscripts per month in Virginia—the largest State! At this rate, how are we to replenish the ranks as they become thinned in battle? It is to be hoped the enemy will find the same difficulty in filling up their regiments, else we have rather a gloomy prospect before us. But God can and will save us if it be His pleasure.

April 15th.—There is a dispatch, unofficial, from the West, contradicting the news of the defeat of Van Dorn. On the Cumberland River, another dispatch says, we have met with new successes, capturing or destroying several more gun-boats. And Wheeler has certainly captured a railroad train in the rear of the enemy, containing a large sum of Federal money, and a number of officers.

We have nothing from the South, except a letter from Gen. Whiting, in regard to some demonstration at Bull Bay, S. C.

Major Griswold, Provost Marshal, is now himself on trial before a court-martial, for allowing 200 barrels of spirits to come into the city. He says he had an order from the Surgeon-General; but what right had he to give such orders? It is understood he will resign, irrespective of the decision of the court.

Congress, yesterday (the House of Representatives), passed a series of resolutions, denying the authority of the government to declare martial law, such as existed in this city under the administration of Gen. Winder. It was a great blunder, and alienated thousands.

We have a seasonable rain to-day.

April 16th.—The Federal papers have heard of the failure to take Charleston, and the sinking of the Keokuk; and yet they strive to mollify the disaster, and represent that but little damage was sustained by the rest of the fleet. Those that escaped, they say, have proved themselves invulnerable. The Keokuk had ninety shots on the water line. No wonder it sunk!

Gen. Longstreet has invested Suffolk, this side of Norfolk, after destroying one gunboat and crippling another in the Nansemond River. Unless the enemy get reinforcements, the garrison at Suffolk may be forced to surrender. Perhaps our general may storm their works!

I learn, to-day, that the remaining eye of the President is failing. Total blindness would incapacitate him for the executive office. A fearful thing to contemplate!

April 17th.—From the Northern papers we learn that the defeat at Charleston is called by the enemy a reconnoissance. This causes us much merriment here; McClellan's defeat was called a "strategical movement," and "change of base."

We have some rumors to-day, to the effect that Gen. Hill is likely to take Washington and Newbern, N. C.; Gen. Longstreet, Suffolk; and Gen. Wise, Fort Magruder, and the Peninsula—he has not troops enough.

Gold advanced 7 per cent. in New York when the news of the "reconnoissance" reached that city.

We are planting almost every acre in grain, to the exclusion of cotton and tobacco—resolved never to be starved, nor even feel a scarcity of provisions in future. We shall be cutting wheat in another month in Alabama and other States.

Among the other rumors, it is said Hooker is falling back toward Washington, but these are merely rumors.

The President is in a very feeble and nervous condition, and is really threatened with the loss of sight altogether. But he works on; and few or no visitors are admitted. He remains at his dwelling, and has not been in the executive office these ten days.

Col. Lay was merry again to-day. He ordered in another foreign substitute (in North Carolina).

Pins are so scarce and costly, that it is now a pretty general practice to stoop down and pick up any found in the street. The boarding-houses are breaking up, and rooms, furnished and unfurnished, are rented out to messes. One dollar and fifty cents for beef, leaves no margin for profit, even at $100 per month, which is charged for board, and most of the boarders cannot afford to pay that price. Therefore they take rooms, and buy their own scanty food. I am inclined to think provisions would not be deficient, to an alarming extent, if they were equally distributed. Wood is no scarcer than before the war, and yet $30 per load (less than a cord) is demanded for it, and obtained.

The other day Wilmington might have been taken, for the troops were sent to Beauregard. Their places have since been filled by a brigade from Longstreet. It is a monstrous undertaking to attempt to subjugate so vast a country as this, even with its disparity of population. We have superior facilities for concentration, while the invader must occupy, or penetrate the outer lines of the circumference. Our danger is from within, not from without. We are distressed more by the extortioners than by the enemy. Eternal infamy on the heads of speculators in articles of prime necessity! After the war, let them be known by the fortunes they have amassed from the sufferings of the patriots and heroes!—the widows and orphans!

This day is the anniversary of the secession of Virginia. The government at Washington did not believe the separation would last two years! Nor do they believe now, perhaps, that it will continue two years longer.

April 18th.—We have nothing more from the Peninsula, Suffolk, N. C., or South Carolina; but it is rumored that the enemy's gun-boats (seven or eight) have passed down the Mississippi in spite of our batteries at Vicksburg, which sunk one of them. If this be true, it is bad news.

We have lovely weather now, and vegetation shows signs of the return of the vernal season. We shall soon have blossoms and roses in abundance, and table vegetables too, to dispel the fears of famine. But we shall also have the horrid sounds of devastating war; and many a cheerful dame and damsel to-day, must soon put on the weeds of mourning.

Gen. Jos. E. Johnston has assumed the command of the army of Tennessee. Gen. Howell Cobb is preparing for the defense of Florida. We do not hear a word from Lee or Jackson—but this is the ominous silence preceding their decisive action.

Bacon fell to-day from $2 to $1.50 per pound, and butter from $3.50 to $3.25; potatoes are $16 per bushel. And yet they say there is no scarcity in the country. Such supplies are hoarded and hidden to extort high prices from the destitute. An intelligent gentleman from North Carolina told me, to-day, that food was never more abundant in his State; nevertheless, the extortioners are demanding there very high prices.

This evening we have dispatches (unofficial) confirmatory of the passing of Vicksburg by the enemy's gun-boats. One of them was destroyed, and two disabled, while five got by uninjured. This is not cheering. No doubt an attack by land will be made, by superior numbers, and blood will gush in streams!

It is now said that Longstreet has captured two gun-boats in the Nansemond, and taken 600 prisoners; and that the Yankees in Norfolk have been thrown into great commotion. The general in command there, Veillé, has adopted very stringent measures to keep the people sympathizing with our cause in subjection. Perhaps he fears an outbreak.

The weather continues fine, and we must soon have important operations in the field.

April 19th, Sunday.—It is now said Longstreet captured two transports, instead of gun-boats, and 600 prisoners.

Mr. Benjamin reports that the enemy's gun-boats, which passed Vicksburg, have recaptured the Queen of the West! It must be so, since he says so.

Mr. Baldwin, the other day, in Congress, asserted a fact, on his own knowledge, that an innocent man had been confined in prison nearly two years, in consequence of a mistake of one of Gen. Winder's subordinates in writing his name, which was Simons; he wrote it Simmons!

April 20th.—We have nothing definite from Suffolk, or from Washington, N. C.

But we have Northern accounts of their great disaster at Charleston. It appears that during the brief engagement on the 7th inst., all their monitors were so badly damaged that they were unable to prolong or to renew the contest. They will have to be taken to New York for repairs; and will not go into service again before autumn. Thus, after nearly a year's preparation, and the expenditure of $100,000,000, all their hopes, so far as Charleston is concerned, have been frustrated in a few brief hours, under the fire of Beauregard's batteries. They complain that England furnished us with the steel-pointed balls that penetrated their iron turrets. To this there can be no objection; indeed it may be productive of good, by involving the Abolitionists in a new quarrel: but it is due to candor to state that the balls complained of were manufactured in this city.

It was a Federal account of the retaking the Queen of the West, reported by Mr. Benjamin; and hence, it is not generally believed.

It is thought by many that Hooker will change his base from the Rappahannock to the Pamunky, embarking his army in transports. If this be so, we shall again have the pleasure of hearing the thunders of battle, this summer, in Richmond.

Gen. Lee has been quite ill, but is now recovering.

April 21st.—Gen. Longstreet lost, it is said, two 32-pounder guns yesterday, with which he was firing on the enemy's gun-boats. A force was landed and captured the battery.

Gen. Lee writes that his men have each, daily, but a quarter pound of meat and 16 ounces of flour. They have, besides, 1 pound of rice to every ten men, two or three times a week. He says this may keep them alive; but that at this season they should have more generous food. The scurvy and the typhoid fever are appearing among them. Longstreet and Hill, however, it is hoped will succeed in bringing off supplies of provision, etc.—such being the object of their demonstrations.

Gen. Wise has fallen back, being ordered by Gen. Elzey not to attempt the capture of Fort Magruder—a feat he could have accomplished.

April 22d.—The President is reported to be very ill to-day—dangerously ill—with inflammation of the throat, etc. While this is a source of grief to nearly all, it is the subject of secret joy to others. I am sure I have seen some officers of rank to-day, not fighting officers, who sincerely hope the President will not recover. He has his faults, but upon the whole is no doubt well qualified for the position he occupies. I trust he will recover.

The destruction of the Queen of the West, and of another of our steamers, is confirmed. Is not Pemberton and Blanchard responsible?

The loss of two guns and forty men the other day, on the Nansemond, is laid at the door of Major-Gen. French, a Northern man! Can it be Gen. Cooper (Northern) who procures the appointment of so many Northern generals in our army?

I cut the following from the Dispatch of yesterday:

Produce, etc.—Bacon has further declined, and we now quote $1.25 to $1.30 for hog-round; butter, $2.25 to $3 per pound; beans in demand at $20 per bushel. Corn is lower—we quote at $6 to $6.50 per bushel; corn meal, $7 to $9 per bushel—the latter figure for a limited quantity; candles, $3.50 to $3.75 per pound; fruit—dried apples, $10 to $12; dried peaches, $15 to $18 per bushel; flour—superfine, $31 to $32; extra, $34; family, $36; hay is in very small supply—sales at $15 per cwt.; lard, $1.65 to $1.70 per pound; potatoes—Irish, $3 to $10; sweet, $10 to $11 per bushel; rice, 25 to 33 cents per pound; wheat, $6.50 to $7 per bushel.

Groceries.—Sugars have a declining tendency: we quote brown at $1.15 to $1.25; molasses, $9 to $10 per gallon; coffee, $4 to $4.50; salt, 45 cents per pound; whisky, $28 to $35; apple brandy, $24 to $25; French brandy, $65 per gallon.

April 23d.—The President's health is improving. His eye is better; and he would have been in his office to-day (the first time for three weeks) if the weather (raining) had been fine.

The expenses of the war amount now to $60,000,000 per month, or $720,000,000 per annum. This enormous expenditure is owing to the absurd prices charged for supplies by the farmers, to save whose slaves and farms the war is waged, in great part. They are charging the government $20 per hundred weight, or $400 per ton for hay! Well, we shall soon see if they be reluctant to pay the taxes soon to be required of them—one-tenth of all their crops, etc. If they refuse to pay, then what will they deserve?

April 24th.—We lost five fine guns and over a hundred men on the Nansemond; and we learn that more of the enemy's gun-boats and transports have passed Vicksburg! These are untoward tidings. Gens. Pemberton and French are severely criticised.

We had a tragedy in the street to-day, near the President's office. It appears that Mr. Dixon, Clerk of the House of Representatives, recently dismissed one of his under clerks, named Ford, for reasons which I have not heard; whereupon the latter notified the former of an intention to assault him whenever they should meet. About two p.m. they met in Bank Street; Ford asked Dixon if he was ready; and upon an affirmative response being given, they both drew their revolvers and commenced firing. Dixon missed Ford, and was wounded by his antagonist, but did not fall. He attempted to fire again, but the pistol missed fire. Ford's next shot missed D. and wounded a man in Main Street, some seventy paces beyond; but his next fire took effect in Dixon's breast, who fell and expired in a few moments.

Many of our people think that because the terms of enlistment of so many in the Federal army will expire next month, we shall not have an active spring campaign. It may be so; but I doubt it. Blood must flow as freely as ever!

April 25th.—We have bad news from the West. The enemy (cavalry, I suppose) have penetrated Mississippi some 200 miles, down to the railroad between Vicksburg and Meridian. This is in the rear and east of Vicksburg, and intercepts supplies. They destroyed two trains. This dispatch was sent to the Secretary of War by the President without remark. The Enquirer this morning contained a paragraph stating that Gen. Pemberton was exchanging civilities with Gen. Sherman, and had sent him a beautiful bouquet! Did he have any conception of the surprise the enemy was executing at the moment? Well, Mississippi is the President's State, and if he is satisfied with Northern generals to defend it, he is as likely to be benefited as any one else.

Gen. Beauregard is urging the government to send more heavy guns to Savannah.

I saw an officer to-day just from Charleston. He says none of the enemy's vessels came nearer than 900 yards of our batteries, and that the Northern statements about the monitors becoming entangled with obstructions are utterly false, for there were no obstructions in the water to impede them. But he says one of the monitors was directly over a torpedo, containing 4000 pounds of powder, which we essayed in vain to ignite.

April 26th.—This being Sunday I shall hear no news, for I will not be in any of the departments.

There is a vague understanding that notwithstanding the repulse of the enemy at Charleston, still the Federal Government collects the duties on merchandise brought into that port, and, indeed, into all other ports. These importations, although purporting to be conducted by British adventurers, it is said are really contrived by Northern merchants, who send hither (with the sanction of the Federal Government, by paying the duty in advance) British and French goods, and in return ship our cotton to Liverpool, etc., whence it is sometimes reshipped to New York. The duties paid the United States are of course paid by the consumers in the Confederate States, in the form of an additional per centum on the prices of merchandise. Some suppose this arrangement has the sanction of certain members of our government. The plausibility of this scheme (if it really exists) is the fact that steamers having munitions of war rarely get through the blockading fleet without trouble, while those having only merchandise arrive in safety almost daily. Gen. D. Green intimates that Mr. Memminger, and Frazer & Co., Charleston, are personally interested in the profits of heavy importations.

April 27th.—A dispatch from Montgomery, Ala., states that the enemy have penetrated as far as Enterprise, Miss., where we had a small body of troops, conscripts. If this be merely a raid, it is an extraordinary one, and I feel some anxiety to learn the conclusion of it. It is hard to suppose a small force of the enemy would evince such temerity. But if it be supported by an army, and the position maintained, Vicksburg is doomed. We shall get no more sugar from Louisiana.

April 28th.—The enemy's raid in Mississippi seems to have terminated at Enterprise, where we collected a force and offered battle, but the invaders retreated. It is said they had 1600 cavalry and 5 guns, and the impression prevails that but few of them will ever return. It is said they sent back a detachment of 200 men some days ago with their booty, watches, spoons, jewelry, etc. rifled from the habitations of the non-combating people.

I saw Brig.-Gen. Chilton to-day, Chief of Gen. Lee's Staff. He says, when the time comes, Gen. Lee will do us all justice. I asked him if Richmond were safe, and he responded in the affirmative.

I am glad the Secretary of War has stopped the blockade-running operations of Gen. Winder and Judge Campbell, Assistant Secretary of War. Until to-day, Gen. W. issued many passports which were invariably approved by Judge Campbell, but for some cause, and Heaven knows there is cause enough, Mr. Secretary has ordered that no more passports be granted Marylanders or foreigners to depart from the Confederacy. I hope Mr. S. will not "back down" from this position.

To-day I returned to the department from the Bureau of Conscription, being required at my old post by Mr. Kean, Chief of the Bureau of War, my friend, Jacques, being out of town with a strangury. Thus it is; when Congress meets I am detailed on service out of the department, and when Congress adjourns they send for me back again. Do they object to my acquaintance with the members?

A few weeks ago I addressed the President a letter suggesting that an alphabetical analysis be made of letter and indorsement books, embracing principles of decisions, and not names. This I did for the Bureau of Conscription, which was found very useful. Precedents could thus be readily referred to when, as was often the case, the names of parties could not be recollected. It happened, singularly enough, that this paper came into my hands with forty-nine others to-day, at the department, where I shall wholly remain hereafter. The President seemed struck with the idea, and indorsed a reference on it to the "State, Treasury, War, and Navy Departments," and also to the Attorney General. I shall be curious to know what the Secretary thinks of this plan. No matter what the Secretary of War thinks of it; he declined my plan of deriving supplies directly from the people, and then adopted it.

April 29th.—Gen. Beauregard is eager to have completed the "Torpedo Ram," building at Charleston, and wants a "great gun" for it. But the Secretary of the Navy wants all the iron for mailing his gun-boats. Mr. Miles, of South Carolina, says the ram will be worth two gun-boats.

The President of the Manassas Gap Railroad says his company is bringing all its old iron to the city. Wherefore?

The merchants of Mobile are protesting against the impressment by government agents of the sugar and molasses in the city. They say this conduct will double the prices. So Congress did not and cannot restrain the military authorities.

Gen. Humphrey Marshall met with no success in Kentucky. He writes that none joined him, when he was led to expect large accessions, and that he could get neither stock nor hogs. Alas, poor Kentucky! The brave hunters of former days have disappeared from the scene.

The Secretary of War was not permitted to see my letter which the President referred to him, in relation to an alphabetical analysis of the decisions of the departments. The Assistant Secretary, Judge Campbell, and the young Chief of the Bureau of War, sent it to the Secretary of the Navy, who, of course, they knew had no decisions to be preserved. Mr. Kean, I learn, indorsed a hearty approval of the plan, and said he would put it in operation in the War Office. But he said (with his concurrence, no doubt) that Judge Campbell had suggested it some time before. Well, that may be; but I first suggested it a year ago, and before either Mr. K. or Judge Campbell were in office. Office makes curious changes in men! Still, I think Mr. Seddon badly used in not being permitted to see the communications the President sends him. I have the privilege, and will use it, of sending papers directly to the Secretary.

Gen. Lee telegraphs the President to-day to send troops to Gordonsville, and to hasten forward supplies. He says Lt.-Gen. Longstreet's corps might now be sent from Suffolk to him. Something of magnitude is on the tapis, whether offensive or defensive, I could not judge from the dispatch.

We had hail this evening as large as pullets' eggs.

The Federal papers have accounts of brilliant successes in Louisiana and Missouri, having taken 1600 prisoners in the former State and defeated Price at Cape Girardeau in the latter. Whether these accounts are authentic or not we have no means of knowing yet. We have nothing further from Mississippi.

It is said there is some despondency in Washington.

Our people will die in the last ditch rather than be subjugated and see the confiscation of their property.

April 30th.—The enemy are advancing across the Rappahannock, and the heavy skirmishing which precedes a battle has begun. We are sending up troops and supplies with all possible expedition. Decisive events are looked for in a few days. But if all of Longstreet's corps be sent up, we leave the southern approach to the city but weakly defended. Hooker must have overwhelming numbers, else he would not venture to advance in the face of Lee's army! Can he believe the silly tale about our troops being sent from Virginia to the Carolinas? If so, he will repent his error.

We hear of fighting in Northwestern Virginia and in Louisiana, but know not the result. The enemy have in possession all of Louisiana west of the Mississippi River. This is bad for us,—sugar and salt will be scarcer still. At Grand Gulf our batteries have repulsed their gun-boats, but the battle is to be renewed.

The railroad presidents have met in this city, and ascertained that to keep the tracks in order for military purposes, 49,500 tons of rails must be manufactured per annum, and that the Tredegar Works here, and the works at Atlanta, cannot produce more than 20,000 tons per annum, even if engaged exclusively in that work! They say that neither individual nor incorporated companies will suffice. The government must manufacture iron or the roads must fail!

A cheering letter was received from Gov. Vance to-day, stating that, upon examination, the State (North Carolina) contains a much larger supply of meat and grain than was supposed. The State Government will, in a week or so, turn over to the Confederate Government 250,000 pounds of bacon, and a quantity of corn; and as speculators are driven out of the market, the Confederate States agents will be able to purchase large supplies from the people, who really have a considerable surplus of provisions. He attributes this auspicious state of things to the cessation of arbitrary impressments.

May 1st.—Gov. Vance writes that Gen. Hill desires him to call out the militia, believing the enemy, balked in the attempt on Charleston, will concentrate their forces against North Carolina. But the Governor is reluctant to call the non-conscripts from the plow in the planting season. He thinks the defense of North Carolina has not been adequately provided for by the government, and that his State has been neglected for the benefit of others. He asks heavy guns; and says half the armament hurled against Charleston would suffice for the capture of Wilmington.

A protest, signed by the thousands of men taken at Arkansas Post, now exchanged, against being kept on this side of the Mississippi, has been received. The protest was also signed by the members of Congress from Texas, Louisiana, Arkansas, and Missouri.

Capt. Causey, of the Signal Corps, writes that there are only a few battalions of the enemy on the Peninsula; but that rations for 40,000 men are sent to Suffolk.

Gen. Lee announces the crossing of the Rappahannock at Port Royal (which the Yankees pillaged) and at places above Fredericksburg. Gen. Stuart is hovering on their flank. A great battle may happen any moment.

L. E. Harvey, president of Richmond and Danville Railroad, asks for details to repair locomotives, else daily trains (freight) must be reduced to tri-weekly trains—and then the army cannot be sustained in Virginia.

Hon. Mr. Garnett asked (and obtained) permission for a Mr. Hurst (Jew?) to pass our lines, and bring Northern merchandise to Richmond for sale. He vouches for his loyalty to Virginia. Congress has before it a bill rendering this traffic criminal.

May 2d.—The awful hour, when thousands of human lives are to be sacrificed in the attempt to wrest this city from the Confederate States, has come again. Now parents, wives, sisters, brothers, and little children, both in the North and in the South, hold their breath in painful expectation. At the last accounts the two armies, yesterday, were drawn up in battle array, facing each other. No water flowed between them, the Northern army being on this side of the Rappahannock. We have no means of knowing their relative numbers; but I suspect Gen. Hooker commands more than 100,000 men, while Gen. Lee's army, perhaps, does not exceed 55,000 efficients.

Accounts by passengers, and reports from the telegraph operators at the northern end of the line, some ten or twelve miles this side of the armies, indicate that the battle was joined early this morning. Certainly heavy cannonading was heard. Yet nothing important transpired up to 3 p.m., when I left the department, else I should have known it. Still, the battle may be raging, without, as yet, decisive result, and the general may not have leisure to be dictating dispatches.

Yet the heavy artillery may be only the preliminary overture to the desperate engagement; and it seems to me that several days might be spent in manœuvring into position before the shock of arms occurs, which will lay so many heads low in the dust.

But a great battle seems inevitable. All the world knows the fighting qualifications of Gen. Lee, and the brave army he commands; and Gen. Hooker will, of course, make every effort to sustain his reputation as "fighting Joe." Besides, he commands, for the first time, an army: and knows well that failure to fight, or failure to win, will consign him to the same disgrace of all his predecessors who have hitherto commanded the "Army of the Potomac."

It is certain that a column of Federal cavalry, yesterday, cut the Central Railroad at Trevillian's depot, which prevents communication with Gordonsville, if we should desire to send heavy stores thither. And some suppose Lee is manœuvring to get in the rear of Hooker, which would place the enemy between him and Richmond! He could then cut off his supplies, now being drawn by wagons some twenty or thirty miles, and spread alarm even to Washington. But, then, how would it be with Richmond, if Hooker should accept the position, and if the force at Suffolk should advance on the south side of the river, and gun-boats and transports were to come, simultaneously, up the York and James? Has Hooker the genius to conceive such a plan? Suppose it were so, and that he has shipped his supplies from the Potomac—the supplies which Stuart expects to capture—with the desperate resolution, abandoning his base on the Rappahannock, to force a junction with the heavy detachments south and east of this city? A Napoleon would get Richmond—but then Lee might get Washington! Longstreet's corps is somewhere in transitu between Petersburg and Gordonsville, and would no doubt be ordered here, and it might arrive in time. Our defenses are strong; but at this moment we have only Gen.

Wise's brigade, and a few battalions at the batteries, to defend the capital—some 5000 in all.

This is mere speculation, to be succeeded speedily by awful facts. The inhabitants here do not doubt the result, although there is a feverish anxiety to get intelligence. There is no such thing as fear, in this community, of personal danger, even among the women and children; but there is some alarm by the opulent inhabitants, some of whom, for the sake of their property, would submit to the invader. One thing is pretty certain, Richmond will not fall by assault without costing the lives of 50,000 men, which is about equal to its population in ordinary times.

Well, I am planting potatoes in my little garden, and hope to reap the benefit of them. I pay 50 cts. per quart for seed potatoes, and should be chagrined to find my expenditure of money and labor had been for the benefit of the invader! Yet it may be so; and if it should be, still there are other little gardens to cultivate where we might fly to. We have too broad and too long a territory in the revolted States to be overrun and possessed by the troops of the United States.

May 3d.—We have no further news from the army, except the usual skirmishing. A number of our wounded arrived last evening. An officer reports that, from what he could see of the enemy's conduct, the soldiers do not come to the point with alacrity. He thinks they fight with reluctance, and are liable to be routed any hour by inferior numbers.

Troops were sent up in special trains last night, and also this morning. These are some of the regiments which Gen. D. P. Hill had in North Carolina; and hence the complaints of Gov. Vance, that his State did not have its just proportion of the protection of the government. Of Longstreet's movements, I am not advised. But there will be news enough in a few days.

The President's health is still precarious, and he is still threatened with the loss of his remaining eye.

The Vice-President was in my office yesterday, and told me his health is quite as good as usual. One would suppose him to be afflicted with all manner of diseases, and doomed to speedy dissolution; but, then, he has worn this appearance during the last twenty years. His eyes are magnificent, and his mind is in the meridian of intellectual vigor.

There has been some commotion in the city this afternoon and evening, but no painful alarm, produced by intelligence that the enemy's cavalry, that cut the road at Trevillian's depot, had reached Ashland and destroyed the depot. Subsequent rumors brought them within eight miles of the city; and we have no force of any consequence here. The account was brought from Ashland by a Mr. Davis, who killed his horse in riding eighteen miles in one hour and a half.

Later in the day a young man, sixteen years old (Shelton), reached the city from Hanover on a United States horse, the enemy having foraged on his father's farm and taken his blooded steed. He says, when he escaped from them (having been taken prisoner this morning) 1500 were at his father's place, and three times as many more, being 6000 in all, were resting a short distance apart on another farm; but such ideas of numbers are generally erroneous. They told him they had been in the saddle five days, and had burnt all the bridges behind them to prevent pursuit. It was after this that they cut the road at Ashland. They professed to have fresh horses taken from our people, leaving their own. I think they will disappear down the Pamunky, and of course will cut the Central and York River Roads, and the wires. Thus communication with Lee's army is interrupted!

The Fredericksburg train, of course, failed to arrive to-day at 6 p.m.; and it is rumored there were 700 of our wounded in it, and that a great battle was fought yesterday by Lee. These are rumors.

May 4th.—This morning early the tocsin sounded, and the din, kept up for several hours, intensified the alarm. The presence of the enemy would not have produced a greater effect. But, in truth, the enemy were almost in sight of the city. Hon. James Lyons told me they were within a mile and a half of his house, which is about that distance from the city. Thousands of men, mostly old men and employees of the government, were instantly organized and marched to the batteries.

But the alarm subsided about 10 a.m. upon information being received that the enemy were flying before Gen. Wise down the Peninsula.

After this the following dispatch was received from Gen. Lee:

"Milford, May 3d, 1863.

"President Davis.

"Yesterday Gen. Jackson, with three of his divisions, penetrated to the rear of the enemy, and drove him from all his positions, from the Wilderness to within one mile of Chancellorville. He was engaged at the same time, in front, by two of Longstreet's divisions. This morning the battle was renewed. He was dislodged from all his positions around Chancellorville, and driven back toward the Rappahannock, over which he is now retreating.

"Many prisoners were taken, and the enemy's loss, in killed and wounded, large.

"We have again to thank Almighty God for a great victory.

"I regret to state that Gen. Paxton was killed. Gen. Jackson severely, and Generals Heth and A. P. Hill slightly, wounded.

"(Signed) R. E. Lee, General."

Enough is known to raise the spirits of all. Gen. Lee gives thanks to God "for a great victory;" and he never misleads, never exaggerates.

My son Custis got a musket and marched in one of the companies—I have not learned which—for the defense of the city. It is a sultry day, and he will suffer.

The President was driven out in a light open carriage after the reception of Gen. Lee's dispatch, and exhibited the finest spirits. He was even diverted at the zeal of the old men and boys marching out with heavy muskets to the batteries.

Brig.-Gen. Pryor, who has been under arrest (I know not for what offense), volunteered in a company of horse, and galloped away with the rest in pursuit of the enemy.

May 5th.—To-day the excitement was quite as great as ever, for bodies of the enemy are still in the vicinity. They are like frightened quails when the hawks are after them, skurrying about the country in battalions and regiments. Fitzhugh Lee defeated one of their parties, and reports that the entire cavalry force of Hooker, in anticipation of certain victory, had been detached in the rear of Lee's army. This force comprises twenty-eight regiments, or 15,000 mounted men! Now that Hooker is defeated—our operator at Guiney's station dispatches to-day that it is reported there, and believed, that Hooker and his staff are prisoners—it may be reasonably doubted whether one-half of this wild cavalry will escape. It was the mad pranks of a desperate commander. Hooker cast all upon the hazard of the die—and lost.

Among the mad pranks of the enemy, they sent a message over the wires to-day from Louisa County, I believe, to this purport: "For Heaven's sake, come and take us. We are broken down, and will surrender."

They captured an engine sent out yesterday to repair the road. The white men escaped, leaving two free negroes. The Yankees made the negroes put on a full head of steam, and run the locomotive into the river.

One of the enemy was taken sleeping at one of our city batteries near the river.

My friend, Dr. Powell, on the Brooke Turnpike, sent his little son, mounted on his finest horse, on an errand to a neighbor. The lad fell in with, as he called, them, "some Yankee Dutchmen," who presented their pistols and made him dismount. They took his horse and allowed him to return.

At the hour we were dining yesterday, the enemy were within two and a half miles of us on the Brooke road, and might have thrown shell into this part of the city.

Col. D. J. Godwin writes a long letter to the Secretary of War, from King and Queen Counties, concerning the great number of suspicious persons continually passing our lines into those of the enemy, with passports from this city; and the great injury done by the information they give. Unquestionably they have not only given information, but have furnished guides to the many regiments of cavalry now skurrying through the country. But the Baltimore Plug Uglies, under the protection of Gen. Winder, are the masters, now Mr. Secretary Seddon has yielded again.

A letter was received from Gen. J. E. Johnston to-day. He is too unwell to take the field, and suggests, if it be desirable to be in regular communication with Gen. Bragg, that the President send out a confidential officer. He says the army is suffering for meat, and if it retires into East Tennessee, supplies must be obtained from its flanks instead of from its rear, which would be dangerous. The letter was dated a week ago, and gives no indications of a battle. The general says he is exchanging sugar for bacon; but condemns the practice of allowing our people to sell cotton to the enemy for supplies. In my opinion none but government cotton should be exchanged for subsistence. He says the people are subjugated by trade. He suggests that our men when paroled, and not exchanged, may do duty otherwise than in arms—as is practiced by the enemy.

H. D. Bird, general superintendent of the railroad, writes from Petersburg that the movements of cars with ammunition, etc. are thrown into confusion by the neglect of telegraph agents in giving timely notice. This is an unfortunate time for confusion. I sent the letter to the Secretary, and know that it was not "filed" on the way to him.

A communication came in to-day from the Committee of Safety at Mobile, Ala., charging that J. S. Clark, Wm. G. Ford, and —— Hurt, have been shipping cotton to New Orleans, after pretending to clear it for Nassau. It says Mr. Clarke was an intimate crony of Gen. Butler's speculating brother. It also intimates that the people believe the government here winks at these violations of the act of Congress of April, 1862.

Very curiously, a letter came from the Assistant Secretary's room to-day for "file," which was written April 22d, 1861, by R. H. Smith to Judge Campbell—a private letter—warning him not to come to Mobile, as nothing was thought of but secession, and it was believed Judge C. had used his influence with Mr. Seward to prevent secession. The writer deprecates civil war. And quite as curiously, the Examiner to-day contains what purports to be Admiral Buchanan's correspondence with the Lincoln government, two letters, the first in April, 1861, tendering his resignation, and the last on May 4th, begging, if it had not been done already, that the government would not accept his resignation.

May 6th.—The excitement has subsided, as troops come pouring in, and many improvised cavalry companies go out in quest of the fox—who has vanished we know not exactly whither.

It is believed we have taken 15,000 or 20,000 prisoners, and that the enemy's killed, wounded, and prisoners must reach the appalling number of 40,000.

On Sunday, the enemy opposite Fredericksburg sent over a flag, asking permission to bury their dead. This was granted. But when they came—two corps under Gen. Sedgwick came over and fell upon our few regiments in the vicinity. So goes the story. Then, it is said, when Gen. Lee ordered two of our divisions to drive Sedgwick back, the men, learning the enemy with the flag of truce had given no quarter to their comrades, refused to fight unless permitted to retaliate in kind. This was promised them; and then their charge was irresistible, never pausing until the Yankees were hurled back across the river. No prisoners were taken. However this may be, Gen. Lee sends the following to the President:

"[Received by telegraph from Guiney's Depot.]

"Headquarters, 10 o'clock a.m.,
"May 5, 1863.

"To his Excellency, President Davis.

"At the close of the battle of Chancellorville, on Sunday, the enemy was reported advancing from Fredericksburg in our rear.

"Gen. McLaws was sent back to arrest his progress, and repulsed him handsomely that afternoon. Learning that this force consisted of two corps, under Gen. Sedgwick, I determined to attack it, and marched back yesterday with Gen. Anderson, and uniting with Gens. McLaws and Early in the afternoon, succeeded by the blessing of Heaven in driving Gen. Sedgwick over the river. We have reoccupied Fredericksburg, and no enemy remains south of the Rappahannock in its vicinity.

"(Signed) R. E. Lee, General."

Another dispatch from Gen. Lee says Hooker is still on this side of the river, at United States Ford, fortifying.

Gen. Longstreet is now closeted with the Secretary of War. No doubt his entire corps will immediately rejoin Lee.

Jackson was wounded (his arm has been amputated) before the great battle was fought, by our own men, in the gloom of the evening, supposing him a Federal officer. He was reconnoitering in front of the line.

S. S. H—— writes to the department, proposing to send an emissary to the North, to organize secret societies to destroy the enemy's stores, ships, railroad bridges, etc. by an unexplained process.

Tillman, Griffin & Co. write to Judge Campbell to obtain them permission to trade with Mexico. Does this mean trading cotton with the enemy? I know not whether the request was granted.

Mr. Benjamin, Secretary of State, writes to the Secretary to-day for permission for some of his Louisiana friends to leave the country in a government steamer.

It is said that the government at Washington is ordering their troops from North Carolina and other places on the Southern seaboard towards Washington, and to reinforce Hooker—or Hooker's army. I think Hooker himself will go the way of all general flesh that fails.

The President sent to the War Department fifty-five letters to-day, written to him on various subjects, but mostly asking appointments. He had read them, and several had indorsed on them, in his own hand, what he wished done in the premises. So he has not lost his sight. He still attends to business at his dwelling, and has not been in his office for more than a month.

Secretary Seddon is gaunt and emaciated, with long straggling hair, mingled gray and black. He looks like a dead man galvanized into muscular animation. His eyes are sunken, and his features have the hue of a man who had been in his grave a full month. But he is an orator, and a man of fine education—but in bad health, being much afflicted with neuralgia. His administrative capacity will be taxed by the results.

May 7th.—A scout came in to-day with the vexatious intelligence that a body of hostile cavalry is still in Louisa County. And later in the day we have information that the Mattapony bridge was burned last night! Thus again is communication interrupted between Gen. Lee and the city! Our wounded cannot be brought to the hospitals here, nor supplies sent to them! It really does seem as if an organization of Union men here were co-operating with the enemy, else they never could disappear and reappear so often with impunity. Every one is asking what Gens. Elzey and Winder are doing—and echo answers, what?

There is a great pressure for passports to leave the country. Mr. Benjamin writes an indignant letter to the Secretary against Gen. Whiting, at Wilmington, for detaining a Mr. Flanner's steamer, laden with cotton for some of the nationalities—Mr. B. intimates a foreign or neutral power. But when once away from our shore, many of these vessels steer for New York, depositing large sums "for those whom it may concern."

Mr. J. B. Campbell, attorney for J. E. Hertz (Jew), writes a long letter to "J. A. Campbell, Assistant Secretary of War," urging the payment of the slight sum of $25,200 for ninety kegs of bicarbonate of soda seized by the agent of the department! The true value is about $250!

At two o'clock this afternoon a note was received by the Secretary of War from Lieut.-Gen. Longstreet (still in the city), stating that the President last night desired him to go to Gen. Lee immediately; but the general, during the day, has become convinced that he should not leave the city until communications are re-established with Gen. Lee, and the city in a condition of defense against the sudden dash of one or two columns of the enemy—an event, he thinks, meditated by the Yankees! And the persistency of the Federal cavalry in hanging round the city in spite of all the generals here, and the many companies, battalions, and regiments vainly sent out in quest of them, would seem to indicate such purpose.

But the raids in the West don't seem to flourish so well. We have an official dispatch from Gen. Bragg, stating that Gen. Forrest has captured 1600 of the enemy's cavalry in a body, near Rome, Georgia.

There are amusing scenes among the horrors of war, as the following, taken from a paper to-day, shows:

"Taking the Oath under Protest.—A few weeks ago a laughable incident occurred in the neighborhood of Nashville, which is worthy of record. A saucy, dashing young girl, of the Southern persuasion, was, with a number of other ladies, brought into the presence of Gen. Rosecrans, in order that their Southern ardor might be checked by the administration of the oath of loyalty. The bold, bright-eyed Juno in question, objected to take the oath, saying that her mother had taught her that it was unlady-like to swear; her sense of morality forbid her to swear, and swear she could and would not. The officer insisted that the lady must take an oath before she left his presence.

"'Well, general,' said bright eyes, 'if I must swear, I will; but all sins of the oath must rest on your shoulders, for I swear on your compulsion: "G—d d—m every Yankee to h—l!"'

"And the defiant beauty tossed her dark curls and swept out of the presence unmolested."—Nashville Union.

7 o'clock p.m. The report that the bridge over the Mattapony had been burned by the enemy was false—invented probably by a spy or emissary, who has enjoyed the freedom of the city under the Dogberrys and Vergises imported hither to preserve the government. A number of trains containing our wounded men, guarded by a detachment of troops, have arrived at the Fredericksburg depot. An officer just arrived from the army says we have taken 15,000 prisoners. If this be so, the loss of the enemy during the week in Virginia will not be less than 40,000. Our loss in killed and wounded is estimated at from 8 to 10,000—we lost a few hundred prisoners. We have taken, it is said, 53 guns, and lost 14.

I think the reports to-day of squadrons of the enemy's cavalry seen in the surrounding counties are not reliable—they were probably our own men in quest of the enemy.

May 8th.—To-day the city is in fine spirits. Hooker had merely thrown up defenses to protect his flight across the river. The following dispatch was received last night from Gen. Lee:

"Chancellorville, May 7th, 1863.

"To His Excellency, President Davis.

"After driving Gen. Sedgwick across the Rappahannock, on the night of the 4th inst., I returned on the 5th to Chancellorville. The march was delayed by a storm, which continued all night and the following day. In placing the troops in position on the morning of the 6th, to attack Gen. Hooker, it was ascertained he had abandoned his fortified position. The line of skirmishers was pressed forward until they came within range of the enemy's batteries, planted north of the Rappahannock, which, from the configuration of the ground, completely commanded this side. His army, therefore, escaped with the loss of a few additional prisoners.

"(Signed) R. E. Lee, General."

Thus ends the career of Gen. Hooker, who, a week ago, was at the head of an army of 150,000 men, perfect in drill, discipline, and all the muniments of war. He came a confident invader against Gen. Lee at the head of 65,000 "butternuts," as our honest poor-clad defenders were called, and we see the result! An active campaign of less than a week, and Hooker is hurled back in disgrace and irreparable disaster! Tens of thousands of his men will never live to "fight another day"—and although the survivors did "run away," it is doubtful whether they can be put in fighting trim again for many a month.

And the raiding cavalry have not been heard from to-day. If they be not back on the north side of the Rappahannock by this time, it is probable they will reach Richmond in a few days without arms, and on foot.

Gens. Hood's and Pickett's divisions (Longstreet's corps) are now passing through the city—perhaps 15,000 of the best fighting men in the South. Oh, what wisdom and foresight were evinced by Gen. Lee, when, some ten days ago, he telegraphed the President to send him Longstreet's corps, via Gordonsville! It was referred to the Secretary of War, who consulted with Gen. Cooper—and of course it was not done. This corps was not in the battle. If it had been on the field, Hooker's destruction would have been speedy and complete; and his routed regiments would have been followed to the very gates of the Federal capital. As it was, Lee lost a day in driving Sedgwick back—and then Hooker "escaped," as Lee expresses it.

I do not understand the Assistant Secretary of War's official correspondence. He sent in the other day a letter addressed to him two years ago to be filed—and to-day an envelope addressed to him as Assistant Secretary by Mr. Benjamin, Secretary of State, merely covering a letter (sealed) for R. S. Bunkee, Mobile, Alabama. Well, it is filed.

The pressure for permits to leave the Confederacy is not renewed to-day. Judge Campbell will not have so many passports to "approve," and I trust confidence in the permanency of the Confederacy will be unshaken. How must they feel who, in anticipation of Lee's defeat, had received, in advance, a pardon from the powers at Washington!

Col. Lay was in to-day; he thinks the North will be cheered a little by their capture of Grand Gulf, in the West. But that is not Vicksburg, or Charleston, or Richmond.

We have had short allowance of food yesterday and to-day; the country people being afraid to come to market, lest their horses should be seized to go in quest of the enemy's cavalry. My family dined to-day on eight fresh herrings, which cost two dollars.

The trains from Fredericksburg brought down several hundred Federal officers; among them was a general, a large number of colonels, lieutenant-colonels, majors, captains, etc. These, when exchanged, as I suppose they will be—for victory makes our government magnanimous—may, if they choose, deny the report that the raiding cavalry destroyed the railroad.

Now what will the Tribune say? It did say, a few months ago, that if the effort to crush the rebellion failed this spring, it would be useless to prolong the war—and that peace should be made on the best practicable terms. Since the beginning of the war, I doubt not 500,000 men have been precipitated upon Virginia. Where are they now? In the third year of the war, we see "the finest army the world ever saw," overthrown by about half its numbers, and in full retreat toward its own frontier. Perhaps 100,000 invaders have found bloody graves in Virginia—and an equal number have died of their wounds, or from disease contracted in this State. The number of maimed and disabled must also be 100,000—and yet Richmond is not taken, or likely to be. To invade and subjugate a vast territory, inhabited by millions of warlike people, the assailants must always have four times as many men as the assailed; therefore we stand on an equal footing with the United States in this war, and they may, if they be insane enough, protract it indefinitely, and in the end reap no substantial benefit. On the contrary, the fortune of war may shift the scene of devastation to their own homes. Perhaps Lee may follow up this blow until he enters Pennsylvania.

May 9th.—The papers contain the following order from Gen. Lee:

"Headquarters Army Northern Virginia, May 7th, 1863.

"General Orders No. 59.

"With heartfelt gratification, the General Commanding expresses to the army his sense of the heroic conduct displayed by officers and men, during the arduous operations in which they have just been engaged.

"Under trying vicissitudes of heat and storm, you attacked the enemy, strongly intrenched in the depths of a tangled wilderness, and again on the hills of Fredericksburg, fifteen miles distant, and by the valor that has triumphed on so many fields, forced him once more to seek safety beyond the Rappahannock. While this glorious victory entitles you to the praise and gratitude of the nation, we are especially called upon to return our grateful thanks to the only Giver of victory for the signal deliverance He has wrought.

"It is, therefore, earnestly recommended that the troops unite on Sunday next in ascribing to the Lord of hosts the glory due unto His name.

"Let us not forget in our rejoicing the brave soldiers who have fallen in defense of their country; and while we mourn their loss, let us resolve to emulate their noble example.

"The army and the country alike lament the absence for a time of one to whose bravery, energy, and skill they are so much indebted for success.

"The following letter from the President of the Confederate States is communicated to the army as an expression of his appreciation of its success:

"'I have received your dispatch, and reverently unite with you in giving praise to God for the success with which He has crowned our arms.

"'In the name of the people, I offer my cordial thanks to yourself and the troops under your command for this addition to the unprecedented series of great victories which your army has achieved.

"'The universal rejoicing produced by this happy result will be mingled with a general regret for the good and the brave who are numbered among the killed and wounded.'

"R. E. Lee, General."

The losses on either side are not yet relatively ascertained. Ours, in killed, wounded, and prisoners, will probably reach 10,000. We have taken about 10,000 prisoners; the enemy's killed and wounded is thought to be 15,000 to 20,000. We have taken about fifty guns—and it is said 40,000 small arms, in good order. They did not have leisure to destroy them as on former occasions. It was a complete and stunning defeat.

Gen. Jackson remains near Fredericksburg, and is doing well since the amputation of his (left) arm. The wound was received, during the battle by moonlight, from his own men, who did not recognize their beloved general.

A letter was received to-day from Gen. Whiting at Wilmington, who refuses to permit the "Lizzie" to leave the port, unless ordered to do so. He intimates that she trades with the enemy. And yet Mr. Benjamin urges the Secretary to allow her to depart! Commodore Lynch also writes that the detention of the "Lizzie" is a prudential measure, as it is the only steamer in port that could conduct our unfinished gun-boat to a place of safety, should the enemy's fleet make a sudden attack on the city.

The President (who still absents himself from the Executive Office, his health being precarious) writes the Secretary to consult Gen. Lee before detaching Gen. Jenkins's cavalry brigade from the West. It would have been better if Gen. Lee's advice had been taken in regard to Gen. Longstreet.

The men from the garrison at Drewry's Bluff, and the crew from the steamer Richmond, were taken away to man the batteries around the city. The President requests the Secretary to order them back at the earliest moment practicable. It would be an ugly picture if our defenses at Drewry's Bluff were surprised and taken by a sudden dash of the enemy up James River.

The raid of the enemy's cavalry, after all, did little or no permanent injury to the roads or canal. They are all in operation again.

It is said Lincoln has called for 500,000 more men. Numbers have now no terror for the Southern people. They are willing to wage the war against quadruple their number.

May 10th.—Detachments of Federal troops are now marching into the city every few hours, guarded by (mostly) South Carolinians, dressed in home-spun, died yellow with the bark of the butternut-tree. Yesterday evening, at 7 o'clock, a body of 2000 arrived, being marched in by way of the Brooke Pike, near to my residence. Only 200 Butternuts had them in charge, and a less number would have sufficed, for they were extremely weary. Some of them, however, attempted to be humorous.

A young officer asked one of the spectators if the "Libby" (the prison) was the best house in the city to put up at. He was answered that it was the best he would find.

Another passed some compliment on a mulatto wench, who replied: "Go long, you nasty Abolition Yankee."

One of our soldiers taken at Arkansas Post, just exchanged, walked along with the column, and kept repeating these words: "Now you know how we felt when you marched us through your cities."

But generally a deep silence was maintained, and neither insult nor indignity offered the fallen foe. Other columns are on the way—and how they are to be subsisted is a vexatious question.

The Washington papers of the day preceding the first battle contain Hooker's address to his army—how different from Lee's! It is short, though:

"Headquarters Army of the Potomac, Camp near Falmouth, April 30th.

"General Orders No. 47.

"It is with heartfelt satisfaction that the Commanding General announces to the army that the operations of the last three days have determined that our enemy must either ingloriously fly or come out from behind his defenses and give us battle on our own ground, where certain destruction awaits him. The operations of the 15th, 11th, and 12th corps have been a succession of splendid achievements.

"By command of Maj.-Gen. Hooker. S. Williams, Ass't. Adj't.-Gen."

Another column of between twelve and fifteen hundred prisoners marched in this afternoon. It is said a copy of the New York Herald is in town, which acknowledges Hooker's loss to be fully 40,000. There are rumors, also, that our army in Tennessee has gained a great victory. Rumors from the West have hitherto been so very unreliable, that I shall wait patiently for the confirmation of any reports from that quarter.

May 11th.—Lieut.-Gen. J. T. Jackson died at 3 p.m. yesterday. His remains will arrive in the city at 5 p.m. this afternoon. The flags are at half-mast, and all the government offices and even places of business are closed. A multitude of people, mostly women and children, are standing silently in the streets, awaiting the arrival of the hero, destined never again to defend their homes and honor.

A letter from Gen. Lee says, emphatically, that if cavalry be not brought from North Carolina and the South, the enemy's cavalry will be enabled to make raids almost anywhere without molestation. I recollect distinctly how he urged the Secretary of War (Randolph), months ago, to send to Texas for horses, but it was not attended to—and now we see the consequences.

The exchanged prisoners here, taken at Arkansas Post, are ordered to the Mississippi. Gen. Longstreet urged the Secretary to send them off, if that were their destination, without a moment's delay, several days ago—else they would be too late to participate in the campaign.

Northern papers set down Hooker's loss at 20,000, a modest figure, subject to revision.

The Federal Secretary of War has issued a statement to mollify the panic. He is bound to acknowledge that, whereas Hooker advanced upon Lee across the river, he is now, after the battle, back again, where he started from. But he says not more than a third of the army was engaged; and as 30,000 reinforcements have been sent from Washington, and as many from Suffolk, the army will soon be as strong as ever, and in condition for another advance—and defeat.

But what credit can we attach to such statements, since McClellan, under oath, said that he had ninety odd thousand men at the battle of Sharpsburg, 75,000 of whom only were actually engaged, while Lee had 100,000? We know that he did not have 40,000 engaged!

Gen. Van Dorn is dead—being killed by a man whose peace he had ruined.

More applications for passports to leave the country are coming in—and they are "allowed" by the Assistant Secretary of War. How could he refuse, since his own family (at least a portion of it) have enjoyed the benefits of sojourning in the North since the war began?

A letter was received to-day from Mr. Ranney, president of the N. C., Jackson, and Great Northern Railroad Co., asking the protection of government from harm for violations of the Act of Congress of April 19th, 1862, prohibiting the transportation of cotton within the enemy's lines. He incloses a number of peremptory orders from Lieut.-Gen. Pemberton, dated January 19th, February 16th and 19th, to take large amounts of cotton into the enemy's lines for S. J. Josephs (Jew?), and for Messrs. Clarke, Ford, and Hust, etc. etc. He says Gen. P. threatened to seize the road if he did not comply, and asserted that he had authority from the Secretary of War to issue the orders. One of these orders was from Gov. Pettus, for a small lot not more than fifty bales, to be exchanged for salt. This was authorized by the President, who most positively forbid the others. The letter from Gen. Johnston the other day said this traffic was subjugating the people. Was that "allowed" to reach the Secretary and the President? I know not; it has not yet passed through my hands from the President back to the department.

May 12th.—The departments and all places of business are still closed in honor of Gen. Jackson, whose funeral will take place to-day. The remains will be placed in state at the Capitol, where the people will be permitted to see him. The grief is universal, and the victory involving such a loss is regarded as a calamity.

The day is bright and excessively hot; and so was yesterday.

Many letters are coming in from the counties in which the enemy's cavalry replenished their horses. It appears that the government has sent out agents to collect the worn-down horses left by the enemy; and this is bitterly objected to by the farmers. It is the corn-planting season, and without horses, they say, they can raise no crops. Some of these writers are almost menacing in their remarks, and intimate that they are about as harshly used, in this war, by one side as the other.

To-day I observed the clerks coming out of the departments with chagrin and mortification. Seventy-five per cent. of them ought to be in the army, for they are young able-bodied men. This applies also to the chiefs of bureaus.

The funeral was very solemn and imposing, because the mourning was sincere and heartfelt. There was no vain ostentation. The pall bearers were generals. The President followed near the hearse in a carriage, looking thin and frail in health. The heads of departments, two and two, followed on foot—Benjamin and Seddon first—at the head of the column of young clerks (who ought to be in the field), the State authorities, municipal authorities, and thousands of soldiers and citizens. The war-horse was led by the general's servant, and flags and black feathers abounded.

Arrived at the Capitol, the whole multitude passed the bier, and gazed upon the hero's face, seen through a glass in the coffin.

Just previous to the melancholy ceremony, a very large body of prisoners (I think 3500) arrived, and were marched through Main Street, to the grated buildings allotted them. But these attracted slight attention,—Jackson, the great hero, was the absorbing thought. Yet there are other Jacksons in the army, who will win victories,—no one doubts it.

The following is Gen. Lee's order to the army after the intelligence of Gen. Jackson's death:

"Headquarters Army Northern Va., May 11th, 1863.

"General Orders No. 61.

"With deep grief the Commanding General announces to the army the death of Lieut.-Gen. T. J. Jackson, who expired on the 10th inst., at 3½ p.m. The daring, skill, and energy of this great and good soldier, by the decree of an all-wise Providence, are now lost to us. But while we mourn his death, we feel that his spirit still lives, and will inspire the whole army with his indomitable courage and unshaken confidence in God as our hope and our strength. Let his name be a watchword to his corps, who have followed him to victory on so many fields. Let officers and soldiers emulate his invincible determination to do everything in the defense of our beloved country.

"R. E. Lee, General."

The Letter of Gen. Lee to Gen. Jackson.

The letter written by Gen. Lee to Gen. Jackson before the death of the latter is as follows:

"Chancellorville, May 4th.

"General:—

"I have just received your note informing me that you were wounded. I cannot express my regret at the occurrence. Could I have dictated events, I should have chosen for the good of the country to have been disabled in your stead.

"I congratulate you upon the victory which is due to your skill and energy.

"Most truly yours,
"R. E. Lee.

"To Gen. T. J. Jackson."

"The nation's agony," as it is termed in a Washington paper, in an appeal for 500,000 more men, now demands a prompt response from the people. And yet that paper, under the eye and in the interest of the Federal Government, would make it appear that "the Army of the Potomac" has sustained no considerable disaster. What, then, constitutes the "nation's agony"? Is it the imminency of war with England? It may be, judging from the debates in Parliament, relating to the liberties the United States have been taking with British commerce. But what do they mean by the "nation?" They have nothing resembling a homogeneous race in the North, and nearly a moiety of the people are Germans and Irish. How ridiculous it would have been even for a Galba to call his people the Roman nation! An idiot may produce a conflagration, but he can never rise to the dignity of a high-minded man. Yet that word "Nation" may raise a million Yankee troops. It is a "new thing."

The Northern papers say Charleston is to be assailed again immediately; that large reinforcements are going to Hooker, and that they captured six or eight thousand prisoners in their flight on the Rappahannock. All these fictions are understood and appreciated here; but they may answer a purpose in the North, by deceiving the people again into the belief that Richmond will certainly fall the next time an advance is made. And really, where we see such extravagant statements in the Federal journals, after a great battle, we are much rejoiced, because we know them to be unfounded, and we are led to believe our victory was even greater than we supposed it to be.

Co. Aytch, Maury Grays, First Tennessee Regiment; Or, A Side Show Of The Big Show.

By Sam. R. Watkins, Columbia, Tenn.

"Quaeque ipse miserima vidi, Et quorum pars magna fui."

(... and those terrible things I saw, and in which I played a great part.)

To The Memory Of My Dead Comrades Of The Maury Grays, And The First Tennessee Regiment, Who Died In Defense Of Southern Homes And Liberties: Also To My Living Comrades, Nearly All Of Whom Shed Their Blood In Defense Of The Same Cause, This Book Is Respectfully Dedicated By The Author . . . . .

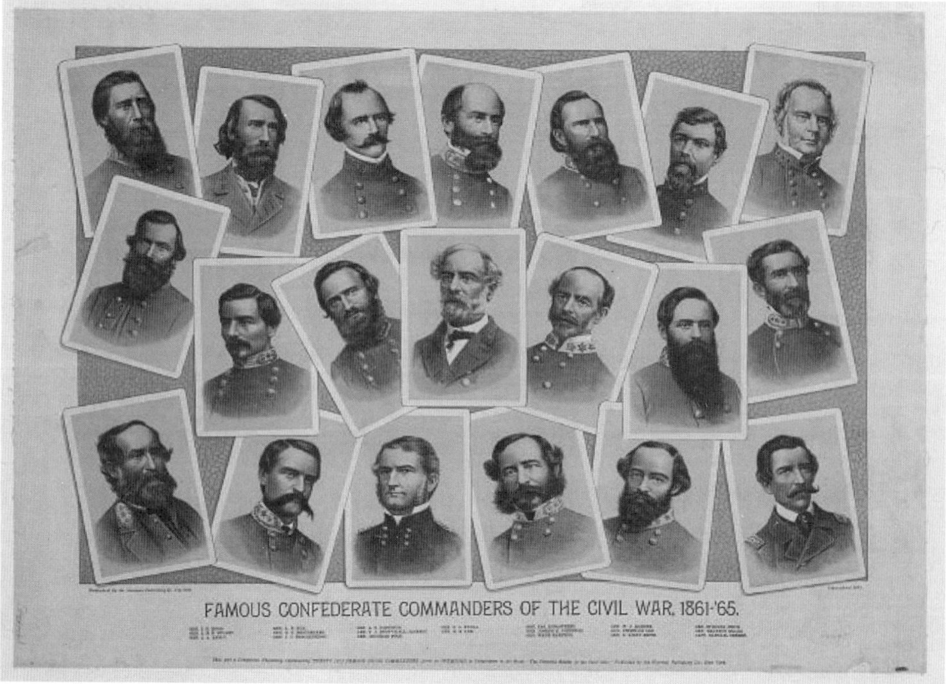

Famous Confederate commanders of the Civil War, 1861-65 [Hood Stuart, Early, Hill, Polk, J.E. Johnston, Hardee, Smith, Bragg, R. E. Lee, Beauregard, Breckinridge, A.S. Johnston, Jackson, Ewell, Hampton, Fitzhugh Lee, Price, Semmes, Longstreet

Chapter I -- Retrospective

"We Are One And Undivided"

About twenty years ago, I think it was--I won't be certain, though--a man whose name, if I remember correctly, was Wm. L. Yancy--I write only from memory, and this was a long time ago--took a strange and peculiar notion that the sun rose in the east and set in the west, and that the compass pointed north and south. Now, everybody knew at the time that it was but the idiosyncrasy of an unbalanced mind, and that the United States of America had no north, no south, no east, no west. Well, he began to preach the strange doctrine of there being such a thing. He began to have followers. As you know, it matters not how absurd, ridiculous and preposterous doctrines may be preached, there will be some followers. Well, one man by the name of (I think it was) Rhett, said it out loud. He was told to "s-h-e-e." Then another fellow by the name (I remember this one because it sounded like a graveyard) Toombs said so, and he was told to "sh-sh-ee-ee." Then after a while whole heaps of people began to say that they thought that there was a north and a south; and after a while hundreds and thousands and millions said that there was a south. But they were the persons who lived in the direction that the water courses run. Now, the people who lived where the water courses started from came down to see about it, and they said, "Gents, you are very much mistaken. We came over in the Mayflower, and we used to burn witches for saying that the sun rose in the east and set in the west, because the sun neither rises nor sets, the earth simply turns on its axis, and we know, because we are Pure(i)tans." The spokesman of the party was named (I think I remember his name because it always gave me the blues when I heard it) Horrors Greeley; and another person by the name of Charles Sumner, said there ain't any north or south, east or west, and you shan't say so, either. Now, the other people who lived in the direction that the water courses run, just raised their bristles and continued saying that there is a north and there is a south. When those at the head of the water courses come out furiously mad, to coerce those in the direction that water courses run, and to make them take it back. Well, they went to gouging and biting, to pulling and scratching at a furious rate. One side elected a captain by the name of Jeff Davis, and known as one-eyed Jeff, and a first lieutenant by the name of Aleck Stephens, commonly styled Smart Aleck. The other side selected as captain a son of Nancy Hanks, of Bowling Green, and a son of old Bob Lincoln, the rail-splitter, and whose name was Abe. Well, after he was elected captain, they elected as first lieutenant an individual of doubtful blood by the name of Hannibal Hamlin, being a descendant of the generation of Ham, the bad son of old Noah, who meant to curse him blue, but overdid the thing, and cursed him black.

Well, as I said before, they went to fighting, but old Abe's side got the best of the argument. But in getting the best of the argument they called in all the people and wise men of other nations of the earth, and they, too, said that America had no cardinal points, and that the sun did not rise in the east and set in the west, and that the compass did not point either north or south. Well, then, Captain Jeff Davis' side gave it up and quit, and they, too, went to saying that there is no north, no south, no east, no west. Well, "us boys" all took a small part in the fracas, and Shep, the prophet, remarked that the day would come when those who once believed that the American continent had cardinal points would be ashamed to own it. That day has arrived. America has no north, no south, no east, no west; the sun rises over the hills and sets over the mountains, the compass just points up and down, and we can laugh now at the absurd notion of there being a north and a south.

Well, reader, let me whisper in your ear. I was in the row, and the following pages will tell what part I took in the little unpleasant misconception of there being such a thing as a north and south.

The Bloody Chasm

In these memoirs, after the lapse of twenty years, we propose to fight our "battles o'er again."

To do this is but a pastime and pleasure, as there is nothing that so much delights the old soldier as to revisit the scenes and battlefields with which he was once so familiar, and to recall the incidents, though trifling they may have been at the time.

The histories of the Lost Cause are all written out by "big bugs," generals and renowned historians, and like the fellow who called a turtle a "cooter," being told that no such word as cooter was in Webster's dictionary, remarked that he had as much right to make a dictionary as Mr. Webster or any other man; so have I to write a history. But in these pages I do not pretend to write the history of the war. I only give a few sketches and incidents that came under the observation of a "high private" in the rear ranks of the rebel army. Of course, the histories are all correct. They tell of great achievements of great men, who wear the laurels of victory; have grand presents given them; high positions in civil life; presidents of corporations; governors of states; official positions, etc., and when they die, long obituaries are published, telling their many virtues, their distinguished victories, etc., and when they are buried, the whole country goes in mourning and is called upon to buy an elegant monument to erect over the remains of so distinguished and brave a general, etc. But in the following pages I propose to tell of the fellows who did the shooting and killing, the fortifying and ditching, the sweeping of the streets, the drilling, the standing guard, picket and videt, and who drew (or were to draw) eleven dollars per month and rations, and also drew the ramrod and tore the cartridge. Pardon me should I use the personal pronoun "I" too frequently, as I do not wish to be called egotistical, for I only write of what I saw as an humble private in the rear rank in an infantry regiment, commonly called "webfoot." Neither do I propose to make this a connected journal, for I write entirely from memory, and you must remember, kind reader, that these things happened twenty years ago, and twenty years is a long time in the life of any individual.

I was twenty-one years old then, and at that time I was not married. Now I have a house full of young "rebels," clustering around my knees and bumping against my elbow, while I write these reminiscences of the war of secession, rebellion, state rights, slavery, or our rights in the territories, or by whatever other name it may be called. These are all with the past now, and the North and South have long ago "shaken hands across the bloody chasm." The flag of the Southern cause has been furled never to be again unfurled; gone like a dream of yesterday, and lives only in the memory of those who lived through those bloody days and times.

Eighteen Hundred And Sixty-One

Reader mine, did you live in that stormy period? In the year of our Lord eighteen hundred and sixty-one, do you remember those stirring times? Do you recollect in that year, for the first time in your life, of hearing Dixie and the Bonnie Blue Flag? Fort Sumter was fired upon from Charleston by troops under General Beauregard, and Major Anderson, of the Federal army, surrendered. The die was cast; war was declared; Lincoln called for troops from Tennessee and all the Southern states, but Tennessee, loyal to her Southern sister states, passed the ordinance of secession, and enlisted under the Stars and Bars. From that day on, every person, almost, was eager for the war, and we were all afraid it would be over and we not be in the fight. Companies were made up, regiments organized; left, left, left, was heard from morning till night. By the right flank, file left, march, were familiar sounds. Everywhere could be seen Southern cockades made by the ladies and our sweethearts. And some who afterwards became Union men made the most fiery secession speeches. Flags made by the ladies were presented to companies, and to hear the young orators tell of how they would protect that flag, and that they would come back with the flag or come not at all, and if they fell they would fall with their backs to the field and their feet to the foe, would fairly make our hair stand on end with intense patriotism, and we wanted to march right off and whip twenty Yankees. But we soon found out that the glory of war was at home among the ladies and not upon the field of blood and carnage of death, where our comrades were mutilated and torn by shot and shell. And to see the cheek blanch and to hear the fervent prayer, aye, I might say the agony of mind were very different indeed from the patriotic times at home.

Camp Cheatham

After being drilled and disciplined at Camp Cheatham, under the administrative ability of General R. C. Foster, 3rd, for two months, we, the First, Third and Eleventh Tennessee Regiments--Maney, Brown and Rains-- learned of the advance of McClelland's army into Virginia, toward Harper's Ferry and Bull Run. The Federal army was advancing all along the line. They expected to march right into the heart of the South, set the negroes free, take our property, and whip the rebels back into the Union. But they soon found that secession was a bigger mouthful than they could swallow at one gobble. They found the people of the South in earnest.

Secession may have been wrong in the abstract, and has been tried and settled by the arbitrament of the sword and bayonet, but I am as firm in my convictions today of the right of secession as I was in 1861. The South is our country, the North is the country of those who live there. We are an agricultural people; they are a manufacturing people. They are the descendants of the good old Puritan Plymouth Rock stock, and we of the South from the proud and aristocratic stock of Cavaliers. We believe in the doctrine of State rights, they in the doctrine of centralization.

John C. Calhoun, Patrick Henry, and Randolph, of Roanoke, saw the venom under their wings, and warned the North of the consequences, but they laughed at them. We only fought for our State rights, they for Union and power. The South fell battling under the banner of State rights, but yet grand and glorious even in death. Now, reader, please pardon the digression. It is every word that we will say in behalf of the rights of secession in the following pages. The question has been long ago settled and is buried forever, never in this age or generation to be resurrected.

The vote of the regiment was taken, and we all voted to go to Virginia. The Southern Confederacy had established its capital at Richmond.

A man by the name of Jackson, who kept a hotel in Maryland, had raised the Stars and Bars, and a Federal officer by the name of Ellsworth tore it down, and Jackson had riddled his body with buckshot from a double- barreled shotgun. First blood for the South.

Everywhere the enemy were advancing; the red clouds of war were booming up everywhere, but at this particular epoch, I refer you to the history of that period.

A private soldier is but an automaton, a machine that works by the command of a good, bad, or indifferent engineer, and is presumed to know nothing of all these great events. His business is to load and shoot, stand picket, videt, etc., while the officers sleep, or perhaps die on the field of battle and glory, and his obituary and epitaph but "one" remembered among the slain, but to what company, regiment, brigade or corps he belongs, there is no account; he is soon forgotten.

A long line of box cars was drawn up at Camp Cheatham one morning in July, the bugle sounded to strike tents and to place everything on board the cars. We old comrades have gotten together and laughed a hundred times at the plunder and property that we had accumulated, compared with our subsequent scanty wardrobe. Every soldier had enough blankets, shirts, pants and old boots to last a year, and the empty bottles and jugs would have set up a first-class drug store. In addition, every one of us had his gun, cartridge-box, knapsack and three days' rations, a pistol on each side and a long Bowie knife, that had been presented to us by William Wood, of Columbia, Tenn. We got in and on top of the box cars, the whistle sounded, and amid the waving of hats, handkerchiefs and flags, we bid a long farewell and forever to old Camp Cheatham.

Arriving at Nashville, the citizens turned out _en masse_ to receive us, and here again we were reminded of the good old times and the "gal we left behind us." Ah, it is worth soldiering to receive such welcomes as this.

The Rev. Mr. Elliott invited us to his college grove, where had been prepared enough of the good things of earth to gratify the tastes of the most fastidious epicure. And what was most novel, we were waited on by the most beautiful young ladies (pupils of his school). It was charming, I tell you. Rev. C. D. Elliott was our Brigade Chaplain all through the war, and Dr. C. T. Quintard the Chaplain of the First Tennessee Regiment-- two of the best men who ever lived. (Quintard is the present Bishop of Tennessee).

On The Road

Leaving Nashville, we went bowling along twenty or thirty miles an hour, as fast as steam could carry us. At every town and station citizens and ladies were waving their handkerchiefs and hurrahing for Jeff Davis and the Southern Confederacy. Magnificent banquets were prepared for us all along the entire route. It was one magnificent festival from one end of the line to the other. At Chattanooga, Knoxville, Bristol, Farmville, Lynchburg, everywhere, the same demonstrations of joy and welcome greeted us. Ah, those were glorious times; and you, reader, see why the old soldier loves to live over again that happy period.

But the Yankees are advancing on Manassas. July 21st finds us a hundred miles from that fierce day's battle. That night, after the battle is fought and won, our train draws up at Manassas Junction.

Well, what news? Everyone was wild, nay, frenzied with the excitement of victory, and we felt very much like the "boy the calf had run over." We felt that the war was over, and we would have to return home without even seeing a Yankee soldier. Ah, how we envied those that were wounded. We thought at that time that we would have given a thousand dollars to have been in the battle, and to have had our arm shot off, so we could have returned home with an empty sleeve. But the battle was over, and we left out.

Staunton

From Manassas our train moved on to Staunton, Virginia. Here we again went into camp, overhauled kettles, pots, buckets, jugs and tents, and found everything so tangled up and mixed that we could not tell tuther from which.

We stretched our tents, and the soldiers once again felt that restraint and discipline which we had almost forgotten en route to this place. But, as the war was over now, our captains, colonels and generals were not "hard on the boys;" in fact, had begun to electioneer a little for the Legislature and for Congress. In fact, some wanted, and were looking forward to the time, to run for Governor of Tennessee. Staunton was a big place; whisky was cheap, and good Virginia tobacco was plentiful, and the currency of the country was gold and silver.

The State Asylums for the blind and insane were here, and we visited all the places of interest.

Here is where we first saw the game called "chuck-a-luck," afterwards so popular in the army. But, I always noticed that chuck won, and luck always lost.

Faro and roulette were in full blast; in fact, the skum had begun to come to the surface, and shoddy was the gentleman. By this, I mean that civil law had been suspended; the ermine of the judges had been overridden by the sword and bayonet. In other words, the military had absorbed the civil. Hence the gambler was in his glory.

Warm Springs, Virginia

One day while we were idling around camp, June Tucker sounded the assembly, and we were ordered aboard the cars. We pulled out for Millboro; from there we had to foot it to Bath Alum and Warm Springs. We went over the Allegheny Mountains.

I was on every march that was ever made by the First Tennessee Regiment during the whole war, and at this time I cannot remember of ever experiencing a harder or more fatiguing march. It seemed that mountain was piled upon mountain. No sooner would we arrive at a place that seemed to be the top than another view of a higher, and yet higher mountain would rise before us. From the foot to the top of the mountain the soldiers lined the road, broken down and exhausted. First one blanket was thrown away, and then another; now and then a good pair of pants, old boots and shoes, Sunday hats, pistols and Bowie knives strewed the road. Old bottles and jugs and various and sundry articles were lying pell-mell everywhere. Up and up, and onward and upward we pulled and toiled, until we reached the very top, when there burst upon our view one of the grandest and most beautiful landscapes we ever beheld.

Nestled in the valley right before us is Bath Alum and Warm Springs. It seemed to me at that time, and since, a glimpse of a better and brighter world beyond, to the weary Christian pilgrim who may have been toiling on his journey for years. A glad shout arose from those who had gained the top, which cheered and encouraged the others to persevere. At last we got to Warm Springs. Here they had a nice warm dinner waiting for us. They had a large bath-house at Warm Springs. A large pool of water arranged so that a person could go in any depth he might desire. It was a free thing, and we pitched in. We had no idea of the enervating effect it would have upon our physical systems, and as the water was but little past tepid, we stayed in a good long time. But when we came out we were as limp as dishrags. About this time the assembly sounded and we were ordered to march. But we couldn't march worth a cent. There we had to stay until our systems had had sufficient recuperation. And we would wonder what all this marching was for, as the war was over anyhow.

The second day after leaving Warm Springs we came to Big Springs. It was in the month of August, and the biggest white frost fell that I ever saw in winter.

The Yankees were reported to be in close proximity to us, and Captain Field with a detail of ten men was sent forward on the scout. I was on the detail, and when we left camp that evening, it was dark and dreary and drizzling rain. After a while the rain began to come down harder and harder, and every one of us was wet and drenched to the skin--

guns, cartridges and powder. The next morning about daylight, while standing videt, I saw a body of twenty-five or thirty Yankees approaching, and I raised my gun for the purpose of shooting, and pulled down, but the cap popped. They discovered me and popped three or four caps at me; their powder was wet also. Before I could get on a fresh cap, Captain Field came running up with his seven-shooting rifle, and the first fire he killed a Yankee. They broke and run. Captain Field did all the firing, but every time he pulled down he brought a Yankee. I have forgotten the number that he did kill, but if I am not mistaken it was either twenty or twenty-one, for I remember the incident was in almost every Southern paper at that time, and the general comments were that one Southern man was equal to twenty Yankees. While we were in hot pursuit, one truly brave and magnanimous Yankee, who had been badly wounded, said, "Gentlemen, you have killed me, but not a hundred yards from here is the main line." We did not go any further, but halted right there, and after getting all the information that we could out of the wounded Yankee, we returned to camp.

One evening, General Robert E. Lee came to our camp. He was a fine- looking gentleman, and wore a moustache. He was dressed in blue cottonade and looked like some good boy's grandpa. I felt like going up to him and saying good evening, Uncle Bob! I am not certain at this late day that I did not do so. I remember going up mighty close and sitting there and listening to his conversation with the officers of our regiment. He had a calm and collected air about him, his voice was kind and tender, and his eye was as gentle as a dove's. His whole make-up of form and person, looks and manner had a kind of gentle and soothing magnetism about it that drew every one to him and made them love, respect, and honor him. I fell in love with the old gentleman and felt like going home with him. I know I have never seen a finer looking man, nor one with more kind and gentle features and manners. His horse was standing nipping the grass, and when I saw that he was getting ready to start I ran and caught his horse and led him up to him. He took the reins of the bridle in his hand and said, "thank you, my son," rode off, and my heart went with him. There was none of his staff with him; he had on no sword or pistol, or anything to show his rank. The only thing that I remember he had was an opera-glass hung over his shoulder by a strap.

Robert E. Lee's home in Richmond, Va.

Leaving Big Springs, we marched on day by day, across Greenbrier and Gauley rivers to Huntersville, a little but sprightly town hid in the very fastnesses of the mountains. The people live exceedingly well in these mountains. They had plenty of honey and buckwheat cakes, and they called buttermilk "sour-milk," and sour-milk weren't fit for pigs; they couldn't see how folks drank sour-milk. But sour-kraut was good. Everything seemed to grow in the mountains--potatoes, Irish and sweet; onions, snap beans, peas--though the country was very thinly populated. Deer, bear, and foxes, as well as wild turkeys, and rabbits and squirrels abounded everywhere. Apples and peaches were abundant, and everywhere the people had apple-butter for every meal; and occasionally we would come across a small-sized distillery, which we would at once start to doing duty. We drank the singlings while they were hot, but like the old woman who could not eat corn bread until she heard that they made whisky out of corn, then she could manage to "worry a little of it down;" so it was with us and the singlings.

From this time forward, we were ever on the march--tramp, tramp, tramp-- always on the march. Lee's corps, Stonewall Jackson's division--I refer you to the histories for the marches and tramps made by these commanders the first year of the war. Well, we followed them.

Cheat Mountain

One evening about 4 o'clock, the drummers of the regiment began to beat their drums as hard as they could stave, and I saw men running in every direction, and the camp soon became one scene of hurry and excitement. I asked some one what all this hubbub meant. He looked at me with utter astonishment. I saw soldiers running to their tents and grabbing their guns and cartridge-boxes and hurry out again, the drums still rolling and rattling. I asked several other fellows what in the dickens did all this mean? Finally one fellow, who seemed scared almost out of his wits, answered between a wail and a shriek, "Why, sir, they are beating the long roll." Says I, "What is the long roll for?" "The long roll, man, the long roll! Get your gun; they are beating the long roll!" This was all the information that I could get. It was the first, last, and only long roll that I ever heard. But, then everything was new, and Colonel Maney, ever prompt, ordered the assembly. Without any command or bugle sound, or anything, every soldier was in his place. Tents, knapsacks and everything was left indiscriminately.

We were soon on the march, and we marched on and on and on. About night it began to rain. All our blankets were back in camp, but we were expected every minute to be ordered into action. That night we came to Mingo Flats. The rain still poured. We had no rations to eat and nowhere to sleep. Some of us got some fence rails and piled them together and worried through the night as best we could. The next morning we were ordered to march again, but we soon began to get hungry, and we had about half halted and about not halted at all. Some of the boys were picking blackberries. The main body of the regiment was marching leisurely along the road, when bang, debang, debang, bang, and a volley of buck and ball came hurling right through the two advance companies of the regiment--companies H and K. We had marched into a Yankee ambuscade.

All at once everything was a scene of consternation and confusion; no one seemed equal to the emergency. We did not know whether to run or stand, when Captain Field gave the command to fire and charge the bushes. We charged the bushes and saw the Yankees running through them, and we fired on them as they retreated. I do not know how many Yankees were killed, if any. Our company (H) had one man killed, Pat Hanley, an Irishman, who had joined our company at Chattanooga. Hugh Padgett and Dr. Hooper, and perhaps one or two others, were wounded.

After the fighting was over, where, O where, was all the fine rigging heretofore on our officers? They could not be seen. Corporals, sergeants, lieutenants, captains, all had torn all the fine lace off their clothing. I noticed that at the time and was surprised and hurt. I asked several of them why they had torn off the insignia of their rank, and they always answered, "Humph, you think that I was going to be a target for the Yankees to shoot at?" You see, this was our first battle, and the officers had not found out that minnie as well as cannon balls were blind; that they had no eyes and could not see. They thought that the balls would hunt for them and not hurt the privates.

I always shot at privates. It was they that did the shooting and killing, and if I could kill or wound a private, why, my chances were so much the better. I always looked upon officers as harmless personages. Colonel Field, I suppose, was about the only Colonel of the war that did as much shooting as the private soldier. If I shot at an officer, it was at long range, but when we got down to close quarters I always tried to kill those that were trying to kill me.

Sewell Mountain

From Cheat Mountain we went by forced marches day and night, over hill and everlasting mountains, and through lovely and smiling valleys, sometimes the country rich and productive, sometimes rough and broken, through towns and villages, the names of which I have forgotten, crossing streams and rivers, but continuing our never ceasing, unending march, passing through the Kanawha Valley and by the salt-works, and nearly back to the Ohio river, when we at last reached Sewell Mountain. Here we found General John B. Floyd strongly entrenched and fortified and facing the advance of the Federal army. Two days before our arrival he had charged and captured one line of the enemy's works. I know nothing of the battle. See the histories for that. I only write from memory, and that was twenty years ago, but I remember reading in the newspapers at that time of some distinguished man, whether he was captain, colonel or general, I have forgotten, but I know the papers said "he sought the bauble, reputation, at the cannon's mouth, and went to glory from the death-bed of fame." I remember it sounded gloriously in print. Now, reader, this is all I know of this grand battle. I only recollect what the newspapers said about it, and you know that a newspaper always tells the truth. I also know that beef livers sold for one dollar apiece in gold; and here is where we were first paid off in Confederate money. Remaining here a few days, we commenced our march again. Sewell Mountain, Harrisonburg, Lewisburg, Kanawha Salt-works, first four, forward and back, seemed to be the programme of that day. Rosecrans, that wiley old fox, kept Lee and Jackson both busy trying to catch him, but Rosey would not be caught. March, march, march; tramp, tramp, tramp, back through the valley to Huntersville and Warm Springs, and up through the most beautiful valley--the Shenandoah--in the world, passing towns and elegant farms and beautiful residences, rich pastures and abundant harvests, which a Federal General (Fighting Joe Hooker), later in the war, ordered to be so sacked and destroyed that a "crow passing over this valley would have to carry his rations." Passing on, we arrived at Winchester. The first night we arrived at this place, the wind blew a perfect hurricane, and every tent and marquee in Lee's and Jackson's army was blown down. This is the first sight we had of Stonewall Jackson, riding upon his old sorrel horse, his feet drawn up as if his stirrups were much too short for him, and his old dingy military cap hanging well forward over his head, and his nose erected in the air, his old rusty sabre rattling by his side. This is the way the grand old hero of a hundred battles looked. His spirit is yonder with the blessed ones that have gone before, but his history is one that the country will ever be proud of, and his memory will be cherished and loved by the old soldiers who followed him through the war.

Photograph of Lieut. General Thomas J. Jackson

Romney

Our march to and from Romney was in midwinter in the month of January, 1862. It was the coldest winter known to the oldest inhabitant of these regions. Situated in the most mountainous country in Virginia, and away up near the Maryland and Pennsylvania line, the storm king seemed to rule in all of his majesty and power. Snow and rain and sleet and tempest seemed to ride and laugh and shriek and howl and moan and groan in all their fury and wrath. The soldiers on this march got very much discouraged and disheartened. As they marched along icicles hung from their clothing, guns, and knapsacks; many were badly frost bitten, and I heard of many freezing to death along the road side. My feet peeled off like a peeled onion on that march, and I have not recovered from its effects to this day. The snow and ice on the ground being packed by the soldiers tramping, the horses hitched to the artillery wagons were continually slipping and sliding and falling and wounding themselves and sometimes killing their riders. The wind whistling with a keen and piercing shriek, seemed as if they would freeze the marrow in our bones. The soldiers in the whole army got rebellious--almost mutinous--and would curse and abuse Stonewall Jackson; in fact, they called him "Fool Tom Jackson." They blamed him for the cold weather; they blamed him for everything, and when he would ride by a regiment they would take occasion, _sotto voce_, to abuse him, and call him "Fool Tom Jackson," and loud enough for him to hear. Soldiers from all commands would fall out of ranks and stop by the road side and swear that they would not follow such a leader any longer.

When Jackson got to Romney, and was ready to strike Banks and Meade in a vital point, and which would have changed, perhaps, the destiny of the war and the South, his troops refused to march any further, and he turned, marched back to Winchester and tendered his resignation to the authorities at Richmond. But the great leader's resignation was not accepted. It was in store for him to do some of the hardest fighting and greatest generalship that was done during the war.

One night at this place (Romney), I was sent forward with two other soldiers across the wire bridge as picket. One of them was named Schwartz and the other Pfifer--he called it Fifer, but spelled it with a P--both full-blooded Dutchmen, and belonging to Company E, or the German Yagers, Captain Harsh, or, as he was more generally called, "God-for-dam."

When we had crossed the bridge and taken our station for the night, I saw another snow storm was coming. The zig-zag lightnings began to flare and flash, and sheet after sheet of wild flames seemed to burst right over our heads and were hissing around us. The very elements seemed to be one aurora borealis with continued lightning. Streak after streak of lightning seemed to be piercing each the other, the one from the north and the other from the south. The white clouds would roll up, looking like huge snow balls, encircled with living fires. The earth and hills and trees were covered with snow, and the lightnings seemed to be playing "King, King Canico" along its crusted surface. If it thundered at all, it seemed to be between a groaning and a rumbling sound. The trees and hills seemed white with livid fire. I can remember that storm now as the grandest picture that has ever made any impression on my memory. As soon as it quit lightning, the most blinding snow storm fell that I ever saw. It fell so thick and fast that I got hot. I felt like pulling off my coat. I was freezing. The winds sounded like sweet music. I felt grand, glorious, peculiar; beautiful things began to play and dance around my head, and I supposed I must have dropped to sleep or something, when I felt Schwartz grab me, and give me a shake, and at the same time raised his gun and fired, and yelled out at the top of his voice, "Here is your mule." The next instant a volley of minnie balls was scattering the snow all around us. I tried to walk, but my pants and boots were stiff and frozen, and the blood had ceased to circulate in my lower limbs. But Schwartz kept on firing, and at every fire he would yell out, "Yer is yer mool!" Pfifer could not speak English, and I reckon he said "Here is your mule" in Dutch. About the same time we were hailed from three Confederate officers, at full gallop right toward us, not to shoot. And as they galloped up to us and thundered right across the bridge, we discovered it was Stonewall Jackson and two of his staff. At the same time the Yankee cavalry charged us, and we, too, ran back across the bridge.

Standing Picket On The Potomac

Leaving Winchester, we continued up the valley.

The night before the attack on Bath or Berkly Springs, there fell the largest snow I ever saw.

Stonewall Jackson had seventeen thousand soldiers at his command. The Yankees were fortified at Bath. An attack was ordered, our regiment marched upon top of a mountain overlooking the movements of both armies in the valley below. About 4 o'clock one grand charge and rush was made, and the Yankees were routed and skedaddled.

By some circumstance or other, Lieutenant J. Lee Bullock came in command of the First Tennessee Regiment. But Lee was not a graduate of West Point, you see.

The Federals had left some spiked batteries on the hill side, as we were informed by an old citizen, and Lee, anxious to capture a battery, gave the new and peculiar command of, "Soldiers, you are ordered to go forward and capture a battery; just piroute up that hill; piroute, march. Forward, men; piroute carefully." The boys "pirouted" as best they could. It may have been a new command, and not laid down in Hardee's or Scott's tactics; but Lee was speaking plain English, and we understood his meaning perfectly, and even at this late day I have no doubt that every soldier who heard the command thought it a legal and technical term used by military graduates to go forward and capture a battery.

At this place (Bath), a beautiful young lady ran across the street. I have seen many beautiful and pretty women in my life, but she was the prettiest one I ever saw. Were you to ask any member of the First Tennessee Regiment who was the prettiest woman he ever saw, he would unhesitatingly answer that he saw her at Berkly Springs during the war, and he would continue the tale, and tell you of Lee Bullock's piroute and Stonewall Jackson's charge.

We rushed down to the big spring bursting out of the mountain side, and it was hot enough to cook an egg. Never did I see soldiers more surprised. The water was so hot we could not drink it.

The snow covered the ground and was still falling.

That night I stood picket on the Potomac with a detail of the Third Arkansas Regiment. I remember how sorry I felt for the poor fellows, because they had enlisted for the war, and we for only twelve months. Before nightfall I took in every object and commenced my weary vigils. I had to stand all night. I could hear the rumblings of the Federal artillery and wagons, and hear the low shuffling sound made by troops on the march. The snow came pelting down as large as goose eggs. About midnight the snow ceased to fall, and became quiet. Now and then the snow would fall off the bushes and make a terrible noise. While I was peering through the darkness, my eyes suddenly fell upon the outlines of a man. The more I looked the more I was convinced that it was a Yankee picket. I could see his hat and coat--yes, see his gun. I was sure that it was a Yankee picket. What was I to do? The relief was several hundred yards in the rear. The more I looked the more sure I was. At last a cold sweat broke out all over my body. Turkey bumps rose. I summoned all the nerves and bravery that I could command, and said: "Halt! who goes there?" There being no response, I became resolute. I did not wish to fire and arouse the camp, but I marched right up to it and stuck my bayonet through and through it. It was a stump. I tell the above, because it illustrates a part of many a private's recollections of the war; in fact, a part of the hardships and suffering that they go through. One secret of Stonewall Jackson's success was that he was such a strict disciplinarian. He did his duty himself and was ever at his post, and he expected and demanded of everybody to do the same thing. He would have a man shot at the drop of a hat, and drop it himself. The first army order that was ever read to us after being attached to his corps, was the shooting to death by musketry of two men who had stopped on the battlefield to carry off a wounded comrade. It was read to us in line of battle at Winchester.

Fort Burnham (previously Confederate Fort Harrison), Va., Confederate Picket Line and Fort in background

Schwartz And Pfifer

At Valley Mountain the finest and fattest beef I ever saw was issued to the soldiers, and it was the custom to use tallow for lard. Tallow made good shortening if the biscuits were eaten hot, but if allowed to get cold they had a strong taste of tallow in their flavor that did not taste like the flavor of vanilla or lemon in ice cream and strawberries; and biscuits fried in tallow were something upon the principle of 'possum and sweet potatoes. Well, Pfifer had got the fat from the kidneys of two hind quarters and made a cake of tallow weighing about twenty-five pounds. He wrapped it up and put it carefully away in his knapsack. When the assembly sounded for the march, Pfifer strapped on his knapsack. It was pretty heavy, but Pfifer was "well heeled." He knew the good frying he would get out of that twenty-five pounds of nice fat tallow, and he was willing to tug and toil all day over a muddy and sloppy road for his anticipated hot tallow gravy for supper. We made a long and hard march that day, and about dark went into camp. Fires were made up and water brought, and the soldiers began to get supper. Pfifer was in a good humor. He went to get that twenty-five pounds of good, nice, fat tallow out of his knapsack, and on opening it, lo and behold! it was a rock that weighed about thirty pounds. Pfifer was struck dumb with amazement. He looked bewildered, yea, even silly. I do not think he cursed, because he could not do the subject justice. He looked at that rock with the death stare of a doomed man. But he suspected Schwartz. He went to Schwartz's knapsack, and there he found his cake of tallow. He went to Schwartz and would have killed him had not soldiers interfered and pulled him off by main force. His eyes blazed and looked like those of a tiger when he has just torn his victim limb from limb. I would not have been in Schwartz's shoes for all the tallow in every beef in Virginia. Captain Harsh made Schwartz carry that rock for two days to pacify Pfifer.

The Court-Martial

One incident came under my observation while in Virginia that made a deep impression on my mind. One morning, about daybreak, the new guard was relieving the old guard. It was a bitter cold morning, and on coming to our extreme outpost, I saw a soldier--he was but a mere boy--either dead or asleep at his post. The sergeant commanding the relief went up to him and shook him. He immediately woke up and seemed very much frightened. He was fast asleep at his post. The sergeant had him arrested and carried to the guard-house.

Two days afterwards I received notice to appear before a court-martial at nine. I was summoned to appear as a witness against him for being asleep at his post in the enemy's country. An example had to be made of some one. He had to be tried for his life. The court-martial was made up of seven or eight officers of a different regiment. The witnesses all testified against him, charges and specifications were read, and by the rules of war he had to be shot to death by musketry. The Advocate- General for the prosecution made the opening speech. He read the law in a plain, straightforward manner, and said that for a soldier to go to sleep at his post of duty, while so much depended upon him, was the most culpable of all crimes, and the most inexcusable. I trembled in my boots, for on several occasions I knew I had taken a short nap, even on the very outpost. The Advocate-General went on further to say, that the picket was the sentinel that held the lives of his countrymen and the liberty of his country in his hands, and it mattered not what may have been his record in the past. At one moment he had forfeited his life to his country. For discipline's sake, if for nothing else, you gentlemen that make up this court-martial find the prisoner guilty. It is necessary for you to be firm, gentlemen, for upon your decision depends the safety of our country. When he had finished, thinks I to myself, "Gone up the spout, sure; we will have a first-class funeral here before night."

Well, as to the lawyer who defended him, I cannot now remember his speeches; but he represented a fair-haired boy leaving his home and family, telling his father and aged mother and darling little sister farewell, and spoke of his proud step, though a mere boy, going to defend his country and his loved ones; but at one weak moment, when nature, tasked and taxed beyond the bounds of human endurance, could stand no longer, and upon the still and silent picket post, when the whole army was hushed in slumber, what wonder is it that he, too, may have fallen asleep while at his post of duty.

Some of you gentlemen of this court-martial may have sons, may have brothers; yes, even fathers, in the army. Where are they tonight? You love your children, or your brother or father. This mere youth has a father and mother and sister away back in Tennessee. They are willing to give him to his country. But oh! gentlemen, let the word go back to Tennessee that he died upon the battlefield, and not by the hands of his own comrades for being asleep at his post of duty. I cannot now remember the speeches, but one thing I do know, that he was acquitted, and I was glad of it.

"The Death Watch"

One more scene I can remember. Kind friends--you that know nothing of a soldier's life--I ask you in all candor not to doubt the following lines in this sketch. You have no doubt read of the old Roman soldier found amid the ruins of Pompeii, who had stood there for sixteen hundred years, and when he was excavated was found at his post with his gun clasped in his skeleton hands. You believe this because it is written in history. I have heard politicians tell it. I have heard it told from the sacred desk. It is true; no one doubts it.

Now, were I to tell something that happened in this nineteenth century exactly similar, you would hardly believe it. But whether you believe it or not, it is for you to say. At a little village called Hampshire Crossing, our regiment was ordered to go to a little stream called St. John's Run, to relieve the 14th Georgia Regiment and the 3rd Arkansas. I cannot tell the facts as I desire to. In fact, my hand trembles so, and my feelings are so overcome, that it is hard for me to write at all. But we went to the place that we were ordered to go to, and when we arrived there we found the guard sure enough. If I remember correctly, there were just eleven of them. Some were sitting down and some were lying down; but each and every one was as cold and as hard frozen as the icicles that hung from their hands and faces and clothing-- dead! They had died at their post of duty. Two of them, a little in advance of the others, were standing with their guns in their hands, as cold and as hard frozen as a monument of marble--standing sentinel with loaded guns in their frozen hands! The tale is told. Were they true men? Does He who noteth the sparrow's fall, and numbers the hairs of our heads, have any interest in one like ourselves? Yes; He doeth all things well. Not a sparrow falls to the ground without His consent.

Virginia, Farewell

After having served through all the valley campaign, and marched through all the wonders of Northwest Virginia, and being associated with the army of Virginia, it was with sorrow and regret that we bade farewell to "Old Virginia's shore," to go to other fields of blood and carnage and death. We had learned to love Virginia; we love her now. The people were kind and good to us. They divided their last crust of bread and rasher of bacon with us. We loved Lee, we loved Jackson; we loved the name, association and people of Virginia. Hatton, Forbes, Anderson, Gilliam, Govan, Loring, Ashby and Schumaker were names with which we had been long associated. We hated to leave all our old comrades behind us. We felt that we were proving recreant to the instincts of our own manhood, and that we were leaving those who had stood by us on the march and battlefield when they most needed our help. We knew the 7th and 14th Tennessee regiments; we knew the 3rd Arkansas, the 14th Georgia, and 42nd Virginia regiments. Their names were as familiar as household words. We were about to leave the bones of Joe Bynum and Gus Allen and Patrick Hanly. We were about to bid farewell to every tender association that we had formed with the good people of Virginia, and to our old associates among the soldiers of the Grand Army of Virginia. _Virginia, farewell!_ Away back yonder, in good old Tennessee, our homes and loved ones are being robbed and insulted, our fields laid waste, our cities sacked, and our people slain. Duty as well as patriotism calls us back to our native home, to try and defend it, as best we can, against an invading army of our then enemies; and, Virginia, once more we bid you a long farewell!

Chapter II -- Shiloh

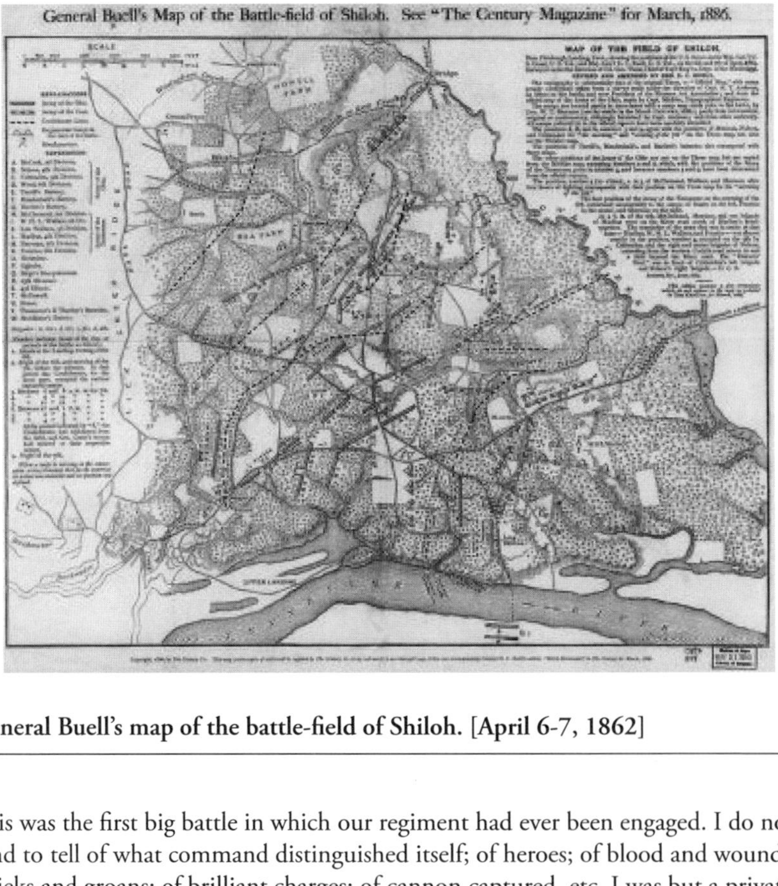

General Buell's map of the battle-field of Shiloh. [April 6-7, 1862]

This was the first big battle in which our regiment had ever been engaged. I do not pretend to tell of what command distinguished itself; of heroes; of blood and wounds; of shrieks and groans; of brilliant charges; of cannon captured, etc. I was but a private soldier, and if I happened to look to see if I could find out anything, "Eyes right, guide center," was the order. "Close up, guide right, halt, forward, right oblique, left oblique, halt, forward, guide center, eyes right, dress up promptly in the rear, steady, double quick, charge bayonets, fire at will," is about all that a private soldier ever knows of a battle. He can see the smoke rise and the flash of the enemy's guns, and he can hear the whistle of the minnie and cannon balls, but he has got to load and shoot as hard as he can tear and ram cartridge, or he will soon find out, like the Irishman who had been shooting blank cartridges, when a ball happened to strike him, and he halloed out, "Faith, Pat, and be jabbers, them fellows are shooting bullets." But I nevertheless remember many things that came under my observation in this battle. I remember a man by the name of Smith stepping deliberately out of the ranks and shooting his finger off to keep out of the fight; of another poor fellow who was accidentally shot and killed by the discharge of another person's gun, and of others suddenly taken sick with colic. Our regiment was the advance guard on Saturday evening, and did a little skirmishing; but General Gladden's brigade passed us and assumed a position in our immediate front. About daylight on Sunday morning, Chalmers' brigade relieved Gladden's. As Gladden rode by us, a courier rode up and told him something. I do not know what it was, but I heard Gladden say, "Tell General Bragg that I have as keen a scent for Yankees as General Chalmers has." On Sunday morning, a clear, beautiful, and still day, the order was given for the whole army to advance, and to attack immediately. We were supporting an Alabama brigade. The fire opened--bang, bang, bang, a rattle de bang, bang, bang, a boom, de bang, bang, bang, boom, bang, boom, bang, boom, bang, boom, bang, boom, whirr-siz-siz-siz--a ripping, roaring boom, bang! The air was full of balls and deadly missiles. The litter corps was carrying off the dying and wounded. We could hear the shout of the charge and the incessant roar of the guns, the rattle of the musketry, and knew that the contending forces were engaged in a breast to breast struggle. But cheering news continued to come back. Every one who passed would be hailed with, "Well, what news from the front?" "Well, boys, we are driving 'em. We have captured all their encampments, everything that they had, and all their provisions and army stores, and everything."

As we were advancing to the attack and to support the Alabama brigade in our front, and which had given way and were stricken with fear, some of the boys of our regiment would laugh at them, and ask what they were running for, and would commence to say "Flicker! flicker! flicker!" like the bird called the yellowhammer, "Flicker! flicker! flicker!" As we advanced, on the edge of the battlefield, we saw a big fat colonel of the 23rd Tennessee regiment badly wounded, whose name, if I remember correctly, was Matt. Martin. He said to us, "Give 'em goss, boys. That's right, my brave First Tennessee. Give 'em Hail Columbia!" We halted but a moment, and said I, "Colonel, where are you wounded?" He answered in a deep bass voice, "My son, I am wounded in the arm, in the leg, in the head, in the body, and in another place which I have a delicacy in mentioning." That is what the gallant old Colonel said. Advancing a little further on, we saw General Albert Sidney Johnson surrounded by his staff and Governor Harris, of Tennessee. We saw some little commotion among those who surrounded him, but we did not know at the time that he was dead. The fact was kept from the troops.

About noon a courier dashed up and ordered us to go forward and support General Bragg's center. We had to pass over the ground where troops had been fighting all day.

I had heard and read of battlefields, seen pictures of battlefields, of horses and men, of cannon and wagons, all jumbled together, while the ground was strewn with dead and dying and wounded, but I must confess that I never realized the "pomp and circumstance" of the thing called glorious war until I saw this. Men were lying in every conceivable position; the dead lying with their eyes wide open, the wounded begging piteously for help, and some waving their hats and shouting to us to go forward. It all seemed to me a dream; I seemed to be in a sort of haze, when siz, siz, siz, the minnie balls from the Yankee line began to whistle around our ears, and I thought of the Irishman when he said, "Sure enough, those fellows are shooting bullets!"

Down would drop first one fellow and then another, either killed or wounded, when we were ordered to charge bayonets. I had been feeling mean all the morning as if I had stolen a sheep, but when the order to charge was given, I got happy. I felt happier than a fellow does when he professes religion at a big Methodist camp-meeting. I shouted. It was fun then. Everybody looked happy. We were crowding them. One more charge, then their lines waver and break. They retreat in wild confusion. We were jubilant; we were triumphant. Officers could not curb the men to keep in line. Discharge after discharge was poured into the retreating line. The Federal dead and wounded covered the ground.

When in the very midst of our victory, here comes an order to halt. What! halt after today's victory? Sidney Johnson killed, General Gladden killed, and a host of generals and other brave men killed, and the whole Yankee army in full retreat.

These four letters, h-a-l-t, O, how harsh they did break upon our ears. The victory was complete, but the word "halt" turned victory into defeat.

The soldiers had passed through the Yankee camps and saw all the good things that they had to eat in their sutlers' stores and officers' marquees, and it was but a short time before every soldier was rummaging to see what he could find.

The harvest was great and the laborers were not few.

The negro boys, who were with their young masters as servants, got rich. Greenbacks were plentiful, good clothes were plentiful, rations were not in demand. The boys were in clover.

This was Sunday.

On Monday the tide was reversed.

Now, those Yankees were whipped, fairly whipped, and according to all the rules of war they ought to have retreated. But they didn't. Flushed with their victories at Fort Henry and Fort Donelson and the capture of Nashville, and the whole State of Tennessee having fallen into their hands, victory was again to perch upon their banners, for Buell's army, by forced marches, had come to Grant's assistance at the eleventh hour.

Gunboats and transports were busily crossing Buell's army all of Sunday night. We could hear their boats ringing their bells, and hear the puff of smoke and steam from their boilers. Our regiment was the advance outpost, and we saw the skirmish line of the

Federals advancing and then their main line and then their artillery. We made a good fight on Monday morning, and I was taken by surprise when the order came for us to retreat instead of advance. But as I said before, reader, a private soldier is but an automaton, and knows nothing of what is going on among the generals, and I am only giving the chronicles of little things and events that came under my own observation as I saw them then and remember them now. Should you desire to find out more about the battle, I refer you to history.

One incident I recollect very well. A Yankee colonel, riding a fine gray mare, was sitting on his horse looking at our advance as if we were on review. W. H. rushed forward and grabbed his horse by the bridle, telling him at the same time to surrender. The Yankee seized the reins, set himself back in the saddle, put the muzzle of his pistol in W. H.'s face and fired. About the time he pulled trigger, a stray ball from some direction struck him in the side and he fell off dead, and his horse becoming frightened, galloped off, dragging him through the Confederate lines. His pistol had missed its aim.

I have heard hundreds of old soldiers tell of the amount of greenback money they saw and picked up on the battlefield of Shiloh, but they thought it valueless and did not trouble themselves with bringing it off with them.

One fellow, a courier, who had had his horse killed, got on a mule he had captured, and in the last charge, before the final and fatal halt was made, just charged right ahead by his lone self, and the soldiers said, "Just look at that brave man, charging right in the jaws of death." He began to seesaw the mule and grit his teeth, and finally yelled out, "It arn't me, boys, it's this blarsted old mule. Whoa! Whoa!"

On Monday morning I too captured me a mule. He was not a fast mule, and I soon found out that he thought he knew as much as I did. He was wise in his own conceit. He had a propensity to take every hog path he came to. All the bombasting that I could give him would not make him accelerate his speed. If blood makes speed, I do not suppose he had a drop of any kind in him. If I wanted him to go on one side of the road he was sure to be possessed of an equal desire to go on the other side. Finally I and my mule fell out. I got a big hickory and would frail him over the head, and he would only shake his head and flop his ears, and seem to say, "Well, now, you think you are smart, don't you?" He was a resolute mule, slow to anger, and would have made an excellent merchant to refuse bad pay, or I will pay your credit, for his whole composition seemed to be made up the one word--no. I frequently thought it would be pleasant to split the difference with that mule, and I would gladly have done so if I could have gotten one-half of his no. Me and mule worried along until we came to a creek. Mule did not desire to cross, while I was trying to persuade him with a big stick, a rock in his ear, and a twister on his nose. The caisson of a battery was about to cross. The driver said, "I'll take your mule over for you." So he got a large two-inch rope, tied one end around the mule's neck and the other to the caisson, and ordered the driver to whip up. The mule was loath to take to the water. He was no Baptist, and did not believe in immersion, and had his views about crossing streams, but the rope began to tighten, the mule to squeal out his protestations against such villainous proceedings. The rope, however, was stronger than the mule's "no," and he was finally prevailed upon by the strength of the rope to cross the creek. On my taking the rope off he shook himself and seemed to say, "You think that you are mighty smart folks, but you are a leetle too smart." I gave it up that that mule's "no" was a little stronger than my determination. He seemed to be in deep meditation. I got on him again, when all of a sudden he lifted his head, pricked up his ears, began to champ his bit, gave a little squeal, got a little faster, and finally into a gallop and then a run. He seemed all at once to have remembered or to have forgotten something, and was now making up for lost time. With all my pulling and seesawing and strength I could not stop him until he brought up with me at Corinth, Mississippi.

Chapter III -- Corinth

Well, here we were, again "reorganizing," and after our lax discipline on the road to and from Virginia, and after a big battle, which always disorganizes an army, what wonder is it that some men had to be shot, merely for discipline's sake? And what wonder that General Bragg's name became a terror to deserters and evil doers? Men were shot by scores, and no wonder the army had to be reorganized. Soldiers had enlisted for twelve months only, and had faithfully complied with their volunteer obligations; the terms for which they had enlisted had expired, and they naturally looked upon it that they had a right to go home. They had done their duty faithfully and well. They wanted to see their families; in fact, wanted to go home anyhow. War had become a reality; they were tired of it. A law had been passed by the Confederate States Congress called the conscript act. A soldier had no right to volunteer and to choose the branch of service he preferred. He was conscripted.

From this time on till the end of the war, a soldier was simply a machine, a conscript. It was mighty rough on rebels. We cursed the war, we cursed Bragg, we cursed the Southern Confederacy. All our pride and valor had gone, and we were sick of war and the Southern Confederacy.

A law was made by the Confederate States Congress about this time allowing every person who owned twenty negroes to go home. It gave us the blues; we wanted twenty negroes. Negro property suddenly became very valuable, and there was raised the howl of "rich man's war, poor man's fight." The glory of the war, the glory of the South, the glory and the pride of our volunteers had no charms for the conscript.

We were directed to re-elect our officers, and the country was surprised to see the sample of a conscript's choice. The conscript had no choice. He was callous, and indifferent whether he had a captain or not. Those who were at first officers had resigned and gone home, because they were officers. The poor private, a contemptible conscript, was left to howl and gnash his teeth. The war might as well have ended then and there. The boys were "hacked," nay, whipped. They were shorn of the locks of their glory. They had but one ambition now, and that was to get out of the army in some way or other. They wanted to join the cavalry or artillery or home guards or pioneer corps or to be "yaller dogs," or anything.

[The average staff officer and courier were always called "yaller dogs," and were regarded as non-combatants and a nuisance, and the average private never let one pass without whistling and calling dogs. In fact, the general had to issue an army order threatening punishment for the ridicule hurled at staff officers and couriers. They were looked upon as simply "hangers on," or in other words, as yellow sheep-killing dogs, that if you would say "booh" at, would yelp and get under their master's heels. Mike Snyder was General George Maney's "yaller dog," and I believe here is where Joe Jefferson, in Rip Van Winkle, got the name of Rip's dog Snyder. At all times of day or night you could hear, "wheer, hyat, hyat, haer, haer, hugh, Snyder, whoopee, hyat, whoopee, Snyder, here, here," when a staff officer or courier happened to pass. The reason of this was that the private knew and felt that there was just that much more loading, shooting and fighting for him; and there are the fewest number of instances on record where a staff officer or courier ever fired a gun in their country's cause; and even at this late day, when I hear an old soldier telling of being on some general's staff, I always think of the letter "E." In fact, later in the war I was detailed as special courier and staff officer for General Hood, which office I held three days. But while I held the office in passing a guard I always told them I was on Hood's staff, and ever afterwards I made those three days' staff business last me the balance of the war. I could pass any guard in the army by using the magic words, "staff officer." It beat all the countersigns ever invented. It was the "open sesame" of war and discipline.]

Their last hope had set. They hated war. To their minds the South was a great tyrant, and the Confederacy a fraud. They were deserting by thousands. They had no love or respect for General Bragg. When men were to be shot or whipped, the whole army was marched to the horrid scene to see a poor trembling wretch tied to a post and a platoon of twelve men drawn up in line to put him to death, and the hushed command of "Ready, aim, fire!" would make the soldier, or conscript, I should say, loathe the very name of Southern Confederacy. And when some miserable wretch was to be whipped and branded for being absent ten days without leave, we had to see him kneel down and have his head shaved smooth and slick as a peeled onion, and then stripped to the naked skin. Then a strapping fellow with a big rawhide would make the blood flow and spurt at every lick, the wretch begging and howling like a hound, and then he was branded with a red hot iron with the letter D on both hips, when he was marched through the army to the music of the "Rogue's March." It was enough. None of General Bragg's soldiers ever loved him. They had no faith in his ability as a general. He was looked upon as a merciless tyrant. The soldiers were very scantily fed. Bragg never was a good feeder or commissary-general. Rations with us were always scarce. No extra rations were ever allowed to the negroes who were with us as servants. No coffee or whisky or tobacco were ever allowed to be issued to the troops. If they obtained these luxuries, they were not from the government. These luxuries were withheld in order to crush the very heart and spirit of his troops. We were crushed. Bragg was the great autocrat. In the mind of the soldier, his word was law. He loved to crush the spirit of his men. The more of a hang-dog look they had about them the better was General Bragg pleased. Not a single soldier in the whole army ever loved or respected him. But he is dead now.

Peace to his ashes!

We became starved skeletons; naked and ragged rebels. The chronic diarrhoea became the scourge of the army. Corinth became one vast hospital. Almost the whole army attended the sick call every morning. All the water courses went dry, and we used water out of filthy pools. Halleck was advancing; we had to fortify Corinth. A vast army, Grant, Buell, Halleck, Sherman, all were advancing on Corinth. Our troops were in no condition to fight. In fact, they had seen enough of this miserable yet tragic farce. They were ready to ring down the curtain, put out the footlights and go home. They loved the Union anyhow, and were always opposed to this war. But breathe softly the name of Bragg. It had more terror than the advancing hosts of Halleck's army. The shot and shell would come tearing through our ranks. Every now and then a soldier was killed or wounded, and we thought what "magnificent" folly. Death was welcome. Halleck's whole army of blue coats had no terror now. When we were drawn up in line of battle, a detail of one-tenth of the army was placed in our rear to shoot us down if we ran. No pack of hounds under the master's lash, or body of penitentiary convicts were ever under greater surveillance. We were tenfold worse than slaves; our morale was a thing of the past; the glory of war and the pride of manhood had been sacrificed upon Bragg's tyrannical holocaust. But enough of this.

Rowland Shot To Death

One morning I went over to the 23rd Tennessee Regiment on a visit to Captain Gray Armstrong and Colonel Jim Niel, both of whom were glad to see me, as we were old ante-bellum friends. While at Colonel Niel's marquee I saw a detail of soldiers bring out a man by the name of Rowland, whom they were going to shoot to death with musketry, by order of a court-martial, for desertion. I learned that he had served out the term for which he had originally volunteered, had quit our army and joined that of the Yankees, and was captured with Prentiss' Yankee brigade at Shiloh. He was being hauled to the place of execution in a wagon, sitting on an old gun box, which was to be his coffin. When they got to the grave, which had been dug the day before, the water had risen in it, and a soldier was baling it out. Rowland spoke up and said, "Please hand me a drink of that water, as I want to drink out of my own grave so the boys will talk about it when I am dead, and remember Rowland." They handed him the water and he drank all there was in the bucket, and handing it back asked them to please hand him a little more, as he had heard that water was very scarce in hell, and it would be the last he would ever drink. He was then carried to the death post, and there he began to cut up jack generally. He began to curse Bragg, Jeff. Davis, and the Southern Confederacy, and all the rebels at a terrible rate. He was simply arrogant and very insulting. I felt that he deserved to die. He said he would show the rebels how a Union man could die. I do not know what all he did say. When the shooting detail came up, he went of his own accord and knelt down at the post. The Captain commanding the squad gave the command, "Ready, aim, fire!" and Rowland tumbled over on his side. It was the last of Rowland.

Killing A Yankee Sharpshooter

In our immediate front, at Corinth, Mississippi, our men were being picked off by sharpshooters, and a great many were killed, but no one could tell where the shots came from. At one particular post it was sure death. Every detail that had been sent to this post for a week had been killed. In distributing the detail this post fell to Tom Webb and myself. They were bringing off a dead boy just as we went on duty. Colonel George C. Porter, of the 6th Tennessee, warned us to keep a good lookout. We took our stands. A minnie ball whistled right by my head. I don't think it missed me an eighth of an inch. Tom had sat down on an old chunk of wood, and just as he took his seat, zip! a ball took the chunk of wood. Tom picked it up and began laughing at our tight place. Happening to glance up towards the tree tops, I saw a smoke rising above a tree, and about the same time I saw a Yankee peep from behind the tree, up among the bushes. I quickly called Tom's attention to it, and pointed out the place. We could see his ramrod as he handled it while loading his gun; saw him raise his gun, as we thought, to put a cap on it. Tom in the meantime had lain flat on his belly and placed his gun across the chunk he had been sitting on. I had taken a rest for my gun by the side of a sapling, and both of us had dead aim at the place where the Yankee was. Finally we saw him sort o' peep round the tree, and we moved about a little so that he might see us, and as we did so, the Yankee stepped out in full view, and bang, bang! Tom and I had both shot. We saw that Yankee tumble out like a squirrel. It sounded like distant thunder when that Yankee struck the ground. We heard the Yankees carry him off. One thing I am certain of, and that is, not another Yankee went up that tree that day, and Colonel George C. Porter complimented Tom and I very highly on our success. This is where I first saw a jack o'lantern (ignis fatui). That night, while Tom and I were on our posts, we saw a number of very dim lights, which seemed to be in motion. At first we took them to be Yankees moving about with lights. Whenever we could get a shot we would blaze away. At last one got up very close, and passed right between Tom and I. I don't think I was ever more scared in my life. My hair stood on end like the quills of the fretful porcupine; I could not imagine what on earth it was. I took it to be some hellish machination of a Yankee trick. I did not know whether to run or stand, until I heard Tom laugh and say, "Well, well, that's a jack o'lantern."

COLONEL FIELD

Before proceeding further with these memoirs, I desire to give short sketches of two personages with whom we were identified and closely associated until the winding up of the ball. The first is Colonel Hume R. Field. Colonel Field was born a soldier. I have read many descriptions of Stonewall Jackson. Colonel Field was his exact counterpart. They looked somewhat alike, spoke alike, and alike were trained military soldiers. The War Department at Richmond made a grand mistake in not making him a "commander of armies." He was not a brilliant man; could not talk at all. He was a soldier. His conversation was yea and nay. But when you could get "yes, sir," and "no, sir," out of him his voice was as soft and gentle as a maid's when she says "yes" to her lover. Fancy, if you please, a man about thirty years old, a dark skin, made swarthy by exposure to sun and rain, very black eyes that seemed to blaze with a gentle luster. I never saw him the least excited in my life. His face was a face of bronze. His form was somewhat slender, but when you looked at him you saw at the first glance that this would be a dangerous man in a ground skuffle, a foot race, or a fight. There was nothing repulsive or forbidding or even domineering in his looks. A child or a dog would make up with him on first sight. He knew not what fear was, or the meaning of the word fear. He had no nerves, or rather, has a rock or tree any nerves? You might as well try to shake the nerves of a rock or tree as those of Colonel Field. He was the bravest man, I think, I ever knew. Later in the war he was known by every soldier in the army; and the First Tennessee Regiment, by his manipulations, became the regiment to occupy "tight places." He knew his men. When he struck the Yankee line they felt the blow. He had, himself, set the example, and so trained his regiment that all the armies in the world could not whip it. They might kill every man in it, is true, but they would die game to the last man. His men all loved him. He was no disciplinarian, but made his regiment what it was by his own example. And every day on the march you would see some poor old ragged rebel riding his fine gray mare, and he was walking.

Captain Joe P. Lee

The other person I wish to speak of is Captain Joe P. Lee. Captain Henry J. Webster was our regular captain, but was captured while on furlough, sent to a northern prison and died there, and Joe went up by promotion. He was quite a young man, about twenty-one years old, but as brave as any old Roman soldier that ever lived. Joe's face was ever wreathed in smiles, and from the beginning to the end he was ever at the head of his company. I do not think that any member of the company ever did call him by his title. He was called simply "Joe Lee," or more frequently "Black Perch." While on duty he was strict and firm, but off duty he was "one of us boys." We all loved and respected him, but everybody knows Joe, and further comment is unnecessary.

I merely mention these two persons because in this rapid sketch I may have cause occasionally to mention them, and only wish to introduce them to the reader, so he may understand more fully my ideas. But, reader, please remember that I am not writing a history at all, and do not propose in these memoirs to be anybody's biographer. I am only giving my own impressions. If other persons think differently from me it is all right, and I forgive them.

Corinth Forsaken

One morning a detail was sent to burn up and destroy all the provisions and army stores, and to blow up the arsenal. The town was in a blaze of fire and the arsenal was roaring and popping and bellowing like pandemonium turned loose as we marched through Corinth on the morning of the evacuation. We bade farewell to Corinth. Its history was black and dark and damning. No little speck of green oasis ever enlivened the dark recesses of our memory while at this place. It's a desert that lives only in bitter memories. It was but one vast graveyard that entombed the life and spirit of once brave and chivalrous men. We left it to the tender mercies of the Yankees without one tear of sorrow or regret, and bade it farewell forever.

Chapter IV – Tupelo

We went into summer quarters at Tupelo. Our principal occupation at this place was playing poker, chuck-a-luck and cracking graybacks (lice). Every soldier had a brigade of lice on him, and I have seen fellows so busily engaged in cracking them that it reminded me of an old woman knitting. At first the boys would go off in the woods and hide to louse themselves, but that was unnecessary, the ground fairly crawled with lice. Pharaoh's people, when they were resisting old Moses, never enjoyed the curse of lice more than we did. The boys would frequently have a louse race. There was one fellow who was winning all the money; his lice would run quicker and crawl faster than anybody's lice. We could not understand it. If some fellow happened to catch a fierce-looking louse, he would call on Dornin for a race. Dornin would come and always win the stake. The lice were placed in plates--this was the race course--and the first that crawled off was the winner. At last we found out D.'s trick; he always heated his plate.

Billy P. said he had no lice on him.

"Did you ever look?"

"No."

"How do you know then?"

"If ignorance is bliss 'tis folly to be wise," said Billy.

"Why, there is one crawling on your bosom now."

Billy took him and put him back in his bosom and said to the louse, "You stay there now; this makes the fourth time I have put you back, and if I catch you out again today I'll martyr you."

Billy was philosophic--the death of one louse did not stop the breed.

The Court Martial At Tupelo

At this place was held the grand court-martial. Almost every day we would hear a discharge of musketry, and knew that some poor, trembling wretch had bid farewell to mortal things here below. It seemed to be but a question of time with all of us as to when we too would be shot. We were afraid to chirp. So far now as patriotism was concerned, we had forgotten all about that, and did not now so much love our country as we feared Bragg. Men were being led to the death stake every day. I heard of many being shot, but did not see but two men shot myself. I do not know to what regiment they belonged, but I remember that they were mere beardless boys. I did not learn for what crime or the magnitude of their offenses. They might have deserved death for all I know.

I saw an old man, about sixty years old, whose name was Dave Brewer, and another man, about forty-five, by the name of Rube Franklin, whipped. There was many a man whipped and branded that I never saw or heard tell of. But the reason I remembered these two was that they belonged to Company A of the 23rd Tennessee Regiment, and I knew many men in the regiment.

These two men were hung up by the hands, after having their heads shaved, to a tree, put there for the purpose, with the prongs left on them, and one hand was stretched toward one prong and the other hand to another prong, their feet, perhaps, just touching the ground. The man who did the whipping had a thick piece of sole-leather, the end of which was cut in three strips, and this tacked on to the end of a paddle. After the charges and specifications had been read (both men being stark naked), the whipper "lit in" on Rube, who was the youngest. I do not think he intended to hit as hard as he did, but, being excited himself, he blistered Rube from head to foot. Thirty-nine lashes was always the number. Now, three times thirty-nine makes one hundred and seventeen. When he struck at all, one lick would make three whelps. When he had finished Rube, the Captain commanding the whipping squad told him to lay it on old man Brewer as light as the law would allow, that old man Brewer was so old that he would die--that he could not stand it. He struck old man Dave Brewer thirty-nine lashes, but they were laid on light. Old Dave didn't beg and squall like Rube did. He j-e-s-t did whip old man Dave. Like the old preacher who caught the bear on Sunday. They had him up before the church, agreed to let him off if he did not again set his trap. "Well," he said, "brethren, I j-e-s-t did set it."

Raiding On Roastingears

At this place General Bragg issued an order authorizing citizens to defend themselves against the depredations of soldiers--to shoot them down if caught depredating.

Well, one day Byron Richardson and myself made a raid on an old citizen's roastingear patch. We had pulled about all the corn that we could carry. I had my arms full and was about starting for camp, when an old citizen raised up and said, "Stop there! drop that corn." He had a double- barreled shotgun cocked and leveled at my breast.

"Come and go with me to General Bragg's headquarters. I intend to take you there, by the living God!"

I was in for it. Directed to go in front, I was being marched to Bragg's headquarters. I could see the devil in the old fellow's eye. I tried to beg off with good promises, but the old fellow was deaf to all entreaty. I represented to him all of our hardships and suffering. But the old fellow was inexorable. I was being steadily carried toward Bragg's headquarters. I was determined not to see General Bragg, even if the old citizen shot me in the back. When all at once a happy thought struck me. Says I, "Mister, Byron Richardson is in your field, and if you will go back we can catch him and you can take both of us to General Bragg." The old fellow's spunk was up. He had captured me so easy, he no doubt thought he could whip a dozen. We went back a short distance, and there was Byron, who had just climbed over the fence and had his arms full, when the old citizen, diverted from me, leveled his double-barrel at Byron, when I made a grab for his gun, which was accidentally discharged in the air, and with the assistance of Byron, we had the old fellow and his gun both. The table was turned. We made the old fellow gather as much as he could carry, and made him carry it nearly to camp, when we dismissed him, a wiser if not a better and richer man. We took his gun and bent it around a black jack tree. He was at the soldiers' mercy.

Chapter V -- Kentucky

We Go Into Kentucky

After being thoroughly reorganized at Tupelo, and the troops had recovered their health and spirits, we made an advance into Kentucky. We took the cars at Tupelo and went to Mobile, from thence across Mobile Bay to Montgomery, Alabama, then to Atlanta, from there to Chattanooga, and then over the mountains afoot to the blue-grass regions of Kentucky-- the dark and bloody ground. Please remember, patient reader, that I write entirely from memory. I have no data or diary or anything to go by, and memory is a peculiar faculty. I find that I cannot remember towns and battles, and remember only the little things. I remember how gladly the citizens of Kentucky received us. I thought they had the prettiest girls that God ever made. They could not do too much for us. They had heaps and stacks of cooked rations along our route, with wine and cider everywhere, and the glad shouts of "Hurrah for our Southern boys!" greeted and welcomed us at every house. Ah, the boys felt like soldiers again. The bands played merrier and livelier tunes. It was the patient convalescing; the fever had left him, he was getting fat and strong; the old fire was seen to illuminate his eyes; his step was buoyant and proud; he felt ashamed that he had ever been "hacked"; he could fight now. It was the same old proud soldier of yore. The bands played "Dixie" and the "Bonnie Blue Flag," the citizens cheered, and the ladies waved their handkerchiefs and threw us bouquets. Ah, those were halcyon days, and your old soldier, kind reader, loves to recall that happy period. Mumfordsville had been captured with five thousand prisoners. New recruits were continually joining our ranks.

Camp Dick Robinson, that immense pile of army stores, had fallen into our hands. We rode upon the summit of the wave of success. The boys had got clean clothes, and had their faces washed. I saw then what I had long since forgotten--a "cockade." The Kentucky girls made cockades for us, and almost every soldier had one pinned on his hat. But stirring events were hastening on, the black cloud of battle and war had begun then to appear much larger than a man's hand, in fact we could see the lightning flash and hear the thunder roar.

We were at Harrodsburg; the Yankees were approaching Perryville under General Buell. The Yankees had been dogging our rear, picking up our stragglers and capturing some of our wagon trains.

This good time that we were having was too good to last. We were in an ecstasy akin to heaven. We were happy; the troops were jubilant; our manhood blood pulsated more warmly; our patriotism was awakened; our pride was renewed and stood ready for any emergency; we felt that one Southern man could whip twenty Yankees. All was lovely and the goose hung high. We went to dances and parties every night.

When General Chalmers marched to Perryville, in flanking and surrounding Mumfordsville, we marched the whole night long. We, the private soldiers, did not know what was going on among the generals. All that we had to do was march, march, march. It mattered not how tired, hungry, or thirsty we were. All that we had to do was to march that whole night long, and every staff officer who would pass, some fellow would say,

"Hey, mister, how far is it to Mumfordsville?" He would answer, "five miles." It seemed to me we traveled a hundred miles and were always within five miles of Mumfordsville. That night we heard a volley of musketry in our immediate front, and did not know what it meant, but soon we came to where a few soldiers had lighted some candles and were holding them over the body of a dead soldier. It was Captain Allison, if I remember rightly, of General Cheatham's staff. He was very bloody, and had his clothes riddled with balls. I heard that he rode on in front of the advance guard of our army, and had no doubt discovered the Yankee picket, and came galloping back at full speed in the dark, when our advance guard fired on and killed him.

We laid down in a graveyard that night and slept, and when we awoke the sun was high in the heavens, shining in our faces. Mumfordsville had surrendered. The next day Dr. C. T. Quintard let me ride his horse nearly all day, while he walked with the webfeet.

The Battle Of Perryville

In giving a description of this most memorable battle, I do not pretend to give you figures, and describe how this general looked and how that one spoke, and the other one charged with drawn sabre, etc. I know nothing of these things--see the history for that. I was simply a soldier of the line, and I only write of the things I saw. I was in every battle, skirmish and march that was made by the First Tennessee Regiment during the war, and I do not remember of a harder contest and more evenly fought battle than that of Perryville. If it had been two men wrestling, it would have been called a "dog fall." Both sides claim the victory--both whipped.

I stood picket in Perryville the night before the battle--a Yankee on one side of the street, and I on the other. We got very friendly during the night, and made a raid upon a citizen's pantry, where we captured a bucket of honey, a pitcher of sweet milk, and three or four biscuit. The old citizen was not at home--he and his whole household had gone visiting, I believe. In fact, I think all of the citizens of Perryville were taken with a sudden notion of promiscuous visiting about this time; at least they were not at home to all callers.

At length the morning dawned. Our line was drawn up on one side of Perryville, the Yankee army on the other. The two enemies that were soon to meet in deadly embrace seemed to be eyeing each other. The blue coats lined the hillside in plain view. You could count the number of their regiments by the number of their flags. We could see the huge war dogs frowning at us, ready at any moment to belch forth their fire and smoke, and hurl their thunderbolts of iron and death in our very midst.

I wondered why the fighting did not begin. Never on earth were our troops more eager for the engagement to open. The Yankees commenced to march toward their left, and we marched almost parallel to our right-- both sides watching each other's maneuvers and movements. It was but the lull that precedes the storm. Colonel Field was commanding our brigade, and Lieutenant-Colonel Patterson our regiment. About 12 o'clock, while we were marching through a corn field, in which the corn had been shocked, they opened their war dogs upon us. The beginning of the end had come. Here is where Captain John F. Wheless was wounded, and three others, whose names I have forgotten. The battle now opened in earnest, and from one end of the line to the other seemed to be a solid sheet of blazing smoke and fire. Our regiment crossed a stream, being preceded by Wharton's Texas Rangers, and we were ordered to attack at once with vigor. Here General Maney's horse was shot. From this moment the battle was a mortal struggle. Two lines of battle confronted us. We killed almost every one in the first line, and were soon charging over the second, when right in our immediate front was their third and main line of battle from which four Napoleon guns poured their deadly fire.

We did not recoil, but our line was fairly hurled back by the leaden hail that was poured into our very faces. Eight color-bearers were killed at one discharge of their cannon. We were right up among the very wheels of their Napoleon guns. It was death to retreat now to either side. Our Lieutenant-Colonel Patterson halloed to charge and take their guns, and we were soon in a hand-to-hand fight--every man for himself--using the butts of our guns and bayonets. One side would waver and fall back a few yards, and would rally, when the other side would fall back, leaving the four Napoleon guns; and yet the battle raged. Such obstinate fighting I never had seen before or since. The guns were discharged so rapidly that it seemed the earth itself was in a volcanic uproar. The iron storm passed through our ranks, mangling and tearing men to pieces. The very air seemed full of stifling smoke and fire which seemed the very pit of hell, peopled by contending demons.

Our men were dead and dying right in the very midst of this grand havoc of battle. It was a life to life and death to death grapple. The sun was poised above us, a great red ball sinking slowly in the west, yet the scene of battle and carnage continued. I cannot describe it. The mantle of night fell upon the scene. I do not know which side whipped, but I know that I helped bring off those four Napoleon guns that night though we were mighty easy about it.

They were given to Turner's Battery of our brigade and had the name of our Lieutenant-Colonel Patterson and our color-bearer, Mitchell, both of whom were killed, inscribed on two of the pieces. I have forgotten the names inscribed on the other two pieces. I saw these very four guns surrendered at Missionary Ridge. But of this another time.

The battle of Perryville presented a strange scene. The dead, dying, and wounded of both armies, Confederate and Federal, were blended in inextricable confusion. Now and then a cluster of dead Yankees and close by a cluster of dead Rebels. It was like the Englishman's grog--'alf and 'alf. Now, if you wish, kind reader, to find out how many were killed and wounded, I refer you to the histories.

I remember one little incident that I laughed at while in the very midst of battle. We were charging through an old citizen's yard, when a big yellow cur dog ran out and commenced snapping at the soldiers' legs-- they kicking at him to keep him off. The next morning he was lying near the same place, but he was a dead dog.

I helped bring off our wounded that night. We worked the whole night. The next morning about daylight a wounded comrade, Sam Campbell, complained of being cold, and asked me to lie down beside him. I did so, and was soon asleep; when I awoke the poor fellow was stiff and cold in death. His spirit had flown to its home beyond the skies.

After the battle was over, John T. Tucker, Scott Stephens, A. S. Horsley and I were detailed to bring off our wounded that night, and we helped to bring off many a poor dying comrade--Joe Thompson, Billy Bond, Byron Richardson, the two Allen boys--brothers, killed side by side--and Colonel Patterson, who was killed standing right by my side. He was first shot through the hand, and was wrapping his handkerchief around it, when another ball struck and killed him. I saw W. J. Whittorne, then a strippling boy of fifteen years of age, fall, shot through the neck and collar-bone. He fell apparently dead, when I saw him all at once jump up, grab his gun and commence loading and firing, and I heard him say, "D--n 'em, I'll fight 'em as long as I live." Whit thought he was killed, but he is living yet. We helped bring off a man by the name of Hodge, with his under jaw shot off, and his tongue lolling out. We brought off Captain Lute B. Irvine. Lute was shot through the lungs and was vomiting blood all the while, and begging us to lay him down and let him die. But Lute is living yet. Also, Lieutenant Woldridge, with both eyes shot out. I found him rambling in a briar-patch. About fifty members of the Rock City Guards were killed and nearly one hundred wounded. They were led by Captains W. D. Kelley, Wheless, and Steele. Lieutenant Thomas H. Maney was badly wounded. I saw dead on the battlefield a Federal General by the name of Jackson. It was his brigade that fought us so obstinately at this place, and I did hear that they were made up in Kentucky. Colonel Field, then commanding our brigade, and on his fine gray mare, rode up almost face to face with General Jackson, before he was killed, and Colonel Field was shooting all the time with his seven-shooting rifle. I cannot tell the one-half, or even remember at this late date, the scenes of blood and suffering that I witnessed on the battlefield of Perryville. But its history, like all the balance, has gone into the history of the war, and it has been twenty years ago, and I write entirely from memory. I remember Lieutenant Joe P. Lee and Captain W. C. Flournoy standing right at the muzzle of the Napoleon guns, and the next moment seemed to be enveloped in smoke and fire from the discharge of the cannon. When the regiment recoiled under the heavy firing and at the first charge, Billy Webster and I stopped behind a large oak tree and continued to fire at the Yankees until the regiment was again charging upon the four Napoleon guns, heavily supported by infantry. We were not more than twenty paces from them; and here I was shot through the hat and cartridge-box. I remember this, because at that time Billy and I were in advance of our line, and whenever we saw a Yankee rise to shoot, we shot him; and I desire to mention here that a braver or more noble boy was never created on earth than was Billy Webster. Everybody liked him. He was the flower and chivalry of our regiment. His record as a brave and noble boy will ever live in the hearts of his old comrades that served with him in Company H. He is up yonder now, and we shall meet again. In these memoirs I only tell what I saw myself, and in this way the world will know the truth.

Now, citizen, let me tell you what you never heard before, and this is this--there were many men with the rank and pay of general, who were not generals; there were many men with the rank and pay of privates who would have honored and adorned the name of general. Now, I will state further that a private soldier was a private.

It mattered not how ignorant a corporal might be, he was always right; it mattered not how intelligent the private might be (and so on up); the sergeant was right over the corporal, the sergeant-major over the sergeant, the lieutenant over him, and the captain over him, and the major over him, and the colonel over him, and the general over him, and so on up to Jeff Davis. You see, a private had no right to know anything, and that is why generals did all the fighting, and that is today why generals and colonels and captains are great men. They fought the battles of our country. The privates did not. The generals risked their reputation, the private soldier his life. No one ever saw a private in battle. His history would never be written. It was the generals that everybody saw charge such and such, with drawn sabre, his eyes flashing fire, his nostrils dilated, and his clarion voice ringing above the din of battle--"in a horn," over the left.

Bill Johns and Marsh Pinkard would have made Generals that would have distinguished themselves and been an honor to the country.

I know today many a private who would have made a good General. I know of many a General who was better fitted to be excused from detail and fights, to hang around a camp and draw rations for the company. A private had no way to distinguish himself. He had to keep in ranks, either in a charge or a retreat. But now, as the Generals and Colonels fill all the positions of honor and emoluments, the least I say, the better.

The Retreat Out Of Kentucky

From Perryville we went to Camp Dick Robinson and drew three days' rations, and then set fire to and destroyed all those great deposits of army stores which would have supplied the South for a year. We ate those rations and commenced our retreat out of Kentucky with empty haversacks and still emptier stomachs.

We supposed our general and commissaries knew what they were doing, and at night we would again draw rations, but we didn't.

The Yankee cavalry are worrying our rear guards. There is danger of an attack at any moment. No soldier is allowed to break ranks.

We thought, well surely we will draw rations tonight. But we didn't. We are marching for Cumberland Gap; the country has long ago been made desolate by the alternate occupation of both armies. There are no provisions in the country. It has long since been laid waste. We wanted rations, but we did not get them.

Fourth day out--Cumberland Gap in the distance--a great indenture in the ranges of Cumberland mountains. The scene was grand. But grand scenery had but little attraction for a hungry soldier. Surely we will get rations at Cumberland Gap. Toil on up the hill, and when half way up the hill, "Halt!"--march back down to the foot of the hill to defend the cavalry. I was hungry. A cavalryman was passing our regiment with a pile of scorched dough on the pummel of his saddle. Says I, "Halt! I am going to have a pattock of that bread." "Don't give it to him! don't give it to him!" was yelled out from all sides. I cocked my gun and was about to raise it to my shoulder, when he handed me over a pattock of scorched dough, and every fellow in Company H made a grab for it, and I only got about two or three mouthfuls. About dark a wild heifer ran by our regiment, and I pulled down on her. We killed and skinned her, and I cut off about five pounds of hindquarter. In three minutes there was no sign of that beef left to tell the tale. We ate that beef raw and without salt.

Only eight miles now to Cumberland Gap, and we will get rations now. But we didn't. We descended the mountain on the southern side. No rations yet.

Well, says I, this won't do me. I am going to hunt something to eat, Bragg or no Bragg. I turned off the road and struck out through the country, but had gone but a short distance before I came across a group of soldiers clambering over something. It was Tom Tuck with a barrel of sorghum that he had captured from a good Union man. He was selling it out at five dollars a quart. I paid my five dollars, and by pushing and scrouging I finally got my quart. I sat down and drank it; it was bully; it was not so good; it was not worth a cent; I was sick, and have never loved sorghum since.

Along the route it was nothing but tramp, tramp, tramp, and no sound or noise but the same inevitable, monotonous tramp, tramp, tramp, up hill and down hill, through long and dusty lanes, weary, wornout and hungry. No cheerful warble of a merry songster would ever greet our ears. It was always tramp, tramp, tramp. You might, every now and then, hear the occasional words, "close up;" but outside of that, it was but the same tramp, tramp, tramp. I have seen soldiers fast asleep, and no doubt dreaming of home and loved ones there, as they staggered along in their places in the ranks. I know that on many a weary night's march I have slept, and slept soundly, while marching along in my proper place in the ranks of the company, stepping to the same step as the soldier in front of me did. Sometimes, when weary, broken down and worn out, some member of the regiment would start a tune, and every man would join in. John Branch was usually the leader of the choir. He would commence a beautiful tune. The words, as I remember them now, were "Dear Paul, Just Twenty Years Ago." After singing this piece he would commence on a lively, spirit-stirring air to the tune of "Old Uncle Ned." Now, reader, it has been twenty years ago since I heard it, but I can remember a part of it now. Here it is:

"There was an ancient individual whose cognomen was Uncle Edward.

He departed this life long since, long since.

He had no capillary substance on the top of his cranium,

The place where the capillary substance ought to vegetate.

"His digits were as long as the bamboo piscatorial implement of the Southern Mississippi.

He had no oculars to observe the beauties of nature.

He had no ossified formation to masticate his daily rations,

So he had to let his daily rations pass by with impunity."

Walker Coleman raises the tune of "I'se a gwine to jine the rebel band, a fightin' for my home."

Now, reader, the above is all I can now remember of that very beautiful and soul-stirring air. But the boys would wake up and step quicker and livelier for some time, and Arthur Fulghum would holloa out, "All right; go ahead!" and then would toot! toot! as if the cars were starting-- puff! puff! puff and then he would say, "Tickets, gentlemen; tickets, gentlemen." like he was conductor on a train of cars. This little episode would be over, and then would commence the same tramp, tramp, tramp, all night long. Step by step, step by step, we continued to plod and nod and stagger and march, tramp, tramp, tramp. After a while we would see the morning star rise in the east, and then after a while the dim gray twilight, and finally we could discover the outlines of our file leader, and after a while could make out the outlines of trees and other objects. And as it would get lighter and lighter, and day would be about to break, cuckoo, cuckoo, cuckoo, would come from Tom Tuck's rooster. [Tom carried a game rooster, that he called "Fed" for Confederacy, all through the war in a haversack.] And then the sun would begin to shoot his slender rays athwart the eastern sky, and the boys would wake up and begin laughing and talking as if they had just risen from a good feather bed, and were perfectly refreshed and happy. We would usually stop at some branch or other about breakfast time, and all wash our hands and faces and eat breakfast, if we had any, and then commence our weary march again. If we were halted for one minute, every soldier would drop down, and resting on his knapsack, would go to sleep. Sometimes the sleeping soldiers were made to get up to let some general and his staff pass by. But whenever that was the case, the general always got a worse cursing than when Noah cursed his son Ham black and blue. I heard Jessee Ely do this once.

We march on. The scene of a few days ago comes unbidden to my mind. Tramp, tramp, tramp, the soldiers are marching. Where are many of my old friends and comrades, whose names were so familiar at every roll call, and whose familiar "Here" is no more? They lie yonder at Perryville, unburied, on the field of battle. They lie where they fell. More than three hundred and fifty members of my regiment, the First Tennessee, numbered among the killed and wounded--one hundred and eighty-five slain on the field of battle. Who are they? Even then I had to try to think up the names of all the slain of Company H alone. Their spirits seemed to be with us on the march, but we know that their souls are with their God. Their bones, today, no doubt, bleach upon the battlefield. They left their homes, families, and loved ones a little more than one short twelve months ago, dressed in their gray uniforms, amid the applause and cheering farewells of those same friends. They lie yonder; no friendly hands ever closed their eyes in death; no kind, gentle, and loving mother was there to shed a tear over and say farewell to her darling boy; no sister's gentle touch ever wiped the death damp from off their dying brows. Noble boys; brave boys! They willingly gave their lives to their country's cause. Their bodies and bones are mangled and torn by the rude missiles of war. They sleep the sleep of the brave. They have given their all to their country. We miss them from our ranks. There are no more hard marches and scant rations for them. They have accomplished all that could be required of them. They are no more; their names are soon forgotten. They are put down in the roll-book as killed. They are forgotten. We will see them no more until the last reveille on the last morning of the final resurrection. Soldiers, comrades, friends, noble boys, farewell we will meet no more on earth, but up yonder some day we will have a grand reunion.

Knoxville

The first night after crossing Cumberland Gap--I have forgotten the date, but I know it was very early in the fall of the year; we had had no frost or cold weather, and our marches all through Kentucky had been characterized by very dry weather, it not having rained a drop on us during the whole time--about four o'clock in the morning it began to snow, and the next morning the ground was covered with a deep snow; the trees and grass and everything of the vegetable kingdom still green.

When we got back to Knoxville we were the lousiest, dirtiest, raggedest looking Rebels you ever saw. I had been shot through the hat and cartridge-box at Perryville, and had both on, and the clothing I then had on was all that I had in the world. William A. Hughes and I were walking up the street looking at the stores, etc., when we met two of the prettiest girls I ever saw. They ran forward with smiling faces, and seemed very glad to see us. I thought they were old acquaintances of Hughes, and Hughes thought they were old acquaintances of mine. We were soon laughing and talking as if we had been old friends, when one of the young ladies spoke up and said, "Gentlemen, there is a supper for the soldiers at the Ladies' Association rooms, and we are sent out to bring in all the soldiers we can find." We spoke up quickly and said, "Thank you, thank you, young ladies," and I picked out the prettiest one and said, "Please take my arm," which she did, and Hughes did the same with the other one, and we went in that style down the street. I imagine we were a funny looking sight. I know one thing, I felt good all over, and as proud as a boy with his first pants, and when we got to that supper room those young ladies waited on us, and we felt as grand as kings. To you, ladies, I say, God bless you!

AH, "SNEAK"

Almost every soldier in the army--generals, colonels, captains, as well as privates--had a nick-name; and I almost believe that had the war continued ten years, we would have forgotten our proper names. John T. Tucker was called "Sneak," A. S. Horsley was called "Don Von One Horsley," W. A. Hughes was called "Apple Jack," Green Rieves was called "Devil Horse," the surgeon of our regiment was called "Old Snake," Bob Brank was called "Count," the colonel of the Fourth was called "Guide Post," E. L. Lansdown was called "Left Tenant," some were called by the name of "Greasy," some "Buzzard," others "Hog," and "Brutus," and "Cassius," and "Caesar," "Left Center," and "Bolderdust," and "Old Hannah;" in fact, the nick-names were singular and peculiar, and when a man got a nick-name it stuck to him like the Old Man of the Sea did to the shoulders of Sinbad, the sailor.

On our retreat the soldiers got very thirsty for tobacco (they always used the word thirsty), and they would sometimes come across an old field off which the tobacco had been cut and the suckers had re-sprouted from the old stalk, and would cut off these suckers and dry them by the fire and chew them. "Sneak" had somehow or other got hold of a plug or two, and knowing that he would be begged for a chew, had cut it up in little bits of pieces about one-fourth of a chew. Some fellow would say, "Sneak, please give me a chew of tobacco." Sneak would say, "I don't believe I have a piece left," and then he would begin to feel in his pockets. He would pull that hand out and feel in another pocket, and then in his coat pockets, and hid away down in an odd corner of his vest pocket he would accidentally find a little chew, just big enough to make "spit come." Sneak had his pockets full all the time. The boys soon found out his inuendoes and subterfuges, but John would all the time appear as innocent of having tobacco as a pet lamb that has just torn down a nice vine that you were so careful in training to run over the front porch. Ah, John, don't deny it now!

I Jine The Cavalry

When we got to Charleston, on the Hiwassee river, there we found the First Tennessee Cavalry and Ninth Battalion, both of which had been made up principally in Maury county, and we knew all the boys. We had a good old-fashioned handshaking all around. Then I wanted to "jine the cavalry." Captain Asa G. Freeman had an extra horse, and I got on him and joined the cavalry for several days, but all the time some passing cavalryman would make some jocose remark about "Here is a webfoot who wants to jine the cavalry, and has got a bayonet on his gun and a knapsack on his back." I felt like I had got into the wrong pen, but anyhow I got to ride all of three days. I remember that Mr. Willis B. Embry gave me a five-pound package of Kallickanick smoking tobacco, for which I was very grateful. I think he was quartermaster of the First Tennessee Cavalry, and as good a man and as clever a person as I ever knew. None knew him but to love him. I was told that he was killed by a lot of Yankee soldiers after he had surrendered to them, all the time begging for his life, asking them please not kill him. But He that noteth the sparrow's fall doeth all things well. Not one ever falls to the ground with His consent.

Chapter XVI-- Battles In Tennessee

Columbia

"This is my own, my native land."

Once more the Maury Grays are permitted to put their feet upon their native heath, and to revisit their homes and friends, after having followed their tattered, and torn, and battle-riddled flag, which they had borne aloft for four long years, on every march, and in every battle that had been fought by the Army of Tennessee. We were a mere handful of devoted braves, who had stood by our colors when sometimes it seemed that God himself had forsaken us. But, parents, here are your noble and brave sons; and, ladies, four years ago you gave us this flag, and we promised you "That we would come back with the flag as victors, or we would come not at all." We have been true to our promise and our trust. On every battlefield the flag that you entrusted to our hands has been borne aloft by brave and heroic men, amid shot and shell, bloody battle, and death. We have never forsaken our colors. Are we worthy to be called the sons of old Maury county? Or have we fought in vain? Have our efforts been appreciated, or have four years of our lives been wasted, while we were battling for constitutional government, the supremacy of our laws over centralization, and our rights, as guaranteed to us by the blood of our forefathers on the battlefields of the Revolution? It is for you to make up your verdict. If our lives as soldiers have been a _failure_, we can but bow our heads on our bosoms, and say, "Surely, four years of our lives have been given for naught, and our efforts to please you have been in vain."

Yet, the invader's foot is still on our soil, but there beats in our bosoms the blood of brave and patriotic men, and we will continue to follow our old and war-worn and battle-riddled flag until it goes down forever.

The Maury Grays, commanded by Captain A. M. Looney, left Columbia, four years ago, with 120 men. How many of those 120 original members are with the company today? Just twelve. Company H has twenty members, but some of this number had subsequently enlisted. But we twelve will stick to our colors till she goes down forever, and until five more of this number fall dead and bleeding on the battlefield.

A Fiasco

When we arrived in sight of Columbia, we found the Yankees still in possession of the town, fortified and determined to resist our advance. We send forward a "feeler," and the "feeler" reports back very promptly, "Yes, the Yankees are there." Well, if that be the case, we'll just make a flank movement. We turn off the main turnpike at J. E. R. Carpenter's, and march through the cedars, and cross Duck river at Davis' ferry, on pontoon bridges, near Lowell's mill. We pass on, and cross Rutherford creek, near Burick's mill, about three o'clock in the afternoon. We had marched through fields in the heavy mud, and the men, weary and worn out, were just dragging themselves along, passing by the old Union Seminary, and then by Mr. Fred Thompson's, until we came to the Rally Hill turnpike-- it being then nearly dark--we heard some skirmishing, but, exhausted as we were, we went into bivouac. The Yankees, it seems to me, might have captured the whole of us. But that is a matter of history. But I desire to state that no blunder was made by either Generals Cheatham or Stewart, neither of whom ever failed to come to time. Jeff Davis is alone responsible for the blunder. About two hours after sun up the next morning we received the order to "Fall in, fall in, quick, make haste, hurrah, promptly, men; each rank count two; by the right flank, quick time, march; keep promptly closed up." Everything indicated an immediate attack. When we got to the turnpike near Spring Hill, lo! and behold; wonder of wonders! the whole Yankee army had passed during the night. The bird had flown. We made a quick and rapid march down the turnpike, finding Yankee guns and knapsacks, and now and then a broken down straggler, also two pieces of howitzer cannon, and at least twenty broken wagons along the road. Everything betokened a rout and a stampede of the Yankee army. Double quick! Forrest is in the rear. Now for fun. All that we want to do now is to catch the blue-coated rascals, ha! ha! We all want to see the surrender, ha! ha! Double quick! A rip, rip, rip; wheuf; pant, pant, pant. First one man drops out, and then another. The Yankees are routed and running, and Forrest has crossed Harpeth river in the rear of Franklin. Hurrah, men! keep closed up; we are going to capture Schofield. Forrest is in the rear; never mind the straggler and cannon. Kerflop we come against the breast-works at Franklin.

Franklin

"The death-angel gathers its last harvest."

Kind reader, right here my pen, and courage, and ability fail me. I shrink from butchery. Would to God I could tear the page from these memoirs and from my own memory. It is the blackest page in the history of the war of the Lost Cause. It was the bloodiest battle of modern times in any war. It was the finishing stroke to the independence of the Southern Confederacy. I was there. I saw it. My flesh trembles, and creeps, and crawls when I think of it today. My heart almost ceases to beat at the horrid recollection. Would to God that I had never witnessed such a scene!

I cannot describe it. It beggars description. I will not attempt to describe it. I could not. The death-angel was there to gather its last harvest. It was the grand coronation of death. Would that I could turn the page. But I feel, though I did so, that page would still be there, teeming with its scenes of horror and blood. I can only tell of what I saw.

Our regiment was resting in the gap of a range of hills in plain view of the city of Franklin. We could see the battle-flags of the enemy waving in the breeze. Our army had been depleted of its strength by a forced march from Spring Hill, and stragglers lined the road. Our artillery had not yet come up, and could not be brought into action. Our cavalry was across Harpeth river, and our army was but in poor condition to make an assault. While resting on this hillside, I saw a courier dash up to our commanding general, B. F. Cheatham, and the word, "Attention!" was given. I knew then that we would soon be in action. Forward, march. We passed over the hill and through a little skirt of woods.

The enemy were fortified right across the Franklin pike, in the suburbs of the town. Right here in these woods a detail of skirmishers was called for. Our regiment was detailed. We deployed as skirmishers, firing as we advanced on the left of the turnpike road. If I had not been a skirmisher on that day, I would not have been writing this today, in the year of our Lord 1882.

It was four o'clock on that dark and dismal December day when the line of battle was formed, and those devoted heroes were ordered forward, to

"Strike for their altars and their fires,

For the green graves of their sires,

For God and their native land."

As they marched on down through an open field toward the rampart of blood and death, the Federal batteries began to open and mow down and gather into the garner of death, as brave, and good, and pure spirits as the world ever saw. The twilight of evening had begun to gather as a precursor of the coming blackness of midnight darkness that was to envelop a scene so sickening and horrible that it is impossible for me to describe it. "Forward, men," is repeated all along the line. A sheet of fire was poured into our very faces, and for a moment we halted as if in despair, as the terrible avalanche of shot and shell laid low those brave and gallant heroes, whose bleeding wounds attested that the struggle would be desperate. Forward, men! The air loaded with death-dealing missiles. Never on this earth did men fight against such terrible odds. It seemed that the very elements of heaven and earth were in one mighty uproar. Forward, men! And the blood spurts in a perfect jet from the dead and wounded. The earth is red with blood. It runs in streams, making little rivulets as it flows. Occasionally there was a little lull in the storm of battle, as the men were loading their guns, and for a few moments it seemed as if night tried to cover the scene with her mantle. The death-angel shrieks and laughs and old Father Time is busy with his sickle, as he gathers in the last harvest of death, crying, More, more, more! while his rapacious maw is glutted with the slain.

But the skirmish line being deployed out, extending a little wider than the battle did--passing through a thicket of small locusts, where Brown, orderly sergeant of Company B, was killed--we advanced on toward the breastworks, on and on. I had made up my mind to die--felt glorious. We pressed forward until I heard the terrific roar of battle open on our right. Cleburne's division was charging their works. I passed on until I got to their works, and got over on their (the Yankees') side. But in fifty yards of where I was the scene was lit up by fires that seemed like hell itself. It appeared to be but one line of streaming fire. Our troops were upon one side of the breastworks, and the Federals on the other. I ran up on the line of works, where our men were engaged. Dead soldiers filled the entrenchments. The firing was kept up until after midnight, and gradually died out. We passed the night where we were. But when the morrow's sun began to light up the eastern sky with its rosy hues, and we looked over the battlefield, O, my God! what did we see! It was a grand holocaust of death. Death had held high carnival there that night. The dead were piled the one on the other all over the ground. I never was so horrified and appalled in my life. Horses, like men, had died game on the gory breastworks. General Adams' horse had his fore feet on one side of the works and his hind feet on the other, dead. The general seems to have been caught so that he was held to the horse's back, sitting almost as if living, riddled, and mangled, and torn with balls. General Cleburne's mare had her fore feet on top of the works, dead in that position. General Cleburne's body was pierced with forty-nine bullets, through and through. General Strahl's horse lay by the roadside and the general by his side, both dead, and all his staff. General Gist, a noble and brave cavalier from South Carolina, was lying with his sword reaching across the breastworks still grasped in his hand. He was lying there dead. All dead! They sleep in the graveyard yonder at Ashwood, almost in sight of my home, where I am writing today. They sleep the sleep of the brave. We love and cherish their memory. They sleep beneath the ivy-mantled walls of St. John's church, where they expressed a wish to be buried. The private soldier sleeps where he fell, piled in one mighty heap. Four thousand five hundred privates! all lying side by side in death! Thirteen generals were killed and wounded. Four thousand five hundred men slain, all piled and heaped together at one place. I cannot tell the number of others killed and wounded. God alone knows that. We'll all find out on the morning of the final resurrection.

Battle of Franklin. November 30, 1864 - Union (Gen. Schofield) and Confederate (Gen. Hood)

Kind friends, I have attempted in my poor and feeble way to tell you of this (I can hardly call it) battle. It should be called by some other name. But, like all other battles, it, too, has gone into history. I leave it with you. I do not know who was to blame. It lives in the memory of the poor old Rebel soldier who went through that trying and terrible ordeal. We shed a tear for the dead. They are buried and forgotten. We meet no more on earth. But up yonder, beyond the sunset and the night, away beyond the clouds and tempest, away beyond the stars that ever twinkle and shine in the blue vault above us, away yonder by the great white throne, and by the river of life, where the Almighty and Eternal God sits, surrounded by the angels and archangels and the redeemed of earth, we will meet again and see those noble and brave spirits who gave up their lives for their country's cause that night at Franklin, Tennessee. A life given for one's country is never lost. It blooms again beyond the grave in a land of beauty and of love. Hanging around the throne of sapphire and gold, a rich garland awaits the coming of him who died for his country, and when the horologe of time has struck its last note upon his dying brow, Justice hands the record of life to Mercy, and Mercy pleads with Jesus, and God, for his sake, receives him in his eternal home beyond the skies at last and forever.

Nashville

A few more scenes, my dear friends, and we close these memoirs. We march toward the city of Nashville. We camp the first night at Brentwood. The next day we can see the fine old building of solid granite, looming up on Capitol Hill--the capitol of Tennessee. We can see the Stars and Stripes flying from the dome. Our pulse leaps with pride when we see the grand old architecture. We can hear the bugle call, and the playing of the bands of the different regiments in the Federal lines. Now and then a shell is thrown into our midst from Fort Negley, but no attack or demonstrations on either side. We bivouac on the cold and hard-frozen ground, and when we walk about, the echo of our footsteps sound like the echo of a tombstone. The earth is crusted with snow, and the wind from the north-west is piercing our very bones. We can see our ragged soldiers, with sunken cheeks and famine-glistening eyes. Where were our generals? Alas! there were none. Not one single general out of Cheatham's division was left--not one. General B. F. Cheatham himself was the only surviving general of his old division. Nearly all our captains and colonels were gone. Companies mingled with companies, regiments with regiments, and brigades with brigades. A few raw-boned horses stood shivering under the ice-covered trees, nibbling the short, scanty grass. Being in range of the Federal guns from Fort Negley, we were not allowed to have fires at night, and our thin and ragged blankets were but poor protection against the cold, raw blasts of December weather--the coldest ever known. The cold stars seem to twinkle with unusual brilliancy, and the pale moon seems to be but one vast heap of frozen snow, which glimmers in the cold gray sky, and the air gets colder by its coming; our breath, forming in little rays, seems to make a thousand little coruscations that scintillate in the cold frosty air. I can tell you nothing of what was going on among the generals. But there we were, and that is all that I can tell you. One morning about daylight our army began to move. Our division was then on the extreme right wing, and then we were transferred to the left wing. The battle had begun. We were continually moving to our left. We would build little temporary breastworks, then we would be moved to another place. Our lines kept on widening out, and stretching further and further apart, until it was not more than a skeleton of a skirmish line from one end to the other. We started at a run. We cared for nothing. Not more than a thousand yards off, we could see the Yankee cavalry, artillery, and infantry, marching apparently still further to our left. We could see regiments advancing at double-quick across the fields, while, with our army, everything seemed confused. The private soldier could not see into things. It seemed to be somewhat like a flock of wild geese when they have lost their leader. We were willing to go anywhere, or to follow anyone who would lead us. We were anxious to flee, fight, or fortify. I have never seen an army so confused and demoralized. The whole thing seemed to be tottering and trembling. When, _Halt! Front! Right dress!_ and Adjutant McKinney reads us the following order:

"SOLDIERS:--The commanding general takes pleasure in announcing to his troops that victory and success are now within their grasp; and the commanding general feels proud and gratified that in every attack and assault the enemy have been repulsed; and the commanding general will further say to his noble and gallant troops, 'Be of good cheer--all is well.'

"GENERAL JOHN B. HOOD,

"General Commanding."

"KINLOCK FALCONER,

"Acting Adjutant-General."

I remember how this order was received. Every soldier said, "O, shucks; that is all shenanigan," for we knew that we had never met the enemy or fired a gun outside of a little skirmishing. And I will further state that that battle order, announcing success and victory, was the cause of a greater demoralization than if our troops had been actually engaged in battle. They at once mistrusted General Hood's judgment as a commander. And every private soldier in the whole army knew the situation of affairs. I remember when passing by Hood, how feeble and decrepit he looked, with an arm in a sling, and a crutch in the other hand, and trying to guide and control his horse. And, reader, I was not a Christian then, and am but little better today; but, as God sees my heart tonight, I prayed in my heart that day for General Hood. Poor fellow, I loved him, not as a General, but as a good man. I knew when that army order was read, that General Hood had been deceived, and that the poor fellow was only trying to encourage his men. Every impulse of his nature was but to do good, and to serve his country as best he could. Ah! reader, some day all will be well.

We continued marching toward our left, our battle-line getting thinner and thinner. We could see the Federals advancing, their blue coats and banners flying, and could see their movements and hear them giving their commands. Our regiment was ordered to double quick to the extreme left wing of the army, and we had to pass up a steep hill, and the dead grass was wet and as slick as glass, and it was with the greatest difficulty that we could get up the steep hill side. When we got to the top, we, as skirmishers, were ordered to deploy still further to the left. Billy Carr and J. E. Jones, two as brave soldiers as ever breathed the breath of life--in fact, it was given up that they were the bravest and most daring men in the Army of Tennessee--and myself, were on the very extreme left wing of our army. While we were deployed as skirmishers, I heard, "Surrender, surrender," and on looking around us, I saw that we were right in the midst of a Yankee line of battle. They were lying down in the bushes, and we were not looking for them so close to us. We immediately threw down our guns and surrendered. J. E. Jones was killed at the first discharge of their guns, when another Yankee raised up and took deliberate aim at Billy Carr, and fired, the ball striking him below the eye and passing through his head. As soon as I could, I picked up my gun, and as the Yankee turned I sent a minnie ball crushing through his head, and broke and run. But I am certain that I killed the Yankee who killed Billy Carr, but it was too late to save the poor boy's life. As I started to run, a fallen dogwood tree tripped me up, and I fell over the log. It was all that saved me. The log was riddled with balls, and thousands, it seemed to me, passed over it. As I got up to run again, I was shot through the middle finger of the very hand that is now penning these lines, and the thigh. But I had just killed a Yankee, and was determined to get away from there as soon as I could. How I did get back I hardly know, for I was wounded and surrounded by Yankees. One rushed forward, and placing the muzzle of his gun in two feet of me, discharged it, but it missed its aim, when I ran at him, grabbed him by the collar, and brought him off a prisoner. Captain Joe P. Lee and Colonel H. R. Field remember this, as would Lieutenant-Colonel John L. House, were he alive; and all the balance of Company H, who were there at the time. I had eight bullet holes in my coat, and two in my hand, beside the one in my thigh and finger. It was a hail storm of bullets. The above is true in every particular, and is but one incident of the war, which happened to hundreds of others. But, alas! all our valor and victories were in vain, when God and the whole world were against us.

Billy Carr was one of the bravest and best men I ever knew. He never knew what fear was, and in consequence of his reckless bravery, had been badly wounded at Perryville, Murfreesboro, Chickamauga, the octagon house, Dead Angle, and the 22nd of July at Atlanta. In every battle he was wounded, and finally, in the very last battle of the war, surrendered up his life for his country's cause. No father and mother of such a brave and gallant boy, should ever sorrow or regret having born to them such a son. He was the flower and chivalry of his company. He was as good as he was brave. His bones rest yonder on the Overton hills today, while I have no doubt in my own mind that his spirit is with the Redeemer of the hosts of heaven. He was my friend. Poor boy, farewell!

When I got back to where I could see our lines, it was one scene of confusion and rout. Finney's Florida brigade had broken before a mere skirmish line, and soon the whole army had caught the infection, had broken, and were running in every direction. Such a scene I never saw. The army was panic-stricken. The woods everywhere were full of running soldiers. Our officers were crying, "Halt! halt!" and trying to rally and re-form their broken ranks. The Federals would dash their cavalry in amongst us, and even their cannon joined in the charge. One piece of Yankee artillery galloped past me, right on the road, unlimbered their gun, fired a few shots, and galloped ahead again.

Hood's whole army was routed and in full retreat. Nearly every man in the entire army had thrown away his gun and accouterments. More than ten thousand had stopped and allowed themselves to be captured, while many, dreading the horrors of a Northern prison, kept on, and I saw many, yea, even thousands, broken down from sheer exhaustion, with despair and pity written on their features. Wagon trains, cannon, artillery, cavalry, and infantry were all blended in inextricable confusion. Broken down and jaded horses and mules refused to pull, and the badly-scared drivers looked like their eyes would pop out of their heads from fright. Wagon wheels, interlocking each other, soon clogged the road, and wagons, horses and provisions were left indiscriminately. The officers soon became effected with the demoralization of their troops, and rode on in dogged indifference. General Frank Cheatham and General Loring tried to form a line at Brentwood, but the line they formed was like trying to stop the current of Duck river with a fish net. I believe the army would have rallied, had there been any colors to rally to. And as the straggling army moves on down the road, every now and then we can hear the sullen roar of the Federal artillery booming in the distance. I saw a wagon and team abandoned, and I unhitched one of the horses and rode on horseback to Franklin, where a surgeon tied up my broken finger, and bandaged up my bleeding thigh. My boot was full of blood, and my clothing saturated with it. I was at General Hood's headquarters. He was much agitated and affected, pulling his hair with his one hand (he had but one), and crying like his heart would break. I pitied him, poor fellow. I asked him for a wounded furlough, and he gave it to me. I never saw him afterward. I always loved and honored him, and will ever revere and cherish his memory. He gave his life in the service of his country, and I know today he wears a garland of glory beyond the grave, where Justice says "well done," and Mercy has erased all his errors and faults.

I only write of the under _strata_ of history; in other words, the _privates' history_--as I saw things then, and remember them now.

The winter of 1864-5 was the coldest that had been known for many years. The ground was frozen and rough, and our soldiers were poorly clad, while many, yes, very many, were entirely barefooted. Our wagon trains had either gone on, we knew not whither, or had been left behind. Everything and nature, too, seemed to be working against us. Even the keen, cutting air that whistled through our tattered clothes and over our poorly covered heads, seemed to lash us in its fury. The floods of waters that had overflowed their banks, seemed to laugh at our calamity, and to mock us in our misfortunes.

All along the route were weary and footsore soldiers. The citizens seemed to shrink and hide from us as we approached them. And, to cap the climax, Tennessee river was overflowing its banks, and several Federal gunboats were anchored just below Mussel Shoals, firing at us while crossing.

The once proud Army of Tennessee had degenerated to a mob. We were pinched by hunger and cold. The rains, and sleet, and snow never ceased falling from the winter sky, while the winds pierced the old, ragged, grayback Rebel soldier to his very marrow. The clothing of many were hanging around them in shreds of rags and tatters, while an old slouched hat covered their frozen ears. Some were on old, raw-boned horses, without saddles.

Hon. Jefferson Davis perhaps made blunders and mistakes, but I honestly believe that he ever did what he thought best for the good of his country. And there never lived on this earth from the days of Hampden to George Washington, a purer patriot or a nobler man than Jefferson Davis; and, like Marius, grand even in ruins.

Hood was a good man, a kind man, a philanthropic man, but he is both harmless and defenseless now. He was a poor general in the capacity of commander-in-chief. Had he been mentally qualified, his physical condition would have disqualified him. His legs and one of his arms had been shot off in the defense of his country. As a soldier, he was brave, good, noble, and gallant, and fought with the ferociousness of the wounded tiger, and with the everlasting grit of the bull-dog; but as a general he was a failure in every particular.

Our country is gone, our cause is lost.

"_Actum est de Republica_."

Chapter XVII -- The Surrender

The Last Act Of The Drama

On the 10th day of May, 1861, our regiment, the First Tennessee, left Nashville for the camp of instruction, with twelve hundred and fifty men, officers and line. Other recruits continually coming in swelled this number to fourteen hundred. In addition to this Major Fulcher's battalion of four companies, with four hundred men (originally), was afterwards attached to the regiment; and the Twenty-seventh Tennessee Regiment was afterwards consolidated with the First. And besides this, there were about two hundred conscripts added to the regiment from time to time. To recapitulate: The First Tennessee, numbering originally, 1,250; recruited from time to time, 150; Fulcher's battalion, 400; the Twenty-seventh Tennessee, 1,200; number of conscripts (at the lowest estimate), 200--making the sum total 3,200 men that belonged to our regiment during the war. The above I think a low estimate. Well, on the 26th day of April, 1865, General Joe E. Johnston surrendered his army at Greensboro, North Carolina. The day that we surrendered our regiment it was a pitiful sight to behold. If I remember correctly, there were just sixty-five men in all, including officers, that were paroled on that day. Now, what became of the original 3,200? A grand army, you may say. Three thousand two hundred men! Only sixty-five left! Now, reader, you may draw your own conclusions. It lacked just four days of four years from the day we were sworn in to the day of the surrender, and it was just four years and twenty four days from the time that we left home for the army to the time that we got back again. It was indeed a sad sight to look at, the Old First Tennessee Regiment. A mere squad of noble and brave men, gathered around the tattered flag that they had followed in every battle through that long war. It was so bullet-riddled and torn that it was but a few blue and red shreds that hung drooping while it, too, was stacked with our guns forever.

Thermopylae had one messenger of defeat, but when General Joe E. Johnston surrendered the Army of the South there were hundreds of regiments, yea, I might safely say thousands, that had not a representative on the 26th day of April, 1865.

Gen. J.E. Johnston, C.S.A.

Our cause was lost from the beginning. Our greatest victories-- Chickamauga and Franklin--were our greatest defeats. Our people were divided upon the question of Union and secession. Our generals were scrambling for "_Who ranked_." The private soldier fought and starved and died for naught. Our hospitals were crowded with sick and wounded, but half provided with food and clothing to sustain life. Our money was depreciated to naught and our cause lost. We left our homes four years previous. Amid the waving of flags and handkerchiefs and the smiles of the ladies, while the fife and drum were playing Dixie and the Bonnie Blue Flag, we bid farewell to home and friends. The bones of our brave Southern boys lie scattered over our loved South. They fought for their "_country_," and gave their lives freely for that country's cause: and now they who survive sit, like Marius amid the wreck of Carthage, sublime even in ruins. Other pens abler than mine will have to chronicle their glorious deeds of valor and devotion. In these sketches I have named but a few persons who fought side by side with me during that long and unholy war. In looking back over these pages, I ask, Where now are many whose names have appeared in these sketches? They are up yonder, and are no doubt waiting and watching for those of us who are left behind. And, my kind reader, the time is coming when we, too, will be called, while the archangel of death is beating the long roll of eternity, and with us it will be the last reveille. God Himself will sound the "assembly" on yonder beautiful and happy shore, where we will again have a grand "reconfederation." We shed a tear over their flower-strewn graves. We live after them. We love their memory yet. But one generation passes away and another generation follows. We know our loved and brave soldiers. We love them yet.

But when we pass away, the impartial historian will render a true verdict, and a history will then be written in justification and vindication of those brave and noble boys who gave their all in fighting the battles of their homes, their country, and their God.

"The United States has no North, no South, no East, no West." "_We are one and undivided_."

ADIEU

My kind friends--soldiers, comrades, brothers, all: The curtain is rung down, the footlights are put out, the audience has all left and gone home, the seats are vacant, and the cold walls are silent. The gaudy tinsel that appears before the footlights is exchanged for the dress of the citizen. Coming generations and historians will be the critics as to how we have acted our parts. The past is buried in oblivion. The blood-red flag, with its crescent and cross, that we followed for four long, bloody, and disastrous years, has been folded never again to be unfurled. We have no regrets for what we did, but we mourn the loss of so many brave and gallant men who perished on the field of battle and honor. I now bid you an affectionate adieu.

But in closing these memoirs, the scenes of my life pass in rapid review before me. In imagination, I am young again tonight. I feel the flush and vigor of my manhood--am just twenty-one years of age. I hear the fife and drum playing Dixie and Bonnie Blue Flag. I see and hear our fire-eating stump-orators tell of the right of secession and disunion. I see our fair and beautiful women waving their handkerchiefs and encouraging their sweethearts to go to the war. I see the marshaling of the hosts for "glorious war." I see the fine banners waving and hear the cry everywhere, "_To arms! to arms!_" And I also see our country at peace and prosperous, our fine cities look grand and gay, our fields rich in abundant harvests, our people happy and contented. All these pass in imagination before me. Then I look and see glorious war in all its splendor. I hear the shout and charge, the boom of artillery and the rattle of small arms. I see gaily-dressed officers charging backwards and forwards upon their mettled war horses, clothed in the panoply of war. I see victory and conquest upon flying banners. I see our arms triumph in every battle. And, O, my friends, I see another scene. I see broken homes and broken hearts. I see war in all of its desolation. I see a country ruined and impoverished. I see a nation disfranchised and maltreated. I see a commonwealth forced to pay dishonest and fraudulent bonds that were issued to crush that people. I see sycophants licking the boots of the country's oppressor. I see other and many wrongs perpetrated upon a conquered people. But maybe it is but the ghosts and phantoms of a dreamy mind, or the wind as it whistles around our lonely cabin-home. The past is buried in oblivion. The mantle of charity has long ago fallen upon those who think differently from us. We remember no longer wrongs and injustice done us by anyone on earth. We are willing to forget and forgive those who have wronged and falsified us. We look up above and beyond all these petty groveling things and shake hands and forget the past. And while my imagination is like the weaver's shuttle, playing backward and forward through these two decades of time, I ask myself, Are these things real? did they happen? are they being enacted today? or are they the fancies of the imagination in forgetful reverie? Is it true that I have seen all these things? that they are real incidents in my life's history? Did I see those brave and noble countrymen of mine laid low in death and weltering in their blood? Did I see our country laid waste and in ruins? Did I see soldiers marching, the earth trembling and jarring beneath their measured tread? Did I see the ruins of smouldering cities and deserted homes? Did I see my comrades buried and see the violet and wild flowers bloom over their graves? Did I see the flag of my country, that I had followed so long, furled to be no more unfurled forever? Surely they are but the vagaries of mine own imagination. Surely my fancies are running wild tonight. But, hush! I now hear the approach of battle. That low, rumbling sound in the west is the roar of cannon in the distance. That rushing sound is the tread of soldiers. That quick, lurid glare is the flash that precedes the cannon's roar. And listen! that loud report that makes the earth tremble and jar and sway, is but the bursting of a shell, as it screams through the dark, tempestuous night. That black, ebon cloud, where the lurid lightning flickers and flares, that is rolling through the heavens, is the smoke of battle; beneath is being enacted a carnage of blood and death. Listen! the soldiers are charging now. The flashes and roaring now are blended with the shouts of soldiers and confusion of battle.

But, reader, time has brought his changes since I, a young ardent and
impetuous youth, burning with a lofty patriotism first shouldered my
musket to defend the rights of my country.

Lifting the veil of the past, I see many manly forms, bright in youth and hope, standing in view by my side in Company H, First Tennessee Regiment. Again I look and half those forms are gone. Again, and gray locks and wrinkled faces and clouded brows stand before me.

Before me, too, I see, not in imagination, but in reality, my own loved Jennie, the partner of my joys and the sharer of my sorrows, sustaining, comforting, and cheering my pathway by her benignant smile; pouring the sunshine of domestic comfort and happiness upon our humble home; making life more worth the living as we toil on up the hill of time together, with the bright pledges of our early and constant love by our side while the sunlight of hope ever brightens our pathway, dispelling darkness and sorrow as we hand in hand approach the valley of the great shadow.

The tale is told. The world moves on, the sun shines as brightly as before, the flowers bloom as beautifully, the birds sing their carols as sweetly, the trees nod and bow their leafy tops as if slumbering in the breeze, the gentle winds fan our brow and kiss our cheek as they pass by, the pale moon sheds her silvery sheen, the blue dome of the sky sparkles with the trembling stars that twinkle and shine and make night beautiful, and the scene melts and gradually disappears forever.

THE END.

VMI Cadet, William Hugh McDowell

photos and letters courtesy of Virginia Military Institute Archives

William Hugh McDowell entered VMI on August 22, 1863, from Mt. Mourne, North Carolina, and was assigned to the fourth (freshman) class. He was killed on May 15, 1864, while serving as a cadet Private in Company B at the Battle of New Market. When ordered to New Market, he was contemplating accepting a position upon the staff of General James Conner, his kinsman. After temporary burial at New Market, McDowell's remains were brought to Lexington in May 1866, and are now buried beneath the New Market Battle Monument at VMI.

Letters

William Hugh McDowell was only 17 and a freshman cadet at VMI when he was killed at the Battle of New Market. His mother, who wrote requesting his entry into the prestigious school, was unaware the school would be sending cadets into battle.

June 1st, 1863

Col. Smith

I write for information concerning the time when the exercises at Lexington commence; as you promised Mrs. Jackson last winter that you would take him in July but did not state what time in July. Please let me know the time, the regulations, and terms.

I might obtain the necessary information from my cousin* but her grief is too recent, too great, & sacred to obtrude upon with my concerns. Virginia had reason to be proud of & thankful for such a chieftain as Jackson. A great & good man, a pure & unselfish patriot, and it is a pleasure to us to think that we can do something by kind offices & soothing attentions, to cheer his widow on her lonely way. We all mourn him, through the length & breadth of this Confederacy.

You will find our child careless & thoughtless, but high principled, & too firm to be led astray. I hope his conduct & deportment may be unexceptionable as it has been hitherto. And let me beg of you to take an interest in him. I can scarce hope to have him with me much more after he goes to you--as when he leaves you twill be to enter the army. He has been a good obedient child to me and I would feel relieved to know that far from home and among strangers he has found one friend and protector.

Please direct your letter to Mrs. R.R. McDowell, Mt. Mourne, P.O. Iredell Cty, N.C.

Very respectfully, R.R. McDowell

**Her cousin was Mary Anna Jackson, the widow of General Stonewall Jackson*

Oct 3d 1863

Genrl Smith

I enclose you $10 for the use of my son William H. McDowell, with which I beg that you will have a good Daguerreotype, or photograph of him taken. He is my eldest child, and is far from me. And should any misfortune befall him, I would wish some likeness of him preserved. I have no idea of the cost of such a thing at the present time, and should this be insufficient for the purpose I will remit more. Should it be more than enough, tis subject to your discretion. Willie can retain the daguerreotype until there is an opportunity of sending it to us. By attending to this request, you will confer a favor on

R.R. McDowell

Mr. R.I. McDowell
Mount Mourne, Iredell Co. N.C.

Sir--

You have doubtless received before this the mournful intelligence that your [noble] son has been added to the long list of the gallant dead who have fallen in defending their country against the invasion of a ruthless foe. The newspapers have furnished you with accounts of the victory gained by Gen. Breckinridge over Sigel near New Market, and every notice of the fight bgears unequivocal testimony to the value of the aid rendered by the Corps of Cadets and the [illegible] valour that they displayed in the action. You have also received, I suppose, an official letter from the Adjutant informing you of the sad event.

I can add nothing more except the statement that the fatal ball passed entirely through his body, entering a little to the [illegible] of the breastbone and coming out on the left of the spine, passing probably through the heart, so that it may be concluded that his death was instantaneous.

This I received from Col. Gilham who examined the body before its interment. I have not been able to see anyone who was near him when he fell, as the cadets have not returned to the Institute, [having been] ordered to Richmond.

The Quartermaster will endeavor to preserve any mementos or any property of the cadets who have fallen, but cannot at present while the Corps is absent identify what belongs to each. The letter which you gave me for him [3 words illegible] and which weighed as a heavy burden on my heart after I heard before I reached home, that the words of affection it contained could never reach the eyes closed in death forever--together with a second one received from the office for him, I have directed to be kept subject to your order not choosing to subject them to the risk of the mail in the present uncertainty of transmission.

I offer no words of condolence. I know how to sympathize with you for my noblest son fell slain in battle not two months after he left the Institute--and I know by experience that the only comfort for so great a sorrow must come from a source higher than any on earth.

Yrs truly,
J.T.L. Preston

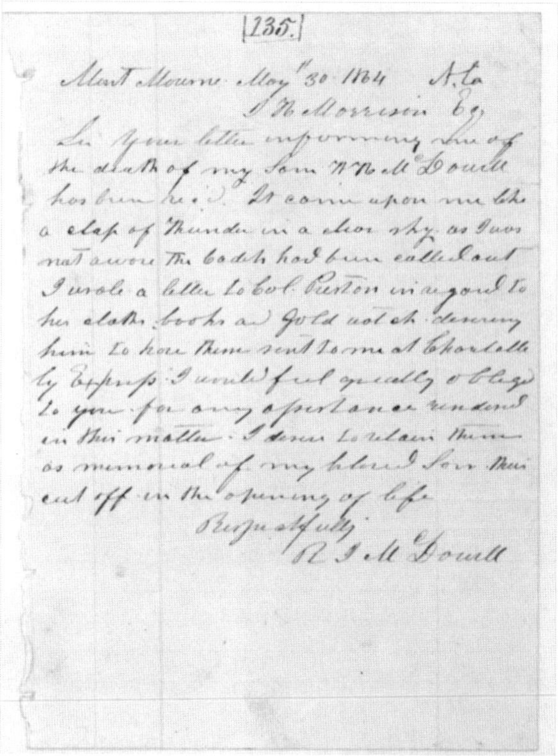

[135]

Mount Mourne May 30 1864 N.Ca
J N Morrison Esq
Sir Your letter informing me of
the death of my Son W H McDowell
has been rec'd. It came upon me like
a clap of Thunder in a clear sky as I was
not aware the Cadets had been called out
I wrote a letter to Col. Preston in regard to
his clothes books and Gold watch desiring
him to have them sent to me at Charlotte
by Express I would feel greatly oblige
to you for any assistance rendered
in this matter. I desire to retain them
as memorial of my beloved Son thus
cut off in the opening of life
Respectfully
R I McDowell

Letter from Robert McDowell, May 30, 1964

Mount Mourne, May 30 1864 N.C.
J.N. Morrison, Esq.

Sir:

Your letter informing me of the death of my son Wm McDowell has been received. It came upon me like a clap of thunder in a clear sky, as I was not aware the cadets had been called out. I wrote a letter to Col. Preston in regard to his clothes, books, and gold watch, desiring him to have them sent to me at Charlotte by Express. I would feel greatly obliged to you for any assistance rendered in this matter. I desire to retain them as memorial of my beloved son, [thus] cut off in the opening of life.

Respectfully
R.I. McDowell

"A little removed from the spot where Cabell fell, and nearer to the position of the enemy, lay McDowell, it was a sight to wring one's heart. That little boy was lying there asleep, more fit, indeed, for the cradle than the grave. He was barely sixteen, I judge, and by no means robust for his age. He was a North Carolinian. He had torn open his jacket and shirt, and, even in death, lay clutching them back, exposing a fair breast with its red wound." (From *An End of an Era* by John S. Wise, copyright 1899)

The Recollections and Letters of General Robert E. Lee

Chapter II & Chapter III

Chapter II

The Confederate General

In February, 1861, after the secession of Texas, my father was ordered to report to General Scott, the Commander-in-Chief of the United States Army. He immediately relinquished the command of his regiment, and departed from Fort Mason, Texas, for Washington. He reached Arlington March 1st. April 17th, Virginia seceded. On the 18th Colonel Lee had a long interview with General Scott. On April 20th he tendered his resignation of his commission in the United States Army. The same day he wrote to General Scott the following letter:

General Lee's Headquarters

Arlington, Virginia, April 20, 1861.

General: Since my interview with you on the 18th inst. I have felt that I ought no longer to retain my commission in the Army. I therefore tender my resignation, which I request you will recommend for acceptance. It would have been presented at once but for the struggle it has cost me to separate myself from a service to which I have devoted the best years of my life, and all the ability I possessed.

During the whole of that time--more than a quarter of a century--I have experienced nothing but kindness from my superiors and a most cordial friendship from my comrades. To no one, General, have I been as much indebted as to yourself for uniform kindness and consideration, and it has always been my ardent desire to merit your approbation. I shall carry tot he grave the most grateful recollections of your kind consideration, and your name and fame shall always be dear to me.

Save in the defense of my native State, I never desire again to draw my sword.

Be pleased to accept my most earnest wishes for the continuance of your happiness and prosperity, and believe me most truly yours,

R. E. Lee
His resignation was written the same day.

Arlington, Washington City P.O., April 20, 1861.

Honourable Simon Cameron, Secretary of War.

Sir: I have the honour to tender the resignation of my command as Colonel of the First Regiment of Cavalry. Very respectfully your obedient servant, R. E. Lee, Colonel First Cavalry.

To show further his great feeling in thus having to leave the army with which he had been associated for so long, I give two more letters, one to his sister, Mrs. Anne Marshall, of Baltimore, the other to his brother, Captain Sydney Smith Lee, of the United States Navy:

R. E. Lee

Arlington, Virginia, April 20, 1861.

My Dear Sister: I am grieved at my inability to see you.... I have been waiting for a 'more convenient season,' which has brought to many before me deep and lasting regret. Now we are in a state of war which will yield to nothing. The whole South is in a state of revolution, into which Virginia, after a long struggle, has been drawn; and though I recognise no necessity for this state of things, and would have forborne and pleaded to the end for redress of grievances, real or supposed, yet in my own person I had to meet the question whether I should take part against my native State.

With all my devotion to the Union and the feeling of loyalty and duty of an American citizen, I have not been able to make up my mind to raise my hand against my relatives, my children, my home. I have therefore resigned my commission in the Army, and save in defense of my native State, with the sincere hope that my poor services may never be needed, I hope I may never be called on to draw my sword. I know you will blame me; but you must think as kindly of me as you can, and believe that I have endeavoured to do what I thought right.

To show you the feeling and struggle it has cost me, I send you a copy of my letter of resignation. I have no time for more. May God guard and protect you and yours, and shower upon you everlasting blessings, is the prayer of your devoted brother,

R. E. Lee.

Arlington, Virginia, April 20, 1860.

My Dear Brother Smith: The question which was the subject of my earnest consultation with you on the 18th inst. has in my own mind been decided. After the most anxious inquiry as to the correct course for me to pursue, I concluded to resign, and sent in my resignation this morning. I wished to wait till the Ordinance of secession should be acted on by the people of Virginia; but war seems to have commenced, and I am liable at any time to be ordered on duty which I could not conscientiously perform. To save me from such a position, and to prevent the necessity of resigning under orders, I had to act at once, and before I could see you again on the subject, as I had wished. I am now a private citizen, and have no other ambition than to remain at home. Save in defense of my native State, I have no desire ever again to draw my sword. I send you my warmest love. Your affectionate brother,

R. E. Lee.

I will give here one of my father's letters, written after the war, in which is his account of his resignation from the United States Army:

Lexington, Virginia, February 25, 1868.
Honourable Reverdy Johnson,
United States Senate, Washington, D. C.

My Dear Sir: My attention has been called to the official report of the debate in the Senate of the United States, on the 19th instant, in which you did my the kindness to doubt the correctness of the statement made by the Honourable Simon Cameron, in regard to myself. I desire that you may feel certain of my conduct on the occasion referred to, so far as my individual statement can make you. I never intimated to any one that I desired the command of the United States Army; nor did I ever have a conversation with but one gentleman, Mr. Francis Preston Blair, on the subject, which was at his invitation, and, as I understood, at the instance of President Lincoln. After listening to his remarks, I declined the offer that he made me, to take command of the army that was to be brought into the field; stating, as candidly and courteously as I could, that, though opposed to secession and deprecating war, I could take no part in an invasion of the Southern States. I went directly from the interview with Mr. Blair to the office of General Scott; told him of the proposition that had been made to me, and my decision. Upon reflection after returning to my home, I concluded that I ought no longer to retain the commission I held in the United States Army, and on the second morning thereafter I forwarded my resignation to General Scott. At the time, I hoped that peace would have been preserved; that some way would have been found to save the country from the calamities of war; and I then had no other intention than to pass the remainder of my life as a private citizen. Two days afterward, upon the invitation of the Governor of Virginia, I repaired to Richmond; found that the Convention then in session had passed the ordinance withdrawing the State from the Union; and accepted the commission of commander of its forces, which was tendered me.

These are the ample facts of the case, and they show that Mr. Cameron has been misinformed.

I am with great respect, Your obedient servant,

R. E. Lee.

My father reached Richmond April 22, 1861. The next day he was introduced to the Virginia Convention, and offered by them the command of the military forces of his State. In his reply to Mr. John Janney, the President, who spoke for the Convention, he said:

Mr. President and Gentlemen of the Convention: Deeply impressed with the solemnity of the occasion on which I appear before you, and profoundly grateful for the honour conferred upon me, I accept the position your partiality has assigned me, though I would greatly have preferred your choice should have fallen on one more capable.

Trusting to Almighty God, an approving conscience, and the aid of my fellow citizens, I will devote myself to the defense and service of my native State, in whose behalf alone would I have ever drawn my sword.

On April 26th, from Richmond, he wrote to his wife:

...I am very anxious about you. You have to move and make arrangements to go to some point of safety, which you must select. The Mount Vernon plate and pictures ought to be secured. Keep quiet while you remain and in your preparation. War is inevitable, and there is no telling when it will burst around you. Virginia, yesterday, I understand, joined the Confederate States. What policy they may adopt I cannot conjecture. May God bless and preserve you, and have mercy upon all our people, is the constant prayer of your affectionate husband, R. E. Lee.

On April 30th:

On going to my room last night I found my trunk and sword there, and opening them this morning discovered the package of letters and was very glad to learn you were all well and as yet peaceful. I fear the latter state will not continue long.... I think therefore you had better prepare all things for removal, that is, the plate, pictures, etc., and be prepared at any moment. Where to go is the difficulty. When the war commences no place will be exempt, in my opinion, and indeed all the avenues into the State will be the scenes of military operations.

There is no prospect or intention of the Government to propose a truce. Do not be deceived by it.... May God preserve you all and bring peace to our distracted country.

Again to my mother at Arlington:

Richmond, May 2, 1861.

My dear Mary: I received last night your letter of the 1st, with contents. It gave me great pleasure to learn that you are all well and in peace. You know how pleased I should be to have you and my dear daughters with me. That I fear can not be. There is no place that I can expect to be but in the field, and there is no rest for me to look to. but I want you to be in a place of safety.... We have only to be resigned to God's will and pleasure, and do all we can for our protection.... I have just received Custis's letter of the 30th, inclosing the acceptance of my resignation. It is stated that it will take effect April 25th. I resigned on the 20th, and wished it to take effect that day. I cannot consent to its running on further, and he must receive no pay, if they tender it, beyond that day, but return the whole, if need be....

From another letter to my mother, dated May 8th:

...I grieve at the necessity that drives you from your home. I can appreciate your feelings on the occasion, and pray that you may receive comfort and strength in the difficulties that surround you. When I reflect upon the calamity impending over the country, my own sorrows sink into insignificance.... Be content and resigned to God's will. I shall be able to write seldom. Write to me, as you letters will be my greatest comfort. I send a check for $500; it is all I have in bank. Pay the children's school expenses....

To my mother, still at Arlington:

Richmond, May 11, 1861.

I have received your letter of the 9th from Arlington. I had supposed you were at Ravensworth.... I am glad to hear that you are at peace, and enjoying the sweet weather and beautiful flowers. You had better complete your arrangements and retire further from the scene of war. It may burst upon you at any time. It is sad to think of the devastation, if not ruin, it may bring upon a spot so endeared to us. But God's will be done. We must be resigned. May He guard and keep you all, is my constant prayer.

All this time my father was very hard at work organising and equipping the volunteers who were pouring into Richmond from the Southern States, but he was in constant correspondence with my mother, helping her all he could in her arrangements for leaving her home. His letters show that he thought of everything, even the least, and he gave the most particular directions about his family, their effects, the servants, the horses, the farm, pictures, plate, and furniture. Being called to Norfolk suddenly, before going he wrote to my mother:

Richmond, May 16, 1861.

My Dear Mary: I am called down to Norfolk and leave this afternoon. I expect to return Friday, but may be delayed. I write to advise you of my absence, in case you should not receive answers to any letters that may arrive. I have not heard from you since I last wrote; nor have I anything to relate. I heard from my dear little Rob, who had an attack of chills and fever. He hoped to escape the next paroxysm.... I witnessed the opening of the convention [The Episcopal Convention of the Diocese of Virginia] yesterday, and heard the good Bishop's [Bishop Meade, of Virginia] sermon, being the 50th anniversary of his ministry. It was a most impressive scene, and more than once I felt the tears coming down my cheek. It was from the text, 'and Pharoh said unto Jacob, how old art thou?' It was full of humility and self-reproach. I saw Mr. Walker, Bishop Johns, Bishop Atkinson, etc. I have not been able to attend any other services, and presume the session will not be prolonged. I suppose it may be considered a small attendance. Should Custis arrive during my absence, I will leave word for him to take my room at the Spotswood till my return. Smith [His brother, S. S. Lee, C. S. N.] is well and enjoys a ride in the afternoon with Mrs. Stannard. The charming women, you know, always find him out. Give much love to Cousin Anna, Nannie, and dear daughters. When Rob leaves the University take him with you. Truly and affectionately, R. E. Lee.

By this time my mother and all the family had left Arlington. My brother, Custis, had joined my father in Richmond, the girls had gone to Fauquier county, to visit relatives, and my mother to Ravensworth, about ten miles from Arlington towards Fairfax Court House, where her aunt, Mrs. A. M. Fitzhugh, lived. Always considerate of the happiness and comfort of others, my father feared that his wife's presence at Ravensworth might possibly bring annoyance to "Cousin Anna," as he called our aunt, and he wrote to my mother, urging her not to remain there. He sympathised with her in having to leave her home, which she never saw again.

Richmond, May 25, 1861.

I have been trying, dearest Mary, ever since the receipt of your letter by Custis, to write to you. I sympathise deeply in your feelings at leaving your dear home. I have experienced them myself, and they are constantly revived. I fear we have not been grateful enough for the happiness there within our reach, and our Heavenly Father has found it necessary to deprive us of what He has given us. I acknowledge my ingratitude, my transgressions, and my unworthiness, and submit with resignation to what he thinks proper to inflict upon me. We must trust all then to him, and I do not think it prudent or right for you to return there, while the United States troops occupy that country. I have gone over all this ground before, and have just written Cousin Anna on the subject.

While writing, I received a telegram from Cousin John Goldsborough [a cousin of Mrs. Fitzhugh], urging your departure 'South.' I suppose he is impressed with the risk of your present position, and in addition to the possibility, or probability, of personal annoyance to yourself, I fear your presence may provoke annoyance in Cousin Anna. But unless Cousin Anna goes with you, I shall be distressed about her being there alone. If the girls went to 'Kinloch' or 'Eastern View,' you and Cousin Anna might take care of yourselves, because you could get in the carriage and go off in an emergency. But I really am afraid that you may prove more harm than comfort to her. Mr. Wm. C. Rives has just been in to say that if you and Cousin Anna will go to his house, he will be very glad for you to stay as long as you please. That his son has a commodious house just opposite his, unoccupied, partially furnished; that you could, if you prefer, take that, bring up servants and what you desire, and remain there as independent as at home.... I must now leave the matter to you, and pray that God may guard you. I have no time for more. I know and feel the discomfort of your position, but it cannot be helped, and we must bear our trials like Christians.... If you and Cousin Anna choose to come here, you know how happy we shall be to see you. I shall take the field as soon now as I can....Ever yours truly and devotedly, R. E. Lee

Three days later he was at Manassas, only a short distance from Ravensworth, and he sent her this short note:

Manassas, May 28, 1861.

I reached here, dearest Mary, this afternoon. I am very much occupied in examining matters, and have to go out to look over the ground. Cousin John tempts me strongly to go down, but I never visit for many reasons. If for no other, to prevent compromising the house, for my visit would certainly be known.

I have written to you fully and to Cousin Anna. I am decidedly of the opinion that it would be better for you to leave, on your account and Cousin Anna's. My only objection is the leaving of Cousin Anna alone, if she will not go with you. If you prefer Richmond, go with Nannie. Otherwise, go to the upper country, as John indicates. I fear I cannot be with you anywhere. I do not think Richmond will be permanent. Truly, R.

I may as well say here, that "Cousin Anna" never did leave "Ravensworth" during the war. She remained there, with only a few faithful servants, and managed to escape any serious molestation. "Nannie" was Mrs. S. S. Lee, who shortly after this time went to Richmond.

On May 25th, my father was transferred, with all the Virginia troops, to the Confederate States Army. He ceased to be a Major-General, and became a Brigadier. No higher rank having been created as yet in the Confederate service. Later, when the rank was created, he was made a full general.

By the end of May, to quote from General Long,

"Lee had organised, equipped, and sent to the field more than thirty thousand men, and various regiments were in a forward state of preparation."

When the Confederate government moved from Montgomery to Richmond, and President Davis took charge of all military movements, my father was kept near him as his constant and trusted adviser. His experience as an engineer was of great service to the young Confederacy, and he was called upon often for advice for the location of batteries and troops on our different defensive lines. In a letter to my mother he speaks of one of these trips to the waters east of Richmond.

Richmond, June 9, 1861.

...I have just returned from a visit to the batteries and troops on James and York rivers, etc., where I was some days. I called a few hours at the White House. Saw Charlotte and Annie. Fitzhugh was away, but got out of the cars as I got in. Our little boy looked very sweet and seemed glad to kiss me good-bye. Charlotte said she was going to prepare to leave for the summer, but had not determined where to go. I could only see some of the servants about the house and the stables. They were all well.... You may be aware that the Confederate Government is established here. Yesterday I turned over to it the command of the military and naval forces of the State, in accordance with the proclamation of the Government and the agreement between the State and the Confederate States. I do not know what my position will be. I should like to retire to private life, if I could be with you and the children, but if I can be of any service to the State or her cause I must continue. Mr. Davis and all his Cabinet are here.... Good-bye. Give much love to kind friends. May God guard and bless you, them, and our suffering country, and enable me to perform my duty. I think of you constantly. Write me what you will do. Direct here.

Always yours, R. E. Lee.

To my mother, who was now in Fauquier County, staying at "Kinloch," Mr. Edward Turner's home, he writes on June 24th, from Richmond:

...Your future arrangements are the source of much anxiety to me. No one can say what is in the future, nor is it wise to anticipate evil. But it is well to prepare for what may reasonably happen and be provided for the worst. There is no saying when you can return to your home or what may be its condition when you do return. What, then, can you do in the meantime? To remain with friends may be incumbent, and where can you go?... My movements are very uncertain, and I wish to take the field as soon as certain arrangements can be made. I may go at any moment, and to any point where it may be necessary.... Many of our old friends are dropping in. E. P. Alexander is here, Jimmy Hill, Alston, Jenifer, etc., and I hear that my old colonel, A. S. Johnston, is crossing the plains from California....As ever, R. E. Lee.

I again quote from a letter to my mother, dated Richmond, July 12, 1861:

...I am very anxious to get into the field, but am detained by matters beyond my control. I have never heard of the appointment, to which you allude, of Commander-in-Chief of the Confederate States Army, nor have I any expectation or wish for it. President Davis holds that position. Since the transfer of the military operations in Virginia to the authorities of the Confederate States, I have only occupied the position of a general in that service, with the duties devolved on me by the President. I have been labouring to prepare and get into the field the Virginia troops, and to strengthen, by those from the other States, the threatened commands of Johnston, Beauregard, Huger, Garnett, etc. Where I shall go I do not know, as that will depend upon President Davis. As usual in getting through with a thing, I have broken down a little and had to take my bed last evening, but am at my office this morning and hope will soon be right again.... My young friend Mr. Vest has just returned from a search in the city for 'Dixie,' and says he has visited every place in Richmond without finding it. I suppose it is exhausted. Always yours, R. E. Lee.

The booksellers say 'Dixie' is not to be had in Virginia. R. E. L.

On July 21st occurred the battle of Manassas. In a letter to my mother written on the 27th, my father says:

...That indeed was a glorious victory and has lightened the pressure upon our front amazingly. Do not grieve for the brave dead. Sorrow for those they left behind--friends, relatives, and families. The former are at rest. The latter must suffer. The battle will be repeated there in greater force. I hope God will again smile on us and strengthen our hearts and arms. I wished to partake in the former struggle, and am mortified at my absence, but the President thought it more important I should be here. I could not have done as well as has been done, but I could have helped, and taken part in the struggle for my home and neighbourhood. So the work is done I care not by whom it is done. I leave to-morrow for the Northwest Army. I wished to go before, as I wrote you, and was all prepared, but the indications were so evident of the coming battle, and in the uncertainty of the result, the President forbade my departure. Now it is necessary and he consents. I cannot say for how long, but will write you.... I inclose you a letter from Markie [Miss Martha Custis Williams--second cousin of my mother, afterward Mrs. Admiral Carter, U.S.N.]. Write to her if you can and thank her for her letter to me. I have not time. My whole time is occupied, and all my thoughts and strength are given to the cause to which my life, be it long or short, will be devoted. Tell her not to mind the reports she sees in the papers. They are made to injure and occasion distrust. Those that know me will not believe them. Those that do not will not care for them. I laugh at them. Give love to all, and for yourself accept the constant prayers and love of truly yours, R. E. Lee.

It was thought best at this time to send General Lee to take command of military operations in West Virginia. The ordinary difficulties of a campaign in this country of mountains and bad roads were greatly increased by incessant rains, sickness of all kinds amongst the new troops, and the hostility of many of the inhabitants of the Southern cause. My father's letters, which I will give here, tell of his trials and troubles, and describe at the same time the beauty of the scenery and some of the military movements.

About August 1st he started for his new command, and he writes to my mother on his arrival at Huntersville, Pocahontas County, now West Virginia:

Huntersville, August 4, 1861.

I reached here yesterday, dearest Mary, to visit this portion of the army. The day after my arrival at Staunton, I set off for Monterey, where the army of General Garnett's command is stationed. Two regiments and a field-battery occupy the Alleghany Mountains in advance, about thirty miles, and this division guards the road to Staunton. The division here guards the road leading to the Warm Springs to Milboro and Covington. Two regiments are advanced about twenty-eight miles to Middle Mountain. Fitzhugh [Major W. H. F. Lee--General Lee's second son] with his squadron is between that point and this. I have not seen him. I understand he is well. South of here again is another column of our enemies, making their way up the Kanawha Valley, and, from General Wise's report, are not far from Lewisburgh. Their object seems to be to get possession of the Virginia Central Railroad and the Virginia and Tennessee Railroad. By the first they can approach

Richmond; by the last interrupt our reinforcements from the South. The points from which we can be attacked are numerous, and their means are unlimited. So we must always be on the alert. My uneasiness on these points brought me out here. It is so difficult to get our people, unaccustomed to the necessities of war, to comprehend and promptly execute the measures required for the occasion. General Jackson of Georgia commands on the Monterey line, General Loring on this line, and General Wise, supported by General Floyd, on the Kanawha line. The soldiers everywhere are sick. The measles are prevalent throughout the whole army, and you know that disease leaves unpleasant results, attacks on the lungs, typhoid, etc., especially in camp, where accommodations for the sick are poor. I travelled from Staunton on horseback. A part of the road, as far as Buffalo Gap, I passed over in the summer of 1840, on my return to St. Louis, after bringing you home. If any one had then told me that the next time I travelled that road would have been on my present errand, I should have supposed him insane. I enjoyed the mountains, as I rode along. The views are magnificent--the valleys so beautiful, the scenery so peaceful. What a glorious world Almighty God has given us. How thankless and ungrateful we are, and how we labour to mar his gifts. I hope you received my letters from Richmond. Give love to daughter and Mildred. I did not see Rob as I passed through Charlottesville. He was at the University and I could not stop."

A few days later there is another letter:

Camp at Valley Mountain, August 9, 1861.

I have been here, dear Mary, three days, coming from Monterey to Huntersville and thence here. We are on the dividing ridge looking north down the Tygart's river valley, whose waters flow into the Monongahela and South towards the Elk River and Greenbriar, flowing into the Kanawha. In the valley north of us lie Huttonsville and Beverly, occupied by our invaders, and the Rich Mountains west, the scene of our former disaster, and the Cheat Mountains east, their present stronghold, are in full view.

The mountains are beautiful, fertile to the tops, covered with the richest sward of bluegrass and white clover, the inclosed fields waving with the natural growth of timothy. The inhabitants are few and population sparse. This is a magnificent grazing country, and all it needs is labour to clear the mountain-sides of its great growth of timber. There surely is no lack of moisture at this time. It has rained, I believe, some portion of every day since I left Staunton. Now it is pouring, and the wind, having veered around to every point of the compass, has settled down to the northeast. What that portends in these regions I do not know. Colonel Washington [John Augustin Washington, great-nephew of General Washington, and Mt. Vernon's last owner bearing that name], Captain Taylor, and myself are in one tent, which as yet protects us. I have enjoyed the company of Fitzhugh since I have been here. He is very well and very active, and as yet the war has not reduced him much. He dined with me yesterday and preserves his fine appetite. To-day he is out reconnoitering and has the full benefit of this rain. I fear he is without his overcoat, as I do not recollect seeing it on his saddle. I told you he had been promoted to a major in cavalry, and is the commanding cavalry officer on this line at present. He is as sanguine, cheerful, and hearty as ever. I sent him some corn-meal this morning and he sent me some butter--a mutual interchange of good things. There are but few of your acquaintances in this army. I find here in the ranks of one company Henry Tiffany. The company is composed principally of Baltimoreans-- George Lemmon and Douglas Mercer are in it. It is a very find company, well drilled and well instructed. I find that our friend, J. J. Reynolds, of West Point memory, is in command of the troops immediately in front of us. He is a brigadier-general. You may recollect him as the Assistant Professor of Philosophy, and lived in the cottage beyond the west gate, with his little, pale-faced wife, a great friend of Lawrence and Markie. He resigned on being relieved from West Point, and was made professor of some college in the West. Fitzhugh was the bearer of a flag the other day, and he recognised him. He was very polite and made inquiries of us all. I am told they feel very safe and are very confident of success. Their numbers are said to be large, ranging from 12,000 to 30,000, but it is impossible for me to get correct information either as to their strength or position. Our citizens beyond this are all on their side. Our movements seem to be rapidly communicated to them, while theirs come to us slowly and indistinctly. I have two regiments here, with others coming up. I think we shall shut up this road to the Central Railroad which they strongly threaten. Our supplies come up slowly. We have plenty of beef and can get some bread. I hope you are well and are content. I have heard nothing of you or the children since I left Richmond. You must write there.... The men are suffering from the measles, etc., as elsewhere, but are cheerful and light-hearted. The atmosphere, when it is not raining, is delightful. You must give much love to daughter and 'Life' [Pet names for his two daughters, Mary and Mildred]. I want to see you all very much, but I know not when that can be. May God guard and protect you all. In Him alone is our hope. Remember me to Ned [M. Edward Carter Turner, of Kinloch, my father's cousin] and all at 'Kinloch' and Avenel [The house of the Berbeleys, in Fauquier County]. Send word to Miss Lou Washington [Eldest daughter of John Augustin Washington] that her father is sitting on his blanket sewing the strap on his haversack. I think she out to be here to do it. Always yours, R. E. Lee.

In a letter to his two daughters who were in Richmond, he writes:

Valley Mountain, August 29, 1861.

My Precious Daughters: I have just received your letters of the 24th and am rejoiced to hear that you are well and enjoying the company of your friends.... It rains here all the time, literally. There has not been sunshine enough since my arrival to dry my clothes. Perry [his servant--had been in the dining-room at Arlington] is my washerman, and socks and towels suffer. But the worst of the rain is that the ground has become so saturated with water that the constant travel on the roads has made them almost impassable, so that I cannot get up sufficient supplies for the troops to move. It is raining now. Has been all day, last night, day before, and day before that, etc., etc. But we must be patient. It is quite cool, too. I have on all my winter clothes and am writing in my overcoat. All the clouds seem to concentrate over this ridge of mountains, and by whatever wind they are driven, give us rain. The mountains are magnificent. The sugar- maples are beginning to turn already, and the grass is luxuriant.

'Richmond' [His horse] has not been accustomed to such fare or such treatment. But he gets along tolerably, complains some, and has not much superfluous flesh. There has been much sickness among the men-- measles, etc.--and the weather has been unfavourable. I hope their attacks are nearly over, and that they will come out with the sun. Our party has kept well.... Although we may be too weak to break through the lines, I feel well satisfied that the enemy cannot at present reach Richmond by either of these routes, leading to Staunton, Milborough or Covington. He must find some other way.... God Bless you, my children, and preserve you from all harm is the constant prayer of Your devoted father, R. E. Lee.

On account of rheumatism, my mother was anxious to go to the Hot Springs in Bath County. She was now staying at "Audley," Clarke County, Virginia, with Mrs. Lorenzo Lewis, who had just sent her six sons into the army. Bath County was not very far from the seat of war in western Virginia, and my father was asked as to the safety of the Hot Springs from occupation by the enemy. He writes as follows to my mother:

Valley Mountain, September 1, 1861.

I have received, dearest Mary, your letter of August 18th from Audley, and am very glad to get news of your whereabouts.... I am very glad you are enabled to see so many of your friends. I hope you have found all well in your tour, and am very glad that our cousin Esther bears the separation from all her sons so bravely. I have no doubt they will do good service in our Southern cause, and wish they could be placed according to their fancies.... I fear you have postponed your visit to the Hot too late. It must be quite cold there now, judging from the temperature here, and it has been raining in these mountains since July 24th.... I see Fitzhugh quite often, though he is encamped four miles from me. He is very well and not at all harmed by the campaign.

We have a great deal of sickness among the soldiers, and now those on the sick-list would form an army. The measles is still among them, though I hope it is dying out. But it is a disease which though light in childhood is severe in manhood, and prepares the system for other attacks. The constant cold rains, with no shelter but tents, have aggravated it. All these drawbacks, with impassable roads, have paralysed our efforts. Still I think you will be safe at the Hot, for the present. We are right up to the enemy on three lines, and in the Kanawha he has been pushed beyond the Gauley.... My poor little Rob I never hear from scarcely. He is busy, I suppose, and knows not where to direct.... With much affection, R. E. Lee.

From the same camp, to my mother, on September 9th:

...I hope from the tone of your letter that you feel better, and wish I could see you and be with you. I trust we may meet this fall somewhere, if only for a little time. I have written to Robert telling him if, after considering what I have previously said to him on the subject of his joining the company he desires under Major Ross, he still thinks it best for him to do so, I will not withhold my consent. It seems he will be eighteen; I thought seventeen. I am unable to judge for him and he must decide for himself. In reply to a recent letter from him to me on the same subject, I said to him all I could. I pray God to bring him to the right conclusion.... For military news, I must refer you to the papers. You will see there more than ever occurs, and what does occur the relation must be taken with some allowance. Do not believe anything you see about me. There has been no battle, only skirmishing with the outposts, and nothing done of any moment. The weather is still unfavourable to us. The roads, or rather tracks of mud, are almost impassable and the number of sick large....Truly and devotedly yours, R. E. Lee.

My mother was at the Hot Springs--I had taken her there and was with her. I don't now remember why, but it was decided that I should return to the University of Virginia, which opened October 1st, and continue my course there. While at the Springs my mother received this letter from my father:

Valley Mount, September 17, 1861.

I received, dear Mary, your letter of the 5th by Beverly Turner [A son of Mr. Edward Turner, of 'Kinloch'], who is a nice young soldier. I am pained to see find young men like him, of education and standing, from all the old and respectable families in the State, serving in the ranks. I hope in time they will receive their reward. I met him as I was returning from an expedition to the enemy's works, which I had hoped to have surprised on the morning of the 12th, both at Cheat Mountain and on Valley River. All the attacking parties with great labour had reached their destination, over mountains considered impassable to bodies of troops, notwithstanding a heavy storm that set in the day before and raged all night, in which they had to stand up till daylight. Their arms were then unserviceable, and they in poor condition for a fierce assault against artillery and superior numbers. After waiting till 10 o'clock for the assault on Cheat Mountain, which did not take place, and which was to have been the signal for the rest, they were withdrawn, and, after waiting three days in front of the enemy, hoping he would come out of his trenches, we returned to our position at this place. I can not tell you my regret and mortification at the untoward events that caused the failure of the plan. I had taken every precaution to ensure success and counted on it. but the Ruler of the Universe willed otherwise and sent a storm to disconcert a well-laid plan, and to destroy my hopes. We are no worse off now than before, except the disclosure of our plan, against which they will guard. We met with one heavy loss which grieves me deeply: Colonel Washington accompanied Fitzhugh on a reconnoitering expedition, and I fear they were carried away by their zeal and approached the enemy's pickets. The first they knew was a volley from a concealed party within a few yards of them. Their balls passed through the Colonel's body, then struck Fitzhugh's horse, and the horse of one of the men was killed. Fitzhugh mounted the Colonel's horse and brought him off. I am much grieved. He was always anxious to go on these expeditions. This was the first day I assented. Since I had been thrown into such intimate relations with him, I had learned to appreciate him very highly. Morning and evening have I seen him on his knees praying to his Maker.

'The righteous perisheth and no man layeth it to heart, and merciful men are taken away, none considering that the righteous is taken away from the evil to come.' May God have mercy on us all! I suppose you are at the Hot Springs and will direct to you there. Our poor sick, I know, suffer much. They bring it on themselves by not doing what they are told. They are worse than children, for the latter can be forced....Truly yours, R. E. Lee.

On the same day he wrote the Governor of Virginia:

Valley Mountain, September 17, 1861.

My Dear Governor: I received your very kind note of the 5th instant, just as I was about to accompany General Loring's command on an expedition to the enemy's works in front, or I would have before thanked you for the interest you take in my welfare, and your too flattering expressions of my ability. Indeed, you overrate me much, and I feel humbled when I weigh myself by your standard. I am, however, very grateful for your confidence, and I can answer for my sincerity in the earnest endeavour I make to advance the cause I have so much at heart, though conscious of the slow progress I make. I was very sanguine of taking the enemy's works on last Thursday morning. I had considered the subject well. With great effort the troops intended for the surprise had reached their destination, having traversed twenty miles of steep, rugged mountain paths; and the last day through a terrible storm, which lasted all night, and in which they had to stand drenched to the skin in cold rain. Still, their spirits were good. When morning broke, I could see the enemy's tents on Valley River, at the point on the Huttonsville road just below me. It was a tempting sight. We waited for the attack on Cheat Mountain, which was to be the signal. Till 10 A. M. the men were cleaning their unserviceable arms. But the signal did not come. All chance for a surprise was gone. The provisions of the men had been destroyed the preceding day by the storm. They had nothing to eat that morning, could not hold out another day, and were obliged to be withdrawn. The party sent to Cheat Mountain to take that in rear had also to be withdrawn. The attack to come off the east side failed from the difficulties in the way; the opportunity was lost, and our plan discovered. It is a grievous disappointment to me, I assure you. but for the rain-storm, I have no doubt it would have succeeded. This, Governor, is for your own eye. Please do not speak of it; we must try again. Our greatest loss is the death of my dear friend, Colonel Washington. He and my son were reconnoitering the front of the enemy. They came unawares upon a concealed party, who fired upon them within twenty yards, and the Colonel fell pierced by three balls. My son's horse received three shots, but he escaped on the Colonel's horse. His zeal for the cause to which he had devoted himself carried him, I fear, too far. We took some seventy prisoners, and killed some twenty-five or thirty of the enemy. Our loss was small besides what I have mentioned. Our greatest difficulty is the roads. It has been raining in these mountains about six weeks. It is impossible to get along. It is that which has paralysed all our efforts. With sincere thanks for your good wishes, I am very truly yours, R. E. Lee.

G.W.C. Lee, Robert E. Lee, Walter Taylor

Chapter III

Letters to Wife and Daughters

The season being too far advanced to attempt any further movements away from our base of supplies, and the same reasons preventing any advance of the Federal forces, the campaign in this part of Virginia ended for the winter. In the Kanawha Valley, however, the enemy had been and were quite active. Large reinforcements under General Rosecrans were sent there to assist General Cox, the officer in command at that point. General Loring, leaving a sufficient force to watch the enemy at Cheat Mountain, moved the rest of his army to join the commands of Generals Floyd and Wise, who were opposing the advance of Cox. General Lee, about September 20th, reached General Floyd's camp, and immediately proceeded to arrange the lines of defense. Shortly after his arrival there he wrote to my mother at the Hot Springs:

Camp on Sewell's Mountain,

September 26, 1881.

I have just received, dear Mary, your letter of the 17th and 19th instants, with one from Robert. I have but little time for writing to-night, and will, therefore, write to you.... Having now disposed of business matters, I will say how glad I am to hear from you, and to learn that you have reached the Hot in safety, with daughter and Rob. I pray that its healing waters may benefit you all. I am glad to hear of Charlotte and the girls, and hope all will go well with them. I infer you received my letter before leaving Valley Mountain, though you did not direct your letter 'via Lewisburg, Greenbrier County,' and hence its delay. I told you of the death of Colonel Washington. I grieve for his loss, though trust him to the mercy of our Heavenly Father. May He have mercy on us all.

It is raining heavily. The men are all exposed on the mountain, with the enemy opposite to us. We are without tents, and for two nights I have lain buttoned up in my overcoat. To-day my tent came up and I am in it. Yet I fear I shall not sleep for thinking of the poor men. I wrote about socks for myself. I have no doubt the yarn ones you mention will be very acceptable to the men here or elsewhere. If you can send them here, I will distribute them to the most needy. Tell Rob I could not write to him for want of time. My heart is always with you and my children. May God guard and bless you all is the constant prayer of Your devoted husband, R. E. Lee.

To my mother, still at the Hot Springs:

Sewell's Mountain, October 7, 1861.

I received, dear Mary, your letter by Doctor Quintard, with the cotton socks. Both were very acceptable, though the latter I have not yet tried. At the time of their reception the enemy was threatening an attack, which was continued till Saturday night, when under cover of darkness we suddenly withdrew. Your letter of the 2d, with the yarn socks, four pairs, was handed to me when I was preparing to follow, and I could not at the time attend to either. But I have since, and as I found Perry in desperate need, I bestowed a couple of pairs on him, as a present from you. the others I have put in my trunk and suppose they will fall to the lot of Meredith [His cook--a servant from the White House], into the state of whose hose I have not yet inquired. Should any sick man require them first, he shall have them, but Meredith will have no one near to supply him but me, and will naturally expect that attention. I hope, dear Mary, you and daughter, as well as poor little Rob, have derived some benefit from the sanitary baths of the Hot. What does daughter intend to do during the winter? And, indeed, what do you? It is time you were determining. There is no prospect of your returning to Arlington. I think you had better select some comfortable place in the Carolinas or Georgia, and all board together. If Mildred goes to school at Raleigh, why not go there? It is a good opportunity to try a warmer climate for your rheumatism. If I thought our enemies would not make a vigorous move against Richmond, I would recommend to rent a house there. But under these circumstances I would not feel as if you were permanently located if there. I am ignorant where I shall be. In the field somewhere, I suspect, so I have little hope of being with you, though I hope to be able to see you.... I heard from Fitzhugh the other day. He is well, though his command is greatly reduced by sickness. I wished much to bring him with me; but there is too much cavalry on this line now, and I am dismounting them. I could not, therefore, order more. The weather is almost as bas here as in the mountains I left. There was a drenching rain yesterday, and as I had left my overcoat in camp I was thoroughly wet from head to foot. It has been raining ever since and is now coming down with a will. But I have my clothes out on the bushes and they will be well washed.

The force of the enemy, by a few prisoners captured yesterday and civilians on the road, is put down from 17,000 to 20,000. Some went as high as 22,000. General Floyd thinks 18,000. I do not think it exceeds 9,000 or 10,000, though it exceeds ours. I wish he had attacked us, as I believe he would have been repulsed with great loss. His plan was to attack us at all points at the same time. The rumbling of his wheels, etc., was heard by our pickets, but as that was customary at night in the moving and placing of his cannon, the officer of the day to whom it was reported paid no particular attention to it, supposing it to be a preparation for attack in the morning. When day appeared, the bird had flown, and the misfortune was that the reduced condition of our horses for want of provender, exposure to cold rains in these mountains, and want of provisions for the men prevented the vigorous pursuit and following up that was proper. We can only get up provisions from day to day--which paralyses our operations.

I am sorry, as you say, that the movements of the armies cannot keep pace with the expectations of the editors of papers. I know they can regulate matters satisfactorily to themselves on paper. I wish they could do so in the field. No one wishes them more success than I do and would be happy to see them have full swing. I hope something will be done to please them. Give much love to the children and everybody, and believe me.

Always yours, R. E. Lee.

Colonel Taylor, in his "Four Years with General Lee," says:

We had now reached the latter days of October. The lateness of the season and the condition of the roads precluded the idea of earnest, aggressive operations, and the campaign in western Virginia was virtually concluded.

Judged from its results, it must be confessed that this series of operations was a failure. At its conclusion, a large portion of the State was in possession of the Federals, including the rich valleys of the Ohio and Kanawha rivers, and so remained until the close of the war. For this, however, General Lee cannot reasonably be held accountable. Disaster had befallen the Confederate arms, and the worst had been accomplished before he had reached the theatre of operations; the Alleghanies there constituted the dividing line between the hostile forces, and in this network of mountains, sterile and rendered absolutely impracticable by a prolonged season of rain, Nature had provided an insurmountable barrier to operations in this transmontane country.... It was doubtless because of similar embarrassments that the Federal general retired, in the face of inferior numbers, to a point near his base of supplies."

Professor William P. Trent, in his "Robert E. Lee," after describing briefly the movements of the contending armies, writes: "There was, then, nothing to do but to acknowledge the campaign a failure. The Confederate Government withdrew its troops and sent them elsewhere. Lee, whom the press abused and even former friends began to regard as overrated, was assigned to command the Department of South Carolina, Georgia, and Florida; and her western counties were lost to the Old Dominion forever. It must have been a crushing blow to Lee at the time, but he bore it uncomplainingly.... And when all is said, no commander, however great, can succeed against bad roads, bad weather, sickness of troops, lack of judgement and harmony among subordinates, and a strong, alert enemy. Yet this is what Lee was expected to do."

Mr. Davis, in an address before a memorial meeting at Richmond in 1870, speaking of General Lee in this campaign, said:

"He came back, carrying the heavy weight of defeat, and unappreciated by the people whom he served, for they could not know, as I knew, that, if his plans and orders had been carried out, the result would have been victory rather than retreat. You did not know it; for I should not have known it had he not breathed it in my ear only at my earnest request, and begging that nothing be said about it. The clamour which then arose followed him when he went to South Carolina, so that it became necessary on his departure to write a letter to the Governor of that State, telling him what manner of man he was. Yet, through all this, with a magnanimity rarely equalled, he stood in silence, without defending himself or allowing others to defend him, for he was unwilling to offend any one who was wearing a sword and striking blows for the Confederacy."

After returning to Richmond, my father resumed his position as advisor and counsellor to Mr. Davis. From there he writes to my mother, who had left the Hot Springs and gone on to "Shirley," on James River:

Richmond, November 5, 1861.

My Dear Mary: I received last night your letter of the 2d, and would have answered it at once, but was detained with the Secretary till after 11 P. M. I fear now I may miss the mail. Saturday evening I tried to get down to you to spend Sunday, but could find no government boat going down, and the passenger boats all go in the morning. I then went to the stable and got out my horse, but it was near night then and I was ignorant both of the road and distance and I gave it up. I was obliged to be here Monday, and as it would have consumed all Sunday to go and come, I have remained for better times. The President said I could not go to-day, so I must see what can be done to-morrow. I will come, however, wherever you are, either Shirley or the White House, as soon as possible, and if not sooner, Saturday at all events.... I am, as ever, Yours, R. E. Lee.

The day after this letter was written, my father was ordered to South Carolina for the purpose of directing and supervising the construction of a line of defense along the southern coast. I give here several letters to members of his family which tell of his duties and manner of life:

Savannah, November 18, 1861.

My Dear Mary: This is the first moment I have had to write to you, and now am waiting the call to breakfast, on my way to Brunswick, Fernandina, etc. This is my second visit to Savannah. Night before last, I returned to Coosawhatchie, South Carolina, from Charleston, where I have placed my headquarters, and last night came here, arriving after midnight. I received in Charleston your letter from Shirley. It was a grievous disappointment to me not to have seen you, but better times will come, I hope.... You probably have seen the operations of the enemy's fleet. Since their first attack they have been quiescent apparently, confining themselves to Hilton Head, where they are apparently fortifying.

I have no time for more. Love to all.

Yours very affectionately and truly, R. E. Lee.

Charleston, November 15, 1861.

My Precious Daughter: I have received your letter forwarded to Richmond by Mr. Powell, and I also got, while in the West, the letter sent by B. Turner. I can write but seldom, but your letters always give me great pleasure. I am glad you had such a pleasant visit to 'Kinloch.' I have passed a great many pleasant days there myself in my young days. Now you must labour at your books and gain knowledge and wisdom. Do not mind what Rob says. I have a beautiful white beard. It is much admired. At least, much remarked on. You know I have told you not to believe what the young men tell you. I was unable to see your poor mother when in Richmond. Before I could get down I was sent off here. Another forlorn hope expedition. Worse than West Virginia.... I have much to do in this country. I have been to Savannah and have to go again. The enemy is quiet after his conquest of Port Royal Harbor and his whole fleet is lying there. May God guard and protect you, my dear child, prays your Affectionate father, R. E. Lee.

The above letter was written to his youngest daughter Mildred, who was at school in Winchester, Virginia. Two of my sisters were in King George County, Virginia, at "Clydale," the summer home of Dr. Richard Stuart, with whose family we had been a long time intimate. From there they had driven to "Stratford," in Westmoreland County, about thirty miles distant, where my father was born. They had written him of this trip, and this is his reply:

Savannah, November 22, 1861.

My Darling Daughters: I have just received your joint letter of October 24th from 'Clydale.' It was very cheering to me, and the affection and sympathy you expressed were very grateful to my feelings. I wish indeed I could see you, be with you, and never again part from you. God only can give me that happiness. I pray for it night and day. But my prayers I know are not worthy to be heard. I received your former letter in western Virginia, but had no opportunity to reply to it. I enjoyed it, nevertheless. I am glad you do not wait to hear from me, as that would deprive me of the pleasure of hearing from you often. I am so pressed with business. I am much pleased at your description of Stratford and your visit. It is endeared to me by many recollections, and it has been always a great desire of my life to be able to purchase it. Now that we have no other home, and the one we so loved has been foully polluted, the desire is stronger with me than ever. The horse-chestnut you mention in the garden was planted by my mother. I am sorry the vault is so dilapidated. You did not mention the spring, on of the objects of my earliest recollections. I am very glad, my precious Agnes, that you have become so early a riser. It is a good habit, and in these times for mighty works advantage should be taken of every hour. I much regretted being obliged to come from Richmond without seeing your poor mother.... This is my second visit to Savannah. I have been down the coast to Amelia Island to examine the defenses. They are poor indeed, and I have laid off work enough to employ our people a month. I hope our enemy will be polite enough to wait for us. It is difficult to get our people to realise their position.... Good-bye, my dear daughters. Your affectionate father, R. E. Lee.

To his daughter Annie:

Coosawhatchie, South Carolina, December 8, 1861.

My Precious Annie: I have taken the only quiet time I have been able to find on this holy day to thank you for your letter of the 29th ulto. One of the miseries of war is that there is no Sabbath, and the current of work and strife has no cessation. How can we be pardoned for all our offenses! I am glad that you have joined your mamma again and that some of you are together at last. It would be a great happiness to me were you all at some quiet place, remote from the vicissitudes of war, where I could consider you safe. You must have had a pleasant time at 'Clydale.' I hope indeed that 'Cedar Grove' may be saved from the ruin and pillage that other places have received at the hands of our enemies, who are pursuing the same course here as the have practised elsewhere. Unfortunately, too, the numerous deep estuaries, all accessible to their ships, expose the multitude of islands to their predatory excursions, and what they leave is finished by the negroes whose masters have deserted their plantations, subject to visitations of the enemy. I am afraid Cousin Julia [Mrs. Richard Stuart] will not be able to defend her home if attacked by the vandals, for they have little respect for anybody, and if they catch the Doctor [Doctor Richard Stuart] they will certainly send him to Fort Warren or La Fayette. I fear, too, the Yankees will bear off their pretty daughters. I am very glad you visited 'Chatham' [the home of the Fitzhughs, where my grandmother Custis was born]. I was there many years ago, when it was the residence of Judge Coulter, and some of the avenues of poplar, so dear to your grandmama, still existed. I presume they have all gone now. The letter that you and Agnes wrote from 'Clydale' I replied to and sent to that place. You know I never have any news. I am trying to get a force to make headway on our defenses, but it comes in very slow. The people do not seem to realise that there is a war.

It is very warm here, if that is news, and as an evidence I inclose some violets I plucked in the yard of a deserted house I occupy. I wish I could see you and give them in person.... Good-bye, my precious child. Give much love to everybody, and believe me,

Your affectionate father, R. E. Lee.

From the same place, on December 2d, he writes to my mother:

I received last night, dear Mary, your letter of the 12th, and am delighted to learn that you are all well and so many of you are together. I am much pleased that Fitzhugh has an opportunity to be with you all and will not be so far removed from his home in his new field of action. I hope to see him at the head of a find regiment and that he will be able to do good service in the cause of his country. If Mary and Rob get to you Christmas, you will have quite a family party, especially if Fitzhugh is not obliged to leave his home and sweet wife before that time. I shall think of you all on that holy day more intensely than usual, and shall pray to the great God of Heaven to shower His blessings upon you in this world, and to unite you all in His courts in the world to come. With a grateful heart I thank Him for His preservation thus far, and trust to His mercy and kindness for the future. Oh, that I were more worthy, more thankful for all He has done and continues to do for me! Perry and Meredith [his two coloured servants] send their respects to all.... Truly and affectionately, R. E. Lee.

From the same place, on Christmas Day, he writes to my mother:

I cannot let this day of grateful rejoicing pass, dear Mary, without some communication with you. I am thankful for the many among the past that I have passed with you, and the remembrance of them fills me with pleasure. For those on which we have been separated we must not repine. Now we must be content with the many blessings we receive. If we can only become sensible of our transgressions, so as to be fully penitent and forgiven, that this heavy punishment under which we labour may with justice be removed from us and the whole nation, what a gracious consummation of all that we have endured it will be!

I hope you had a pleasant visit to Richmond.... If you were to see this place, I think you would have it, too. I am here but little myself. The days I am not here I visit some point exposed to the enemy, and after our dinner at early candle-light, am engaged in writing till eleven or twelve o'clock at night.... AS to our old home, if not destroyed, it will be difficult ever to be recognised. Even if the enemy had wished to preserve it, it would almost have been impossible. With the number of troops encamped around it, the change of officers, etc., the want of fuel, shelter, etc., and all the dire necessities of war, it is vain to think of its being in a habitable condition. I fear, too, books, furniture, and the relics of Mount Vernon will be gone. It is better to make up our minds to a general loss. They cannot take away the remembrance of the spot, and the memories of those that to us rendered it sacred. That will remain to us as long as life will last, and that we can preserve. In the absence of a home, I wish I could purchase 'Stratford.' That is the only other place that I could go to, now accessible to us, that would inspire me with feelings of pleasure and local love. You and the girls could remain there in quiet. It is a poor place, but we could make enough cornbread and bacon for our support, and the girls could weave us clothes. I wonder if it is for sale and at how much. Ask Fitzhugh to try to find out, when he gets to Fredericksburg. You must not build your hopes on peace on account of the

United States going into a war with England [on account of the Trent affair]. She will be very loath to do that, notwithstanding the bluster of the Northern papers. Her rulers are not entirely mad, and if they find England is in earnest, and that war or a restitution of their captives must be the consequence, they will adopt the latter. We must make up our minds to fight our battles and win our independence alone. No one will help us. We require no extraneous aid, if true to ourselves. But we must be patient. It is not a light achievement and cannot be accomplished at once.... I wrote a few days since, giving you all the news, and have now therefore nothing to relate. The enemy is still quiet and increasing in strength. We grow in size slowly but are working hard. I have had a day of labour instead of rest, and have written intervals to some of the children. I hope they are with you, and inclose my letters....Affectionately and truly, R. E. Lee.

In the next letter to my mother he describes a visit to the grave of his father at Dungeness, on Cumberland Island, Georgia. Dungeness was presented to General Nathaniel Green by the State of Georgia for services rendered her in the Revolution. General Henry Lee, returning from the West Indies, where he had been for some months on account of his health, landed there, and in a few days died, March 15, 1818. He was most kindly cared for by the daughter of his old commander, and was buried there in the garden of Dungeness. At the time of my father's visit the place belonged to a great-nephew of General Green, Mr. Nightingale.

Coosawhatchie, South Carolina, January 18, 1862.

On my return, day before yesterday, from Florida, dear Mary, I received your letter of the 1st inst. I am very glad to find that you had a pleasant family meeting Christmas, and that it was so large. I am truly grateful for all the mercies we enjoy, notwithstanding the miseries of war, and join heartily in the wish that the next year may find us at peace with all the world. I am delighted to hear that our little grandson [his first grandchild--son of my brother Fitzhugh. He died in 1863] is improving so fast and is becoming such a perfect gentleman. May his path be strewn with flowers and his life with happiness. I am very glad to hear also that his dear papa is promoted. It will be gratifying to him and increase, I hope, his means of usefulness. Robert wrote me he saw him on his way through Charlottesville with his squadron, and that he was well. While at Fernandina I went over to Cumberland Island and walked up to 'Dungeness,' the former residence of General Green. It was my first visit to the house, and I had the gratification at length of visiting my father's grave. He died there, you may recollect, on his way from the West Indies, and was interred in one corner of the family cemetery. The spot is marked by a plain marble slab, with his name, age, and her daughter, Mrs. Shaw, and her husband. The place is at present owned by Mr. Nightingale, nephew of Mrs. Shaw, who married a daughter of Mr. James King. The family have moved into the interior of Georgia, leaving only a few servants and a white gardener on the place. The garden was beautiful, inclosed by the finest hedge I have ever seen. It was of the wild olive, which, in Mrs. Shaw's lifetime, during my tour of duty in Savannah in early life, was so productive, had been destroyed by an insect that has proved fatal to the orange on the coast of Georgia and Florida. There was a fine grove of olives, from which, I learn, Mr. Nightingale procures oil. The garden was filled with roses and beautiful vines, the names of which I do not know. Among them was the tomato-vine in full bearing, with the ripe fruit on it. There has yet been no frost in that region of country this winter. I went in the dining-room and parlour, in which the furniture still remained.... The house has never been finished, but is a fine, large one and beautifully located. A magnificent grove of live-oaks envelops the road from the landing to the house.... Love to everybody and God bless you all. Truly and faithfully yours, R. E. Lee.

From the same place there is another letter to my mother:

Coosawhatchie, South Carolina, January 28, 1862.

I have just returned from Charleston, and received your letter of the 14th, dear Mary.... I was called to Charleston by the appearance off the bar of a fleet of vessels the true character and intent of which could not be discerned during the continuance of the storm which obscured the view. Saturday, however, all doubt was dispelled, and from the beach on Sullivan's Island the preparations for sinking them were plainly seen. Twenty-one were visible the first day of my arrival, but at the end of the storm, Saturday, only seventeen were seen. Five of these were vessels of war: what became of the other four is not known. The twelve old merchantmen were being stripped of their spars, masts, etc., and by sunset seven were prepared apparently for sinking across the mouth of the Maffitt Channel. they were placed in a line about two hundred yards apart, about four miles from Fort Moultrie. They will do but little harm to the channel, I think, but may deter vessels from running out at night for fear of getting on them. There now seem to be indications of a movement against Savannah. The enemy's gunboats are pushing up the creek to cut off communication between the city and Fort Pulaski on Cockspur Island. Unless I have better news, I must go there to-day. There are so many points of attack, and so little means to meet them on the water, that there is but little rest.... Perry and Meredith are well and send regards to everybody....Very truly and sincerely yours, R. E. Lee.

It was most important that the defenses of Charleston and Savannah should be made as strong as possible. The difficulties in the way were many and great, but General Lee's perseverance overcame most of them. The result was that neither of those cities fell till the close of the war, and a region of country was preserved to the Confederacy necessary for the feeding of its armies. Of course all of this was not accomplished by my father alone in the four months he was there; but the plans of defense he laid down were successfully followed.

While in Savannah, he writes to my mother:

Savannah, February 8, 1862.

I wrote to you, dear Mary, the day I left Coosawhatchie for this place. I have been here ever since, endeavouring to push forward the work for the defense of the city, which has lagged terribly and which ought to have been finished. But it is difficult to arouse ourselves from ease and comfort to labour and self-denial.

Guns are scarce, as well as ammunition, and I shall have to break up batteries on the coast to provide, I fear, for this city. Our enemies are endeavouring to work their way through the creeks that traverse the impassable marshes stretching along the interior of the coast and communicating with the sounds and sea, through which the Savannah flows, and thus avoid the entrance of the river commanded by Fort Pulaski. Their boats require only seven feet of water to float them, and the tide rises seven feet, so that at high water they can work their way and rest on the mud at low. They are also provided with dredges and appliancances for removing obstructions through the creeks in question, which cannot be guarded by batteries. I hope, however, we shall be able to stop them, and I daily pray to the Giver of all victories to enable us to do so.... I trust you are all well and doing well, and wish I could do anything to promote either. I have more here than I can do, and more, I fear, than I can well accomplish. It is so very hard to get anything done, and while all wish well and mean well, it is so different to get them to act energetically and promptly.... The news from Kentucky and Tennessee is not favourable, but we must make up our minds to meet with reverses and overcome them. I hope God will at last crown our efforts with success. But the contest must be long and severe, and the whole country has to go through much suffering. It is necessary we should be humbled and taught to be less boastful, less selfish, and more devoted to right and justice to all the world.... Always yours, R. E. Lee.

To my mother:

Savannah, February 23, 1862.

I have been wishing, dear Mary, to write to you for more than a week, but every day and every hour seem so taken up that I have found it impossible.... The news from Tennessee and North Carolina is not all cheering, and disasters seem to be thickening around us. It calls for renewed energies and redoubled strength on our part, and, I hope, will produce it. I fear our soldiers have not realised the necessity for the endurance and labour they are called upon to undergo, and that it is better to sacrifice themselves than our cause. God, I hope, will shield us and give us success. Here the enemy is progressing slowly in his designs, and does not seem prepared, or to have determined when or where to make his attack. His gunboats are pushing up all the creeks and marshes of the Savannah, and have attained a position so near the river as to shell the steamers navigating it. None have as yet been struck. I am engaged in constructing a line of defense at Fort Jackson which, if time permits and guns can be obtained, I hope will keep them out. They can bring such overwhelming force in all their movements that it has the effect to demoralise our new troops. The accounts given in the papers of the quantity of cotton shipped to New York are, of course, exaggerated. It is cotton in the seed and dirt, and has to be ginned and cleaned after its arrival. It is said that the negroes are employed in picking and collecting it, and are paid a certain amount. But all these things are gathered from rumour, and can only be believed as they appear probable, which this seems to be....

I went yesterday to church, being the day appointed for fasting and prayer. I wish I could have passed it more devoutly. The bishop (Elliott) gave a most beautiful prayer for the President, which I hope may be heard and answered.... Here the yellow jasmine, red-bud, orange-tree, etc., perfume the whole woods, and the japonicas and azaleas cover the garden. Perry and Meredith are well. May God bless and keep you always is the constant prayer of your husband, R. E. Lee.

To his daughter Annie:

Savannah, March 2, 1862.

My Precious Annie: It has been a long time since I have written to you, but you have been constantly in my thoughts. I think of you all, separately and collectively, in the busy hours of the day and the silent hours of the night, and the recollection of each and every one whiles away the long night, in which my anxious thoughts drive away sleep. But I always feel that you and Agnes at those times are sound asleep, and that is immaterial to either where the blockaders are or what their progress is in the river. I hope you are all well, and as happy as you can be in these perilous times to our country. They look dark at present, and it is plain we have not suffered enough, laboured enough, repented enough, to deserve success. But they will brighten after awhile, and I trust that a merciful God will arouse us to a sense of our danger, bless our honest efforts, and drive back our enemies to their homes. Our people have not been earnest enough, have thought too much of themselves and their ease, and instead of turning out to a man, have been content to nurse themselves and their dimes, and leave the protection of themselves and families to others. To satisfy their consciences, they have been clamorous in criticising what others have done, and endeavoured to prove that they ought to do nothing. This is not the way to accomplish our independence. I have been doing all I can with our small means and slow workmen to defend the cities and coast here. Against ordinary numbers we are pretty strong, but against the hosts our enemies seem able to bring everywhere there is no calculating. But if our men will stand to their work, we shall give them trouble and damage them yet. They have worked their way across the marshes, with their dredges, under cover of their gunboats, to the Savannah River, about Fort Pulaski. I presume they will endeavour to reduce the fort and thus open a way for their vessels up the river. But we have an interior line they must force before reaching the city. It is on this line we are working, slowly to my anxious mind, but as fast as I can drive them.... Good-bye, my dear child. May God bless you and our poor country. Your devoted father, R. E. Lee.

Soon after this letter was written my father was recalled to Richmond, "and was assigned on the 13th of March, under the direction of the President, to the conduct of the military operations of all the armies of the Confederate States" ["Four Years with General Lee"]. My mother was still at the White House, my brother's place on the Pamunkey, and there my father wrote to her:

Richmond, March 14, 1862.

My Dear Mary: I have been trying all the week to write to you, but have not been able. I have been placed on duty here to conduct operations under the direction of the President. It will give me great pleasure to do anything I can to relieve him and serve the country, but I do not see either advantage or pleasure in my duties. But I will not complain, but do my best. I do not see at present either that it will enable me to see much more of you. In the present condition of affairs no one can foresee what may happen, nor in my judgement is it advisable for any one to make arrangements with a view to permanency or pleasure. The presence of some one at the White House is necessary as long as practicable. How long it will be practicable for you an Charlotte to remain there I cannot say. The enemy is pushing us back in all directions, and how far he will be successful depends much upon our efforts and the mercy of Providence. I shall, in all human probability, soon have to take the field, so for the present I think things had better remain as they are. Write me your views. If you think it best for you to come to Richmond I can soon make arrangements for your comfort and shall be very glad of your company and presence. We have experienced a great affliction both in our private and public relations. Our good and noble Bishop Meade died last night. He was very anxious to see you, sent you his love and kindest remembrances, and had I known in time yesterday I should have sent expressly for you to come up. But I did not know of his wish or condition till after the departure of the cars yesterday. Between 6 and 7 P. M. yesterday he sent for me, said he wished to bid me good-bye, and to give me his blessing, which he did in the most affecting manner. Called me Robert and reverted to the time I used to say the catechism to him. He invoked the blessing of God upon me and the country. He spoke with difficulty and pain, but was perfectly calm and clear. His hand was then cold and pulseless, yet he shook mine warmly. 'I ne'er shall look upon his like again.' He died during the night. I presume the papers of to-morrow will tell you all....Very truly and sincerely, R. E. Lee.

The next day he again writes to my mother.

Richmond, March 15, 1861.

My Dear Mary: I wrote you yesterday by mail. On returning to my quarters last night after 11 P. M. Custis informed me Robert had arrived and had made up his mind to go into the army. He stayed at the Spottswood, and this morning I went with him to get his overcoat, blankets, etc. There is great difficulty in procuring what is good. They all have to be made, and he has gone to the office of the adjutant- general of Virginia to engage in the service. God grant it may be for his good as He has permitted it. I must be resigned. I told him of the exemption granted by the Secretary of War to the professors and students of the university, but he expressed no desire to take advantage of it. It would be useless for him to go, if he did not improve himself, nor would I wish him to go merely for exemption. As I have done all in the matter that seems proper and right, I must now leave the rest in the hands of our merciful God. I hope our son will do his duty and make a good soldier.... I had expected yesterday to go to North Carolina this morning, but the President changed his mind. I should like to go to see you to-morrow, but in the present condition of things do not feel that I ought to be absent.... I may have to go to North Carolina or Norfolk yet. New Berne, N. C., has fallen into the hands of the enemy. In Arkansas our troops under Van Dorn have had a hard battle, but nothing decisive gained. Four general skilled-- McIntosh, McCullogh, Herbert, and Slack. General Price wounded. Loss on both sides said to be heavy....Very truly yours, R. E. Lee.

Death of Colonel Ellsworth

Resolved by the Congress of the Confederate States of America,

That the Seal of the Confederate States shall consist of a device representing an equestrian portrait of Washington (after the statue which surmounts his monument in the Capitol Square at Richmond), surrounded with a wreath composed of the principal agricultural products of the Confederacy (cotton, tobacco, sugar-cane, corn, wheat and rice) and having around its margin the words: "The Confederate States of America, Twenty-second February, Eighteen Hundred and Sixty-two," with the following motto: "Deo Vindice."

Designed by the late Thomas J. Semmes, of Louisiana, Engraved by the late Joseph S. Wyon, Chief Engraver of Her Majesty's Seals, London, England.

FRANK LESLIE'S ILLUSTRATED NEWSPAPER

Entered according to the Act of Congress, in the year 1860, by Frank Leslie, in the Clerk's Office of the District Court for the Southern District of New York.

No. 276—Vol. XI.] NEW YORK, MARCH 9, 1861. [Price 6 Cents.

Our Portrait of the President.

On the eve of the Presidential Inauguration we present to our readers the only correct portrait yet given to the public of Abraham Lincoln, President of the United States. Great labor and care have been bestowed upon its preparation, and we feel assured that as a work of art, and as a life-like portraiture of the man who has been chosen to fill the highest office in the gift of the people at a time of great trouble and difficulty, it will be conceded by all to be unequalled in excellence and truthfulness.

The elegant border which forms the framework of the Portrait contains a series of spirited sketches illustrating incidents in the life of President Lincoln and his father.

JEFFERSON DAVIS,

President of the Southern Confederacy.

Jefferson Davis, lately elected President of the new Southern Confederacy, is the son of Samuel Davis, a Revolutionary soldier, and was born in Kentucky in 1806—8. When a boy he went with his father to Mississippi, where he was educated at Transylvania University, whence he passed to West Point, from which he graduated in 1828, passing at once into service under General Taylor. As the captor of the celebrated Black Hawk he attained an eminent place in the history of our Indian wars. After his marriage, in 1835, to a daughter of General (then Colonel) Taylor, he settled down on a plantation, where he devoted some attention to study, and qualified himself for a Southern political life. In 1843 he entered the campaign on the Democratic side, and with such success as to become one of the

JEFFERSON DAVIS, FIRST PRESIDENT OF THE NEW SOUTHERN CONFEDERACY.—PHOTOGRAPHED BY BRADY.

Jefferson Davis, first president of the new Southern Confederacy

Mrs. Jefferson Davis, full-length studio portrait, standing, facing slightly right with left hand resting on the back of a chair

Confederate White House, home of Jefferson Davis in Richmond

The ordnance armory, Charleston, South Carolina, the volunteer troops trying the arms

Deck of iron-clad gunboat Galena, showing stack damaged by fire from Fort Darling

Thomas Jonathan Jackson, full-length portrait, on horseback, facing left, holding up hat in his right hand

General Robert E. Lee on horseback flanked by Stonewall Jackson and Jeb Stuart, riding in review before a crowd of cheering soldiers.

Great Battle of Murfreesboro, Tennessee between the Union Forces, under General Rosecrans and the Rebel Army under General Bragg

Atlanta, before being burnt, taken by order of General Sherman

The Rebel forces under General Jackson advancing upon the Rappahannock Station at the river

Mrs. Robert E. Lee

General Robert E. Lee, C.S.A

Unidentified soldier in Confederate frock coat with gold trim,
The Liljenquist Collection, Library of Congress

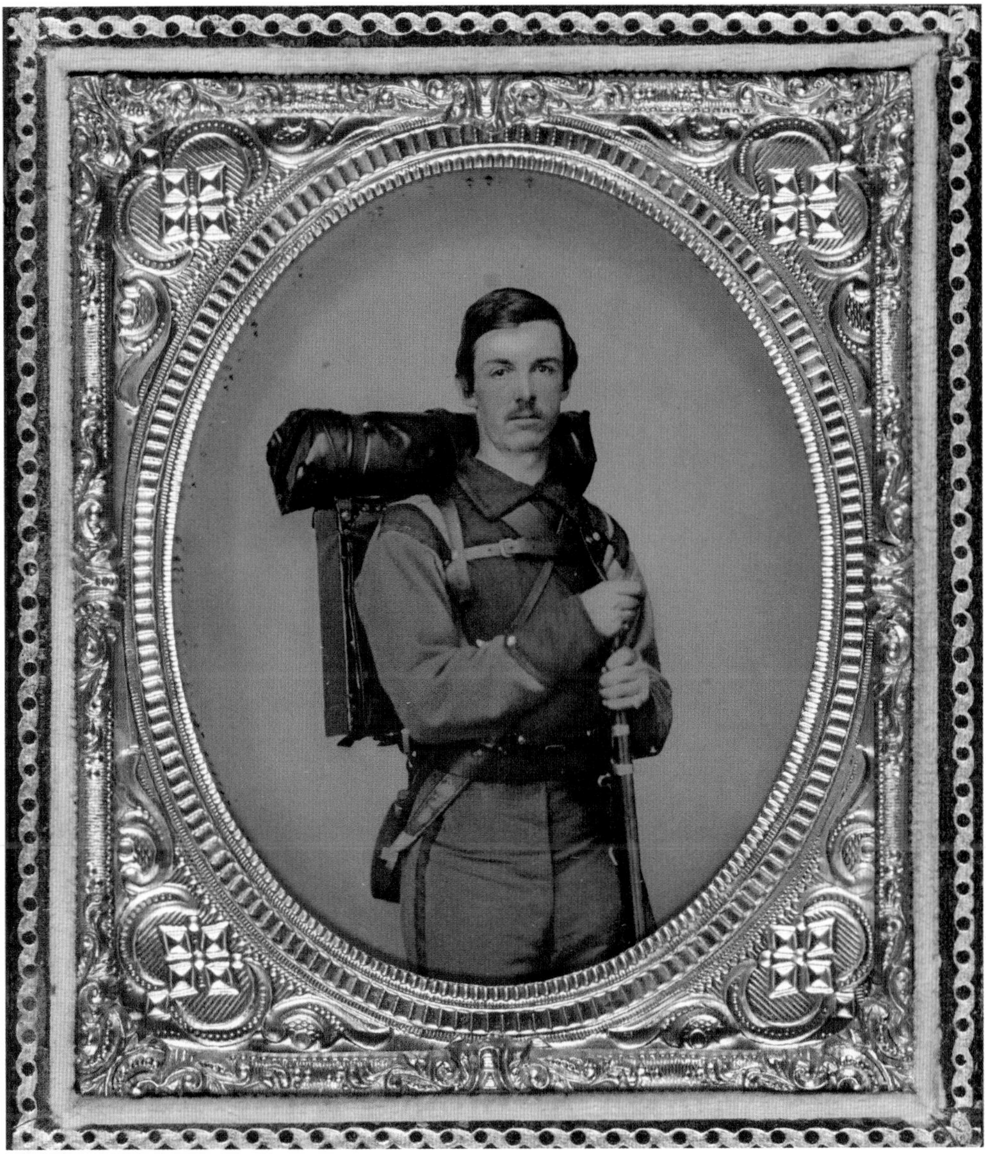

Unidentified soldier in Confederate uniform of Co. E, "Lynchburg Rifles," 11th Virginia Infantry Volunteers holding 1841 "Mississippi" rifle, Sheffield-type Bowie knife, canteen, box knapsack, blanket roll, and cartridge box, The Liljenquist Collection, Library of Congress

Struggle on a bridge during the retreat from Manassas

Battle of Corinth

The Monitor And The Merrimac

Both Sides Of The Story Told By Lieut. J.L. Worden, U.S.N. Lieut. Greene, U.S.N. Of The Monitor And H. Ashton Ramsay, C.S.N. Chief Engineer Of The Merrimac

Introduction

This is the first-hand story of what was done and seen and felt on each side in the battle of the Monitor and the Merrimac. The actual experiences on both vessels are pictured, in one case by the commander of the Monitor, then a lieutenant, and the next in rank, Lieutenant Greene, and in the other by Chief-Engineer Ramsay of the Merrimac. Clearly such a record of personal experiences has a place by itself in the literature of the subject.

It is quite unnecessary to dwell upon the various controversies which this battle has involved. As to the first use of armor, we know that France experimented with floating armored batteries in the Crimean War, and England had armored ships before 1862. As to the invention of the movable turret, which has been a bone of contention, the pages of Colonel Church's Life of John Ericsson and other books are open to the curious. The struggle of Ericsson to obtain official recognition, the raising of money, the hasty equipment of the Monitor, and the restraining orders under which she fought form a story supplementary to the battle, but of peculiar interest. The Monitor was ordered to act on the defensive. It was her mission first to protect the wooden ships. That explains certain misconceptions of her cautious attitude. And the fact that the powder charges for her Dahlgren guns were officially limited to fifteen pounds, although thirty and even fifty pounds were used with safety afterward, invites speculation upon the results if she had fought with a free hand.

But the main result was reached. The Union fleet was saved. The career of the Merrimac was checked. No Union vessel was destroyed after the Monitor appeared. It seems proper to note these facts here, in view of the fact that Mr. Ramsay's fresh and striking story of the Merrimac, which is presented for the first time, enters upon the details of the battle more fully than the narrative of Lieutenant Worden and Lieutenant Greene. Fortunately the discussion has become academic in the half-century that has passed since Southern cheers over the first conquests of the Merrimac faltered before the acclaim which greeted the Monitor's achievement of her task. One may disagree with the phrasing of various historians on both sides, one may find it difficult to accept the inscription upon the shaft of the Merrimac outside the "Confederate White House" in Richmond, but no American can cease to wonder at the fortitude and daring of those other Americans who fought to the death in those hastily improvised crafts, bearing the brunt not only of battle, but of a strange and terrible experiment. It is not an argument that this book offers, but a saga of heroes, an illumination of qualities which have made our history in times of crisis.

The year of this battle witnessed the destruction of both the vessels engaged. Mr. Ramsay describes the blowing-up of the Merrimac. An eye-witness of the sinking of the

Monitor off Hatteras, Rear-Admiral E.W. Watson, who was an officer of the Rhode Island, which was towing the Monitor on that eventful night, has very kindly written a brief description of the tragedy for this book.

The publishers desire to make acknowledgment to the representatives of the late Lucius E. Chittenden for the use of Part I of this book, which appears in Mr. Chittenden's most interesting volume, Recollections of President Lincoln and his Administration.

I

Told by Lieutenant Worden and Lieutenant S.D. Greene of the "Monitor"

Some weeks after the historic battle between the Monitor and the Merrimac in Hampton Roads, on March 9, 1862, the former vessel came to the Washington Navy-yard unchanged, in the same condition as when she discharged her parting shot at the Merrimac. There she lay until her heroic commander had so far recovered from his injuries as to be able to rejoin his vessel. All leaves of absence had been revoked, the absentees had returned, and were ready to welcome their captain. President Lincoln, Captain Fox, and a limited number of Captain Worden's personal friends had been invited to his informal reception. Lieutenant Greene received the President and the guests. He was a boy in years—not too young to volunteer, however, when volunteers were scarce, and to fight the Merrimac during the last half of the battle, after the captain was disabled.

The President and the other guests stood on the deck, near the turret. The men were formed in lines, with their officers a little in advance, when Captain Worden ascended the gangway. The heavy guns in the navy-yard began firing the customary salute when he stepped upon the deck. One side of his face was permanently blackened by the powder shot into it from the muzzle of a cannon carrying a shell of one hundred pounds' weight, discharged less than twenty yards away. The President advanced to welcome him, and introduced him to the few strangers present. The officers and men passed in review and were dismissed. Then there was a scene worth witnessing. The old tars swarmed around their loved captain, they grasped his hand, crowded to touch him, thanked God for his recovery and return, and invoked blessings upon his head in the name of all the saints in the calendar. He called them by their names, had a pleasant word for each of them, and for a few moments we looked upon an exhibition of a species of affection that could only have been the product of a common danger.

When order was restored, the President gave a brief sketch of Captain Worden's career. Commodore Paulding had been the first, Captain Worden the second officer, of the navy, he said, to give an unqualified opinion in favor of armored vessels. Their opinions had been influential with him and with the Board of Construction. Captain Worden had volunteered to take command of the Monitor, at the risk of his life and reputation, before the keel was laid. He had watched her construction, and his energy had made it possible to send her to sea in time to arrest the destructive operations of the Merrimac. What he had done with a new crew, and a vessel of novel construction, we all knew. He, the President, cordially acknowledged his indebtedness to Captain Worden, and he hoped the whole country would unite in the feeling of obligation. The debt was a heavy one, and would not be repudiated when its nature was understood. The details of the first battle between ironclads would interest every one. At the request of Captain Fox, Captain Worden had consented to give an account of his voyage from New York to Hampton Roads, and of what had afterward happened there on board the Monitor.

In an easy conversational manner, without any effort at display, Captain Worden told the story, of which the following is the substance:

"I suppose," he began, "that every one knows that we left New York Harbor in some haste. We had information that the Merrimac was nearly completed, and if we were to fight her on her first appearance, we must be on the ground. The Monitor had been hurried from the laying of her keel. Her engines were new, and her machinery did not move smoothly. Never was a vessel launched that so much needed trial-trips to test her machinery and get her crew accustomed to their novel duties. We went to sea practically without them. No part of the vessel was finished; there was one omission that was serious, and came very near causing her failure and the loss of many lives. In heavy weather it was intended that her hatches and all her openings should be closed and battened down. In that case all the men would be below, and would have to depend upon artificial ventilation. Our machinery for that purpose proved wholly inadequate.

"We were in a heavy gale of wind as soon as we passed Sandy Hook. The vessel behaved splendidly. The seas rolled over her, and we found her the most comfortable vessel we had ever seen, except for the ventilation, which gave us more trouble than I have time to tell you about. We had to run into port and anchor on account of the weather, and, as you know, it was two o'clock in the morning of Sunday before we were alongside the Minnesota. Captain Van Brunt gave us an account of Saturday's experience. He was very glad to make our acquaintance, and notified us that we must be prepared to receive the Merrimac at daylight. We had had a very hard trip down the coast, and officers and men were weary and sleepy. But when informed that our fight would probably open at daylight, and that the Monitor must be put in order, every man went to his post with a cheer. That night there was no sleep on board the Monitor.

"In the gray of the early morning we saw a vessel approaching, which our friends on the Minnesota said was the Merrimac. Our fastenings were cast off, our machinery started, and we moved out to meet her half-way. We had come a long way to fight her, and did not intend to lose our opportunity.

"Before showing you over the vessel, let me say that there were three possible points of weakness in the Monitor, two of which might have been guarded against in her construction, if there had been more time to perfect her plans. One of them was in the turret, which, as you see, is constructed of eight plates of inch iron—on the side of the ports, nine—set on end so as to break joints, and firmly bolted together, making a hollow cylinder eight inches thick. It rests on a metal ring on a vertical shaft, which is revolved by power from the boilers. If a projectile struck the turret at an acute angle, it was expected to glance off without doing damage. But what would happen if it was fired in a straight line to the center of the turret, which in that case would receive the whole force of the blow? It might break off the bolt-heads on the interior, which, flying across, would kill the men at the guns; it might disarrange the revolving mechanism, and then we would be wholly disabled.

"I laid the Monitor close alongside the Merrimac, and gave her a shot. She returned our compliment by a shell weighing one hundred and fifty pounds, fired when we were close together, which struck the turret so squarely that it received the whole force. Here you see the scar, two and a half inches deep in the wrought iron, a perfect mold of the shell. If anything could test the turret, it was that shot. It did not start a rivet-head or a nut! It stunned the two men who were nearest where the ball struck, and that was all. I touched the lever—the turret revolved as smoothly as before. The turret had stood the test; I could mark that point of weakness off my list forever.

"You notice that the deck is joined to the side of the hull by a right angle, at what sailors call the 'plank-shear.' If a projectile struck that angle what would happen? It would not be deflected; its whole force would be expended there. It might open a seam in the hull below the water-line, or pierce the wooden hull, and sink us. Here was our second point of weakness.

"I had decided how I would fight her in advance. I would keep the Monitor moving in a circle just large enough to give time for loading the guns. At the point where the circle impinged upon the Merrimac our guns should be fired, and loaded while we were moving around the circuit. Evidently the Merrimac would return the compliment every time. At our second exchange of shots, she returning six or eight to our two, another of her large shells struck our 'plank-shear' at its angle, and tore up one of the deck-plates, as you see. The shell had struck what I believed to be the weakest point in the Monitor. We had already learned that the Merrimac swarmed with sharpshooters, for their bullets were constantly spattering against our turret and our deck. If a man showed himself on deck he would draw their fire. But I did not much consider the sharpshooters. It was my duty to investigate the effects of that shot. I ordered one of the pendulums to be hauled aside, and, crawling out of the port, walked to the side, lay down upon my chest, and examined it thoroughly. The hull was uninjured, except for a few splinters in the wood. I walked back and crawled into the turret—the bullets were falling on the iron deck all about me as thick as hail-stones in a storm. None struck me, I suppose because the vessel was moving, and at the angle, and when I was lying on the deck my body made a small mark, difficult to hit. We gave them two more guns, and then I told the men, what was true, that the Merrimac could not sink us if we let her pound us for a month. The men cheered; the knowledge put new life into all.

"We had more exchanges, and then the Merrimac tried new tactics. She endeavored to ram us, to run us down. Once she struck us about amidships with her iron ram. Here you see its mark. It gave us a shock, pushed us around, and that was all the harm. But the movement placed our sides together. I gave her two guns, which I think lodged in her side, for, from my lookout crack, I could not see that either shot rebounded. Ours being the smaller vessel, and more easily handled, I had no difficulty in avoiding her ram. I ran around her several times, planting our shot in what seemed to be the most vulnerable places. In this way, reserving my fire until I got the range and the mark, I planted two more shots almost in the very spot I had hit when she tried to ram us. Those shots must have been effective, for they were followed by a shower of bars of iron.

"The third weak spot was our pilot-house. You see that it is built a little more than three feet above the deck, of bars of iron, ten by twelve inches square, built up like a log-house, bolted with very large bolts at the corners where the bars interlock. The pilot stands upon a platform below, his head and shoulders in the pilot-house. The upper tier of bars is separated from the second by an open space of an inch, through which the pilot may look out at every point of the compass. The pilot-house, as you see, is a foursquare mass of iron, provided with no means of deflecting a ball. I expected trouble from it, and I was not disappointed. Until my accident happened, as we approached the enemy I stood in the pilot-house and gave the signals. Lieutenant Greene fired the guns, and Engineer Stimers, here, revolved the turret.

"I was below the deck when the corner of the pilot-house was first struck by a shot or a shell. It either burst or was broken, and no harm was done. A short time after I had given the signal and, with my eye close against the lookout crack, was watching the effect of our shot, something happened to me—my part in the fight was ended. Lieutenant Greene, who fought the Merrimac until she had no longer stomach for fighting, will tell you the rest of the story."

Can it be possible that this beardless boy fought one of the historic battles of the world? This was the thought of every one, as the modest, diffident young Greene was half pushed forward into the circle.

"I cannot add much to the Captain's story," he began. "He had cut out the work for us, and we had only to follow his pattern. I kept the Monitor either moving around the circle or around the enemy, and endeavored to place our shots as near her amidships as possible, where Captain Worden believed he had already broken through her armor. We knew that she could not sink us, and I thought I would keep right on pounding her as long as she would stand it. There is really nothing new to be added to Captain Worden's account. We could strike her wherever we chose. Weary as they must have been, our men were full of enthusiasm, and I do not think we wasted a shot. Once we ran out of the circle for a moment to adjust a piece of machinery, and I learn that some of our friends feared that we were drawing out of the fight. The Merrimac took the opportunity to start for Norfolk. As soon as our machinery was adjusted we followed her, and got near enough to give her a parting shot. But I was not familiar with the locality; there might be torpedoes planted in the channel, and I did not wish to take any risk of losing our vessel, so I came back to the company of our friends. But except that we were, all of us, tired and hungry when we came back to the Minnesota at half-past twelve P.M., the Monitor was just as well prepared to fight as she was at eight o'clock in the morning when she fired the first gun."

We were then shown the injury to the pilot-house. The mark of the ball was plain upon the two upper bars, the principal impact being upon the lower of the two. This huge bar was broken in the middle, but held firmly at either end. The farther it was pressed in, the stronger was the resistance on the exterior. On the inside the fracture in the bar was half an inch wide. Captain Worden's eye was very near to the lookout crack, so that when the gun was discharged the shock of the ball knocked him senseless, while the mass of flame filled one side of his face with coarse grains of powder. He remained insensible for some hours.

"Have you heard what Captain Worden's first inquiry was when he recovered his senses after the general shock to his system?" asked Captain Fox of the President.

"I think I have," replied Mr. Lincoln, "but it is worth relating to these gentlemen."

"His question was," said Captain Fox, "'Have I saved the Minnesota?'

"'Yes, and whipped the Merrimac!' some one answered.

"'Then,' said Captain Worden, 'I don't care what becomes of me.'

"Mr. President," said Captain Fox, "not much of the history to which we have listened is new to me. I saw this battle from eight o'clock until midday. There was one marvel in it which has not been mentioned—the splendid handling of the Monitor throughout the battle. The first bold advance of this diminutive vessel against a giant like the Merrimac was superlatively grand. She seemed inspired by Nelson's order at Trafalgar: 'He will make no mistake who lays his vessel alongside the enemy.' One would have thought the Monitor a living thing. No man was visible. You saw her moving around that circle, delivering her fire invariably at the point of contact, and heard the crash of the missile against her enemy's armor above the thunder of her guns, on the bank where we stood. It was indescribably grand!

"Now," he continued, "standing here on the deck of this battle-scarred vessel, the first genuine ironclad—the victor in the first fight of the ironclads—let me make a confession and perform an act of simple justice: I never fully believed in armored vessels until I saw this battle. I know all the facts which united to give us the Monitor. I withhold no credit from Captain Ericsson, her inventor, but I know that the country is principally indebted for the construction of this vessel to President Lincoln, and for the success of her trial to Captain Worden, her commander."

The Merrimac And The Monitor II

Told by H. Ashton Ramsay, Major C.S.A.,
Chief Engineer of the "Merrimac"

The naval engagement between the Merrimac and the Monitor at Hampton Roads - on the 9th of March 1862

The Merrimac was built in 1856 as a full-rigged war-frigate, of thirty-one hundred tons' burden, with auxiliary steam power to be used only in case of head winds. She was a hybrid from her birth, marking the transition from sails to steam as well as from wooden ships to ironclads.

I became her second assistant engineer in Panama Bay in 1859, cruising in her around the Horn and back to Norfolk. Her chief engineer was Alban C. Stimers. Little did we dream that he was to be the right-hand man of Ericsson in the construction of the Monitor, while I was to hold a similar post in the conversion of our own ship into an ironclad, or that, in less than a year and a half, we would be seeking to destroy each other, he as chief engineer of the Monitor and I in the corresponding position on the Merrimac.

In the harbor of Rio on our return voyage we met the Congress, and as we sailed away after coaling she fired a friendly salute and cheered us, and we responded with a will. When the two ships next met it was in one of the deadliest combats of naval history.

The machinery of the Merrimac was condemned, and she went out of commission on our return. She was still at Norfolk when the war broke out, and was set on fire by the Federals when Norfolk was evacuated. Some of the workmen in the navy-yard scuttled and sank her, thus putting out the flames. When she was raised by the Confederates she was nothing but a burned and blackened hulk.

Her charred upper works were cut away, and in the center a casement shield one hundred and eighty feet long was built of pitch-pine and oak, two feet thick. This was covered with iron plates, one to two inches thick and eight inches wide, bolted over each other and through and through the woodwork, giving a protective armor four inches in thickness. The shield sloped at an angle of about thirty-six degrees, and was covered with an iron grating that served as an upper deck. For fifty feet forward and aft her decks were submerged below the water, and the prow was shod with an iron beak to receive the impact when ramming.

Even naval officers were skeptical as to the result. The plates were rolled at the Tredegar mills at Richmond, and arrived so slowly that we were nearly a year in finishing her. We could have rolled them at Norfolk and built four Merrimacs in that time, had the South understood the importance of a navy at the outbreak of the war.

I remember that my old friend and comrade, Captain Charles MacIntosh, while awaiting orders, used to come over and stand on the granite curbing of the dock to watch the work as it crawled along.

"Good-by, Ramsay," he said, sadly, on the eve of starting to command a ram at New Orleans. "I shall never see you again. She will prove your coffin." A short time afterward the poor fellow had both legs shot from under him and died almost immediately.

Rifled guns were just coming into use, and Lieutenant Brooke, who designed the Merrimac, considered the question of having some of her guns rifled. How to procure such cannon was not easily discovered, as we had no foundries in the South. There were many cast-iron cannon that had fallen into our hands at Norfolk, and he conceived the idea of turning some of this ordnance into rifles. In order to enable them to stand the additional bursting strain we forged wrought-iron bands and shrank them over the chambers, and we devised a special tool for rifling the bore of the guns. They gave effective service.

Many details remained uncompleted when we were at last floated out of dry-dock, but there was great pressure for us to make some demonstration that might serve to check McClellan in his advance up the Peninsula.

The ship was still full of workmen hurrying her to completion when Commodore Franklin Buchanan arrived from Richmond one March morning and ordered every one out of the ship, except her crew of three hundred and fifty men which had been hastily drilled on shore in the management of the big guns, and directed Executive Officer Jones to prepare to sail at once.

At that time nothing was known of our destination. All we knew was that we were off at last. Buchanan sent for me. The veteran sailor, the beau ideal of a naval officer of the old school, with his tall form, harsh features, and clear, piercing eyes, was pacing the deck with a stride I found it difficult to match, although he was then over sixty and I but twenty-four.

"Ramsay," he asked, "what would happen to your engines and boilers if there should be a collision?"

"They are braced tight," I assured him. "Though the boilers stand fourteen feet, they are so securely fastened that no collision could budge them."

"I am going to ram the Cumberland," said my commander. "I'm told she has the new rifled guns, the only ones in their whole fleet we have cause to fear. The moment we are in the Roads I'm going to make right for her and ram her. How about your engines? They were in bad shape in the old ship, I understand. Can we rely on them? Should they be tested by a trial trip?"

"She will have to travel some ten miles down the river before we get to the Roads," I said. "If any trouble develops I'll report it. I think that will be sufficient trial trip."

I watched the machinery carefully as we sped down the Elizabeth River, and soon satisfied myself that all was well. Then I went on deck.

"How fast is she going do you think?" I asked one of the pilots.

"Eight or nine knots an hour," he replied, making a rapid calculation from objects ashore. The Merrimac as an ironclad was faster under steam than she had ever been before with her top hamper of masts and sails.

I presented myself to the commodore. "The machinery is all right, sir," I assured him.

Across the river at Newport News gleamed the batteries and white tents of the Federal camp and the vessels of the fleet blockading the mouth of the James, chief among them the Congress and the Cumberland, tall and stately, with every line and spar clearly defined against the blue March sky, their decks and ports bristling with guns, while the rigging of the Cumberland was gay with the red, white, and blue of sailors' garments hung out to dry.

As we rounded into view the white-winged sailing craft that sprinkled the bay and long lines of tugs and small boats scurried to the far shore like chickens on the approach of a hovering hawk. They had seen our black hulk which looked like the roof of a barn afloat. Suddenly huge volumes of smoke began to pour from the funnels of the frigates Minnesota and Roanoke at Old Point. They had seen us, too, and were getting up steam. Bright-colored signal flags were run up and down the masts of all the ships of the Federal fleet. The Congress shook out her topsails. Down came the clothes-line on the Cumberland, and boats were lowered and dropped astern.

Our crew was summoned to the gun-deck, and Buchanan addressed us: "Sailors, in a few minutes you will have the long-looked-for opportunity of showing your devotion to our cause. Remember that you are about to strike for your country and your homes. The

Confederacy expects every man to do his duty. Beat to quarters." Every terse, burning word is engraved on my memory, though fifty years have passed since they were spoken.

Just as he had finished, the mess caterer touched my elbow and whispered: "Better get your lunch now, Mr. Ramsay. It will be your last chance. The galley-fires must be put out when the magazines are opened."

On my way I saw Assistant-Surgeon Garnett at a table laying out lint and surgical implements. I had no appetite, and merely tasted some cold tongue and a cup of coffee. Passing along the gun-deck, I saw the pale and determined countenances of the guns' crews, as they stood motionless at their posts, with set lips unsmiling, contrasting with the careless expression of sailors when practised at "fighting quarters" on a man-of-war. This was the real thing.

As we approached the Federal ships we were met by a veritable storm of shells which must have sunk any ship then afloat—except the Merrimac. They struck our sloping sides, were deflected upward to burst harmlessly in the air, or rolled down and fell hissing into the water, dashing the spray up into our ports.

As we drew nearer the Cumberland, above the roar of battle rang the voice of Buchanan, "Do you surrender?"

"Never!" retorted the gallant Morris.

The crux of what followed was down in the engine-room. Two gongs, the signal to stop, were quickly followed by three, the signal to reverse. There was an ominous pause, then a crash, shaking us all off our feet. The engines labored. The vessel was shaken in every fiber. Our bow was visibly depressed. We seemed to be bearing down with a weight on our prow. Thud, thud, thud, came the rain of shot on our shield from the double-decked battery of the Congress. There was a terrible crash in the fire-room. For a moment we thought one of the boilers had burst. No, it was the explosion of a shell in our stack. Was any one hit? No, thank God! The firemen had been warned to keep away from the up-take, so the fragments of shell fell harmlessly on the iron floor-plates.

We had rushed on the doomed ship, relentless as fate, crashing through her barricade of heavy spars and torpedo fenders, striking her below her starboard fore-chains, and crushing far into her. For a moment the whole weight of her hung on our prow and threatened to carry us down with her, the return wave of the collision curling up into our bow port.

The Cumberland began to sink slowly, bow first, but continued to fight desperately for the forty minutes that elapsed after her doom was sealed, while we were engaged with both the Cumberland and the Congress, being right between them.

We had left our cast-iron beak in the side of the Cumberland. Like the wasp, we could sting but once, leaving it in the wound.

Our smoke-stack was riddled, our flag was shot down several times, and was finally secured to a rent in the stack. On our gun-deck the men were fighting like demons. There was no thought or time for the wounded and dying as they tugged away at their guns, training and sighting their pieces while the orders rang out, "Sponge, load, fire!"

"The muzzle of our gun has been shot away," cried one of the gunners.

"No matter, keep on loading and firing—do the best you can with it," replied Lieutenant Jones.

"Keep away from the side ports, don't lean against the shield, look out for the sharpshooters," rang the warnings. Some of our men who failed to heed them and leaned against the shield were stunned and carried below, bleeding at the ears. All were full of courage and worked with a will; they were so begrimed with powder that they looked like negroes.

"Pass along the cartridges."

"More powder."

"A shell for number six."

"A wet wad for the hot-shot gun."

"Put out that pipe and don't light it again on peril of your life."

Such were the directions and commands, issued like clockwork amid the confusion of battle. Our executive officer seemed to be in a dozen places at once.

This gives some faint notion of the scene passing behind our grim iron casement, which to the beholders without seemed a machine of destruction. Human hearts were beating and bleeding there. Human lives were being sacrificed. Pain, death, wounds, glory—that was the sum of it.

On the doomed ship Cumberland the battle raged with equal fury. The sanded deck was red and slippery with blood. Delirium seized the crew. They stripped to their trousers, kicked off their shoes, tied handkerchiefs about their heads, and fought and cheered as their ship sank beneath their feet. Then the order came, "All save who can." There was a scramble for the spar-deck and a rush overboard. The ship listed. The after pivot-gun broke loose and rushed down the decline like a furious animal, rolling over a man as it bounded overboard, leaving a mass of mangled flesh on deck.

We now turned to the Congress, which had tried to escape but had grounded, and the battle raged once more, broadside upon broadside, delivered at close range, the Merrimac working closer all the time with her bow pointed as if to ram the Congress. A shell from Lieutenant Wood's gun sped through their line of powder-passers, not only cutting down the men, but exploding the powder buckets in their hands, spreading death and destruction and setting fire to the ship.

At last came the order, "Cease firing."

"The Congress has surrendered," some one cried. "Look out of the port. See, she has run up white flags. The officers are waving their handkerchiefs."

At this several of the officers started to leave their posts and rush on deck, but Lieutenant Jones in his stentorian voice sang out: "Stand by your guns, and, lieutenants, be ready to resume firing at the word. See that your guns are well supplied with ammunition during the lull. Dr. Garnett, see how those poor fellows yonder are coming on. Mr. Littlepage, tell Paymaster Semple to have a care of the berth-deck and use every precaution against fire. Mr. Hasker, call away the cutter's crew and have them in readiness. Mr. Lindsay [to the carpenter], sound the well, examine the forehold, and report if you find anything wrong." Such was Catesby Ap. R. Jones, the executive officer of the Merrimac.

When it was fully evident that there was to be a suspension of hostilities, and these details had all been attended to, several of the officers went to stand beside Buchanan on the upper grating.

The whole scene was changed. A pall of black smoke hung about the ships and obscured the clean-cut outlines of the shore. Down the river were the three frigates St. Lawrence, Roanoke, and Minnesota, also enveloped in the clouds of battle that now and then reflected the crimson lightnings of the god of war. The masts of the Cumberland were protruding above the water. The Congress presented a terrible scene of carnage.

The gunboats Beaufort and Raleigh were signaled to take off the wounded and fire the ship. They were driven away by sharpshooters on shore, who suddenly turned their fire on us, notwithstanding the white flag of the Congress. Buchanan fell, severely wounded in the groin.

As he was being carried below he said to Executive Officer Jones: "Plug hot shot into her and don't leave her until she's afire. They must look after their own wounded, since they won't let us"—a characteristic command when it is remembered that his own brother, McKean Buchanan, was paymaster of the Congress and might have been numbered among the wounded.

We had kept two furnaces for the purpose of heating shot. They were rolled into the flames on a grating, rolled out into iron buckets, hoisted to the gun-deck, and rolled into the guns, which had been prepared with wads of wet hemp. Then the gun would be touched off quickly and the shot sent on its errand of destruction.

Leaving the Congress wrapped in sheets of flame, we made for the three other frigates. The St. Lawrence and Roanoke had run aground, but were pulled off by tugs and made their escape. The Minnesota was not so fortunate, but we drew twenty-three feet of water and could not get near enough to destroy her, while our guns could not be elevated owing to the narrow embrasures, and their range was only a mile; so we made for our moorings at Sewall's Point.

All the evening we stood on deck watching the brilliant display of the burning ship. Every part of her was on fire at the same time, the red-tongued flames running up shrouds, masts, and stays, and extending out to the yard-arms. She stood in bold relief against the black background, lighting up the Roads and reflecting her lurid lights on the bosom of the now placid and hushed waters. Every now and then the flames would reach one of the loaded cannon and a shell would hiss at random through the darkness. About midnight came the grand finale. The magazines exploded, shooting up a huge column of firebrands hundreds of feet in the air, and then the burning hulk burst asunder and melted into the waters, while the calm night spread her sable mantle over Hampton Roads.

The Monitor arrived during the evening and anchored under the stern of the Minnesota, her lighter draught enabling her to do so without danger. To us the ensuing engagement was in the nature of a surprise. If we had known we were to meet her we would have at least been supplied with solid shot for our rifled guns. We might even have thought best to wait until our iron beak, lost in the side of the Cumberland, could be replaced. Buchanan was incapacitated by his wound, and the command devolved upon Lieutenant Jones.

We left our anchorage shortly before eight o'clock next morning and steamed across and up stream toward the Minnesota, thinking to make short work of her and soon return with her colors trailing under ours. We approached her slowly, feeling our way cautiously along the edge of the channel, when suddenly, to our astonishment, a black object that looked like the historic description, "a barrel-head afloat with a cheese-box on top of it," moved slowly out from under the Minnesota and boldly confronted us. It must be confessed that both ships were queer-looking craft, as grotesque to the eyes of the men of '62 as they would appear to those of the present generation.

And now the great fight was on, a fight the like of which the world had never seen. With the battle of yesterday old methods had passed away, and with them the experience of a thousand years "of battle and of breeze" was brought to naught.

We hovered about each other in spirals, gradually contracting the circuits until we were within point-blank range, but our shell glanced from the Monitor's turret just as hers did from our sloping sides. For two hours the cannonade continued without perceptible damage to either of the combatants.

On our gun-deck all was bustle, smoke, grimy figures, and stern commands, while down in the engine and boiler rooms the sixteen furnaces were belching out fire and smoke, and the firemen standing in front of them, like so many gladiators, tugged away with devil's-claw and slice-bar, inducing by their exertions more and more intense combustion and heat. The noise of the cracking, roaring fires, escaping steam, and the loud and labored pulsations of the engines, together with the roar of battle above and the thud and vibration of the huge masses of iron which were hurled against us produced a scene and sound to be compared only with the poet's picture of the lower regions.

And then an accident occurred that threatened our utter destruction. We stuck fast aground on a sand-bar.

Our situation was critical. The Monitor could, at her leisure, come close up to us and yet be out of our reach, owing to our inability to deflect our guns. In she came and began to sound every chink in our armor—every one but that which was actually vulnerable, had she known it.

The coal consumption of the two days' fight had lightened our prow until our unprotected submerged deck was almost awash. The armor on our sides below the water-line had been extended but about three feet, owing to our hasty departure before the work was finished. Lightened as we were, these exposed portions rendered us no longer an ironclad, and the Monitor might have pierced us between wind and water had she depressed her guns.

Fearing that she might discover our vulnerable "heel of Achilles" we had to take all chances. We lashed down the safety valves, heaped quick-burning combustibles into the already raging fires, and brought the boilers to a pressure that would have been unsafe under ordinary circumstances. The propeller churned the mud and water furiously, but the ship did not stir. We piled on oiled cotton waste, splints of wood, anything that would burn faster than coal. It seemed impossible that the boilers could stand the pressure we were crowding upon them. Just as we were beginning to despair there was a perceptible movement, and the Merrimac slowly dragged herself off the shoal by main strength. We were saved.

Before our adversary saw that we were again afloat we made a dash for her, catching her quite unprepared, and tried to ram her, but our commander was dubious about the result of a collision without our iron-shod beak, and gave the signal to reverse the engines long before we reached the Monitor. As a result I did not feel the slightest shock down in the engine-room, though we struck her fairly enough.

The carpenter reported that the effect was to spring a leak forward. Lieutenant Jones sent for me and asked me about it.

"It is impossible we can be making much water," I replied, "for the skin of the vessel is plainly visible in the crank-pits."

A second time he sent for me and asked if we were making any water in the engine-room.

"With the two large Worthington pumps, besides the bilge injections, we could keep her afloat for hours, even with a ten-inch shell in her hull," I assured him, repeating that there was no water in the engine and boiler rooms.

We glided past, leaving the Monitor unscathed, but got between her and the Minnesota and opened fire on the latter. The Monitor gallantly rushed to her rescue, passing so close under our submerged stern that she almost snapped off our propeller. As she was passing, so near that we could have leaped aboard her, Lieutenant Wood trained the stern-gun on her when she was only twenty yards from its muzzle and delivered a rifle-pointed shell which dislodged the iron logs sheltering the Monitor's conning-tower, carrying away the steering-gear and signal apparatus, and blinding Captain Worden. It was a mistake to place the conning-tower so far from the turret and the vitals of the ship. Since that time it has been located over the turret. The Monitor's turret was a death-trap. It was only twenty feet in diameter, and every shot knocked off bolt-heads and sent them flying against the gunners. If one of them barely touched the side of the turret he would be stunned and momentarily paralyzed. Lieutenant Greene had been taken below in a dazed condition and never fully recovered from the effects. One of the port shutters had been jammed, putting a gun out of commission, and there was nothing for the Monitor to do but to retreat and leave the Minnesota to her fate.

Captain Van Brunt, of the latter vessel, thought he was now doomed and was preparing to fire his ship when he saw the Merrimac also withdrawing toward Norfolk.

It was at this juncture that Lieutenant Jones had sent for me and said: "The pilots will not place us nearer to the Minnesota, and we cannot afford to run the risk of getting aground again. I'm going to haul off under the guns of Sewall's Point and renew the attack on the rise of the tide. Bank your fires and make any necessary adjustments to the machinery, but be prepared to start up again later in the afternoon."

I went below to comply with his instructions, and later was astonished to hear cheering. Rushing on deck, I found we were passing Craney Island on our way to Norfolk, and were being cheered by the soldiers of the battery.

Our captain had consulted with some of his lieutenants. He explained afterward that as the Monitor had proved herself so formidable an adversary he had thought best to get a supply of solid shot, have the prow replaced, the port shutters put on, the armor belt extended below water, and the guns whose muzzles had been shot away replaced, and then renew the engagement with every chance of victory. I remember feeling as though a wet blanket had been thrown over me. His reasoning was doubtless good, but it ignored the moral effect of leaving the Roads without forcing the Minnesota to surrender.

As the Merrimac passed up the river, trailing the ensign of the Congress under the stars and bars, she received a tremendous ovation from the crowds that lined the shores, while hundreds of small boats, gay with flags and bunting, converted our course into a triumphal procession.

We went into dry-dock that very afternoon, and in about three weeks were ready to renew the battle upon more advantageous terms, but the Monitor, though reinforced by two other ironclads, the Galena and the Naugatuck, and every available vessel of the United States navy, was under orders from Washington to refuse our challenge and bottle us up in the Roads. This strategy filled us with rage and dismay, but it proved very effective.

Our new commander, Commodore Josiah Tatnall, was burning to distinguish himself, but he was under orders not to risk the destruction or capture of the Merrimac by leaving the Roads, as General Huger's division at Norfolk would then be at the mercy of the Federal fleet. Week after week was passing and with it his golden opportunity. At last we went to Richmond and pressed a plan for a sortie upon the President. He returned one afternoon and ordered every one aboard. That night we slipped down the Roads and were soon passing Fort Monroe on our way out into the Chesapeake.

Presently our army signal officer began waving his lantern communicating with our distant batteries, and then told the result to Officer Jones, who reported to Tatnall. "We have been ordered to return, sir," he said.

Tatnall was viewing the dim outlines of the fort through his glass and pretended not to hear.

"The order is peremptory," repeated Jones.

Tatnall hesitated. He was of half a mind to disobey. "Old Huger has outwitted me," he muttered. "Do what you please. I leave you in command. I'm going to bed," and he went below in a high dudgeon. Tatnall was a striking-looking man, standing over six feet, with florid complexion, deep-sunken blue eyes, and a protruding under lip. That he did not have a chance to fight was no fault of his.

Our life on board for the weeks that followed was far from comfortable. We were within sight of the enemy, and at every movement of the opposing fleet it was "clear away for action." Steam was kept up continually. Our cabins were without air ports and no ray of light even penetrated the ward-rooms. There was nowhere to walk but on the upper grating—a modern prison is far more comfortable. Sometimes the sailors waded on the submerged deck, giving rise to the superstition among the darkies that they were the crew of the "debble ship" with power to walk on the water.

Norfolk was now being evacuated and we were covering Huger's retreat. When this was effected we were to receive the signal and to make our own way up the James. Norfolk was in Federal hands, and Huger had disappeared without signaling us, when our pilots informed us that Harrison's Bar, which we must cross, drew only eighteen feet of water. Under their advice, on the night of May 11th we lightened ship by throwing overboard all our coal and ballast, thus raising our unprotected decks above water. At last all was ready—and then we found that the wind which had been blowing down-stream all day had swept the water off the bar. When morning dawned the Federal fleet must discover our defenseless condition, and defeat and capture were certain, for we were now no longer an ironclad.

It was decided to abandon the vessel and set her on fire. We took the Merrimac to the bight of Craney Island, and about midnight the work of disembarking the crew began. We had but two boats, and it was sunrise before our three hundred and fifty men were all ashore. Cotton waste and trains of powder were strewn about the deck, and Executive Officer Jones, who was the last to leave the ship, applied the slow match. Then we marched silently through the woods to join Huger, fifteen miles away at Suffolk.

Still unconquered, we hauled down our drooping colors, their laurels all fresh and green, with mingled pride and grief, gave her to the flames, and set the lambent fires roaring about the shotted guns. The slow match, the magazine, and that last, deep, low, sullen, mournful boom told our people, now far away on the march, that their gallant ship was no more.

The Last Of The Monitor

By an eye-witness, Rear-Admiral E.W. Watson, U.S.N.

James River, Va. Deck and turret of U.S.S. Monitor seen from the bow

On the 29th of December, 1862, nine months after her memorable combat with the Merrimac, the Monitor, Commander John P. Bankhead, left Hampton Roads in tow of the Rhode Island, commanded by Captain Stephen Decatur Trenchard, for Beaufort, North Carolina. The weather at the time of starting looked favorable for the trip, but on the following day, when nearing Cape Hatteras, the wind came out from the southeast and gradually freshened until by evening it was blowing a moderate gale, with a tolerably heavy sea running. It was soon seen that the Monitor was making heavy weather of it, and the engines were slowed down, but the course was still kept head to the wind and sea.

This was a mistake, for experience later on in towing other vessels of her class proved that the safest way to handle them in heavy weather was to let them lie in the trough of the sea, when the waves would wash over their decks and the roll would not be excessive. The Monitor was closely watched, all on board the Rhode Island feeling anxious for her safety. Toward the end of the first watch—between 8 P.M. and midnight—the signal of distress, a red lantern, was hoisted on the Monitor, and, unknown to those on the Rhode Island, the hawser was cut and the anchor of the Monitor let go.

The Rhode Island immediately stopped her engine, and three boats were called away with an officer in charge of each, and were sent to take off the Monitor's people. With the heavy sea running it was a difficult matter to go alongside of her, and the first boat to reach her was thrown by a wave upon the deck and a hole stove in her. The next wave washed the boat off, and with considerable difficulty she took on board as many of the men as in her leaky condition could make the return trip safely.

When the boats came alongside of the Monitor, her captain and executive officer went upon the deck and, clinging to the life-lines with the waves washing over them, called to the crew to come down from the turret and get into the boats, which they were reluctant to do at first. Some were able to jump into the boats, and some landed in the water and were hauled in. Seeing an old quartermaster with a large bundle under his arm, the executive officer, thinking that it was his clothes-bag, told him that that was no time to be trying to save his effects. He said nothing, but threw it into the boat. When the bundle was passed up over the side of the Rhode Island it proved to be a little messenger-boy—probably the smallest and youngest one in the service. The three boats were finally loaded and made their way back to the ship.

In the mean while the Rhode Island, in backing her engines, had fouled the hawser with her port paddle-wheel, and being directly to windward of the Monitor, with her engines helpless, drifted down upon her. It looked at one time as if she would strike the bow of the Monitor, but, fortunately, she just missed it, and, scraping along her side, drifted off to leeward.

Another boat was sent to bring off the remainder of the Monitor's crew, but, being to leeward now, she could make only slow headway against the seas, and before she got to her the men saw the Monitor's light disappear, and knew that she had gone down. The hawser having finally been cleared from the Rhode Island's wheel, she steamed around searching for the boat, sending up rockets and burning blue lights to show her position. When the day dawned nothing could be seen. After hailing a passing government vessel and telling them to search for the boat, the Rhode Island steamed with all speed for Fortress Monroe to report the loss.

When the survivors of the ill-fated vessel were mustered on the deck of the Rhode Island, four officers and twelve men were found missing, all of them probably buried in an iron coffin in a watery grave about fifty miles to the southward and eastward of Cape Hatteras Light.

The missing boat and crew of the Rhode Island were found by that vessel a week later safe in Beaufort, North Carolina. They had been picked up by a schooner and taken into that port. The officer in charge of the boat reported that in the early morning he had sighted a schooner standing toward them, and had hoisted a black silk handkerchief belonging to one of the crew on an oar as a signal of distress, but the people in the schooner, evidently thinking them pirates who had come out of some one of the inlets of the coast, turned tail and scudded away from them. A second schooner, coming along soon after, was more hospitable and took them aboard.

History of the Confederate Powder Works

by Col. (General) Geo. W. Rains

The Newburgh Daily News Print, Newburgh, N. Y.

An Address Delivered by Invitation Before the Confederate Survivors' Association, at its Fourth Annual Meeting, on Memorial Day, April 26th, 1882

Fellow Confederate Survivors:

In accepting your invitation to address you on the general history of the Confederate Powder Works, I do so with some hesitation, on account of my close personal connection with a subject which absorbed my thought, time and energies.

In the history of a war we find, generally, but little reference to the manufactories engaged in the preparation of material; they had been previously established, and were in active operation before its commencement, their products being immediately available for active operations. An instance can scarcely be found in modern warfare where previous preparations had not been made, and where the necessary manufacturing works did not already exist.

The late war was entered upon unexpectedly. Throughout the Southern country it was supposed that the North would not seriously oppose a secession of the States from the

Federal compact, hence no previous provision had been made for such contingency, and no material of war gathered.

Manufactories existed on a very limited scale, and none for war purposes, hence their speedy erection was of extreme importance, and had to be accomplished under the most unfavorable conditions.

The entire supply of gunpowder in the Confederacy at the beginning of the conflict, was scarcely sufficient for one month of active operations, and not a pound was being made throughout its limits. To enter upon a great war without a supply of this essential material, and without effective means of procuring it from abroad, or of manufacturing it at home, was appalling.

No one was so well aware of this condition of things as the President of the Confederate States, who, being an educated soldier, was fully alive to the requirements of war, and at once took active measures for the creation of war material. Among these, was the erection of a great gunpowder manufactory.

It is the custom of the different nations, in addition to the private factories of gunpowder, to have erected at different points national [p] works to supply the demand for war. The very limited resources of the Confederacy not admitting of division, had to be accumulated at one point. Mr. Davis was necessarily acquainted with most of the officers of the old army, as he was graduated at West Point, served with great distinction in the war with Mexico, and had been Secretary of War under the Federal Government; he was thus enabled to select his agents for the different services required. Thus that very competent officer, General Gorgas, was placed at the head of the Ordnance Department; I had the honor of being appointed to take charge of the manufactory of gunpowder, a carte blanche being given. The necessary works were to be erected as nearly central as practical; to be permanent structures, and of sufficient magnitude to supply the armies in the field and the artillery of the forts and defences.

On the 10th July, 1861, I left Richmond to enter upon this duty. Making a rapid tour through the South to find a suitable site, Augusta was selected, for several reasons: for its central position; for its canal transportation and water-power; for its railroad facilities; and for its security from attack—since the loss of the works would have been followed by disastrous consequences.

The small amount, comparatively, of gunpowder captured with the Navy Yard at Norfolk, with that on hand from other sources, had been distributed to the army gathering on the Potomac, to Richmond, Yorktown, Pensacola, Mobile, New Orleans, and other places; scarcely any being left for the force assembling under the command of General Albert Sidney Johnson, in Kentucky. The Federal forces, having the requisite advantages for equipment and transportation, were assembling in large bodies, and the utmost energy was required to prevent the loss of a battle by failure in ammunition. General Johnson's command was the most urgent in its wants, hence required the first attention.

The State of Tennessee, through the energy of Governor Harris, and its Military Committee consisting of General Harding and Colonel Bailey, had at the earliest moment taken measures to supply his army by making contracts for saltpetre, to be supplied from the limestone caves, and with the Sycamore Powder Mill, not far from Nashville, which was to be enlarged and put into immediate operation. These contracts were turned over to the Confederate Government on my arrival in that city, and every assistance possible given [p] by the State authorities. Mr. S. D. Morgan, a private citizen of Nashville, but a gentleman of great energy and influence, rendered essential service to the officers of the Confederacy. The Sycamore Stamping Mill was soon put into operation, but its limited arrangements, particularly for preparing the saltpetre, caused the product to be small. Notwithstanding the rapid construction of new stampers, and other parts, it was only in the latter part of September that five hundred pounds of powder daily were produced.

It was soon perceived that to increase the supply, a special refinery for saltpetre would have to be erected; works accordingly were projected, commenced, and mainly completed, at Nashville, by the 9th October, on which day 1,500 lbs. were refined, and this amount was gradually increased to 3,000 lbs. daily. Experts were not to be found, and for some days every part of the operations were carried on under my personal instruction.

Gunpowder contains three-fourths of its weight of saltpetre, and to have its proper and enduring strength, this constituent must be refined to almost chemical purity. Thus the obtaining of this material and its preparation, became matters of the highest consideration.

The Governor of Georgia, at the suggestion of Lieutenant Boggs, late of the Ordnance Department of the old army, had purchased a small cargo of saltpetre and sulphur in Philadelphia, which fortunately arrived safely at Savannah just before that port was blockaded. This store of material, although comparatively small, was of extraordinary value, as from it mainly the gunpowder for General A. S. Johnson's army was supplied, as well as the Batteries at Fort Pillow, Island Number 10, and Memphis, on the Mississippi river.

The earth of the limestone caves of Tennessee, Alabama, Georgia, Arkansas, and other States, was rich in nitrate of lime, and this salt was convertible into saltpetre by lixiviation and saturating with the lye of wood ashes. Some of these caves were personally visited, and great efforts made to have them worked to full capacity. Agents were sent out to investigate their capabilities with authority to make contracts, and supply the necessary information for their working; the last was accomplished by means of a pamphlet which I published in Nashville giving detailed instructions, and which was distributed throughout the country; it was republished in Richmond, New Orleans and other places. As rapidly as the crude saltpetre was [p] received from the caves it was refined and sent to the powder mills, and the products mostly sent to General A. S. Johnson's command. About 100,000 pounds of gunpowder were thus supplied before the fall of Nashville, besides a considerable amount sent to New Orleans and other places.

The caves of Arkansas were rich in nitrous earth, and those of Texas still more so, and these supplied the armies west of the Mississippi river with material for gunpowder. As early as practicable I sent out instructed powder-makers to both those States, who under the directions of the military authorities, assisted to put up the necessary powder mills for the Trans-Mississippi department, which after the fall of Nashville was left necessarily to its own resources.

In the early part of November my time had become so much occupied that it was no longer practicable to attend to the production of saltpetre, and Mr. F. H. Smith was sent from Richmond by the Chief of Ordnance to relieve me from its duties. At a later day a separate department was established, called the Nitre and Mining Bureau, which then had the entire charge of its production.

In the latter part of November, by the desire of General Lovell—the able officer in command at New Orleans—I proceeded to that city and examined the temporary arrangements for making gunpowder, and also conferred with him relative to procuring a supply of saltpetre from abroad. He suggested the chartering of the steamship Tennessee, then lying idle in the river near the city, to proceed at once to Liverpool and take in a cargo of saltpetre and return to New Orleans, or, in case of necessity, to put in at Charleston or Wilmington. The suggestion met my views, and was approved by Mr. Benjamin, then Secretary of War, but was not carried out on account of the effective blockade of the mouth of the Mississippi.

The Confederate Government, however, by its agents in Europe, purchased saltpetre which was shipped on swift blockade runners which arrived from time to time at Charleston and Wilmington. This proved to be adequate to our wants, and about two millions, seven hundred thousand pounds were thus received during the war and sent to the Confederate Powder Works. The amount obtained from the caves amounted to about three hundred thousand pounds for the same period. Thus the total amount received at the works amounted to about 1,500 tons.

The Governor and Military Committee of Tennessee, in making [p] the contracts for war material, had engaged Mr. Whiteman, of Nashville, an energetic citizen, to construct a Powder Mill at Manchester, who at my suggestion adopted the incorporating process of heavy rollers on an iron circular bed, such as I had proposed to employ at the Confederate Powder Works erected at Augusta. The construction of this mill was urged on so successfully, that by the middle of October one set of rollers was in operation, and a second set in course of erection; a month later, by supplying saltpetre and charcoal from the refinery at Nashville, 1,500 pounds of gunpowder were daily produced.

I had proposed at an early period to make this Powder Mill a school of instruction for a few selected men, so as to have them ready for service at the Augusta Powder Works when they should commence operations—similarly to what had been done at the Refinery at Nashville, where men were being taught to refine saltpetre and distill charcoal. Before the occupation of Nashville by the Federal forces, these men, together with the machinery and articles of the Refinery in that city, were removed to the Augusta Works; thus they were supplied at the commencement with the necessary means of operation, which could not have been otherwise accomplished. But one man—Wright—could be found in the Southern States who had seen gunpowder made by the incorporating mill—the only kind that can make it of the first quality; he had been a workman at the Waltham Abbey Government Gunpowder Works, in England. He was made available in the operation of the Manchester Mill, and afterwards for a short time at the Augusta Confederate Works, and although sadly defective in a certain way, I was much indebted to his knowledge and experience.

A singular good fortune happened at the commencement of my labors. I came into possession of an invaluable pamphlet by Major Bradley, the Superintendent of the Waltham Abbey Works; in this the entire process and machinery employed at that Factory—the best existing in any country—was succinctly stated; drawings, or working plans, or details of the buildings, or apparatus, however, were not given.

Nowhere could be found a publication in which this was done of any powder factory, hence in the projection of the Confederate Powder Works, I was thrown upon my own resources to supply these deficiencies.

During the many hours spent in railroad cars, these matters were thought over and planned separately as necessity required. A rough sketch was made, dimensions given, and location designated; this data was placed in the hands of capable men to carry out. In my young Architect and Civil Engineer, C. Shaler Smith, recommended by the proprietors of the Richmond Tredegar Iron Works, I at once recognised genius of a high order, and placed in his hands my rough sketches of buildings to elaborate and give architectural finish. All know with what result, the fine taste exhibited in the massive and beautiful structures which ornamented the banks of the Augusta Canal, for two miles, bore witness of his success.

Good fortune also brought to my notice, by a casual encounter with General Pendleton, Chief of Artillery at Richmond, a skilled machinist, who had served his time at the Tredegar Works, and was then a Sergeant in the Confederate army. He, William Pendleton, was applied for, and in his acquisition, was gained a man of capability and integrity, into whose hands could be confidently placed the erection of all the extensive machinery then in process of construction. The responsible duties of Superintendent of the Works were also committed to his charge.

The Tredegar Iron Works

The Tredegar Iron and Machine Works, at Richmond, were the only ones throughout the South, having adequate capabilities for the construction of the heavy and extensive machinery required in the projected Confederate Powder Works. They were only partially available for the purpose, however, as the demands made upon them for heavy artillery, and for all kinds of urgent work required by the Government, absorbed their resources, nevertheless, I was compelled to call upon them for most of the twelve circular iron beds, and twenty-four ponderous five ton iron rollers, with other work required for the incorporating Mills, which, together, weighed 240 tons; two of the rollers were made in Macon and two in Chattanooga.

The immense iron shaft, nearly three hundred feet long, varying from twelve inches in diameter at the central portions, to ten inches and eight inches, toward the extremities, was cast and completed in sections, mainly, at the Webster Foundry and Machine Works at the latter city; here, also, were made the twelve heavy spur wheels, and twelve powerful friction arrangements to start and stop gradually each set of rollers separately, as the main shaft, working in the [p] extensive subterranean archway, which extended below the line of mills, continued its incessant revolutions.

The great gear-wheel, sixteen feet in diameter, attached to the centre of this shaft, giving it motion, with its corresponding massive pinion on the engine shaft, were cast and accurately finished at Atlanta.

The fine steam engine of 130-horse power, having two cylinders and a fly wheel of fourteen tons weight, and five boilers was made at the North just before the war, and brought to that city to be used in a flouring mill. This was purchased as being exactly the motive power required.

It was designed to make use of the water power of the canal for all purposes, but its available capacities at that time would not permit this, for the large amount required by the incorporating mills; it was employed at the other and more dangerous buildings, which required a smaller amount of power. Two smaller steam engines—one procured at Macon and the other at Selma—were employed in the Refining building. Two Hydraulic Presses were procured at Richmond; the twelve iron evaporating pans, each holding five hundred gallons, were cast at the large Iron Works on the Cumberland River, in Tennessee. The extensive copper drying pans for the powdered saltpetre, being together forty feet long by nine feet broad, were made at Nashville; the four cast iron Retorts, four feet long by three feet in diameter, with eight cast iron coolers, and twelve sheet iron slip cylinders of nearly the same dimensions, were made at the Augusta Confederate Foundry and Machine Works, where also all the smaller machinery required was constructed. Copper boilers were procured from Wilmington, N. C., being made of large turpentine stills; pumps, pipe and cement from Charleston; sheet copper from Savannah and Nashville; tin and zinc for roofing from Mobile; the larger steam pipes from Hight's Foundry, in Augusta, and the smaller from New Orleans; iron and coal for castings were had from North Georgia and Alabama, and copper from Ducktown, in Tennessee.

Thus material was gathered from all the Southern States to unite with the resources of the City of Augusta, to construct the largest and finest Gunpowder Factory to be found in any country.

On the 20th of July, 1861, I examined the Augusta Canal and resources of the city, and later selected the location of the Powder [p] Works, beginning at the site of the United States old Magazine, half a mile from the western city limit. Land adjacent was purchased, and also that between the canal and the river for a distance of two miles, so that the different buildings required, might be separated by intervals of at least one thousand feet for safety in case any one of them should have an explosion.

It was remarkable that the most favorable conditions required in the erection of an extensive Powder manufactory, were all met at this location, and nowhere else attainable. These are:

1. A central point of the country, for obvious reasons.
2. On a main line of railroad communication, to distribute the products to all parts of the country.
3. On a canal or river, which could afford a safe and economical means of transportation of the pulverized materials in process of manufacture, at the same time affording the necessary water-power to the different buildings.
4. In the neighborhood of a town or city, from which mechanics and employees, as well as necessary articles, could be obtained.
5. A location near which the best building materials could be procured for permanent structures.
6. A temperate climate, where operations could be continued throughout the year without obstructions from ice, and to avoid the hazard and expense of warming the building.
7. A district of country free from lime and earthy salts, so that the large amount of water required in the operations of the Saltpetre Refinery should be as nearly pure as possible.
8. A location which would insure an abundant and cheap supply of the proper kind of wood required in the making of gunpowder.
9. A situation which, whilst sufficiently near a town to procure readily supplies and workmen, should, at the same time, be removed so far off that the dangerous structures, should an explosion occur, would cause no damage to the nearest inhabitant.
10. Hence, also, the canal or stream on which the works exist, should have but little traffic or commerce, and, in the vicinity of the works, should pass through a sparsely inhabited district.

The Augusta Canal, having been selected for the site of the Confederate Powder Works, contracts were immediately entered into for the brick, stone and carpenter's work, on very favorable terms.

At the beginning of the war, business was more or less paralyzed, [] so that the manufacturers and builders were, to a considerable extent, thrown out of employment, which enabled contracts to be made advantageously at the usual prices. Thus, the total cost of the entire works did not exceed three hundred and eighty-five thousand dollars.

The erection of these works on the ground of economy alone, was of great service to the Confederate Government. The extreme hazard of importing gunpowder through the blockade, raised its average price, the first year of the war, to three dollars per pound. There were made one million pounds at the works in that period, at a total cost, including the materials, of one million and eighty thousand dollars; thus saving to the Government in one year, one million, nine hundred and twenty thousand dollars.

The requisite land having been purchased, and contracts made for building materials, the site of the main buildings were located by myself, and construction commenced on the 13th of September, 1861, under the immediate supervision of Mr. —— Grant, a young civil engineer from Savannah. These buildings were erected of the excellent bricks supplied by the Augusta and Hamburg yards, which were worked to their full capacity, and above five millions were supplied. The handsome granite of Stone Mountain, on the Georgia Railroad, was employed for the sills, lintels, copings, and foundation stones. The whole of the buildings were erected by Messrs. Denning and Bowe, of Augusta, the former having immediate charge, and could not be surpassed for excellence of workmanship.

The first structure—or the one nearest the city—was called the Refinery building, because the central portion was used for such purposes, but it included a saltpetre and sulphur warehouse, of a capacity of fifteen hundred tons, on the east end, and a charcoal department and machine shop with a steam engine on the west end. Rifle and ballistic pendulums on the northeast, and the steam boiler house on the northwest portions. There were four square towers at the corners, used as offices; the entire structure forming three sides of a square, fronting two hundred and fifty feet along the canal, and extending back two hundred and seventy-five feet. The north side was mostly a brick enclosure with high walls, but having no roof, and temporarily used for storing wood—its ultimate destination was for workshops.

Within the square were located the kilns for drying the wood to] be distilled in the charcoal retorts; the copper boilers and other apparatus for the extraction of the saltpetre from damaged powder; as also the arrangement for the final extraction of the saltpetre from the refuse of the Refinery; lastly, the great chimney, into which all the smoke flues of the entire structure terminated.

In the projection of this part of the Powder Works, I conceived the design of making the central portion present the appearance of a grand monumental structure. For this purpose the chimney was placed centrally, and its exterior dimensions considerably enlarged; in fact, it is composed of two distinct parts, the chimney and outside obelisk; the former being enclosed at its base by a square tower, nineteen by thirty-five feet in height, whose battlements arose to view above the front walls. From the top of this tower the enveloping obelisk commenced, and ascended one hundred and fifteen feet, making the complete structure one hundred and fifty feet from the ground to the coping. The interior chimney flue is five feet square from bottom to top. The corner stone, or rather the box, containing the usual documents, was, by a fancy of the architect, placed in one of the corners of the top coping of the obelisk.

The saltpetre refinery occupied the right central portion of the front, being sixty-five feet long, fifty-five feet broad and thirty feet high, open from the floor to the ventilated roof. At the east end were four of the large evaporating iron pans, placed side by side, and elevated three feet above the floor by the brick work which surrounded them; five similar pans were in a corresponding position at the west end, and the large copper drying pans occupied forty feet along the north side at the same height. Each evaporating pan had a separate furnace, and the heated air from the whole passed beneath, and in contact with the bottoms of the drying pans on its way to the great chimney; the furnaces opened into side rooms communicating with the outside open space in the rear of the building. Thus the refining room was entirely free from ashes, dust and smoke.

The centre space of the floor, about thirty-six feet square, was sunk four feet to allow water from the canal to pass around the bottoms of two of the large evaporating pans, which were placed therein near the centre of this area, and nine feet apart; these were used for a special purpose.

The best quality of gunpowder can only be made from the purest [p] saltpetre; the impurities of the crude material are mainly deliquescent salts, which rapidly deteriorate the strength of the powder by the moisture absorbed. To refine more or less the rough saltpetre of commerce is then a necessity even in producing an inferior article.

To carry the refining process to the extent of nearly absolute purity, required several successive crystallizations and washings, involving a large amount of manual labor in the manipulation, and consuming much time. This was particularly the case in the very large amount of saltpetre, eight to ten thousand pounds per day, used by the Works, the refining of which would demand extended buildings and apparatus, as well as requiring a large number of operatives. Hence, it became desirable to devise methods by which hand labor could be superseded by motive power and machinery; in this I was entirely successful. Thus, in the operations of filling the various boiling pans with water or mother-liquor; the transference of the boiling solution of saltpetre to the draining trough, and thence to the crystallizing machines; the cooling down of the solutions, and their constant agitation to break up the forming crystals into fine particles, and transferring of these to an adjoining tank; the washing of the crystallized mass, and the subsequent removal of the mother-liquor and wash-waters, were all accomplished by machinery, with the assistance of two or three workmen only.

The saving of time and labor was thus manifest, and the rapidity with which these operations were performed, permitted a double and triple process in a single day; thus allowing a degree of purity in the product of refined saltpetre not attained in any other refinery. Its purity was such generally, that there was not the one-hundred-thousandth part of chlorides left in the salt.

Of the machinery used, the most important was a bronze revolving wheel with buckets attached to the periphery, which worked into an iron pan or kettle, whose section was an arc of a circle; the buckets grazed the surface of the bottom and sides of this kettle, the bottom of the latter being immersed in a current of cold water. The hot filtered solution of the crude saltpetre was received into this kettle, and thus kept into a state of rapid agitation, the effect being to produce a wet mass of minute crystals, which, as fast as formed, were taken up by the sharp edged buckets, and lifted sufficiently high to pour into a receiving vat; this permitted the liquid part to flow back [p] into the kettle. By this means in a short time the entire mass of fine deposited crystals from the rapidly cooled liquid, were removed to the vat. When the operation was completed the remaining liquid in the kettle was by the revolutions of the bronze wheel, discharged into one of the eight capacious cisterns below the floor; there were two of these machines employed.

The facility for work which this apparatus, with the other mechanical appliances afforded, enabled the refinery to carry the purification of the saltpetre beyond that of the most celebrated powder factories.

Adjoining this part of the Works was the Sulphur Refinery, where this material was prepared from the crude stock, and made ready for the incorporating process. About one hundred and thirty tons of very impure sulphur had been received from Louisiana, for the use of the Powder Works; it had been purchased before the war by the planters for use in the making of sugar, and was bought up by the Confederate officers. The best quality of gunpowder has its sulphur chemically pure, which could be demonstrated by showing no trace of acid when powdered and boiled in water, and should entirely evaporate on a piece of glass when heated, leaving no stain. This can only be accomplished practically by distillation. The crude article was melted and poured into upright, thick wooden boxes five feet high and ten inches square at the bottom, tapering upwards; when cold the earthy matters would be found in the lower portion by subsidence, leaving about three feet apparently pure. This was broken off and placed into two kettles of suitable form and dimensions, having furnaces; the tops of these kettles were connected by a bent iron pipe to an enlarged portion, which was surrounded with water. On the application of heat the sulphur vaporized, and passing over through the pipe was condensed in the cooled portion, whence it trickled in a thick stream into a receiving vessel below; the first portions being rejected, the remainder was of a beautiful citron yellow when cold, and entirely pure.

Unlike the refined saltpetre, the purified sulphur had to be pulverized and bolted like flour before being used. The former was done by two iron wheels of twelve inches face and five feet diameter, weighing six hundred pounds each, revolving on a bed circle of iron like the incorporating rollers; the later was accomplished by bolters, but when these were worn out and could not be replaced, for want [p] of the silk cloth, which was not to be found in the South, necessity compelled me to devise a different, and as it proved, a superior method.

The pulverized sulphur was placed in barrels or cylinders, with hollow axles, which were made to revolve slowly by machinery; there were ledges on the interior which caused the sulphur to be lifted and poured over as the cylinders revolved; a light current of air was blown through each, entering the hollow axle at one end, and passing out through the axle at the other end, which led into an adjoining room; there the impalpable sulphur dust was deposited, much finer than by the usual bolting process.

Adjoining this Refinery was the department in which charcoal was made and pulverized. Charcoal for gunpowder has to be made of a porous fine-grained wood, having very little ashes when burned; willow is generally preferred, and was used at first in the Powder Works, but the exigencies of the war taking away those who would ordinarily have supplied it, rendered it impracticable to procure a sufficient quantity. Recourse was had to the cotton wood, which was abundant; on trial its charcoal was found fully equal to that of the willow for the purpose, and was, thereafter always used.

Charcoal for gunpowder must be made by what is termed the distilling process; that is, the wood must be heated in iron retorts to the proper degree, to have it of the best quality and free from sand or grit. For this purpose cast iron cylinders, or retorts, six feet long and four feet in diameter were used, placed over furnaces, each having one end solid and the other with a movable cover; into these were run the slip cylinders, which contained the kiln dried cotton wood, split up into sticks about one and a half inches in diameter, and entirely filling it.

The slip cylinders were charged with the wood in an outside apartment, their covers put on, then readily moved by cranes to the retorts, into which they were pushed; the covers of which were then luted with clay and closely applied. The bottoms of the retorts being perforated, permitted the escape of the vapors and gases into the furnaces beneath, where inflaming, they supplied mainly the heat required in the operation. In about two hours the slip cylinders were withdrawn from the retorts and moved by the cranes over, and lowered into the cast iron coolers beneath the floor; these had water from the canal circulating around them; the covers being then put [p] on to exclude the air, the mass of charcoal was rapidly cooled. As soon as a slip cylinder was removed from a retort a freshly charged one would take its place, and thus the process was continued. The slip cylinders were taken out of the coolers in succession by the cranes, and swung over a long and broad table upon which their contents were dropped; here the sticks of charcoal were separately examined and the imperfect rejected. The charcoal was then placed in pulverizing barrels with bronze balls, which revolving by machinery, soon reduced it more or less to a fine powder; it was then bolted, and with the sulphur and saltpetre taken to the weighing house. Here the three materials were arranged into sixty pounds charges, by mingling forty-five pounds of saltpetre, nine pounds of charcoal and six pounds of sulphur, which was then moistened and ready for incorporation.

Reflecting over the processes for making gunpowder, it suggested itself that the chemical reactions would necessarily have the most favorable conditions, when there should be the most intimate approximation of the component molecules. That, as the charcoal by its combustion with the oxygen of the saltpetre, supplied the expanded gases which produced the explosive force, it was of the first consideration that there should be the most perfect mixture practicable between these two ingredients. Under the microscope a fine particle of charcoal was seen to be a mass of carbon penetrated by numerous pores, hence it became necessary to completely fill these minute pores with the saltpetre to have the best condition. This might be accomplished by the usual processes, as the charge is kept moistened when stamped or rolled, but as it will not answer to have the mass wet during the incorporating operation, only moist or damp, the completion of the process was necessarily delayed. If this mass of material could be made into a semi-liquid condition by the action of steam, the hot solution of saltpetre would speedily penetrate the minute pores of the charcoal, and thus the desired end would be rapidly attained.

Accordingly, the following process was devised: The moistened sixty pounds charges, roughly mixed and moistened with water, were introduced into horizontal cylinders of sheet copper thirty inches long by eighteen inches in diameter. These cylinders revolved slowly on a common axis, consisting of a heavy brass tube three inches in diameter, perforated with holes. High pressure [p] steam was introduced through the tube raising the temperature to the boiling point while the water produced by condensation, added to that originally used to moisten the materials, reduced them to a semi-liquid slush, which was run out of the cylinders after about eight minutes rotation. On cooling, this mud became a damp solid cake, the saltpetre which in the state of boiling hot saturated solution had entered the minutest pores of the charcoal, now crystallizing. The cake as produced was transferred to the incorporating mills, and under the five ton rollers was in an hour brought to the condition of finished mill cake, ready to be cooled and granulated, while without the steaming process, four hours incorporation in the mills had previously been necessary to produce powder of the same first-class character. The capacity of the work of the mills was thus practically quadrupled, the thorough saturation of the charcoal with saltpetre being accomplished by the steaming, while it remained for the rollers merely to complete the incorporation of the whole mass and give the required density to the mill cake.

The Incorporating Mills, twelve in number, extended along the canal beyond the Refinery building and further back from its bank, having the Laboratory between the two; they were two hundred and ninety-six feet long. This separation was for safety, as they worked explosive material. The walls were massive, being four to ten feet thick, the horizontal section of each being that of a huge mortar of seventeen feet wide by twenty-four feet long; the height of the walls was twenty-eight feet; they faced alternately in opposite directions, so that an explosion of one would not be communicated to those adjoining.

The fronts were constructed of light wood and glass, and the roofs of sheet zinc, so that but slight resistance would be offered, upwards and outwards, to the explosive force. A wing wall, nearly as high as the main walls, and three feet thick, extended outwards from the centre of the exterior back wall of each mill twenty feet, to guard still further against the effects of an explosion. Behind these the powder-makers stood, for safety, while starting or stopping the motion of the ponderous rollers. This was done by means of a long lever, which threw in or out of gear the friction arrangement, which worked each set beneath the floor, in the thick archway which extended from end to end beneath the mills. It has already been stated that this archway contained the great iron shaft [p18] which imparted motion to all the mills, and which derived its own from the large steam engine, which was located above, in the centre apartments separating the mills into two divisions.

In addition to the above precautions to prevent the explosion of a mill from extending to the others, above each set of rollers was balanced a vessel containing about thirty gallons of water. This was connected by means of a small iron shaft with a similar vessel to each mill of the division. Thus, on an explosion in one mill, its bed-plate was instantly drenched with water, and this caused the same to take place at the same moment with all the others.

These precautions were rendered the more necessary by the carelessness of the powder-makers, who might not remove the broke up powder cake from the mill enclosure before placing a new charge under the rollers, thus having one hundred and twenty pounds of material to take fire at the same time—as once happened—producing a powerful explosion. There occurred only three explosions at these mills—all before the steaming process was adopted—and in the first only was any one injured. In that one no material harm was done, as the two powder-makers—exposed by their own carelessness—were at work again in a few days. This explosion completely destroyed the slight roof, as well as the wood and glass front, but did scarcely any other damage to the mill, and had no action on the other mills further than drenching their beds with water. The other two explosions were insignificant.

These incorporating mills consisted, each, of an iron circular flat bed of seven feet diameter, fixed in a mass of masonry built up above the brick archway, through the center of the floor, to a convenient height. On this bed two massive iron rollers, six feet in diameter and fifteen inches face, revolved. Each weighed five tons. They had a common axle of wrought iron, of five inches diameter, and a vertical shaft of cast iron passing through the centre of the bed, having a rectangular cross-head through which the axle worked. This shaft connected below with the machinery which gave it motion from the main shaft.

These rollers were not equi-distant from the centre of revolution, by which arrangement every part of the charge of materials on the bed was subjected to their action—which was crushing, grinding, mixing and compressing; grinding and mixing from the twisting motion which followed from so large a diameter revolving in so [p] small a circle, and crushing and compressing from the weight of the rollers.

To keep the powder on the bed, a wooden curb, funnel-shaped, two feet high was placed around the circumference, fitting closely, extending outwards at an angle of forty-five degrees. In the centre of the bed was a short cylinder of metal, two feet in diameter and six inches high, through the top of which the vertical shaft passed. This prevented the powder working inwards. It also acted as a steam-chamber to keep the bed-plate warm; but this was not used for the purpose, since the steaming process rendered it unnecessary. A scraper, or plow, followed each roller, which continually broke up the powder-cake, mixed its fragments, and kept them in the path of the rollers.

At the commencement of the operation the charge of sixty pounds of steamed materials was uniformly distributed over the bed; the rollers were then set into motion, revolving about ten times each minute, which continued for an hour; the broken up powder, or mill cake, which was about five-eighths of an inch thick, was then removed from the bed, having a blackish grey color and taken to the cooling magazines. These were excavated in the clay and rock on the other side of the canal, about one hundred yards distant; were four in number and separated from each other; here the mill cake became cold and hard, and was ready for the next operation, that of granulation. The permanent building in which this was done was about fifteen hundred feet distant from the Powder Mills, on the same side, further up the canal; this, as well as each of the other permanent structures, was made of brick, having thin walls and light roofs. Wood in the damp atmosphere of the canal speedily decayed.

A natural growth of trees and brush-wood intervened between the buildings along the canal, which were generally situated about one thousand feet apart; thus the explosion of any one of them would be harmless to the remainder. There was a temporary structure of wood used at first for granulation, about one hundred yards distant from the permanent building, on the opposite side of the canal; this, after a use of some months, exploded with about three tons of gunpowder.

The explosion was heavy, shaking the earth for some distance, and throwing up a convolving column of flame and white smoke [p] five hundred feet in height. It was composed of a series of confused masses of smoke and heated air revolving in vertical planes with extraordinary velocity, through which the flames flashed outwards in all directions; this was followed by the thundering sound of the explosion, which vibrated the air for a mile around, and was heard within the limits of the city.

There were seven men within the structure, a sentinel outside, and a boy with a mule in a shed adjoining. The bodies of the seven men and the boy, with the debris, were carried up with the ascending column, and by its revolving action, reduced mainly to small fragments and dispersed; the sentinel was killed by the shock, but his body was not otherwise disturbed. A growth of small pines surrounded the place, which effectually intercepted the lateral flying fragments; in fact the force of the explosion did not extend outside a diameter of one hundred feet, but within that area the trees were destroyed and the space where the structure stood was ploughed up and nothing remained. At the time there was no work being done, as the workmen were awaiting the arrival of the boat with the mill cake. The careful foreman, Gibson, had been called away, and probably the accident happened from matches falling on the floor, as it had been found impossible to prevent their use by the workmen, for smoking, when off duty. This was the only explosion at the Works during the war, except the three at the Mills, already mentioned. It demonstrated the safety of the arrangements, since there was no damage to any portion of the Works except the destruction of the glass sashes, and a slight movement of the roof of the permanent granulating building, about one hundred yards distant. This was about to be occupied, having been completed.

In the granulating building the cold mill cake was broken up into fragments by bronze toothed cylinders of small diameter, and then by smooth ones; these worked in pairs, and successively, in connection with vibratory screens and sieving, all in one machine. By the action of this arrangement the powder cake was broken into fragments, separated into different sizes of grain, and each delivered into its proper receptacle. A very large grained powder, each grain being a cube of one inch in dimensions, and weighing about one ounce, was made by a separate manipulation of the powder cake, and used for the very largest guns only.

From the granulating building the powder was taken to the [p] drying, dusting and glazing department, 2500 feet further up the canal. There was an intermediate building designed and used for several months, as the dusting and glazing department, the drying alone being done in the one above mentioned; afterwards the three processes were carried on together in one structure. It was soon perceived that the drying process, which was done by similar arrangements to those used at the government works at Waltham Abbey, England, that is, by placing the powder in small quantities in shallow trays in a frame work, over steam heated pipes, required considerable manual labor and occupied much time. It occurred to me that the same could be accomplished more speedily and with far less labor, by a single operation, which would likewise perform the glazing and dusting.

To accomplish this the powder from the granulating house was placed in revolving cylinders having hollow axles, and a current of air warmed by passing through an arrangement of steam pipes was blown through, carrying the dust into its receptacle, leaving the grains clear. This also dried and glazed them at the same time. Thus by one operation, by machinery, all three processes were accomplished, resulting in a large saving of labor and time. In addition, a beautiful jet black glazing was given by admitting a small quantity of steam at the proper time to the current of air, while the barrels revolved. This was not generally done, however, as it was regarded of but slight, if any, practical value, the usual glazing answering all required purposes.

Two hundred yards from this department was the boiler house supplying the steam required for the pipes used in the drying process. Its chimney was one hundred yards still further removed, communicating with the furnace by a subterranean arched flue; thus sparks would have had to drift over three hundred yards to reach the clean metal roof of the drying building.

The finished gunpowder was taken to the next building, one thousand five hundred feet beyond, up the canal, where it was weighed out and put into strong wood boxes about two and a half feet long, by one foot square, having the ends let into grooves; one of the ends had a strong wood screw, two inches diameter, with an octagonal head. Experience proved that these powder boxes, a devise of my own from necessity, were superior to barrels, being stronger, occupying less room, standing transportation better, and [p] safer in use. No explosion ever occurred in their transportation, notwithstanding the occasional Railroad accidents, and the many thousands that were sent from the Powder Works during the war.

The powder boxes being filled, were then transported to the magazine, three quarters of a mile still further up the canal. This wood structure was on a rising ground one hundred yards from the canal, enclosed by a high fence. Its capacity was about one hundred tons of gunpowder.

At this, and every other separate building of the Powder Works, a sentinel was stationed day and night, and the utmost vigilance used. Also, each of the separate buildings along the canal, except the magazine, containing large amounts of gunpowder, were enclosed with high brick walls, having a single entrance.

At the Waltham Abbey Works, in England, the gunpowder cake after being crushed, is subjected to compression by the hydraulic press to give it sufficient density. I found that by using five ton rollers, the proper compression could be given in the powder mills during the incorporation, thus saving much labor and time. The hydraulic press, consequently was only used to compress the powder dust into thin cakes, which were sent to the granulating department to be used for fine grain powder only.

The press house was located between the Cooling Magazines and the granulating building on the same side of the canal as the former. It was a large brick structure provided with two hydraulic presses, cranes, and other appliances, with a turbine water wheel to supply the required motive power. After the discovery that the proper density could be better given to the powder cake, by using sufficiently heavy rollers during the incorporation, this department was used only for the purpose above stated.

The interval of ninety feet between the Refinery building and the Incorporating Mills, was mainly occupied by a fine building called the Laboratory. It had a projecting tower in the front centre, twenty-five feet square at the lower stories, which together were forty-five feet in elevation. From this the upper portion fifteen feet square ascended to the height of thirty feet, making seventy-five feet in all. The upper part of this constituted the clock tower with its four large circular openings for dials. These could be seen for a long distance.

This building which was very striking in its appearance, was [p] never completed in its interior, as the different work to be here performed was being done at the Arsenal sufficiently well, in temporary structures. Awaiting the completion of the clock, the time was struck by hand, every half hour on the large bell suspended temporarily, in the open building in rear of the Refinery.

The continual testing of the powder, as it was being manufactured to insure its equality in strength, and to ascertain its exact propelling force, was done for the fine graded powders, by excellent musket and ballistic pendulums constructed at the Confederate Machine Works in Augusta under my direction. For the cannon or large grain powders, by the initial velocities given to the proper projectiles in an eight inch Columbia. To determine these velocities an accurately made electro-ballistic machine, such as was employed at the West Point Military Academy, was constructed at the same works. Also Rodman's apparatus for determining the absolute pressure on each square inch of the bore of the gun, exerted by the charge. In addition to these instruments, complete arrangements for determining the gravimetric densities and hygrometric properties of different samples of gunpowder were made.

The foregoing appliances enabled accurate comparisons to be made at all points between different gunpowders, and to determine the various matters required in the manufacture of the first quality for the various arms of service. That this was successfully done was certified to by Boards of Artillery and Infantry Officers; after the war the captured powder of these works was used in the School of Artillery practice at Fort Monroe, on account of its superiority.

Mr. Davis, whilst President of the Confederacy, visited the works, then in active operation, and in his recent valuable book, speaks in more than one place in flattering terms of their products. Articles published in the London Times were highly commendatory of the

Works and their results, which were copied in Continental papers. They were visited by many distinguished civil and military gentlemen, both native and foreign.

The great extent of the Powder Works and their immense capabilities, were the admiration of all visitors. This was mainly due to the foresight of the President of the Confederacy, who, comprehending the requirements of a great war, then scarcely commenced, strongly drew my attention to the probable necessity of very large supplies of gunpowder to meet the service of artillery of great [p] calibre, which would probably be employed, as well as the largely increased quantities necessary to meet the rapid firing of the improved small arms, with which infantry and cavalry were now supplied.

The daily product of the Works varied with the demand for gunpowder, and with the amount of saltpetre on hand. At no time after their completion were they worked to their full capacity; indeed, were only worked during daylight. Even when supplying the urgent call of General Ripley at Charleston for cannon powder, to replace the twenty-two thousand pounds consumed during the action with the iron-clad fleet; two days' work nearly supplied that amount.

Notwithstanding the admirable serving of the heavy artillery at Fort Sumter during that engagement, it would have fallen and Charleston captured, had any but the strongest gunpowder been used. The armor of the iron-clads, though constructed expressly to withstand the heaviest charges and projectiles, gave way before its propelling force. Mr. Davis makes the statement that the engagement between the Alabama and Kearsarge would have resulted in a victory for the former, had Admiral Semmes been supplied with the powder from these works. Any failure in their construction and products would have rested with myself. A carte blanche had been given, and there was no one to share the appalling responsibility.

There were made at the Confederate Powder Works at Augusta, commencing April 10, 1862, and terminating April 18, 1865, 2,750,000 pounds, or one thousand, three hundred and seventy-five tons of gunpowder. This was distributed throughout the Confederacy, mostly east of the Mississippi river. There remained on hand, at the Magazine, at the end of operations, about seventy thousand pounds, besides considerable amounts of saltpetre and other material.

The Navy Department during the war established a manufactory of gunpowder at Petersburg, Virginia, which was afterwards removed to Charlotte, North Carolina, and then to Columbia, South Carolina. A powder mill was put into operation at Richmond, Virginia, also, at Raleigh, North Carolina, but the extent of their operations is unknown. Two small stamping mills in the northwestern portion of South Carolina, near the mountains, which were erected to make blasting powder for the neighboring tunnel, were [p] visited, but I found that they could be made available only to a very limited extent.

The Confederate Powder Works were so constructed that the rough materials were received at the building nearest the city; thence successively passed up the canal from building to building in the progressive stages of manufacture, until it arrived finished and ready for shipping at the Magazine.

To facilitate the transportation, a short branch of railroad was constructed connecting the canal basin with the Georgia Railroad. The safe, economical, and ready means of transportation by the canal were invaluable; no accident ever happened, notwithstanding the immense amount of combustible material—over two thousand five hundred tons—which had passed to and fro over it during the three years of operations. From the canal bank to the entrance of each building, the walks were covered with compressed sawdust, and rubber shoes were worn by all operatives in the departments containing gunpowder.

It is an interesting fact that Augusta was the only city of note in the South, which was not occupied at some time by the Federal forces during the war; here the flag of the Confederacy floated undisturbed to the end.

The extensive Sibley Cotton Factory has been erected on a portion of the site of the Refinery, Laboratory and Incorporating Mills, and so arranged that the Confederate obelisk stands conspicuously in front of the centre; the battlemented and ornamental architecture of the Powder Works was adopted in the construction of the Factory buildings, which give them a fine and noble appearance.

Here was once heard the noise of the clanking wheels and muffled sounds of the ponderous rollers of war, as they slowly concentrated into black masses the enormous energies which were to shake the earth and air, with the roar and deafening explosions of the battle field. Now the air is again filled with the sounds of moving machinery, but it is the busy hum of peaceful occupations which assist to clothe the world from the white cotton fields of Georgia. The black material of war has given away to the white staple of peace.

Of the extensive Confederate Powder Works nothing remains [] except the obelisk enclosing the great Chimney. Its battlemented tower and lofty shaft, large proportions and beautiful workmanship, will bear evidence of the magnitude and style of their construction to future generations.

Appendix.

To the special duties of the manufacture of gunpowder were added the command of the Augusta Arsenal, on the 7th April, 1862, and at a later period that of the Military District of Augusta. In the early part of February, 1863, in connection with Captain Fairfax, of the Confederate Navy, the duties of getting into effective operation the extensive and unfinished Foundry Works constructed at Selma, Alabama, under contract with the War and Navy Departments, were superadded. When the communication with Richmond was endangered, in the latter part of the war, all the Arsenals south of Virginia, were committed to my charge.

It had been the design at an early period, of the Chief of Ordnance, to convert the Arsenal at Augusta into one of construction, and Capt. Gill was placed in charge with that object in view. On taking command, I found there were no existing facilities for large constructive works; thus the intention had to be for the time, abandoned, but it was found available, by the erection of several wood structures, for lighter work, such as the preparation of cartridges, fixed ammunition, signal rockets, fuses, primers, grenades, nitric acid, fulminates and percussion caps, etc.

Charleston, S.C. Confederate torpedoes, shot, and shell in the Arsenal yard

It was necessary for works of construction to make available the water power of the canal within the city; accordingly, a Machine and Foundry establishment, then lying idle, was purchased. Air and cupola furnaces, etc., were added to the Foundry, and lathes, planers, drills, etc., were purchased from Holly Springs, Mississippi, and Columbus, Georgia, and from Selma, Alabama, and other places, and added to those already present in the Machine Works. Also an extensive and complete gun-carriage department was erected, and a powder-box manufactory established, together with several houses for the preparation of small arm cartridges, and other purposes. These structures were rapidly erected, and machinists, founders, blacksmiths, tinners, harness makers, armorers, etc., and the various material required, were gathered from all available sources. The large brick building erected by Captain Gill at the Arsenal was converted into a harness and equipment department for field artillery; also used for tin and blacksmith shops, hospital and warehouse.

I was fortunate in obtaining skilled men for the heads of the several departments; among these were, at the Arsenal, Professor Wilson, Chemist; Master Armorer Oliver and F. Smyth; the last had charge of the Tinners' department, and also was Captain of the Operatives' Military company.

At the City Works were Foundry Superintendent Van Buren, of Clarksville; Superintendent Markey, of the Gun Carriage Department; Superintendent Walker, of the Machine Works. Mr. Wyman had charge of the Harness and Saddle and Equipment Department, but the artillery harness was mostly manufactured in the city, very satisfactorily, by Messrs. Jessup, Hatch and Day. There were several valuable foremen in the different shops, among them were Jaillet, Sharky, Shehan, Barr, and others, whose names are not recalled.

I was also materially assisted by Military Store-Keeper Girardey and several young officers—Captain Finney, and Lieutenants Waller, Collier, Sparrow, Hallam, and Cadet Lewis, and towards the close of operations by Captain Warren.

At the several works under my charge at Augusta, a large amount of war material was manufactured, in 1863, 1864 and part of 1865. The record of the last year has been lost. Among the various articles of the two above years were the following, copied from my official reports to the Chief of Ordnance:

110 Field Guns, mostly bronze, 12-pounder Napoleons. These guns were cast, turned, bored and finished complete at all points. Four of them now ornament the principal entrance to Washington's Headquarters, at Newburgh, New York.

174 Gun Carriages.

115 Caissons.

343 Limbers to Field Artillery.

21 Battery Wagons.

31 Traveling Forges.

10,535 Powder Boxes.

11,811 boxes for Small Arm Ammunition.

73,521 Horse Shoes.

12,630 Nitric Acid, pounds of.

2,227 ounces of Fulminate of Mercury.

2,455 Saddles, complete.

2,535 Artillery Harness, single sets of.

2,477 Signal Rockets.

85,800 rounds of Fixed Ammunition.

136,642 Artillery Cartridge Bags.

200,113 Time Fuses.

476,207 pounds of Artillery Projectiles.

4,580,000 Buckshot.

4,626,000 Lead Balls.

1,000,000 Percussion Caps.

10,760,000 Cartridges for Small Arms.

Together with an immense amount of Infantry, Artillery and Calvary equipments.

One hundred of the 12-pounder Napoleon guns were formed [p] into complete Batteries, and sent to the Army of Tennessee and North Georgia; the metal being received from Ducktown, Tennessee, and other places wherever it could be procured, including Church and other bells, and captured 6-pounder bronze cannon. The improved Hand-Grenades with General G. J. Raines' sensitive tubes were here manufactured, and many thousand sent to the Confederate armies.

The Army of Tennessee, before the fall of Atlanta, being at one period about to run short of small arm ammunition, and finding it impracticable to procure sufficient additional labor in time, a call was made on the ladies of Summerville and Augusta, to assist in making cartridges. This call was answered with all the promptness which their devotion to the cause inspired, and by their invaluable aid the danger was tided over by the production of 75,000 cartridges per day.

Letter from W.M. Cloer, 62nd Infantry, North Carolina
October 16, 1862

Dear Ann,

I an very glad to tell you that since I was writing on the 12th of October, my health is a good deal better than it was at that time and I would be glad to know that you are all well. I am about as well as ever only I am very weak yet.

Nothing new has happend. We have 2 more Tories in the guard house but that is not new to us. It is a old thing with us. We get some good news from Kentucky. There has been a big fight in KY. Our men joined the battle and took the near of 1000 prisoners besides arms and other goods and a heavy loss on each side and Kentucky in 3 weeks past has made up 32 Regiments for Southern service and is still making more but we hear more talk of peace. Now we hear have no more talk of us moving to Charleston, S.C. We will take winter quarters here. I expect that is the talk.

The Tennessee volunteers that turned out since se came here won't be took, they have to go as conscripts and by that there is none but us to guard this railroad and I think we will stay here during (the) war and I will be glad if we do for it is a first rate place here. Good cleaner people and good health and plenty to eat. When we have it to buy we can get it easy and we have that to do plenty often but we have been getting plenty for a few days.

Our regiment is the 62 Regt. instead of the first. I would note have wrote this letter but Gaffer did not get off as soon as he expected and I thought it proper to write a few and slip in with what I had wrote but I did not think I would write as much as I have but I don't care how I write when I begin.

The health of the company is generally good. Some of the boys is complaining but all is on foot and all in good heart playing like school boys and all friendly and clever good and kind to each other. Kelley and Enlow is as good to us as they can be. Henry is hardly ever here. Norton is gone home and none of us cares if he ever comes back. I would be glad to be with you now and I would talk better than I can write and a heap more things I could tell you than I can write for I can't write with any satisfaction and my hand trembles so that you know nobody else can read anything that I write but do the best you can with it and I will try to do better next time.

Tell the old women about there if they want needles for each one to send me 40 cents and what number of needles they want and I will get them. I have got you a paper of them but as this letter will be left in Franklin, I won't send them and if you need some let me know it and I will get them for you. I don't think there is any danger but I will get a furlough to go home when I want it and that will be the 15th day of November and if I have no bad luck I will be at home the 20th. I can't get anything to bring to the children when I come. There is nothing to get. I have tried to get a knife for Bud till I have give out trying anymore but maybe I can get something before I go home to take to them.

I want to see you all worse everyday and every day seems longer and the nights is very lonesome.

The weather is getting cool. There has been no frost here yet we get fruit to eat now, no chestnuts and if I was at home I would show you how to eat apples.

I will write you enough to back a letter to me commence.

W. M. Cloer

Zollicoffer P.O. Tenn
62 Regt NC troops

Co. D. in care of Capt. R. M. Henry

You may look for me the 20th or the 21st and you will see me if we don't move from here and I am able to travel. I love you better than I ever did. Take good care of the children and be good to them.

So I must conclude for this time. God bless you all. I am your best friend until death.

W. M. Cloer

Letter from Susann Cloer, Macon County, North Carolina

Dear Husband,

With pleasure I take the opportunity to write you a few lines to let you know that me and the children are all well and I hope that when these lines come to hand they will find you enjoying good health.

I received your letters and envelope and one paper that you sent by Ben Carpenter last Sunday evening. I was glad to still hear that you was coming home and we intend to watch for you that day and Sary keeps asking when that day will come. She says she will run to meet you before Bud or Lucy can get to you. I have nothing particular to write you. The sheep have been scattered but we have got them all but the old ram and I have never heard anything of him yet. We have plenty war news but none worth writing. The neighbors are all well except Liza Haston's oldest child and it is very low and is thought will not recover.

Lucy grows the fastest you ever saw and Bud is as fat as a bacon hog. Sary wants you to write word if you still read your little testament. I still look forward to the time when this bloody war shall cease and all the soldiers come home and stay and enjoy the peace and liberty that they did in gone by days when we will hear of war no more

And Abe shall quelled lie

And we will work around our door

And make our own supply.

I want you to take care of your knee and don't get cold in it. I want you to live in peace with all the company and particular with the officers. Gain their favor and affection. I would be glad to see you I know but I do the best I can believing you will discharge your duty as a brave and faithful soldier so that nothing else can be said to a rising generation and hope the time is not far off when this confusion will cease.

We have not had but 1 wedding about here since you left. That was John Maffat and Edy Spinzez.

You told me to prepare for kisses. You may fix your mouth too. So I will close and remain your loving companion until death.

Susann Cloer

A Confederate Girl's Diary

By Sarah Morgan Dawson

Books I & II

April 26th, 1862.

There is no word in the English language that can express the state in which we are, and have been, these last three days. Day before yesterday, news came early in the morning of three of the enemy's boats passing the Forts, and then the excitement began. It increased rapidly on hearing of the sinking of eight of our gunboats in the engagement, the capture of the Forts, and last night, of the burning of the wharves and cotton in the city while the Yankees were taking possession. To-day, the excitement has reached the point of delirium. I believe I am one of the most self-possessed in my small circle; and yet I feel such a craving for news of Miriam, and mother, and Jimmy, who are in the city, that I suppose I am as wild as the rest. It is nonsense to tell me I am cool, with all these patriotic and enthusiastic sentiments. Nothing can be positively ascertained, save that our gunboats are sunk, and theirs are coming up to the city. Everything else has been contradicted until we really do not know whether the city has been taken or not. We only know we had best be prepared for anything. So day before yesterday, Lilly and I sewed up our jewelry, which may be of use if we have to fly. I vow I will not move one step, unless carried away. Come what will, here I remain.

We went this morning to see the cotton burning - a sight never before witnessed, and probably never again to be seen. Wagons, drays, - everything that can be driven or rolled, - were loaded with the bales and taken a few squares back to burn on the commons. Negroes were running around, cutting them open, piling them up, and setting them afire. All were as busy as though their salvation depended on disappointing the Yankees. Later, Charlie sent for us to come to the river and see him fire a flatboat loaded with the precious material for which the Yankees are risking their bodies and souls. Up and down the levee, as far as we could see, negroes were rolling it down to the brink of the river where they would set them afire and push the bales in to float burning down the tide. Each sent up its wreath of smoke and looked like a tiny steamer puffing away. Only I doubt that from the source to the mouth of the river there are as many boats afloat on the Mississippi. The flatboat was piled with as many bales as it could hold without sinking. Most of them were cut open, while negroes staved in the heads of barrels of alcohol, whiskey, etc., and dashed bucketsful over the cotton. Others built up little chimneys of pine every few feet, lined with pine knots and loose cotton, to burn more quickly. There, piled the length of the whole levee, or burning in the river, lay the work of thousands of negroes for more than a year past. It had come from every side. Men stood by who owned the cotton that was burning or waiting to burn. They either helped, or looked on cheerfully. Charlie owned but sixteen bales - a matter of some fifteen hundred dollars; but he was the head man of the whole affair, and burned his own, as well as the property of others. A single barrel of whiskey that was thrown on the cotton, cost the man who gave it one hundred and twenty-five dollars. (It shows what a nation in earnest is capable of doing.) Only two men got on the flatboat with Charlie when it was ready. It was towed to the middle of the river, set afire in every place, and then they jumped into a little skiff fastened in front, and rowed to land. The cotton floated down the Mississippi one sheet of living flame, even in the sunlight. It would have been grand at night. But then we will have fun watching it this evening anyway; for they cannot get through to-day, though no time is to be lost. Hundreds of bales remained untouched. An incredible amount of property has been destroyed to-day; but no one begrudges it. Every grog-shop has been emptied, and gutters and pavements are floating with liquors of all kinds. So that if the Yankees are fond of strong drink, they will fare ill.

Yesterday, Mr. Hutchinson and a Dr. Moffat called to ask for me, with a message about Jimmy. I was absent, but they saw Lilly. Jimmy, they said, was safe. Though sick in bed, he had sprung up and had rushed to the wharf at the first tap of the alarm bell in New Orleans. But as nothing could be done, he would probably be with us to-day, bringing mother and Miriam. I have neither heard nor seen more. The McRae, they said, went to the bottom with the others. They did not know whether any one aboard had escaped. God be praised that Jimmy was not on her then! The new boat to which he was appointed is not yet finished. So he is saved! I am distressed about Captain Huger, and could not refrain from crying, he was so good to Jimmy. But I remembered Miss Cammack might think it rather tender and obtrusive, so I dried my eyes and began to hope he had escaped. Oh! how glad I should be to know he has suffered no harm. Mr. Hutchinson was on his way above, going to join others where the final battle is to be fought on the Mississippi. He had not even time to sit down; so I was doubly grateful to him for his kindness. I wish I could have thanked him for being so considerate of me in my distress now. In her agitation, Lilly gave him a letter I had been writing to George when I was called away; and begged him to address it and mail it at Vicksburg, or somewhere; for no mail will leave here for Norfolk for a long while to come. The odd part is, that he does not know George. But he said he would gladly take charge of it and remember the address, which Lilly told him was Richmond. Well! if the Yankees get it they will take it for an insane scrawl. I wanted to calm his anxiety about us, though I was so wildly excited that I could only say, "Don't mind us! We are safe. But fight, George! Fight for us!" The repetition was ludicrous. I meant so much, too! I only wanted him to understand he could best defend us there. Ah! Mr. Yankee! if you had but your brothers in this world, and their lives hanging by a thread, you too might write wild letters! And if you want to know what an excited girl can do, just call and let me show you the use of a small seven-shooter and a large carving-knife which vibrate between my belt and my pocket, always ready for emergencies.

U.S. iron clad gunboat Essex

April 27th.

What a day! Last night came a dispatch that New Orleans was under British protection, and could not be bombarded; consequently, the enemy's gunboats would probably be here this morning, such few as had succeeded in passing the Forts; from nine to fifteen, it was said. And the Forts, they said, had not surrendered. I went to church; but I grew very anxious before it was over, feeling that I was needed at home. When I returned, I found Lilly wild with excitement, picking up hastily whatever came to hand, preparing for instant flight, she knew not where. The Yankees were in sight; the town was to be burned; we were to run to the woods, etc. If the house had to be burned, I had to make up my mind to run, too. So my treasure-bag tied around my waist as a bustle, a sack with a few necessary articles hanging on my arm, some few quite unnecessary ones, too, as I had not the heart to leave the old and new prayer books father had given me, and Miriam's, too; - pistol and carving-knife ready, I stood awaiting the exodus. I heaped on the bed the treasures I wanted to burn, matches lying ready to fire the whole at the last minute. I may here say that, when all was over, I found I had omitted many things from the holocaust. This very diary was not included. It would have afforded vast amusement to the Yankees. There may yet be occasion to burn them, and the house also. People fortunately changed their minds about the auto-da-fé just then; and the Yankees have not yet arrived, at sundown. So, when the excitement calmed down, poor Lilly tumbled in bed in a high fever in consequence of terror and exertion.

[A page torn out]

I was right in that prophecy. For this was not the Will Pinckney I saw last. So woebegone! so subdued, careworn, and sad! No trace of his once merry self. He is good-looking, which he never was before. But I would rather never have seen him than have found him so changed. I was talking to a ghost. His was a sad story. He had held one bank of the river until forced to retreat with his men, as their cartridges were exhausted, and General

Lovell omitted sending more. They had to pass through swamps, wading seven and a half miles, up to their waists in water. He gained the edge of the swamp, saw they were over the worst, and fell senseless. Two of his men brought him milk, and "woke him up," he said. His men fell from exhaustion, were lost, and died in the swamp; so that out of five hundred, but one hundred escaped. This he told quietly and sadly, looking so heartbroken that it was piteous to see such pain. He showed me his feet, with thick clumsy shoes which an old negro had pulled off to give him; for his were lost in the swamp, and he came out bare-footed. They reached the Lafourche River, I believe, seized a boat, and arrived here last night. His wife and child were aboard. Heaven knows how they got there! The men he sent on to Port Hudson, while he stopped here. I wanted to bring his wife to stay with us; but he said she could not bear to be seen, as she had run off just as she had happened to be at that moment. In half an hour he would be off to take her to his old home in a carriage. There he would rejoin his men, on the railroad, and march from Clinton to the Jackson road, and so on to Corinth. A long journey for men so disheartened! But they will conquer in the end. Beauregard's army will increase rapidly at this rate. The whole country is aroused, and every man who owns a gun, and many who do not, are on the road to Corinth. We will conquer yet.

May 5th.

Vile old Yankee boats, four in number, passed up this morning without stopping. After all our excitement, this "silent contempt" annihilated me! What in the world do they mean? The river was covered with burning cotton; perhaps they want to see where it came from.

May 9th.

Our lawful (?) owners have at last arrived. About sunset, day before yesterday, the Iroquois anchored here, and a graceful young Federal stepped ashore, carrying a Yankee flag over his shoulder, and asked the way to the Mayor's office. I like the style! If we girls of Baton Rouge had been at the landing, instead of the men, that Yankee would never have insulted us by flying his flag in our faces! We would have opposed his landing except under a flag of truce, but the men let him alone, and he even found a poor Dutchman willing to show him the road!

He did not accomplish much; said a formal demand would be made next day, and asked if it was safe for the men to come ashore and buy a few necessaries, when he was assured the air of Baton Rouge was very unhealthy for Yankee soldiers at night. He promised very magnanimously not to shell us out if we did not molest him; but I notice none of them dare set their feet on terra firma, except the officer who has now called three times on the Mayor, and who is said to tremble visibly as he walks the streets.

Last evening came the demand: the town must be surrendered immediately; the Federal flag Must be raised; they would grant us the same terms they granted New Orleans. Jolly terms those were! The answer was worthy of a Southerner. It was, "The town was defenseless; if we had cannon, there were not men enough to resist; but if forty vessels lay at the landing, - it was intimated we were in their power, and more ships coming up, - we would not surrender; if they wanted, they might come and Take us; if they wished the Federal flag hoisted over the Arsenal, they might put it up for themselves, the town had no control over Government property." Glorious! What a pity they did not shell the town! But they are taking us at our word, and this morning they are landing at the Garrison.

"All devices, signs, and flags of the Confederacy shall be suppressed." So says Picayune Butler. Good. I devote all my red, white, and blue silk to the manufacture of Confederate flags. As soon as one is confiscated, I make another, until my ribbon is exhausted, when I will sport a duster emblazoned in high colors, "Hurra! for the Bonny blue flag!" Henceforth, I wear one pinned to my bosom - not a duster, but a little flag; the man who says take it off will have to pull it off for himself; the man who dares attempt it - well! a pistol in my pocket fills up the gap. I am capable, too.

This is a dreadful war, to make even the hearts of women so bitter! I hardly know myself these last few weeks. I, who have such a horror of bloodshed, consider even killing in self-defense murder, who cannot wish them the slightest evil, whose only prayer is to have them sent back in peace to their own country, - I talk of killing them! For what else do I wear a pistol and carving-knife? I am afraid I will try them on the first one who says an insolent word to me. Yes, and repent for it ever after in sackcloth and ashes. O! if I was only a man! Then I could don the breeches, and slay them with a will! If some few Southern women were in the ranks, they could set the men an example they would not blush to follow. Pshaw! there are no women here! We are all men!

May 10th.

Last night about one o'clock I was wakened and told that mother and Miriam had come. Oh, how glad I was! I tumbled out of bed half asleep and hugged Miriam in a dream, but waked up when I got to mother. They came up under a flag of truce, on a boat going up for provisions, which, by the way, was brought to by half a dozen Yankee ships in succession, with a threat to send a broadside into her if she did not stop - the wretches knew it must be under a flag of truce; no boats leave, except by special order to procure provisions.

What tales they had to tell! They were on the wharf, and saw the ships sail up the river, saw the broadside fired into Will Pinckney's regiment, the boats we fired, our gunboats, floating down to meet them all wrapped in flames; twenty thousand bales of cotton blazing in a single pile; molasses and sugar thrown over everything. They stood there opposite to where one of the ships landed, expecting a broadside, and resolute not to be shot in the back. I wish I had been there! And Captain Huger is not dead! They had hopes of his life for the first time day before yesterday. Miriam saw the ball that had just been extracted. He will probably be lame for the rest of his life. It will be a glory to him. For even the Federal officers say that never did they see so gallant a little ship, or one that fought so desperately as the McRae. Men and officers fought like devils. Think of all those great leviathans after the poor little "Widow Mickey"! One came tearing down on her sideways, while the Brooklyn fired on her from the other side, when brave Captain Warley put the nose of the Manassas under the first, and tilted her over so that the whole broadside passed over, instead of through, the McRae, who spit back its poor little fire at both.

And after all was lost, she carried the wounded and the prisoners to New Orleans, and was scuttled by her own men in port. Glorious Captain Huger! And think of his sending word to Jimmy, suffering as he was, that "his little brass cannon was game to the last." Oh! I hope he will recover. Brave, dare-devil Captain Warley is prisoner, and on the way to Fort Warren, that home of all brave, patriotic men. We'll have him out. And my poor little Jimmy! If I have not spoken of him, it is not because I have lost sight of him for a moment. The day the McRae went down, he arose from his bed, ill as he was, and determined to rejoin her, as his own boat, the Mississippi, was not ready. When he reached the St. Charles, he fell so very ill that he had to be carried back to Brother's. Only his desperate illness saved him from being among the killed or wounded on that gallant little ship. A few days after, he learned the fate of the ship, and was told that Captain Huger was dead. No wonder he should cry so bitterly! For Captain Huger was as tender and as kind to him as his own dear father. God bless him for it! The enemy's ships were sailing up; so he threw a few articles in a carpet-bag and started off for Richmond, Corinth, anywhere, to fight. Sick, weak, hardly able to stand, he went off, two weeks ago yesterday. We know not where, and we have never heard from him since. Whether he succumbed to that jaundice and the rest, and lies dead or dying on the road, God only knows. We can only wait and pray God to send dear little Jimmy home in safety.

And this is WAR! Heaven save me from like scenes and experiences again. I was wild with excitement last night when Miriam described how the soldiers, marching to the depot, waved their hats to the crowds of women and children, shouting, "God bless you, ladies! We will fight for you!" and they, waving their handkerchiefs, sobbed with one voice, "God bless you, Soldiers! Fight for us!"

We, too, have been having our fun. Early in the evening, four more gunboats sailed up here. We saw them from the corner, three squares off, crowded with men even up in the riggings. The American flag was flying from every peak. It was received in profound silence, by the hundreds gathered on the banks. I could hardly refrain from a groan. Much as I once loved that flag, I hate it now! I came back and made myself a Confederate flag about five inches long, slipped the staff in my belt, pinned the flag to my shoulder, and walked downtown, to the consternation of women and children, who expected something awful to follow. An old negro cried, "My young missus got her flag flyin', anyhow!" Nettie made one and hid it in the folds of her dress. But we were the only two who ventured. We went to the State House terrace, and took a good look at the Brooklyn which was crowded with people who took a good look at us, likewise. The picket stationed at the Garrison took alarm at half a dozen men on horseback and ran, saying that the citizens were attacking. The kind officers aboard the ship sent us word that if they were molested, the town would be shelled. Let them! Butchers! Does it take thirty thousand men and millions of dollars to murder defenseless women and children? O the great nation! Bravo!

May 11th.

I - I am disgusted with myself. No unusual thing, but I am peculiarly disgusted this time. Last evening, I went to Mrs. Brunot's, without an idea of going beyond, with my flag flying again. They were all going to the State House, so I went with them; to my great distress, some fifteen or twenty Federal officers were standing on the first terrace, stared at like wild beasts by the curious crowd. I had not expected to meet them, and felt a painful conviction that I was unnecessarily attracting attention, by an unladylike display of defiance, from the crowd gathered there. But what was I to do? I felt humiliated, conspicuous, everything that is painful and disagreeable; but - strike my colors in the face of the enemy? Never! Nettie and Sophie had them, too, but that was no consolation for the shame I suffered by such a display so totally distasteful to me. How I wished myself away, and chafed at my folly, and hated myself for being there, and every one for seeing me. I hope it will be a lesson to me always to remember a lady can gain nothing by such display.

I was not ashamed of the flag of my country, - I proved that by never attempting to remove it in spite of my mortification, - but I was ashamed of my position; for these are evidently gentlemen, not the Billy Wilson's crew we were threatened with. Fine, noble-looking men they were, showing refinement and gentlemanly bearing in every motion. One cannot help but admire such foes! They set us an example worthy of our imitation, and one we would be benefited by following. They come as visitors without either pretensions to superiority, or the insolence of conquerors; they walk quietly their way, offering no annoyance to the citizens, though they themselves are stared at most unmercifully, and pursued by crowds of ragged little boys, while even men gape at them with open mouths. They prove themselves gentlemen, while many of our citizens have proved themselves boors, and I admire them for their conduct. With a conviction that I had allowed myself to be influenced by bigoted, narrow minded people, in believing them to be unworthy of respect or regard, I came home wonderfully changed in all my newly acquired sentiments, resolved never more to wound their feelings, who were so careful of ours, by such unnecessary display. And I hung my flag on the parlor mantel, there to wave, if it will, in the shades of private life; but to make a show, make me conspicuous and ill at ease, as I was yesterday, - never again !

There was a dozen officers in church this morning, and the psalms for the 11th day seemed so singularly appropriate to the feelings of the people, that I felt uncomfortable for them. They answered with us, though.

May 14th.

I am beginning to believe that we are even of more importance in Baton Rouge than we thought we were. It is laughable to hear the things a certain set of people, who know they can't visit us, say about the whole family. . . . When father was alive, they dared not talk about us aloud, beyond calling us the "Proud Morgans" and the "Aristocracy of Baton Rouge" . . . But now father is gone, the people imagine we are public property, to be criticized, vilified, and abused to their hearts' content . . . .

And now, because they find absurdities don't succeed, they try improbabilities. So yesterday the town was in a ferment because it was reported the Federal officers had called on the Miss Morgans, and all the gentlemen were anxious to hear how they had been received. One had the grace to say, "If they did, they received the best lesson there that they could get in town; those young ladies would meet them with the true Southern spirit." The rest did not know; they would like to find out.

I suppose the story originated from the fact that we were unwilling to blackguard - yes, that is the word - the Federal officers here, and would not agree with many of our friends in saying they were liars, thieves, murderers, scoundrels, the scum of the earth, etc. Such epithets are unworthy of ladies, I say, and do harm, rather than advance our cause. Let them be what they will, it shall not make me less the lady; I say it is unworthy of anything except low newspaper war, such abuse, and I will not join in.

I have a brother-in-law in the Federal army whom I love and respect as much as any one in the world, and shall not readily agree that his being a Northerner would give him an irresistible desire to pick my pockets, and take from him all power of telling the truth. No! There are few men I admire more than Major Drum, and I honor him for his independence in doing what he believes right. Let us have liberty of speech and action in our land, I say, but not gross abuse and calumny. Shall I acknowledge that the people we so recently called our brothers are unworthy of consideration, and are liars, cowards, dogs? Not I! If they conquer us, I acknowledge them as a superior race; I will not say that we were conquered by cowards, for where would that place us? It will take a brave people to gain us, and that the Northerners undoubtedly are. I would scorn to have an inferior foe; I fight only my equals. These women may acknowledge that cowards have won battles in which their brothers were engaged, but I, I will ever say mine fought against brave men, and won the day. Which is most honorable?

I was never a Secessionist, for I quietly adopted father's views on political subjects without meddling with them. But even father went over with his State, and when so many outrages were committed by the fanatical leaders of the North, though he regretted the Union, said, "Fight to the death for our liberty." I say so, too. I want to fight until we win the cause so many have died for. I don't believe in Secession, but I do in Liberty. I want the South to conquer, dictate its own terms, and go back to the Union, for I believe that, apart, inevitable ruin awaits both. It is a rope of sand, this Confederacy, founded on the doctrine of Secession, and will not last many years - not five. The North Cannot subdue us. We are too determined to be free. They have no right to confiscate our property to pay debts they themselves have incurred. Death as a nation, rather than Union on such terms. We will have our rights secured on so firm a basis that it can never be shaken. If by power of overwhelming numbers they conquer us, it will be a barren victory over a desolate land.

We, the natives of this loved soil, will be beggars in a foreign land; we will not submit to despotism under the garb of Liberty. The North will find herself burdened with an unparalleled debt, with nothing to show for it except deserted towns, burning homes, a standing army which will govern with no small caprice, and an impoverished land.

If that be treason, make the best of it!

May 17th.

One of these days, when peace is restored and we are quietly settled in our allotted corners of this wide world without any particularly exciting event to alarm us; and with the knowledge of what is now the future, and will then be the dead past; seeing that all has been for the best for us in the end; that all has come right in spite of us, we will wonder how we could ever have been foolish enough to await each hour in such breathless anxiety. We will ask ourselves if it was really true that nightly, as we lay down to sleep, we did not dare plan for the morning, feeling that we might be homeless and beggars before the dawn. How unreal it will then seem! We will say it was our wild imagination, perhaps. But how bitterly, horribly true it is now!

Four days ago the Yankees left us, to attack Vicksburg, leaving their flag flying in the Garrison without a man to guard it, and with the understanding that the town would be held responsible for it. It was intended for a trap; and it succeeded. For night before last, it was pulled down and torn to pieces.

Now, unless Will will have the kindness to sink a dozen of their ships up there, - I hear he has command of the lower batteries, - they will be back in a few days, and will execute their threat of shelling the town. If they do, what will become of us? All we expect in the way of earthly property is as yet mere paper, which will be so much trash if the South is ruined, as it consists of debts due father by many planters for professional services rendered, who, of course, will be ruined, too, so all money is gone. That is nothing, we will not be ashamed to earn our bread, so let it go.

But this house is at least a shelter from the weather, all sentiment apart. And our servants, too; how could they manage without us? The Yankees, on the river, and a band of guerrillas in the woods, are equally anxious to precipitate a fight. Between the two fires, what chance for us? It would take only a little while to burn the city over our heads. They say the women and children must be removed, these guerrillas. Where, please? Charlie says we must go to Greenwell. And have this house pillaged? For Butler has decreed that no unoccupied house shall be respected. If we stay through the battle, if the Federals are victorious, we will suffer. For the officers here were reported to have said, "If the people here did not treat them decently, they would know what it was when Billy Wilson's crew arrived. They would give them a lesson!" That select crowd is now in New Orleans. Heaven help us when they reach here! It is in these small cities that the greatest outrages are perpetrated. What are we to do?

A new proclamation from Butler has just come. It seems that the ladies have an ugly way of gathering their skirts when the Federals pass, to avoid any possible contact. Some even turn up their noses. Unladylike, to say the least. But it is, maybe, owing to the odor they have, which is said to be unbearable even at this early season of the year. Butler says, whereas the so-called ladies of New Orleans insult his men and officers, he gives one and all permission to insult any or all who so treat them, then and there, with the assurance that the women will not receive the slightest protection from the Government, and that the men will all be justified. I did not have time to read it, but repeat it as it was told to me by mother, who is in utter despair at the brutality of the thing. These men our brothers? Not mine! Let us hope for the honor of their nation that Butler is not counted among the gentlemen of the land. And so, if any man should fancy he cared to kiss me, he could do so under the pretext that I had pulled my dress from under his feet! That will justify them! And if we decline their visits, they can insult us under the plea of a prior affront. Oh! Gibbes! George! Jimmy! never did we need your protection as sorely as now. And not to know even whether you are alive! When Charlie joins the army, we will be defenseless, indeed. Come to my bosom, O my discarded carving-knife, laid aside under the impression that these men were gentlemen. We will be close friends once more. And if you must have a sheath, perhaps I may find one for you in the heart of the first man who attempts to Butlerize me. I never dreamed of kissing any man save my father and brothers. And why any one should care to kiss any one else, I fail to understand. And I do not propose to learn to make exceptions.

Still no word from the boys. We hear that Norfolk has been evacuated; but no details. George was there. Gibbes is wherever Johnston is, presumably on the Rappahannock; but it is more than six weeks since we have heard from either of them, and all communication is cut off.

May 21st.

I have had such a search for shoes this week that I am disgusted with shopping. I am triumphant now, for after traversing the town in every direction and finding nothing, I finally discovered a pair of boots just made for a little negro to go fishing with, and only an inch and a half too long for me, besides being unbendable; but I seized them with avidity, and the little negro would have been outbid if I had not soon after discovered a pair more seemly, if not more serviceable, which I took without further difficulty. Behold my tender feet cased in crocodile skin, patent-leather tipped, low-quarter boy's shoes, No. 2! "What a fall was there, my country," from my pretty English glove-kid, to sabots made of some animal closely connected with the hippopotamus! A dernier ressort, vraiment! for my choice was that, or cooling my feet on the burning pavement au naturel; I who have such a terror of any one seeing my naked foot! And this is thanks to war and blockade! Not a decent shoe in the whole community! N'importe! "Better days are coming, we'll all" - have shoes - after a while - perhaps! Why did not Mark Tapley leave me a song calculated to keep the spirits up, under depressing circumstances? I need one very much, and have nothing more suggestive than the old Methodist hymn, "Better days are coming, we'll all go right," which I shout so constantly, as our prospects darken, that it begins to sound stale.

May 27th.

The cry is "Ho! for Greenwell!" Very probably this day week will see us there. I don't want to go. If we were at peace, and were to spend a few months of the warmest season out there, none would be more eager and delighted than I: but to leave our comfortable home, and all it contains, for a rough pine cottage seventeen miles away even from this scanty civilization, is sad. It must be! We are hourly expecting two regiments of Yankees to occupy the Garrison, and some fifteen hundred of our men are awaiting them a little way off, so the fight seems inevitable. And we must go, leaving what little has already been spared us to the tender mercies of Northern volunteers, who, from the specimen of plundering they gave us two weeks ago, will hardly leave us even the shelter of our roof. O my dear Home! How can I help but cry at leaving you forever? For if this fight occurs, never again shall I pass the threshold of this house, where we have been so happy and sad, the scene of joyous meetings and mournful partings, the place where we greeted each other with glad shouts after even so short a parting, the place where Harry and father kissed us good-bye and never came back again!

I know what Lavinia has suffered this long year, by what we have suffered these last six weeks. Poor Lavinia, so far away! How easier poverty, if it must come, would be if we could bear it together! I wonder if the real fate of the boys, if we ever hear, can be so dreadful as this suspense? Still no news of them. My poor little Jimmy! And think how desperate Gibbes and George will be when they read Butler's proclamation, and they not able to defend us! Gibbes was in our late victory of Fredericksburg, I know.

In other days, going to Greenwell was the signal for general noise and confusion. All the boys gathered their guns and fishing-tackle, and thousand and one amusements; father sent out provisions; we helped mother pack; Hal and I tumbled over the libraries to lay in a supply of reading material; and all was bustle until the carriage drove to the door at daylight one morning, and swept us off. It is not so gay this time. I wandered around this morning selecting books alone. We can only take what is necessary, the rest being left to the care of the Northern militia in general. I never knew before how many articles were perfectly "indispensable" to me. This or that little token or keepsake, piles of letters I hate to burn, many dresses, etc., I cannot take conveniently, lie around me, and I hardly know which to choose among them, yet half must be sacrificed; I can only take one trunk.

May 30th, GREENWELL.

After all our trials and tribulations, here we are at last, and no limbs lost! How many weeks ago was it since I wrote here? It seems very long after all these events; let me try to recall them.

Wednesday the 28th, - a day to be forever remembered, - as luck would have it, we rose very early, and had breakfast sooner than usual, it would seem for the express design of becoming famished before dinner. I picked up some of my letters and papers and set them where I could find them whenever we were ready to go to Greenwell, burning a pile of trash and leaving a quantity equally worthless, which were of no value even to myself except from association. I was packing up my traveling-desk with all Harry's little articles that were left to me, and other things, and I was saying to myself that my affairs were in such confusion that if obliged to run unexpectedly I would not know what to save, when I heard Lilly's voice downstairs, crying as she ran in - she had been out shopping - "Mr. Castle has killed a Federal officer on a ship, and they are going to shell -" Bang! went a cannon at the word, and that was all our warning.

Mother had just come in, and was lying down, but sprang to her feet and added her screams to the general confusion. Miriam, who had been searching the libraries, ran up to quiet her; Lilly gathered her children, crying hysterically all the time, and ran to the front door with them as they were; Lucy saved the baby, naked as she took her from her bath, only throwing a quilt over her. I bethought me of my "running-bag" which I had used on a former case, and in a moment my few precious articles were secured under my hoops, and with a sunbonnet on, I stood ready for anything.

The firing still continued; they must have fired half a dozen times before we could coax mother off. What awful screams! I had hoped never to hear them again, after Harry died. Charlie had gone to Greenwell before daybreak, to prepare the house, so we four women, with all those children and servants, were left to save ourselves. I did not forget my poor little Jimmy; I caught up his cage and ran down. Just at this moment mother recovered enough to insist on saving father's papers - which was impossible, as she had not an idea of where the important ones were. I heard Miriam plead, argue, insist, command her to run; Lilly shriek, and cry she should go; the children screaming within; women running by without, crying and moaning; but I could not join in. I was going I knew not where; it was impossible to take my bird, for even if I could carry him, he would starve. So I took him out of his cage, kissed his little yellow head, and tossed him up. He gave one feeble little chirp as if to ascertain where to go, and then for the first and last time I cried, laying my head against the gate-post, and with my eyes too dim to see him. Oh, how it hurt me to lose my little bird, one Jimmy had given me, too!

But the next minute we were all off, in safety. A square from home, I discovered that boy shoes were not the most comfortable things to run in, so I ran back, in spite of cannonading, entreaties, etc., to get another pair. I got home, found an old pair that were by no means respectable, which I seized without hesitation; and being perfectly at ease, thought it would be so nice to save at least Miriam's and my tooth-brushes, so slipped them in my corsets. These in, of course we must have a comb - that was added - then how could we stand the sun without starch to cool our faces? This included the powder-bag; then I must save that beautiful lace collar; and my hair was tumbling down, so in went the tuckingcomb and hair-pins with the rest; until, if there had been any one to speculate, they would have wondered a long while at the singular appearance of a girl who is considered as very slight, usually. By this time, Miriam, alarmed for me, returned to find me, though urged by Dr. Castleton not to risk her life by attempting it, and we started off together.

We had hardly gone a square when we decided to return a second time, and get at least a few articles for the children and ourselves, who had nothing except what we happened to have on when the shelling commenced. She picked up any little things and threw them to me, while I filled a pillow-case jerked from the bed, and placed my powder and brushes in it with the rest. Before we could leave, mother, alarmed for us both, came to find us, with Tiche. All this time they had been shelling, but there was quite a lull when she got there, and she commenced picking up father's papers, vowing all the time she would not leave. Every argument we could use was of no avail, and we were desperate as to what course to pursue, when the shelling recommenced in a few minutes. Then mother recommenced her screaming and was ready to fly anywhere; and holding her box of papers, with a faint idea of saving something, she picked up two dirty underskirts and an old cloak.

By dint of Miriam's vehement appeals, aided by a great deal of pulling, we got her down to the back door. We had given our pillow-case to Tiche, who added another bundle and all our silver to it, and had already departed.

As we stood in the door, four or five shells sailed over our heads at the same time, seeming to make a perfect corkscrew of the air, - for it sounded as though it went in circles. Miriam cried, "Never mind the door!" mother screamed anew, and I stayed behind to lock the door, with this new music in my ears. We reached the back gate, that was on the street, when another shell passed us, and Miriam jumped behind the fence for protection.

We had only gone half a square when Dr. Castleton begged us to take another street, as they were firing up that one. We took his advice, but found our new street worse than the old, for the shells seemed to whistle their strange songs with redoubled vigor. The height of my ambition was now attained. I had heard Jimmy laugh about the singular sensation produced by the rifled balls spinning around one's head; and here I heard the same peculiar sound, ran the same risk, and was equal to the rest of the boys, for was I not in the midst of flying shells, in the middle of a bombardment? I think I was rather proud of it.

We were alone on the road, - all had run away before, - so I thought it was for our especial entertainment, this little affair. I cannot remember how long it lasted; I am positive that the clock struck ten before I left home, but I had been up so long, I know not what time it began, though I am told it was between eight and nine. We passed the graveyard, we did not even stop, and about a mile and a half from home, when mother was perfectly exhausted with fatigue and unable to proceed farther, we met a gentleman in a buggy who kindly took charge of her and our bundles. We could have walked miles beyond, then, for as soon as she was safe we felt as though a load had been removed from our shoulders; and after exhorting her not to be uneasy about us, and reminding her we had a pistol and a dagger, - I had secured a "for true" one the day before, fortunately, - she drove off, and we trudged on alone, the only people in sight on foot, though occasionally carriages and buggies would pass, going towards town. One party of gentlemen put their heads out and one said, "There are Judge Morgan's daughters sitting by the road!" - but I observed he did not offer them the slightest assistance. However, others were very kind. One I never heard of had volunteered to go for us, and bring us to mother, when she was uneasy about our staying so long, when we went home to get clothes. We heard him ring and knock, but, thinking it must be next door, paid no attention, so he went back and mother came herself.

We were two miles away when we sat down by the road to rest, and have a laugh. Here were two women married, and able to take care of themselves, flying for their lives and leaving two lorn girls alone on the road, to protect each other! To be sure, neither could help us, and one was not able to walk, and the other had helpless children to save; but it was so funny when we talked about it, and thought how sorry both would be when they regained their reason! While we were yet resting, we saw a cart coming, and, giving up all idea of our walking to Greenwell, called the people to stop. To our great delight, it proved to be a cart loaded with Mrs. Brunot's affairs, driven by two of her negroes, who kindly took us up with them, on the top of their luggage; and we drove off in state, as much pleased at riding in that novel place as though we were accustomed to ride in wheelbarrows. Miriam was in a hollow between a flour barrel and a mattress, and I at the end, astride, I am afraid, of a tremendous bundle, for my face was down the road and each foot resting very near the sides of the cart. I tried to make a better arrangement, though, after a while. These servants were good enough to lend us their umbrella, without which I am afraid we would have suffered severely, for the day was intensely warm.

Three miles from town we began to overtake the fugitives. Hundreds of women and children were walking along, some bareheaded, and in all costumes. Little girls of twelve and fourteen were wandering on alone. I called to one I knew, and asked where her mother was; she did n't know; she would walk on until she found out. It seems her mother lost a nursing baby, too, which was not found until ten that night. White and black were all mixed together, and were as confidential as though related. All called to us and asked where we were going, and many we knew laughed at us for riding on a cart; but as they had walked only five miles, I imagined they would like even these poor accommodations if they were in their reach.

The negroes deserve the greatest praise for their conduct. Hundreds were walking with babies or bundles; ask them what they had saved, it was invariably, "My mistress's clothes, or silver, or baby." Ask what they had for themselves, it was, "Bless your heart, honey, I was glad to get away with mistress's things; I did n't think 'bout mine."

It was a heart-rending scene. Women searching for their babies along the road, where they had been lost; others sitting in the dust crying and wringing their hands; for by this time we had not an idea but what Baton Rouge was either in ashes, or being plundered, and we had saved nothing. I had one dress, Miriam two, but Tiche had them, and we had lost her before we left home.

Presently we came on a guerrilla camp. Men and horses were resting on each side of the road, some sick, some moving about carrying water to the women and children, and all looking like a monster barbecue, for as far as the eye could see through the woods, was the same repetition of men and horses. They would ask for the news, and one, drunk with excitement or whiskey, informed us that it was our own fault if we had saved nothing, the people must have been - fools not to have known trouble would come before long, and that it was the fault of the men, who were aware of it, that the women were thus forced to fly. In vain we pleaded that there was no warning, no means of foreseeing this; he cried, "You are ruined; so am I; and my brothers, too! And by - there is nothing left but to die now, and I'll die!" "Good!" I said. "But die fighting for us!" He waved his hand, black with powder, and shouted, "That I will!" after us. That was the only swearing guerrilla we met; the others seemed to have too much respect for us to talk loud.

Lucy had met us before this; early in the action, Lilly had sent her back to get some baby-clothes, but a shell exploding within a few feet of her, she took alarm, and ran up another road, for three miles, when she cut across the plantations and regained the Greenwell route. It is fortunate that, without consultation, the thought of running here should have seized us all.

May 31st.

I was interrupted so frequently yesterday that I know not how I continued to write so much. First, I was sent for, to go to Mrs. Brunot, who had just heard of her son's death, and who was alone with Dena; and some hours after, I was sent for, to see Fanny, now Mrs. Trezevant, who had just come with her husband to bring us news of George. A Mrs. Montgomery, who saw him every day at Norfolk, said Jimmy was with him, and though very sick at first, was now in good health. The first news in all that long time! When the city was evacuated, George went with his regiment seven miles from Richmond, Jimmy to the city itself, as aide to Com. Hollins. This lady brought George's opal ring and diamond pin. Howell and Mr. Badger, who had just joined the guerrillas as independents, spent the day with me. We were all in such confusion that I felt ashamed: ever

y one as dirty as possible; I had on the same dress I had escaped in, which, though then perfectly clean, was now rather - dirty. But they knew what a time we had had.

To return to my journal.

Lucy met mother some long way ahead of us, whose conscience was already reproaching her for leaving us, and in answer to her "What has become of my poor girls?" ran down the road to find us, for Lucy thinks the world can't keep on moving without us. When she met us, she walked by the cart, and it was with difficulty we persuaded her to ride a mile; she said she felt "used" to walking now. About five miles from home, we overtook mother. The gentleman had been obliged to go for his wife, so Mary gave her her seat on the cart, and walked with Lucy three miles beyond, where we heard that Lilly and the children had arrived in a cart, early in the day. All the talk by the roadside was of burning homes, houses knocked to pieces by balls, famine, murder, desolation; so I comforted myself singing, "Better days are coming" and "I hope to die shouting, the Lord will provide"; while Lucy toiled through the sun and dust, and answered with a chorus of "I'm a-runnin', a-runnin' up to glo-ry!"

It was three o'clock when we reached Mr. David's and found Lilly. How warm and tired we were! A hasty meal, which tasted like a feast after our fatigue, gave us fresh strength, and Lilly and Miriam got in an old cart with the children to drive out here, leaving me with mother and Dellie to follow next day. About sunset, Charlie came flying down the road, on his way to town. I decided to go, and after an obstinate debate with mother, in which I am afraid I showed more determination than amiability, I wrung a reluctant consent from her, and, promising not to enter if it was being fired or plundered, drove off in triumph. It was a desperate enterprise for a young girl, to enter a town full of soldiers on such an expedition at night; but I knew Charlie could take care of me, and if he was killed I could take care of myself; so I went.

It was long after nine when we got there, and my first act was to look around the deserted house. What a scene of confusion! armoirs spread open, with clothes tumbled in every direction, inside and out; ribbons, laces on floors; chairs overturned; my desk wide open covered with letters, trinkets, etc.; bureau drawers half out, the bed filled with odds and ends of everything. I no longer recognized my little room. On the bolster was a little box, at the sight of which I burst out laughing. Five minutes before the alarm, Miriam had been selecting those articles she meant to take to Greenwell, and, holding up her box, said, "If we were forced to run for our lives without a moment's warning, I 'd risk my life to save this, rather than leave it!" Yet here lay the box, and she was safe at Greenwell!

It took me two hours to pack father's papers, then I packed Miriam's trunk, then some of mother's and mine, listening all the while for a cannon; for men were constantly tramping past the house, and only on condition our guerrillas did not disturb them had they promised not to recommence the shelling. Charlie went out to hear the news, and I packed alone.

Com. Farragut's fleet, passing the forts on the Mississippi, April 24th 1862 The U.S. Frigate Mississippi destroying the rebel ram Manassas

It seems the only thing that saved the town was two gentlemen who rowed out to the ships, and informed the illustrious commander that there were no men there to be hurt, and he was only killing women and children. The answer was, "He was sorry he had hurt them; he thought of course the town had been evacuated before the men were fools enough to fire on them, and had only shelled the principal streets to intimidate the people." These streets were the very ones crowded with flying women and children, which they must have seen with their own eyes, for those lying parallel to the river led to the Garrison at one end and the crevasse at the other, which cut off all the lower roads, so that the streets he shelled were the only ones that the women could follow, unless they wished to be drowned. As for the firing, four guerrillas were rash enough to fire on a yawl which was about to land without a flag of truce, killing one, wounding three, one of whom afterwards died.

They were the only ones in town, there was not a cannon in our hands, even if a dozen men could be collected, and this cannonading was kept up in return for half a dozen shots from as many rifles, without even a show of resistance after! So ended the momentous shelling of Baton Rouge, during which the valiant Farragut killed one whole woman, wounded three, struck some twenty houses several times apiece, and indirectly caused the death of two little children who were drowned in their flight, one poor little baby that was born in the woods, and several cases of the same kind, besides those who will yet die from the fatigue, as Mrs. W. D. Phillips who had not left her room since January, who was carried out in her nightgown, and is now supposed to be in a dying condition. The man who took mother told us he had taken a dying woman - in the act of expiring - in his buggy, from her bed, and had left her a little way off, where she had probably breathed her last a few moments after. There were many similar cases. Hurrah for the illustrious Farragut, the Woman Killer! ! !

It was three o'clock before I left off packing, and took refuge in a tub of cold water, from the dust and heat of the morning. What a luxury the water was! and when I changed my underclothes I felt like a new being. To be sure I pulled off the skin of my heel entirely, where it had been blistered by the walk, dust, sun, etc., but that was a trifle, though still quite sore now. For three hours I dreamed of rifled shells and battles, and at half-past six I was up and at work again. Mother came soon after, and after hard work we got safely off at three, saving nothing but our clothes and silver. All else is gone. It cost me a pang to leave my guitar, and Miriam's piano, but it seems there was no help for it, so I had to submit.

It was dark night when we reached here. A bright fire was blazing in front, but the house looked so desolate that I wanted to cry. Miriam cried when I told her her piano was left behind. Supper was a new sensation, after having been without anything except a glass of clabber (no saucers) and a piece of bread since half-past six. I laid down on the hard floor to rest my weary bones, thankful that I was so fortunate as to be able to lie down at all. In my dozing state, I heard the wagon come, and Miriam ordering a mattress to be put in the room for me. I could make out, "Very well! you may take that one to Miss Eliza, but the next one shall be brought to Miss Sarah!" Poor Miriam! She is always fighting my battles. She and the servants are always taking my part against the rest of the world. . . . She and Lucy made a bed and rolled me in it with no more questions, and left me with damp eyes at the thought of how good and tender every one is to me. Poor Lucy picked me a dish of blackberries to await my arrival, and I was just as grateful for it, though they were eaten by some one else before I came.

Early yesterday morning, Miriam, Nettie, and Sophie, who did not then know of their brother's death, went to town in a cart, determined to save some things, Miriam to save her piano. As soon as they were halfway, news reached us that any one was allowed to enter, but none allowed to leave the town, and all vehicles confiscated as soon as they reached there. Alarmed for their safety, mother started off to find them, and we have heard of none of them since. What will happen next? I am not uneasy. They dare not harm them. It is glorious to shell a town full of women, but to kill four lone ones is not exciting enough.

June 1st, Sunday.

From the news brought by one or two persons who managed to reach here yesterday, I am more uneasy about mother and the girls. A gentleman tells me that no one is permitted to leave without a pass, and of these, only such as are separated from their families, who may have left before. All families are prohibited to leave, and furniture and other valuables also. Here is an agreeable arrangement! I saw the "pass," just such as we give our negroes, signed by a Wisconsin colonel. Think of being obliged to ask permission from some low plowman to go in or out of our own house! Cannon are planted as far out as Colonel Davidson's, six of them at our graveyard, and one or more on all the other roads. If the guerrillas do not attempt their capture, I shall take it upon myself to suggest it to the very next one I see. Even if they cannot use them, it will frighten the Yankees, who are in a state of constant alarm about them. Their reason for keeping people in town is that they hope they will not be attacked so long as our own friends remain; thereby placing us above themselves in the scale of humanity, since they acknowledge we are not brute enough to kill women and children as they did not hesitate to do.

Farragut pleads that he could not restrain his men, they were so enraged when the order was once given to fire, and says they would strike a few houses, though he ordered them to fire solely at horses, and the clouds of dust in the street, where guerrillas were supposed to be. The dust was by no means thick enough to conceal that these "guerrillas" were women, carrying babies instead of guns, and the horses were drawing buggies in which many a sick woman was lying.

A young lady who applied to the Yankee general for a pass to come out here, having doubtless spoken of the number of women here who had fled, and the position of the place, was advised to remain in town and write to the ladies to return immediately, and assure them that they would be respected and protected, etc., but that it was madness to remain at Greenwell, for a terrific battle would be fought there in a few days, and they would be exposed to the greatest danger. The girl wrote the letter, but, Mr. Fox, we are not quite such fools as to return there to afford you the protection our petticoats would secure to you, thereby preventing you from receiving condign punishment for the injuries and loss of property already inflicted upon us by you. No! we remain here; and if you are not laid low before you pass the Comite Bridge, we can take to the woods again, and camp out, as many a poor woman is doing now, a few miles from town. Many citizens have been arrested, and after being confined a while, and closely questioned, have been released, if the information is satisfactory. A negro man is informing on all cotton burners and violent Secessionists, etc.

Sunday night.

The girls have just got back, riding in a mule team, on top of baggage, but without either mother or any of our affairs. Our condition is perfectly desperate. Miriam had an interview with General Williams, which was by no means satisfactory. He gave her a pass to leave, and bring us back, for he says there is no safety here for us; he will restrain his men in town, and protect the women, but once outside, he will answer neither for his men, nor the women and children. As soon as he gets horses enough, he passes this road, going to Camp Moore with his cavalry, and then we are in greater danger than ever. Any house shut up shall be occupied by soldiers. Five thousand are there now, five more expected. What shall we do? Mother remained, sending Miriam for me, determined to keep us there, rather than sacrifice both our lives and property by remaining here. But then - two weeks from now the yellow fever will break out; mother has the greatest horror of it, and we have never had it; dying is not much in the present state of our affairs, but the survivor will suffer even more than we do now. If we stay, how shall we live? I have seventeen hundred dollars in Confederate notes now in my "running-bag," and three or four in silver. The former will not be received there, the latter might last two days. If we save our house and furniture, it is at the price of starving. I am of opinion that we should send for mother, and with what money we have, make our way somewhere in the interior, to some city where we can communicate with the boys, and be advised by them. This is not living. Home is lost beyond all hope of recovery; if we wait, what we have already saved will go, too; so we had better leave at once, with what clothing we have, which will certainly establish us on the footing of ladies, if we chance to fall among vulgar people who never look beyond. I fear the guerrillas will attack the town to-night; if they do, God help mother!

General Williams offered Miriam an escort when he found she was without a protector, in the most fatherly way; he must be a good man. She thanked him, but said "she felt perfectly safe on that road." He bit his lip, understanding the allusion, and did not insist. She was to deliver a message from parties in town to the first guerrillas they met, concerning the safest roads, and presently six met them, and entered into conversation. She told them of the proffered escort, when one sprang forward crying, "Why did n't you accept, Miss? The next time, ask for one, and if it is at all disagreeable to you, I am the very man to rid you of such an inconvenience! I'll see that you are not annoyed long." I am glad it was not sent; she would have reproached herself with murder forever after. I wonder if the General would have risked it?

Baton Rouge, June 3d.

Well! Day before yesterday, I almost vowed I would not return, and last evening I reached here. Verily, consistency, thou art a jewel! I determined to get to town to lay both sides of the question before mother; saving home and property, by remaining, thereby cutting ourselves off forever from the boys and dying of yellow fever; or flying to Mississippi, losing all save our lives. So as Mrs. Brunot was panic-stricken and determined to die in town rather than be starved at Greenwell, and was going in on the same wagon that came out the night before, I got up with her and Nettie, and left Greenwell at ten yesterday morning, bringing nothing except this old book, which I would rather not lose, as it has been an old and kind friend during these days of trouble. At first, I avoided all mention of political affairs, but now there is nothing else to be thought of; if it is not burnt for treason, I will like to look it over some day - if I live. I left Greenwell, without ever looking around it, beyond one walk to the hotel, so I may say I hardly know what it looks like. Miriam stayed, much against her will, I fear, to bring in our trunks, if I could send a wagon.

A guerrilla picket stopped us before we had gone a mile, and seemed disposed to turn us back. We said we must pass; our all was at stake. They then entreated us not to enter, saying it was not safe. I asked if they meant to burn it; "We will help try it," was the answer. I begged them to delay the experiment until we could get away. One waved his hat to me and said he would fight for me. Hope he will - at a distance. They asked if we had no protectors; "None," we said. "Don't go, then"; and they all looked so sorry for us. We said we must; starvation, and another panic awaited us out there, our brothers were fighting, our fathers dead; we had only our own judgment to rely on, and that told us home was the best place for us; if the town must burn, let us burn in our houses, rather than be murdered in the woods. They looked still more sorry, but still begged us not to remain. We would, though, and one young boy called out as we drove off, "What's the name of that young lady who refused the escort?" I told him, and they too expressed the greatest regret that she had not accepted. We met many on the road, nearly all of whom talked to us, and as they were most respectful in their manner (though they saw us in a mule team!), we gave them all the information we could, which was all news to them, though very little. Such a ride in the hot sun, perched up in the air! One of the servants remarked, "Miss Sarah ain't ashamed to ride in a wagon!" With truth I replied, "No, I was never so high before."

Two miles from home we met the first Federal pickets, and then they grew more numerous, until we came on a large camp near our graveyard, filled with soldiers and cannon. From first to last none refrained from laughing at us; not aloud, but they would grin and be inwardly convulsed with laughter as we passed. One laughed so comically that I dropped my veil hastily for fear he would see me smile. I could not help it; if any one smiled at me while I was dying, I believe I would return it. We passed crowds, for it was now five o'clock, and all seemed to be promenading. There were several officers standing at the corner, near our house, who were very much amused at our vehicle. I did not feel like smiling then. After reducing us to riding in a mule team, they were heartless enough to laugh! I forgot them presently, and gave my whole attention to getting out respectably. Now getting in a wagon is bad enough; but getting out -! I hardly know how I managed it. I had fully three feet to step down before reaching the wheel; once there, the driver picked me up and set me on the pavement. The net I had gathered my hair in, fell in my descent, and my hair swept down halfway between my knee and ankle in one stream. As I turned to get my little bundle, the officers had moved their position to one directly opposite to me, where they could examine me at leisure. Queens used to ride drawn by oxen hundreds of years ago, so I played this was old times, the mules were oxen, I a queen, and stalked off in a style I am satisfied would have imposed on Juno herself. When I saw them as I turned, they were perfectly quiet; but Nettie says up to that moment they had been in convulsions of laughter, with their handkerchiefs to their faces. It was not polite!

I found mother safe, but the house was in the most horrible confusion. Jimmy's empty cage stood by the door; it had the same effect on me that empty coffins produce on others. Oh, my birdie! At six, I could no longer stand my hunger. I had fasted for twelve hours, with the exception of a mouthful of hoecake at eleven; I that never fasted in my life! - except last Ash Wednesday when Lydia and I tried it for breakfast, and got so sick we were glad to atone for it at dinner. So I got a little piece of bread and corn beef from Mrs. Daigre's servant, for there was not a morsel here, and I did not know where or what to buy. Presently some kind friend sent me a great short-cake, a dish of strawberry preserves, and some butter, which I was grateful for, for the fact that the old negro was giving me part of her supper made me rather sparing, though she cried, "Eat it all honey! I get plenty more!"

Mother went to Cousin Will's, and I went to Mrs. Brunot's to sleep, and so ended my first day's ride on a mule team. Bah! A lady can make anything respectable by the way she does it! What do I care if I had been driving mules? Better that than walk seventeen miles.

I met Dr. DuChêne and Dr. Castleton twice each, this morning. They were as kind to me as they were to the girls the other day. The latter saved them a disagreeable visit, while here. He and those three were packing some things in the hall, when two officers passed, and prepared to come in, seeing three good-looking girls seemingly alone, for Miriam's dress hid Dr. Castleton as he leaned over the box. Just then she moved, the Doctor raised his head, and the officers started back with an "Ah!" of surprise. The Doctor called them as they turned away, and asked for a pass for the young ladies. They came back bowing and smiling, said they would write one in the house, but they were told very dryly that there were no writing accommodations there. They tried the fascinating, and were much mortified by the coldness they met. Dear me! "Why was n't I born old and ugly?" Suppose I should unconsciously entrap some magnificent Yankee! What an awful thing it would be!

Sentinels are stationed at every corner; Dr. Castleton piloted me safely through one expedition; but on the next, we had to part company, and I passed through a crowd of at least fifty, alone. They were playing cards in the ditch, and swearing dreadfully, these pious Yankees; many were marching up and down, some sleeping on the pavement, others - picking odious bugs out of each other's heads! I thought of the guerrillas, yellow fever, and all, and wished they were all safe at home with their mothers and sisters, and we at peace again.

What a day I have had! Here mother and I are alone, not a servant on the lot. We will sleep here to-night, and I know she will be too nervous to let me sleep. The dirt and confusion were extraordinary in the house. I could not stand it, so I applied myself to making it better. I actually swept two whole rooms! I ruined my hands at gardening, so it made no difference. I replaced piles of books, crockery, china, that Miriam had left packed for Greenwell; I discovered I could empty a dirty hearth, dust, move heavy weights, make myself generally useful and dirty, and all this is thanks to the Yankees! Poor me! This time last year I thought I would never walk again! If I am not laid up forever after the fatigue of this last week, I shall always maintain I have a Constitution. But it all seems nothing in this confusion; everything is almost as bad as ever. Besides that, I have been flying around to get Miriam a wagon. I know she is half distracted at being there alone. Mother chose staying with all its evils. Charlie's life would pay the penalty of a cotton burner if he returned, so Lilly remains at Greenwell with him. We three will get on as best we can here. I wrote to the country to get a wagon, sent a pass from Headquarters, but I will never know if it reached her until I see her in town. I hope it will; I would be better satisfied with Miriam.

Miriam and Mattie drove in, in the little buggy, last evening after sunset, to find out what we were to do. Our condition is desperate. Beauregard is about attacking these Federals. They say he is coming from Corinth, and the fight will be in town. If true, we are lost again. Starvation at Greenwell, fever and bullets here, will put an end to us soon enough. There is no refuge for us, no one to consult. Brother, whose judgment we rely on as implicitly as we did on father's, we hear has gone to New York; there is no one to advise or direct us, for, if he is gone, there is no man in Louisiana whose decision I would blindly abide by. Let us stay and die. We can only die once; we can suffer a thousand deaths with suspense and uncertainty; the shortest is the best. Do you think the few words here can give an idea of our agony and despair? Nothing can express it. I feel a thousand years old to-day. I have shed the bitterest tears to-day that I have shed since father died. I can't stand it much longer; I'll give way presently, and I know my heart will break. Shame! Where is God? A fig for your religion, if it only lasts while the sun shines! "Better days are coming" - I can't!

Troops are constantly passing and repassing. They have scoured the country for ten miles out, in search of guerrillas. We are here without servants, clothing, or the bare necessaries of life: suppose they should seize them on the way! I procured a pass for the wagon, but it now seems doubtful if I can get the latter - a very faint chance. Well! let them go; our home next; then we can die sure enough. With God's help, I can stand anything yet in store for me. "I hope to die shouting, the Lord will provide!" Poor Lavinia! if she could only see us! I am glad she does not know our condition.

5 P.M.

What a day of agony, doubt, uncertainty, and despair! Heaven save me from another such! Every hour fresh difficulties arose, until I believe we were almost crazy, every one of us.

As Miriam was about stepping in the buggy, to go to Greenwell to bring in our trunks, mother's heart misgave her, and she decided to sacrifice her properly rather than remain in this state any longer. After a desperate discussion which proved that each argument was death, she decided to go back to Greenwell and give up the keys of the house to General Williams, and let him do as he pleased, rather than have it broken open during her absence. Mattie and Mr. Tunnard were present at the discussion, which ended by the latter stepping in the buggy and driving Miriam to the Garrison. General Williams called her by name, and asked her about Major Drum. It seems all these people, native and foreign, know us, while we know none. Miriam told him our condition, how our brothers were away, father dead, and mother afraid to remain, yet unwilling to lose her property by going away; how we three were alone and unprotected here, but would remain rather than have our home confiscated. He assured her the house should not be touched, that it would be respected in our absence as though we were in it, and he would place a sentinel at the door to guard it against his own men who might be disposed to enter. The latter she declined, but he said he would send his aide to mark the house, that it might be known. A moment after they got back, the aide, Mr. Biddle (I have his name to so many passes that I know it now), came to the door. Mr. Tunnard left him there, uncertain how we would receive a Christian, and I went out and asked him in. He looked uncertain of his reception, too, when we put an end to his doubt by treating him as we invariably treat gentlemen who appear such. He behaved remarkably well under the trying circumstances, and insisted on a sentinel; for, he said, though they would respect the property, there were many bad characters among the soldiers who might attempt to rob it, and the sentinel would protect it. After a visit of ten minutes, devoted exclusively to the affair, he arose and took his leave, leaving me under the impression that he was a gentleman wherever he came from, even if there were a few grammatical errors in the pass he wrote me yesterday; but "thou that judgest another, dost thou sin?"

Well, now we say, fly to Greenwell. Yes! and by tonight, a most exaggerated account of the whole affair will be spread over the whole country, and we will be equally suspected by our own people. Those who spread useless falsehoods about us will gladly have a foundation for a monstrous one. Did n't Camp Moore ring with the story of our entertaining the Federal officers? did n't they spread the report that Miriam danced with one to the tune of "Yankee Doodle" in the State House garden? What will they stop at now? O! if I was only a man, and knew what to do!

Night.

We were so distressed by the false position in which we would be placed by a Federal sentinel, that we did not know what course to pursue. As all our friends shook their heads and said it was dangerous, we knew full well what our enemies would say. If we win Baton Rouge, as I pray we will, they will say we asked protection from Yankees against our own men, are consequently traitors, and our property will be confiscated by our own Government. To decline General Williams's kind offer exposes the house to being plundered. In our dilemma, we made up our minds to stay, so we could say the sentinel was unnecessary.

Presently a file of six soldiers marched to the gate, an officer came to the steps and introduced himself as Colonel McMillan, of 21st Indiana Volunteers. He asked if this was Mrs. Morgan's; the General had ordered a guard placed around the house; he would suggest placing them in different parts of the yard. "Madam, the pickets await your orders." Miriam in a desperate fright undertook to speak for mother, and asked if he thought there was any necessity. No, but it was an additional security, he said.

"Then, if no actual necessity, we will relieve you of the disagreeable duty, as we expect to remain in town," she said. He was very kind, and discussed the whole affair with us, saying when we made up our minds to leave, - we told him after we could not decide, - to write him word, and he would place a guard around to prevent his men and the negroes from breaking in. It was a singular situation: our brothers off fighting them, while these Federal officers leaned over our fence, and an officer standing on our steps offered to protect us. These people are certainly very kind to us. General Williams especially must be a dear old gentleman; he is so good.

How many good, and how many mean people these troubles have shown us! I am beginning to see my true friends, now; there is a large number of them, too. Everybody from whom we least expected attention has agreeably surprised us. . . .

General Williams will believe we are insane from our changing so often.

His guard positively refused.

June 5th.

Last night I determined to stay. Miriam went after our trunks at daylight. A few hours after, Lilly wrote we must go back. McClellan's army was cut to pieces and driven back to Maryland, by Jackson; the Federals were being driven into the swamp from Richmond, too. Beauregard is undoubtedly coming to attack Baton Rouge; his fire would burn the town, if the gunboats do not; the Yankees will shell, at all events, if forced to retire. It cannot stand. We can't go to New Orleans. Butler says he will lay it in ashes if he is forced to evacuate it, from yellow fever or other causes. Both must be burned. Greenwell is not worth the powder it would cost, so we must stand the chance of murder and starvation there, rather than the certainty of being placed between two fires here. Well, I see nothing but bloodshed and beggary staring us in the face. Let it come. "I hope to die shouting, the Lord will provide."

June 6th.

We dined at Mrs. Brunot's yesterday, and sitting on the gallery later, had the full benefit of a Yankee drill. They stopped in front of the house and went through some very curious manoeuvres, and then marched out to their drill-ground beyond. In returning, the whole regiment drew up directly before us, and we were dreadfully quiet for five minutes, the most uncomfortable I have experienced for some time. For it was absurd to look at the sky, and I looked in vain for one man with downcast eyes whereon I might rest mine; but from the officers down to the last private, they were all looking at us. I believe I would have cried with embarrassment if the command had not been given at that moment. They drilled splendidly, and knew it, too, so went through it as though they had not been at it for an hour before. One conceited, red-headed lieutenant smiled at us in the most fascinating way; perhaps he smiled to think how fine he was, and what an impression he was making.

We got back to our solitary house before twilight, and were sitting on the balcony, when Mr. Biddle entered. He came to ask if the guard had been placed here last night. It seems to me it would have saved him such a long walk if he had asked Colonel McMillan. He sat down, though, and got talking in the moonlight, and people passing, some citizens, some officers, looked wonderingly at this unheard-of occurrence. I won't be rude to any one in my own house, Yankee or Southern, say what they will. He talked a great deal, and was very entertaining; what tempted him, I cannot imagine. It was two hours before he thought of leaving. He was certainly very kind. He spoke of the scarcity of flour in town; said they had quantities at the Garrison, and asked permission to send us a barrel, which of course we refused. It showed a very good heart, though. He offered to take charge of any letters I would write; said he had heard General Williams speak of Harry; and when he at last left, I was still more pleased with him for this kindness to us. He says Captain Huger is dead. I am very, very much distressed. They are related, he says. He talked so reasonably of the war, that it was quite a novelty after reading the abusive newspapers of both sides. I like him, and was sorry I could not ask him to repeat his visit. We are unaccustomed to treat gentlemen that way; but it won't do in the present state to act as we please. Mob governs.

Mother kept me awake all night to listen to the mice in the garret. Every time I would doze she would ask, "What's that?" and insist that the mice were men. I had to get up and look for an imaginary host, so I am tired enough this morning.

Miriam has just got in with all the servants, our baggage is on the way, so we will be obliged to stay whether we will or no. I don't care; it is all the same starve or burn. Oh! I forgot. Mr. Biddle did not write that pass! It was his clerk. He speaks very grammatically, so far as I can judge! !

June 8th, Sunday.

These people mean to kill us with kindness. There is such a thing as being too kind. Yesterday General Williams sent a barrel of flour to mother accompanied by a note begging her to accept it "in consideration of the present condition of the circulating currency," and the intention was so kind, the way it was done so delicate, that there was no refusing it. I had to write her thanks, and got in a violent fit of the "trembles" at the idea of writing to a stranger. One consolation is, that I am not a very big fool, for it took only three lines to prove myself one. If I had been a thundering big one, I would have occupied two pages to show myself fully. And to think it is out of our power to prove them our appreciation of the kindness we have universally met with! Many officers were in church this morning and as they passed us while we waited for the door to be opened, General Williams bowed profoundly, another followed his example; we returned the salute, of course. But by to-morrow, those he did not bow to will cry treason against us. Let them howl. I am tired of lies, scandal, and deceit. All the loudest gossips have been frightened into the country, but enough remain to keep them well supplied with town talk. . . . It is such a consolation to turn to the dear good people of the world after coming in contact with such cattle. Here, for instance, is Mr. Bonnecase on whom we have not the slightest claims. Every day since we have been here, he has sent a great pitcher of milk, knowing our cow is out; one day he sent rice, the next sardines, yesterday two bottles of Port and Madeira, which cannot be purchased in the whole South. What a duck of an old man! That is only one instance.

June 10th.

This morning while I was attending to my flowers . . . several soldiers stopped in front of me, and holding on the fence, commenced to talk about some brave Colonel, and a shooting affair last night. When all had gone except one who was watching me attentively, as he seemed to wish to tell me, I let him go ahead. The story was that Colonel McMillan was shot through the shoulder, breast, and liver, by three guerrillas while four miles from town last night, on a scout. He was a quarter of a mile from his own men at the time, killed one who shot him, took the other two prisoners, and fell from his horse himself, when he got within the lines. The soldier said these two guerrillas would probably be hanged, while the six we saw pass captives, Sunday, would probably be sent to Fort Jackson for life. I think the guerrilla affair mere murder, I confess; but what a dreadful fate for these young men! One who passed Sunday was Jimmy's schoolmate, a boy of sixteen; another, Willie Garig, the pet of a whole family of good, honest country people. . . .

These soldiers will get in the habit of talking to me after a while, through my own fault. Yesterday I could not resist the temptation to ask the fate of the six guerrillas, and stopped two volunteers who were going by, to ask them. They discussed the fate of the country, told me Fort Pillow and Vicksburg were evacuated, the Mississippi opened from source to mouth; I told them of Banks's and McClellan's defeat; they assured me it would all be over in a month, - which I fervently prey may be so; told me they were from Michigan (one was Mr. Bee, he laid, cousin of our General); and they would probably have talked all day if I had not bowed myself away with thanks for their information.

It made me ashamed to contrast the quiet, gentlemanly, liberal way these volunteers spoke of us and our cause, with the rabid, fanatical, abusive violence of our own female Secession declaimers. Thank heaven, I have never yet made my appearance as a Billingsgate orator on these occasions. All my violent feelings, which in moments of intense excitement were really violent, I have recorded in this book; I am happy to say only the reasonable dislike to seeing my country subjugated has been confided to the public ear, when necessary; and that even now, I confess that nothing but the reign of terror and gross prejudice by which I was surrounded at that time could justify many expressions I have here applied to them. Fact is, these people have disarmed me by their kindness. I expected to be in a crowd of ruffian soldiers, who would think nothing of cutting your throat or doing anything they felt like; and I find, among all these thousands, not one who offers the slightest annoyance or disrespect. The former is the thing as it is believed by the whole country, the latter the true state of affairs. I admire foes who show so much consideration for our feelings.

Contrast these with our volunteers from New Orleans - all gentlemen - who came to take the Garrison from Major Haskins. Several of them passing our gate where we were standing with the Brunots, one exclaimed, "What pretty girls!" It was a stage aside that we were supposed not to hear. "Yes," said another; "beautiful! but they look as though they could be fast." Fast! and we were not even speaking! not even looking at them! Sophie and I were walking presently, and met half a dozen. We had to stop to let them pass the crossing; they did not think of making way for us; No. 1 sighed - such a sigh! No. 2 followed, and so on, when they all sighed in chorus for our edification, while we dared not raise our eyes from the ground. That is the time I would have made use of a dagger. Two passed in a buggy, and trusting to our not recognizing them from the rapidity of their vehicle, kissed their hands to us until they were out of sight! All went back to New Orleans vowing Baton Rouge had the prettiest girls in the world. These were our own people, the élite of New Orleans, loyal Southerners and gentlemen. These Northerners pass us satisfied with a simple glance; some take off their hats, for all these officers know our name, though we may not know theirs; how, I can't say.

When I heard of Colonel McMillan's misfortune, mother conspired with me to send over some bandages, and something Tiche manufactured of flour under the name of "nourishment," for he is across the street at Heroman's. Miriam objected on account of what "our people" will say, and what we will suffer for it if the guerrillas reach town, but we persuaded her we were right. . . . You can imagine our condition at present, many years hence, Sarah, when you reflect that it is the brave, noble-hearted, generous Miriam who is afraid to do that deed on account of "public opinion," which indeed is "down" on us. At Greenwell they are frantic about our returning to town, and call us traitors, Yankees, and vow vengeance. . . . A lady said to me, "The guerrillas have a black list containing the names of those remaining in town. All the men are to be hanged, their houses burned, and all the women are to be tarred and feathered." I said, "Madam, if I believed them capable of such a vile threat, even, much less the execution, I would see them cut down without a feeling of compassion" (which is not true), "and swear I was a Yankee rather than claim being a native of the same country with such brutes." She has a long tongue; when I next hear of it, it will be that I told the story, and called them brutes and hoped they would be shot, etc. And so goes the world. No one will think of saying that I did not believe them guilty of the thought, even. Our three brothers may be sick or wounded at this minute; what I do for this man, God will send some one to do for them, and with that belief I do it. . . .

June 11th.

Last evening mother and Miriam went to the Arsenal to see if they would be allowed to do anything for the prisoners. General Williams received them, and fascinated Miriam by his manner, as usual. Poor Miriam is always being fascinated, according to her own account. He sent for little Nathan Castle and Willie Garig, and left them alone in the room with them, showing his confidence and delicacy by walking away. The poor young men were very grateful to be remembered; one had his eyes too full of tears to speak. Mr. Garig told Miriam that when the story of her refusing the escort was told in camp, the woods rang with shouts of "Three cheers for Miss Morgan!" They said they were treated very well, and had no want, except clean clothes, and to let their mothers know they were well and content.

I have been hard at work mending three or four suits of the boys' clothing for those poor young men. Some needed thread and needle very much, but it was the best we could do. So I packed them all up - not forgetting a row of pins - and sent Tiche off with the bundle, perched real Congo fashion on her many-colored head-handkerchief, which was tied in the most superb Creole style in honor of the occasion.

June 16th, Monday.

My poor old diary comes to a very abrupt end, to my great distress. The hardest thing in the world is to break off journalizing when you are once accustomed to it, and mine has proved such a resource to me in these dark days of trouble that I feel as though I were saying good-bye to an old and tried friend. Thanks to my liberal supply of pens, ink, and paper, how many inexpressibly dreary days I have filled up to my own satisfaction, if not to that of others! How many disagreeable affairs it has caused me to pass over without another thought, how many times it has proved a relief to me where my tongue was forced to remain quiet! Without the blessed materials, I would have fallen victim to despair and "the Blues" long since; but they have kept my eyes fixed on "Better days a-coming" while slightly alluding to present woes; kept me from making a fool of myself many a day; acted as lightning rod to my mental thunder, and have made me happy generally. For all of which I cry, "Vivent pen, ink, and paper!" and add with regret, "Adieu, my mental Conductor. I fear this unchained lightning will strike somewhere, in your absence!"

Book II

"I hope to die shouting, the Lord will provide!"

Monday, June 16th, 1862.

THERE is no use in trying to break off journalizing, particularly in "these trying times." It has become a necessity to me. I believe I should go off in a rapid decline if Butler took it in his head to prohibit that among other things. . . . I reserve to myself the privilege of writing my opinions, since I trouble no one with the expression of them. . . . I insist, that if the valor and chivalry of our men cannot save our country, I would rather have it conquered by a brave race than owe its liberty to the Billingsgate oratory and demonstrations of some of these "ladies." If the women have the upper hand then, as they have now, I would not like to live in a country governed by such tongues. Do I consider the female who could spit in a gentleman's face, merely because he wore United States buttons, as a fit associate for me? Lieutenant Biddle assured me he did not pass a street in New Orleans without being most grossly insulted by ladies. It was a friend of his into whose face a lady spit as he walked quietly by without looking at her. (Wonder if she did it to attract his attention?) He had the sense to apply to her husband and give him two minutes to apologize or die, and of course he chose the former. Such things are enough to disgust any one. "Loud" women, what a contempt I have for you! How I despise your vulgarity!

Some of these Ultra-Secessionists, evidently very recently from "down East," who think themselves obliged to "kick up their heels over the Bonny Blue Flag," as Brother describes female patriotism, shriek out, "What! see those vile Northerners pass patiently! No true Southerner could see it without rage. I could kill them! I hate them with all my soul, the murderers, liars, thieves, rascals! You are no Southerner if you do not hate them as much as I!" Ah ça! a true-blue Yankee tell me that I, born and bred here, am no Southerner! I always think, "It is well for you, my friend, to save your credit, else you might be suspected by some people, though your violence is enough for me." I always say, "You may do as you please; my brothers are fighting for me, and doing their duty, so that excess of patriotism is unnecessary for me, as my position is too well known to make any demonstrations requisite."

This war has brought out wicked, malignant feelings that I did not believe could dwell in woman's heart. I see some of the holiest eyes, so holy one would think the very spirit of charity lived in them, and all Christian meekness, go off in a mad tirade of abuse and say, with the holy eyes wondrously

I hope God will send down plague, yellow fever, famine, on these vile Yankees, and that not one will escape death. O, what unutterable horror that remark causes me as often as I hear it! I think of the many mothers, wives, and sisters who wait as anxiously, pray as fervently in their faraway homes for their dear ones, as we do here; I fancy them waiting day after day for the footsteps that will never come, growing more sad, lonely, and heart-broken as the days wear on; I think of how awful it would be if one would say, "Your brothers are dead"; how it would crush all life and happiness out of me; and I say, "God forgive these poor women! They know not what they say!" O women! into what loathsome violence you have abased your holy mission! God will punish us for our hard-heartedness. Not a square off, in the new theatre, lie more than a hundred sick soldiers. What woman has stretched out her hand to save them, to give them a cup of cold water? Where is the charity which should ignore nations and creeds, and administer help to the Indian and Heathen indifferently? Gone! All gone in a Union versus Secession! That is what the American War has brought us. If I was independent, if I could work my own will without causing others to suffer for my deeds, I would not be poring over this stupid page; I would not be idly reading or sewing. I would put aside woman's trash, take up woman's duty, and I would stand by some forsaken man and bid him Godspeed as he closes his dying eyes. That is woman's mission! and not Preaching and Politics. I say I would, yet here I sit! O for liberty! the liberty that dares do what conscience dictates, and scorns all smaller rules! If I could help these dying men! Yet it is as impossible as though I was a chained bear. I can't put out my hand. I am threatened with Coventry because I sent a custard to a sick man who is in the army, and with the anathema of society because I said if I could possibly do anything for Mr. Biddle - at a distance - (he is sick) I would like to very much. Charlie thinks we have acted shockingly in helping Colonel McMillan, and that we will suffer for it when the Federals leave. I would like to see any man who dared harm my father's daughter! But as he seems to think our conduct reflects on him, there is no alternative. Die, poor men, without a woman's hand to close your eyes! We women are too patriotic to help you! I look eagerly on, cry in my soul, "I wish -"; you die; God judges me. Behold the woman who dares not risk private ties for God's glory and her professed religion! Coward, helpless woman that I am! If I was free -!

June 17th.

Yesterday, and day before, boats were constantly arriving and troops embarking from here, destined for Vicksburg. There will be another fight, and of course it will fall. I wish Will was out of it; I don't want him to die. I got the kindest, sweetest letter from Will when Miriam came from Greenwell. It was given to her by a guerrilla on the road who asked if she was not Miss Sarah Morgan.

June 18th.

How long, O how long, is it since I have lain down in peace, thinking, "This night I will rest in safety"? Certainly not since the fall of Fort Jackson. If left to myself, I would not anticipate evil, but would quietly await the issue of all these dreadful events; but when I hear men, who certainly should know better than I, express their belief that in twenty-four hours the town will be laid in ashes, I begin to grow uneasy, and think it must be so, since they say it. These last few days, since the news arrived of the intervention of the English and French, I have alternately risen and fallen from the depth of despair to the height of delight and expectation, as the probability of another exodus diminishes, and peace appears more probable. If these men would not prophesy the burning of the city, I would be perfectly satisfied. . . .

Well! I packed up a few articles to satisfy my conscience, since these men insist that another run is inevitable, though against my own conviction. I am afraid I was partly influenced by my dream last night of being shelled out unexpectedly and flying without saving an article. It was the same dream I had a night or two before we fled so ingloriously from Baton Rouge, when I dreamed of meeting Will Pinckney suddenly, who greeted me in the most extraordinarily affectionate manner, and told me that Vicksburg had fallen. He said he had been chiefly to blame, and the Southerners were so incensed at his losing, the Northerners at his defending, that both were determined to hang him; he was running for his life. He took me to a hill from which I could see the Garrison, and the American flag flying over it. I looked, and saw we were standing in blood up to our knees, while here and there ghastly white bones shone above the red surface. Just then, below me I saw crowds of people running. "What is it?" I asked. "It means that in another instant they will commence to shell the town. Save yourself." "But Will - I must save some clothes, too! How can I go among strangers with a single dress? I will get some!" I cried. He smiled and said, "You will run with only what articles you happen to have on." Bang! went the first shell, the people rushed by with screams, and I awakened to tell Miriam what an absurd dream I had had. It happened as Will had said, either that same day or the day after; for the change of clothes we saved apiece were given to Tiche, who lost sight of us and quietly came home when all was over, and the two dirty skirts and old cloak mother saved, after carrying them a mile and a half, I put in the buggy that took her up; so I saved nothing except the bag that was tied under my hoops. Will was right. I saved not even my powder-bag. (Tiche had it in the bundle.) My handkerchief I gave mother before we had walked three squares, and throughout that long fearfully warm day, riding and walking through the fiery sunshine and stifling dust, I had neither to cool or comfort me.

June 19th.

Miriam and I have disgraced ourselves! This morning I was quietly hearing Dellie's lessons, when I was startled by mother's shrieks of "Send for a guard - they've murdered him!" I saw through the window a soldier sitting in the road just opposite with blood streaming from his hand in a great pool in the dust. I was downstairs in three bounds, and snatching up some water, ran to where he sat alone not a creature near, though all the inhabitants of our side of the street were looking on from the balconies all crying "Murder!" and "Help!" without moving themselves. I poured some water on the man's bloody hand, as he held it streaming with gore up to me, saying, "The man in there did it," meaning the one who keeps the little grog-shop, though it puzzled me at the time to see that all the doors were closed and not a face visible. I had hardly time to speak when Tiche called loudly to me to come away, - she was safe at the front gate, - and looking up, I found myself in a knot of a dozen soldiers, and took her advice and retreated home. It proved to be the guard Miriam had roused. She ran out as I did and seeing a gentleman, begged him to call the guard for that murdered man. The individual - he must have been a "patriot "

- said he did n't know where to find one. She cried out they were at Heroman's; he said he did n't believe they were. "Go! I tell you!" she screamed at last; but the brave man said he did n't like to, so she ran to the corner and called the soldiers herself. O most brave man! Before we got back from our several expeditions, we heard mother, Lilly, Mrs. Day, all shouting, "Bring in the children! lock the doors!" etc. All for a poor wounded soldier!

We after discovered that the man was drunk, and had cursed the woman of the grog-shop, whereupon her husband had pitched him out in the street, where they found him. They say he hurt his hand against a post; but wood could never have cut deep enough to shed all that gore. I don't care if he was drunk or sober, soldier or officer, Federal or Confederate! If he had been Satan himself lying helpless and bleeding in the street, I would have gone to him! I can't believe it was as criminal as though I had watched quietly from a distance, believing him dying and contenting myself with looking on. Yet it seems it was dreadfully indecorous; Miriam and I did very wrong; we should have shouted murder with the rest of the women and servants. Whereas the man who declined committing himself by calling one soldier to the rescue of another, supposed to be dying, acted most discreetly, and showed his wisdom in the most striking manner.

May I never be discreet, or wise, if this is Christian conduct, or a sample of either! I would rather be a rash, impetuous fool! Charlie says he would not open his mouth to save a dozen from being murdered. I say I am not Stoic enough for that. Lilly agrees with him, Miriam with me; so here we two culprits stand alone before the tribunal of "patriotism." Madame Roland, I take the liberty of altering your words and cry, "O Patriotism! How many base deeds are sanctioned by your name!" Don't I wish I was a heathen! In twenty-four hours the whole country will be down on us.

O for a pen to paint the slaves
Whose "country" like a deadly blight;
Closes all hearts when Pity craves
And turns God's spirit to darkest night!
May life's patriotic cup for such
Be filled with glory overmuch;
And when their spirits go above in pride,
Spirit of Patriotism, let these valiant abide
Full in the sight of grand mass-meeting - I don't
Want you to cuss them,
But put them where they can hear politics,
And yet can't discuss them!
(I can't say worse than that!)

June 26th.

Yesterday morning, just as I stepped out of bed I heard the report of four cannon fired in rapid succession, and everybody asked everybody else, "Did you hear that?" so significantly, that I must say my heart beat very rapidly for a few moments, at the thought of another stampede. At half-past six this morning I was wakened by another report, followed by seven others, and heard again the question, "Did you hear that?" on a higher key than yesterday. - It did not take me many minutes to get out of bed, and to slip on a few articles, I confess. My chief desire was to wash my face before running, if they were actually shelling us again. It appears that they were only practicing, however, and no harm was intended. But we are living on such a volcano, that, not knowing what to expect, we are rather nervous.

I am afraid this close confinement will prove too much for me; my long walks are cut off, on account of the soldiers. One month to-morrow since my last visit to the graveyard! That haunts me always; it must be so dreary out there! Here is a sketch of my daily life, enough to finish me off forever, if much longer persisted in.

First, get up a little before seven. After breakfast, which is generally within a few minutes after I get down (it used to be just as I got ready, and sometimes before, last winter), I attend to my garden, which consists of two strips of ground the length of the house, in front, where I can find an hour's work in examining and admiring my flowers, replanting those that the cows and horses occasionally (once a day) pull up for me, and in turning the soil over and over again to see which side grows best. O my garden! abode of rare delights! how many pleasant hours I have passed in you, armed with scissors, knife, hoe, or rake, only pausing when Mr. This or Mr. That leaned over the fence to have a talk! - last spring, that was; ever so many are dead now, for all I know, and all off at the war. Now I work for the edification of proper young women, who look in astonishment at me, as they would consider themselves degraded by the pursuit. A delicate pair of hands my flower mania will leave me!

Then I hear Dellie's and Morgan's lessons, after which I open my desk and am lost in the mysteries of Arithmetic, Geography, Blair's Lectures, Noël et Chapsal, Ollendorff, and reading aloud in French and English, besides writing occasionally in each, and sometimes a peep at Lavoisne, until very nearly dinner. The day is not half long enough for me. Many things I would like to study I am forced to give up, for want of leisure to devote to them. But one of these days, I will make up for present deficiencies. I study only what I absolutely love, now; but then, if I can, I will study what I am at present ignorant of, and cultivate a taste for something new.

The few moments before dinner, and all the time after, I devote to writing, sewing, knitting, etc., and if I included darning, repairs, alterations, etc., my list would be tremendous, for I get through with a great deal of sewing. Somewhere in the day, I find half an hour, or more, to spend at the piano. Before sunset I dress, and am free to spend the evening at home, or else walk to Mrs. Brunot's, for it is not safe to go farther than those three squares, away from home. From early twilight until supper, Miriam and I sing with the guitar, generally, and after, sit comfortably under the chandelier and read until about ten. What little reading I do, is almost exclusively done at that time. It sounds woefully little, but my list of books grows to quite a respectable size, in the course of a year.

At ten comes my Bible class for the servants. Lucy, Rose, Nancy, and Dophy assemble in my room, and hear me read the Bible, or stories from the Bible for a while. Then one by one say their prayers - they cannot be persuaded to say them together; Dophy says "she can't say with Rose, 'cause she ain't got no brothers and sisters to pray for," and Lucy has no father or mother, and so they go. All difficulties and grievances during the day are laid before me, and I sit like Moses judging the children of Israel, until I can appease the discord. Sometimes it is not so easy. For instance, that memorable night when I had to work Rose's stubborn heart to a proper pitch of repentance for having stabbed a carving fork in Lucy's arm in a fit of temper. I don't know that I was ever as much astonished as I was at seeing the dogged, sullen girl throw herself on the floor in a burst of tears, and say if God would forgive her she would never do it again. I was lashing myself internally for not being able to speak as I should, furious at myself for talking so weakly, and lo! here the girl tumbles over wailing and weeping! And Dophy, overcome by her feelings, sobs, "Lucy, I scratched you last week! please forgive me this once !" And amazed and bewildered I look at the touching tableau before me of kissing and reconciliation, for Lucy can bear malice toward no one, and is ready to forgive before others repent, and I look from one to the other, wondering what it was that upset them so completely, for certainly no words of mine caused it. Sometimes Lucy sings a wild hymn, "Did you ever hear the heaven bells ring?" "Come, my loving brothers," "When I put on my starry crown," etc.; and after some such scene as that just described, it is pleasant to hear them going out of the room saying, "Good-night, Miss Sarah!" "God bless Miss Sarah!" and all that.

June 27th.

A proclamation of Van Dorn has just been smuggled into town, that advises all persons living within eight miles of the Mississippi to remove into the interior, as he is determined to defend his department at all hazards to the last extremity. Does not look like the Peace I have been deluding myself with, does it? That means another Exodus. How are we to leave, when we are not allowed to pass the limits of the corporation by the Federals? Where are we to go? We are between the two armies, and here we must remain patiently awaiting the result. Some of these dark nights, bang! we will hear the cannon, and then it will be sauve qui peut in a shower of shells Bah! I don't believe God will suffer that we should be murdered in such a dreadful way! I don't believe He will suffer us to be turned homeless and naked on the world! "Something will turn up" before we are attacked, and we will be spared, I am certain. We can't look forward more than an hour at a time now, sometimes not a minute ahead (witness the shelling frolic), so I must resume my old habit of laying a clean dress on my bed before going to sleep, which I did every night for six weeks before the shelling of Baton Rouge, in order to run respectably, as muslin cross-bar nightgowns are not suitable for day dresses.

June 28th.

I am afraid I shall be nervous when the moment of the bombardment actually arrives. This suspense is not calculated to soothe one's nerves. A few moments since, a salute was fired in honor of General Butler's arrival, when women, children, and servants rushed to the front of the houses, confident of a repetition of the shelling which occurred a month ago to-day. The children have not forgotten the scene, for they all actually howled with fear. Poor little Sarah stopped her screams to say, "Mother, don't you wish we was dogs 'stead o' white folks?" in such piteous accents that we had to laugh. Don't I wish I was a dog! Sarah is right. I don't know if I showed my uneasiness a while ago, but certainly my heart has hardly yet ceased beating rather rapidly. If I knew what moment to expect the stampede, I would not mind; but this way - to expect it every instant - it is too much!' Again, if I knew where we could go for refuge from the shells! -

A window banging unexpectedly just then gave me a curious twinge; not that I thought it was the signal, oh, dear, no! I just thought - what, I wonder? Pshaw! "Picayune Butler's coming, coming" has upset my nervous system. He interrupted me in the middle of my arithmetic; and I have not the energy to resume my studies. I shall try what effect an hour's practice will have on my spirits, and will see that I have a pair of clean stockings in my stampede sack, and that the fastenings of my "running-bag" are safe. Though if I expect to take either, I should keep in harness constantly. How long, O Lord! how long?

June 29th, Sunday.

"Any more, Mr. Lincoln, any more?" Can't you leave our racked homes in repose? We are all wild. Last night, five citizens were arrested, on no charge at all, and carried down to Picayune Butler's ship. What a thrill of terror ran through the whole community! We all felt so helpless, so powerless under the hand of our tyrant, the man who swore to uphold the Constitution and the laws, who is professedly only fighting to give us all Liberty, the birthright of every American, and who, nevertheless, has ground us down to a state where we would not reduce our negroes, who tortures and sneers at us, and rules us with an iron hand! Ah! Liberty! what a humbug! I would rather belong to England or France, than to the North! Bondage, woman that I am, I can never stand! Even now, the Northern papers, distributed among us, taunt us with our subjection and tell us "how coolly Butler will grind them down, paying no regard to their writhing and torture beyond tightening the bonds still more!" Ah, truly! this is the bitterness of slavery, to be insulted and reviled by cowards who are safe at home and enjoy the protection of the laws, while we, captive and overpowered, dare not raise our voices to throw back the insult, and are governed by the despotism of one man, whose word is our law! And that man, they tell us, "is the right man in the right place. He will develop a Union sentiment among the people, if the thing can be done!" Come and see if he can! Hear the curse that arises from thousands of hearts at that man's name and say if he will "speedily bring us to our senses." Will he accomplish it by love, tenderness, mercy, compassion? He might have done it; but did he try? When he came, he assumed his natural rôle as tyrant, and bravely has he acted it through, never once turning aside for Justice or Mercy. . . . This degradation is worse than the bitterness of death!

I see no salvation on either side. No glory awaits the Southern Confederacy, even if it does achieve its independence; it will be a mere speck in the world, with no weight or authority. The North confesses itself lost without us, and has paid an unheard-of ransom to regain us. On the other hand, conquered, what hope is there in this world for us? Broken in health and fortune, reviled, contemned, abused by those who claim already to have subdued us, without a prospect of future support for those few of our brothers who return; outcasts without home or honor, would not death or exile be preferable? Oh, let us abandon our loved home to these implacable enemies, and find refuge elsewhere! Take from us property, everything, only grant us liberty! Is this rather frantic, considering I abhor politics, and women who meddle with them, above all? My opinion has not yet changed; I still feel the same contempt for a woman who would talk at the top of her voice for the edification of Federal officers, as though anxious to receive an invitation requesting her presence at the Garrison. "I can suffer and be still" as far as outward signs are concerned; but as no word of this has passed my lips, I give it vent in writing which is more lasting than words, partly to relieve my heart, partly to prove to my own satisfaction that I am no coward; for one line of this, surrounded as we are by soldiers, and liable to have our houses searched at any instant, would be a sufficient indictment for high treason.

Under General Williams's rule, I was perfectly satisfied that whatever was done, was done through necessity, and under orders from Headquarters, beyond his control; we all liked him. But now, since Butler's arrival, I believe I am as frantic in secret as the others are openly. I know that war sanctions many hard things, and that both sides practice them; but now we are so completely lost in Louisiana, Is it fair to gibe and taunt us with our humiliation? I could stand anything save the cowardly ridicule and triumph of their papers. Honestly, I believe if all vile abusive papers on both sides were suppressed, and some of the fire-eating editors who make a living by lying were soundly cowhided or had their ears clipped, it would do more towards establishing peace, than all the bloodshedding either side can afford. I hope to live to see it, too. Seems to me, more liberty is allowed to the press than would be tolerated in speech. Let us speak as freely as any paper, and see if to-morrow we do not sleep at Fort Jackson!

This morning the excitement is rare; fifteen more citizens were arrested and carried off, and all the rest grew wild with expectation. So great a martyrdom is it considered, that I am sure those who are not arrested will be woefully disappointed. It is ludicrous to see how each man thinks he is the very one they are in search of! We asked a twopenny lawyer, of no more importance in the community than Dophy is, if it was possible he was not arrested. "But I am expecting to be every instant!" So much for his self-assurance! Those arrested have, some, been quietly released (those are so smiling and mysterious that I suspect them), some been obliged to take the oath, some sent to Fort Jackson. Ah, Liberty! What a blessing it is to enjoy thy privileges! If some of these poor men are not taken prisoners, they will die of mortification at the slight.

Our valiant Governor, the brave Moore, has by order of the real Governor, Moïse, made himself visible at some far-distant point, and issued a proclamation, saying, whereas we of Baton Rouge were held forcibly in town, he therefore considered men, women, and children prisoners of war, and as such the Yankees are bound to supply us with all necessaries, and consequently any one sending us aid or comfort or provisions from the country will be severely punished. Only Moore is fool enough for such an order. Held down by the Federals, our paper money so much trash, with hardly any other to buy food and no way of earning it; threatened with starvation and utter ruin, our own friends, by way of making our burden lighter, forbid our receiving the means of prolonging life, and after generously warning us to leave town, which they know is perfectly impossible, prepare to burn it over our heads, and let the women run the same risk as the men. Penned in on one little square mile, here we await our fate like sheep in the slaughter-pen. Our hour may be at hand now, it may be to-night; we have only to wait; the booming of the cannon will announce it to us soon enough.

Of the six sentenced to Fort Jackson, one is the Methodist minister, Mr. Craven. The only charge is, that he was heard to pray for the Confederate States by some officers who passed his house during his family prayers. According to that, which of us would escape unhung? I do not believe there is a woman in the land who closes her eyes before praying for God's blessing on the side on which her brothers are engaged. Are we all to cease? Show me the dungeon deep enough to keep me from praying for them! The man represented that he had a large family totally dependent on him, who must starve. "Let them get up a subscription," was General Butler's humane answer. "I will head it myself." It is useless to say the generous offer was declined.

June 30th.

As a specimen of the humanity of General Butler, let me record a threat of his uttered with all the force and meaning language can convey, and certainly enough to strike terror in the hearts of frail women, since all these men believe him fully equal to carry it into execution; some even believe it will be done. In speaking to Mr. Solomon Benjamin of foreign intervention in our favor, he said, "Let England or France try it, and I'll be - if I don't arm every negro in the South, and make them cut the throat of every man, woman, and child in it! I'll make them lay the whole country waste with fire and sword, and leave it desolate!" Draw me a finer picture of Coward, Brute, or Bully than that one sentence portrays! O men of the North! you do your noble hearts wrong in sending such ruffians among us as the representatives of a great people! Was ever a more brutal thought uttered in a more brutal way? Mother, like many another, is crazy to go away from here, even to New Orleans; but like the rest, will be obliged to stand and await her fate. I don't believe Butler would dare execute his threat, for at the first attempt, thousands, who are passive now, would cut the brutal heart from his inhuman breast.

Tuesday, July 1st.

I heard such a good joke last night! If I had belonged to the female declaiming club, I fear me I would have resigned instantly through mere terror. (Thank Heaven, I don't!) These officers say the women talk too much, which is undeniable. They then said, they meant to get up a sewing society, and place in it every woman who makes herself conspicuous by her loud talking about them. Fancy what a refinement of torture! But only a few would suffer; the majority would be only too happy to enjoy the usual privilege of sewing societies, slander, abuse, and insinuations. How some would revel in it. The mere threat makes me quake! If I could so far forget my dignity, and my father's name, as to court the notice of gentlemen by contemptible insult, etc., and if I should be ordered to take my seat at the sewing society - ! ! ! I would never hold my head up again! Member of a select sewing circle! Fancy me! (I know "there is never any gossip in our society, though the one over the way gets up dreadful reports"; I have heard all that, but would rather try neither.) Oh, how I would beg and plead! Fifty years at Fort Jackson, good, kind General Butler, rather than half an hour in your sewing society! Gentle, humane ruler, spare me and I split my throat in shouting "Yankee Doodle" and "Hurrah for Lincoln!" Any, every thing, so I am not disgraced! Deliver me from your sewing society, and I'll say and do what you please!

Butler told some of these gentlemen that he had a detective watching almost every house in town, and he knew everything. True or not, it looks suspicious. We are certainly watched. Every evening two men may be seen in the shadow on the other side of the street, standing there until ever so late, sometimes until after we have gone to bed. It may be that, far from home, they are attracted by the bright light and singing, and watch us for their amusement. A few nights ago, so many officers passed and repassed while we were singing on the balcony, that I felt as though our habit of long standing had suddenly become improper. Saturday night, having secured a paper, we were all crowding around, Lilly and I reading every now and then a piece of news from opposite ends of the paper, Charlie, walking on the balcony, found five officers leaning over the fence watching us as we stood under the light, through the open window. Hope they won't elect me to the sewing society!

Thursday night, July 3d.

Another day of sickening suspense. This evening, about three, came the rumor that there was to be an attack on the town to-night, or early in the morning, and we had best be prepared for anything. I can't say I believe it, but in spite of my distrust, I made my preparations. First of all I made a charming improvement in my knapsack, alias pillow-case, by sewing a strong black band down each side of the centre from the bottom to the top, when it is carried back and fastened below again, allowing me to pass my arms through, and thus present the appearance of an old peddler. Miriam's I secured also, and tied all our laces in a handkerchief ready to lay it in the last thing.

But the interior of my bag! - what a medley it is! First, I believe, I have secured four underskirts; three chemises, as many pairs of stockings, two underbodies, the prayer book father gave me, "Tennyson" that Harry gave me when I was fourteen, two unmade muslins, a white mull, English grenadine trimmed with lilac, and a purple linen, and nightgown. Then, I must have Lavinia's daguerreotype, and how could I leave Will's, when perhaps he was dead? Besides, Howell's and Will Carter's were with him, and one single case did not matter. But there was Tom Barker's I would like to keep, and oh! let's take Mr. Stone's! and I can't slight Mr. Dunnington, for these two have been too kind to Jimmy for me to forget; and poor Captain Huger is dead, and I will keep his, so they all went together. A box of pens, too, was indispensable, and a case of French notepaper, and a bundle of Harry's letters were added. Miriam insisted on the old diary that preceded this and found place for it, though I am afraid if she knew what trash she was to carry, she would retract before going farther.

It makes me heartsick to see the utter ruin we will be plunged in if forced to run to-night. Not a hundredth part of what I most value can be saved - if I counted my letters and papers, not a thousandth. But I cannot believe we will run to-night. The soldiers tell whoever questions them that there will be a fight before morning, but I believe it must be to alarm them. Though what looks suspicious is, that the officers said - to whom is not stated - that the ladies must not be uneasy if they heard cannon tonight, as they would probably commence to celebrate the Fourth of July about twelve o'clock. What does it mean? I repeat, I don't believe a word of it; yet I have not yet met the woman or child who is not prepared to fly. Rose knocked at the door just now to show her preparations. Her only thought seems to be mother's silver, so she has quietly taken possession of our shoe-bag, which is a long sack for odds and ends with cases for shoes outside, and has filled it with all the contents of the silver-box; this hung over her arm, and carrying Louis and Sarah, this young Samson says she will be ready to fly.

I don't believe it, yet here I sit, my knapsack serving me for a desk, my seat the chair on which I have carefully spread my clothes in order. At my elbow lies my running- or treasure-bag, surrounded by my cabas filled with hair-pins, starch, and a band I was embroidering, etc.; near it lie our combs, etc., and the whole is crowned by my dagger; - by the way, I must add Miriam's pistol which she has forgotten, though over there lies her knapsack ready, too, with our bonnets and veils.

It is long past eleven, and no sound of the cannon Bah! I do not expect it. "I'll lay me down and sleep in peace, for Thou only, Lord, makest me to dwell in safety." Good-night! I wake up to-morrow the same as usual, and be disappointed that my trouble was unnecessary.

July 4th.

Here I am, and still alive, having wakened but once in the night, and that only in consequence of Louis and Morgan crying; nothing more alarming than that. I ought to feel foolish; but I do not. I am glad I was prepared, even though there was no occasion for it.

While I was taking my early bath, Lilly came to the bath-house and told me through the weather-boarding of another battle. Stonewall Jackson has surrounded McClellan completely, and victory is again ours. This is said to be the sixth battle he has fought in twenty days, and they say he has won them all. And the Seventh Regiment distinguished itself, and was presented with four cannon on the battlefield in acknowledgment of its gallant conduct! Gibbes belongs to the "ragged howling regiment that rushed on the field yelling like unchained devils and spread a panic through the army," as the Northern papers said, describing the battle of Manassas. Oh, how I hope he has escaped!

And they say "Palmerston has urged the recognition of the Confederacy, and an armed intervention on our side." Would it not be glorious? Oh, for peace, blessed peace, and our brothers once more! Palmerston is said to have painted Butler as the vilest oppressor, and having added he was ashamed to acknowledge him of Anglo-Saxon origin. Perhaps knowing the opinion entertained of him by foreign nations, caused Butler to turn such a somersault. For a few days before his arrival here, we saw a leading article in the leading Union paper of New Orleans, threatening us with the arming of the slaves for our extermination if England interfered, in the same language almost as Butler used when here; three days ago the same paper ridiculed the idea, and said such a brutal, inhuman thing was never for a moment thought of, it was too absurd. And so the world goes! We all turn somersaults occasionally.

And yet, I would rather we would achieve our independence alone, if possible. It would be so much more glorious. And then I would hate to see England conquer the North, even if for our sake; my love for the old Union is still too great to be willing to see it so humiliated. If England would just make Lincoln come to his senses, and put an end to all this confiscation which is sweeping over everything, make him agree to let us alone and behave himself, that will be quite enough. But what a task! If it were put to the vote to-morrow to return free and unmolested to the Union, or stay out, I am sure Union would have the majority; but this way, to think we are to be sent to Fort Jackson and all the other prisons for expressing our ideas, however harmless, to have our houses burned over our heads, and all the prominent men hanged, who would be eager for it? - unless, indeed, it was to escape even the greater horrors of a war of extermination.

July 5th.

Think, that since the 28th of May, I have not walked three squares at a time, for my only walks are to Mrs. Brunot's!

It is enough to kill any one; I might as well be at Ship Island, where Butler has sentenced Mrs. Phillips for laughing while the corpse of a Federal officer was passing - at least, that is to be the principal charge, though I hope, for the sake of Butler's soul, that he had better reasons. Shocking as her conduct was, she hardly deserved two years' close confinement in such a dreadful place as that, because she happened to have no sense of delicacy, and no feeling.

"The darkest hour is just before the day"; we have had the blackest night for almost three months, and I don't see the light yet. "Better days are coming -" I am getting skeptical, I fear me.

I look forward to my future life with a shudder. This one cannot last long; I will be "up and doing" before many months are past. Doing what ? Why, if all father left us is lost forever, if we are to be penniless as well as homeless, I'll work for my living. How, I wonder? I will teach. I know I am not capable, but I can do my best. I would rather die than be dependent; I would rather die than teach. There now, you know how I feel! Teaching before dependence, death before teaching. My soul revolts from the drudgery. I never see a governess that my heart does not ache for her. I think of the nameless, numberless insults and trials she is forced to submit to; of the hopeless, thankless task that is imposed on her, to which she is expected to submit without a murmur; of all her griefs and agony shut up in her heart, and I cry Heaven help a governess. My heart bleeds for them and -

1 o'clock P.M.

Thus far had I reached when news came that our forces were attacking the town, and had already driven the pickets in! I am well now.

We all rushed to make preparations instantly. I had just finished washing my hair, before I commenced writing, and had it all streaming around me; but it did not take a minute to thrust it into a loose net. Then we each put on a fresh dress, except myself, as I preferred to have a linen cambric worn several times before, to a clean one not quite so nice, for that can do good service when washed. The excitement is intense; mother is securing a few of father's most valuable papers; Lilly running around after the children, and waiting for Charlie who cannot be found; Miriam, after securing all things needful, has gone downstairs to wait the issue; and I, dressed for instant flight, with my running-bag tied to my waist, and knapsack, bonnet, veil, etc., on the bed, occupy my last few moments at home in this profitable way.

Nobody knows what it is. A regiment has been marched out to meet our troops, some say commanded by Van Dorn, which I doubt. The gunboats are preparing to second them; we hear the Garrison drum and see people running, that is all. We don't know what is coming. I believe it will prove nothing, after all. But - ! The gunboat is drawn up so as to command our street here; the guns aimed up the street Just below, and if a house falls, ours will be about the first. Well! this time next year, we will know all of which we are now ignorant. That is one consolation! The house will either be down or standing, then.

6 P.M.

We have once more subsided; how foolish all this seems! Miriam and I laughed while preparing, and laughed while unpacking; it is the only way to take such things, and we agree on that, as on most other subjects. "They say" the affair originated from half a dozen shots fired by some Federal soldiers through idleness, whereupon the pickets rushed in screaming Van Dorn was after them at the head of six thousand men. I have my reasons for doubting the story; it must have been something more than that, to spread such a panic; for they certainly had time to ascertain the truth of the attack before they beat the long roll and sent out their troops, for if it had been Van Dorn, he would have been on them before that. Whatever it was, I am glad of the excitement, for it gave me new life for several hours; I was really sick before. Oh, this life! When will it end? Evermore and forevermore shall we live in this suspense? I wish we were in the Sandwich Islands.

July 7th.

As we have no longer a minister - Mr. Gierlow having gone to Europe - and no papers, I am in danger of forgetting the days of the week, as well as those of the month; but I am positive that yesterday was Sunday because I heard the Sunday-School bells, and Friday I am sure was the Fourth, because I heard the national salute fired. I must remember that to find my dates by.

Well, last night being Sunday, a son of Captain Hooper, who died in the Fort Jackson fight, having just come from New Orleans, stopped here on his way to Jackson, to tell us the news, or rather to see Charlie, and told us afterwards. He says a boat from Mobile reached the city Saturday evening, and the captain told Mr. La Noue that he brought an extra from the former place, containing news of McClellan's surrender with his entire army, his being mortally wounded, and the instant departure of a French, and English, man-of-war, from Hampton Roads, with the news. That revived my spirits considerably - all except McClellan's being wounded; I could dispense with that. But if it were true, and if peace would follow, and the boys come home - ! Oh, what bliss! I would die of joy as rapidly as I am pining away with suspense now, I am afraid!

About ten o'clock, as we came up, mother went to the window in the entry to tell the news to Mrs. Day, and while speaking, saw a man creeping by under the window, in the narrow little alley on the side of the house, evidently listening, for he had previously been standing in the shadow of a tree, and left the street to be nearer. When mother ran to give the alarm to Charlie, I looked down, and there the man was, looking up, as I could dimly see, for he crouched down in the shadow of the fence. Presently, stooping still, he ran fast towards the front of the house, making quite a noise in the long tangled grass. When he got near the pepper-bush, he drew himself up to his full height, paused a moment as though listening, and then walked quietly towards the front gate. By that time Charlie reached the front gallery above, and called to him, asking what he wanted. Without answering the man walked steadily out, closed the gate deliberately; then, suddenly remembering drunkenness would be the best excuse, gave a lurch towards the house, walked off perfectly straight in the moonlight, until seeing Dr. Day fastening his gate, he reeled again.

That man was not drunk! Drunken men cannot run crouching, do not shut gates carefully after them, would have no inclination to creep in a dim little alley merely to creep out again. It may have been one of our detectives. Standing in the full moonlight, which was very bright, he certainly looked like a gentleman, for he was dressed in a handsome suit of black. He was no citizen. Form your own conclusions! Well! after all, he heard no treason. Let him play eavesdropper if he finds it consistent with his character as a gentleman.

The captain who brought the extra from Mobile wished to have it reprinted, but it was instantly seized by a Federal officer, who carried it to Butler, who monopolized it; so that will never be heard of again; we must wait for other means of information. The young boy who told us, reminds me very much of Jimmy; he is by no means so handsome, but yet there is something that recalls him; and his voice, though more childish, sounds like Jimmy's, too. I had an opportunity of writing to Lydia by him, of which I gladly availed myself, and have just finished a really tremendous epistle.

Wednesday, 9th July.

Poor Miriam! Poor Sarah! they are disgraced again! Last night we were all sitting on the balcony in the moonlight, singing as usual with our guitar. I have been so accustomed to hear father say in the evening, "Come, girls! where is my concert?" and he took so much pleasure in listening, that I could not think singing in the balcony was so very dreadful, since he encouraged us in it. But last night changed all my ideas. We noticed Federals, both officers and soldiers, pass singly, or by twos or threes at different times, but as we were not singing for their benefit, and they were evidently attending to their own affairs, there was no necessity of noticing them at all.

But about half-past nine, after we had sung two or three dozen others, we commenced "Mary of Argyle." As the last word died away, while the chords were still vibrating, came a sound of - clapping hands, in short! Down went every string of the guitar; Charlie cried, "I told you so!" and ordered an immediate retreat; Miriam objected, as undignified, but renounced the guitar; mother sprang to her feet, and closed the front windows in an instant, whereupon, dignified or not, we all evacuated the gallery and fell back into the house. All this was done in a few minutes, and as quietly as possible; and while the gas was being turned off downstairs, Miriam and I flew upstairs, - I confess I was mortified to death, very, very much ashamed, - but we wanted to see the guilty party, for from below they were invisible. We stole out on the front balcony above, and in front of the house that used to be Gibbes's, we beheld one of the culprits. At the sight of the creature, my mortification vanished in intense compassion for his. He was standing under the tree, half in the moonlight, his hands in his pockets, looking at the extinction of light below, with the true state of affairs dawning on his astonished mind, and looking by no means satisfied with himself! Such an abashed creature! He looked just as though he had received a kick, that, conscious of deserving, he dared not return! While he yet gazed on the house in silent amazement and consternation, hands still forlornly searching his pockets, as though for a reason for our behavior, from under the dark shadow of the tree another slowly picked himself up from the ground - hope he was not knocked down by surprise - and joined the first. His hands sought his pockets, too, and, if possible, he looked more mortified than the other. After looking for some time at the house, satisfied that they had put an end to future singing from the gallery, they walked slowly away, turning back every now and then to be certain that it was a fact. If ever I saw two mortified, hangdog-looking men, they were these two as they took their way home. Was it not shocking?

But they could not have meant it merely to be insulting or they would have placed themselves in full view of us, rather than out of sight, under the trees. Perhaps they were thinking of their own homes, instead of us.

July 10th.

A proclamation is out announcing that any one talking about the war, or present state of affairs, will be "summarily" dealt with. Now, seems to me "summarily" is not exactly the word they mean, but still it has an imposing effect. What a sad state their affairs must be in, if they can't bear comment. An officer arrived day before yesterday, bringing the surprising intelligence that McClellan had captured Richmond and fifty thousand prisoners; that is the time they talked. But when we received yesterday confirmation of his being finally defeated by our troops, and the capture of his railroad train twelve miles in length, they forbid further mention of the subject. I wonder if they expect to be obeyed? What a stretch of tyranny! O free America! You who uphold free people, free speech, free everything, what a foul blot of despotism rests on a once spotless name! A nation of brave men, who wage war on women and lock them up in prisons for using their woman weapon, the tongue; a nation of free people who advocate despotism; a nation of Brothers who bind the weaker ones hand and foot, and scourge them with military tyrants and other Free, Brotherly institutions; what a picture! Who would not be an American? One consolation is, that this proclamation, and the extraordinary care they take to suppress all news except what they themselves manufacture, proves me our cause is prospering more than they like us to know. I do believe day is about to break!

If our troops are determined to burn our houses over our heads to spite the Yankees, I wish they would hurry and have it over at once. Ten regiments of infantry are stationed at Camp Moore, and Scott's cavalry was expected at Greenwell yesterday, both preparing for an attack on Baton Rouge. If we must be beggars, let it come at once; I can't endure this suspense.

July 11th.

A letter from George this morning! It was written on the 20th of June, and he speaks of being on crutches in consequence of his horse having fallen with him, and injured his knee. Perhaps, then, he was not in the first battle of the 25th? But bah! I know George too well to imagine he would keep quiet at such a moment, if he could possibly stand! I am sure he was there with the rest of the Louisiana regiment. The papers say "the conduct of the First Louisiana is beyond all praise"; of course, George was there!

And Jimmy is with him at Richmond; but whether in the army, or navy, or what rank if in the first, he does not say; he only says he is looking remarkably well. Gibbes he had heard from in a letter dated the 16th, and up to then he was in perfect health. His last letter here was dated 10th of March, so we are thankful enough now. I was so delighted to read the accounts of the "gallant Seventh" in some paper we fortunately procured. At Jackson's address, and presentation of the battery they had so bravely won, I was beside myself with delight; I was thinking that Gibbes, of course, was "the" regiment, had taken the battery with his single sword, and I know not what besides. Strange to say, I have not an idea of the names of the half-dozen battles he was in, in June, but believe that one to be Port Republic.

June 12th [sic].

Brother writes that rumors of the capture of Baton Rouge by our troops have made him very uneasy about us; and he wishes us to go down to New Orleans if possible. I wish we could. The impression here, is that an attack is inevitable, and the city papers found it necessary to contradict the rumor of Ruggles having occupied it already. I wish mother would go. I can see no difference there or here, except that there, we will be safe, for a while at least. . . .

I grow desperate when I read these Northern papers reviling and abusing us, reproaching us for being broken and dispersed, taunting us with their victories, sparing no humiliating name in speaking of us, and laughing as to what "we'll see" when we vile rebels are "driven out of Virginia, and the glorious Union firmly established." I can't bear these taunts! I grow sick to read these vile, insulting papers that seem written expressly to goad us into madness! . . . There must be many humane, reasonable men in the North; can they not teach their editors decency in this their hour of triumph?

July 13th, Sunday.

A profitable way to spend such a day! Being forced to dispense with church-going, I have occupied myself in reading a great deal, and writing a little, which latter duty is a favorite task of mine after church on Sundays. But this evening, the mosquitoes are so savage that writing became impossible, until Miriam and I instituted a grand extermination process, which we partly accomplished by extraordinary efforts. She lay on the bed with the bar half-drawn over her, and half-looped up, while I was commissioned to fan the wretches from all corners into the pen. It was rather fatiguing, and in spite of the numbers slain, hardly recompensed me for the trouble of hunting them around the room; but still, Miriam says exercise is good for me, and she ought to know.

I have been reading that old disguster, Boswell. Bah! I have no patience with the toady! I suppose "my mind is not yet thoroughly impregnated with the Johnsonian ether," and that is the reason why I cannot appreciate him, or his work. I admire him for his patience and minuteness in compiling such trivial details. He must have been an amiable man, to bear Johnson's brutal, ill-humored remarks; but seems to me if I had not spirit enough to resent the indignity, I would at least not publish it to the world! Briefly, my opinion, which this book has only tended to confirm, is that Boswell was a vain, conceited prig, a fool of a jackanape, an insupportable sycophant, a - whatever mean thing you please; there is no word small enough to suit him. As to Johnson, he is a surly old bear; in short, an old brute of a tyrant. All his knowledge and attainments could not have made me tolerate him, I am sure. I could have no respect for a man who was so coarse in speech and manners, and who eat like an animal. Fact is, I am not a Boswellian, or a Johnsonian, either. I do not think him such an extraordinary man. I have heard many conversations as worthy of being recorded as nineteen-twentieths of his. In spite of his learning, he was narrow-minded and bigoted, which I despise above all earthly failings. Witness his tirades against Americans, calling us Rascals, Robbers, Pirates, and saying he would like to burn us! Now I have railed at many of these ordinary women here, for using like epithets for the Yankees, and have felt the greatest contempt for their absurd abuse. These poor women do not aspire to Johnsonian wisdom, and their ignorance may serve as an excuse for their narrow-mindedness; but the wondrous Johnson to rave and bellow like any Billingsgate nymph! Bah! He is an old disguster!

July 14th, 3 P.M.

Another pleasant excitement. News has just arrived that Scott's cavalry was having a hard fight with the Yankees eight miles from town. Everybody immediately commenced to pick up stray articles, and get ready to fly, in spite of the intense heat. I am resigned, as I hardly expect a shelling. Another report places the fight fourteen miles from here. A man on horseback came in for reinforcements. Heaven help poor Howell, if it is true. I am beginning to doubt half I hear. People tell me the most extravagant things, and if I am fool enough to believe them and repeat them, I suddenly discover that it is not half so true as it might be, and as they themselves frequently deny having told it, all the odium of "manufacturing" rests on my shoulders, which have not been accustomed to bear lies of any kind. I mean to cease believing anything, unless it rests on the word of some responsible person. By the way - the order I so confidently believed, concerning the proclamation, turns out not quite so bad. I was told women were included, and it extended to private houses as well as public ones, though I fortunately omitted that when I recorded it. When I read it, it said, "All discussions concerning the war are prohibited in bar-rooms, public assemblies, and street corners." As women do not frequent such places, and private houses are not mentioned, I cannot imagine how my informant made the mistake, unless, like me, it was through hearing it repeated. Odious as I thought it then, I think it wise now; for more than one man has lost his life through discussions of the kind.

July 17th, Thursday.

It is decided that I am to go to New Orleans next week. I hardly know which I dislike most, going or staying. I know I shall be dreadfully homesick; but -

Remember - and keep quiet, Sarah, I beg of you. Everything points to an early attack here. Some say this week. The Federals are cutting down all our beautiful woods near the Penitentiary, to throw up breastworks, some say. Cannon are to be planted on the foundation of Mr. Pike's new house; everybody is in a state of expectation. Honestly, if Baton Rouge has to be shelled, I shall hate to miss the fun. It will be worth seeing, and I would like to be present, even at the risk of losing my big toe by a shell. But then, by going, I can save many of my clothes, and then Miriam and I can divide when everything is burned - that is one advantage, besides being beneficial by the change of air. They say the town is to be attacked to-night. I don't believe a word of it.

Oh, I was so distressed this evening! They tell me Mr. Biddle was killed at Vicksburg. I hope it is not true. Suppose it was a shot from Will's battery?

July 20th, Sunday.

Last night the town was in a dreadful state of excitement. Before sunset a regiment, that had been camped out of town, came in, and pitched their tents around the new theatre, in front of our church. All was commotion and bustle; and as the pickets had been drawn in, and the soldiers talked freely of expecting an attack, everybody believed it, and was consequently in rather an unpleasant state of anticipation. Their cannon were on the commons back of the church, the artillery horses tied to the wheels; while some dozen tents were placed around, filled with men who were ready to harness them at the first alarm. With all these preparations in full view, we went to bed as usual. I did not even take the trouble of gathering my things which I had removed from my "peddler sack"; and slept, satisfied that, if forced to fly, I would lose almost everything in spite of my precaution in making a bag.

Well! night passed, and here is morning, and nothing is heard yet. The attack is delayed until this evening, or to-morrow, they say. Woman though I am, I am by no means as frightened as some of these men are. I can't get excited about it. Perhaps it is because they know the danger, and I do not. But I hate to see men uneasy! I have been so accustomed to brave, fearless ones, who would beard the Devil himself, that it gives me a great disgust to see any one less daring than father and the boys.

I have been so busy preparing to go to the city that I think if the frolic should intervene and prevent my departure, I would be disappointed, though I do not want to go. It would be unpleasant, for instance, to pack all I own in my trunk, and just as I place the key in my pocket to hear the shriek of "Van Dorn!" raised again. This time it is to be Ruggles, though. I would not mind if he came before I was packed. Besides, even if I miss the fun here, they say the boats are fired into from Plaquemine; and then I have the pleasure of being in a fight anyhow. Mother is alarmed about that part of my voyage, but Miriam and I persuaded her it is nothing.

If I was a man - oh, would n't I be in Richmond with the boys! . . . What is the use of all these worthless women, in war times? If they attack, I shall don the breeches, and join the assailants, and fight, though I think they would be hopeless fools to attempt to capture a town they could not hold for ten minutes under the gunboats. How do breeches and coats feel, I wonder? I am actually afraid of them. I kept a suit of Jimmy's hanging in the armoir for six weeks waiting for the Yankees to come, thinking fright would give me courage to try it (what a seeming paradox!), but I never succeeded. Lilly one day insisted on my trying it, and I advanced so far as to lay it on the bed, and then carried my bird out - I was ashamed to let even my canary see me; - but when I took a second look, my courage deserted me, and there ended my first and last attempt at disguise. I have heard so many girls boast of having worn men's clothes; I wonder where they get the courage.

To think half the men in town sat up all night in expectation of a stampede, while we poor women slept serenely! Everybody is digging pits to hide in when the ball opens. The Days have dug a tremendous one; the Wolffs, Sheppers, and some fifty others have taken the same precaution. They may as well dig their graves at once; what if a tremendous shell should burst over them, and bury in the dirt those who were not killed? Oh, no! let me see all the danger, and the way it is coming, at once. To-morrow, - or day after, - in case no unexpected little incident occurs in the interval, I purpose going to New Orleans, taking father's papers and part of Miriam's and mother's valuables for safe-keeping. I hate to go, but they all think I should, as it will be one less to look after if we are shelled - which I doubt. I don't know that I require much protection, but I might as well be agreeable and go. Ouf! how I will grow homesick, before I am out of sight!

Midnight.

Here we go, sure enough. At precisely eleven o'clock, while we were enjoying our first dreams, we were startled by the long roll which was beat half a square below us. At first I only repeated "The roll of the drum," without an idea connected with it; but hearing the soldiers running, in another instant I was up, and was putting on my stockings when Miriam ran in, in her nightgown. The children were roused and dressed quickly, and it did not take us many instants to prepare, - the report of two shots, and the tramp of soldiers, cries of "Double-quick," and sound as of cannon moving, rather hastening our movements. Armoirs, bureaus, and everything else were thrown open, and Miriam and

I hastily packed our sacks with any articles that came to hand, having previously taken the precaution to put on everything fresh from the armoir. We have saved what we can; but I find myself obliged to leave one of my new muslins I had just finished, as it occupied more room than I can afford, the body of my lovely lilac, and my beauteous white mull. But then, I have saved eight half-made linen chemises! that will be better than the outward show.

Here comes an alarm of fire - at least a dreadful odor of burning cotton which has set everybody wild with fear that conflagration is to be added to these horrors. The cavalry swept past on their way to the river ten minutes ago, and here comes the news that the gunboats are drawing up their anchors and making ready. Well! here an hour has passed; suppose they do not come after all? I have been watching two sentinels at the corner, who are singing and dancing in the gayest way. One reminds me of Gibbes; I have seen him dance that way often. I was glad to see a good-humored man again. I wish I was in bed. I am only sitting up to satisfy my conscience, for I have long since ceased to expect a real bombardment. If it must come, let it be now; I am tired of waiting. A crowd of women have sought the protection of the gunboats. I am distressed about the Brunots; suppose they did not hear the noise? O girls! if I was a man, I wonder what would induce me to leave you four lone, unprotected women sleeping in that house, unconscious of all this? Is manhood a dream that is past? Is humanity an idle name? Fatherless, brotherless girls, if I was honored with the title of Man, I do believe I would be fool enough to run around and wake you, at least! Not another word, though. I shall go mad with rage and disgust. I am going to bed. This must be a humbug. Morgan came running in, once more in his nightgear, begging Lilly to hear his prayers. In answer to her "Why? You have said them to-night!" he says, "Yes! but I've been getting up so often!" Poor child! no wonder he is perplexed!

One hour and a half of this nonsense, and no result known. We are told the firing commenced, and the pickets were driven in, twenty minutes before the long roll beat.

July 21st.

It is impossible to discover the true story of last night's alarm. Some say it was a gang of negroes who attacked the pickets in revenge for having been turned out of the Garrison; others say it was a number of our soldiers who fired from the bushes; and the most amusing story is that they took alarm at an old white horse, which they killed, mistaking him for the Confederates. One regiment has refused to do picket duty; and the story runs among these poor soldiers that our army, which is within a mile, is perfectly overwhelming. The excitement still continues.

I have been writing to the Brunots the news confirming the death of McClellan, the surrender of his army, and the good tidings of our Ram's recent exploits above Vicksburg, and her arriving safely under the guns there. If we could keep all the dispatches that have passed between us since the battle of the forts, what a collection of absurdity and contradiction it would be! "Forts have been taken." "Their ships have passed; forts safe ; Yankees at our mercy." "Ships at New Orleans. City to be bombarded in twelve hours." "Forts surrendered." "City under British protection." "No, it is n't." "City surrendered." "Mistake."

"Baton Rouge to be burned when Yankee ships come." And soon, sometimes three times a day, each dispatch contradicting the other, and all equally ridiculous.

The crowd here seems to increase. The streets are thronged with the military, and it will soon be impossible to go even to Mrs. Brunot's, which will be a great privation to me. . . . Five thousand are to come next week, and then it will really be impossible to go in the streets.

July 22d, Tuesday.

Another such day, and there is the end of me! Charlie decided to send Lilly and the children into the country early to-morrow morning, and get them safely out of this doomed town. Mother, Miriam, and I were to remain here alone. Take the children away, and I can stand whatever is to come; but this constant alarm, with five babies in the house, is too much for any of us. So we gladly packed their trunks and got them ready, and then news came pouring in.

First a negro man just from the country told Lilly that our soldiers were swarming out there, that he had never seen so many men. Then Dena wrote us that a Mrs. Bryan had received a letter from her son, praying her not to be in Baton Rouge after Wednesday morning, as they were to attack to-morrow. Then a man came to Charlie, and told him that though he was on parole, yet as a Mason he must beg him not to let his wife sleep in town to-night; to get her away before sunset. But it is impossible for her to start before morning. Hearing so many rumors, all pointing to the same time, we began to believe there might be some danger; so I packed all necessary clothing that could be dispensed with now in a large trunk for mother, Miriam, and me, and got it ready to send out in the country to Mrs. Williams. All told, I have but eight dresses left; so I'll have to be particular. I am wealthy, compared to what I would have been Sunday night, for then I had but two in my sack, and now I have my best in the trunk. If the attack comes before the trunk gets off, or if the trunk is lost, we will verily be beggars; for I pack well, and it contains everything of any value in clothing.

The excitement is on the increase, I think. Everybody is crazy to leave town.

Thursday, July 24th.

Yes; that must be the date, for one day and two nights have passed since I was writing here. Where shall I begin the story of my wanderings? I don't know that it has a beginning, it is all so hurried and confused.

But it was Tuesday evening that the Federals were seized with a panic which threw the whole town in alarm. They said our troops were within eight miles, ten thousand in number. The report was even started that the advance guard was skirmishing with the Federals; the shots were heard distinctly, a dozen people were ready to swear. The Yankees struck their tents, galloped with their cannon through the streets with the most terrific din, troops passed at double-quick on their way to the Garrison, everything was confusion. Mr. Tunnard told us yesterday he was present when part of them reached the gate of the Garrison, and saw one of the officers spring forward, waving his sword, and heard him cry, "Trot, men! Gallop, I say! Damn you! run in!" - with a perfect yell at the close; whereupon all lookers-on raised a shout of laughter, for the man was frightened out of his wits. A Federal officer told him that their fright was really a disgrace; and if one thousand of our men had come in town, the whole thirty-five hundred would have been at their mercy. Even the naval officers denounce it as a most arrant piece of cowardice; for instead of marching their troops out to meet ours, they all rushed into the Garrison, where, if attacked, their only retreat would have been into the river. The gunboats were ordered into the middle of the stream, in front of the Garrison; and cooped up there, these valiant men awaited the assault in such trepidation that yesterday they freely said the force could be purchased for fifty cents, they are so ashamed of their panic.

Imagine what effect this had on the inhabitants! Soon, an exodus took place, in the direction of the Asylum, and we needs must follow the general example and run, too. In haste we packed a trunk with our remaining clothes, - what we could get in, - and the greatest confusion prevailed for an hour. Beatrice had commenced to cry early in the evening, and redoubled her screams when she saw the preparations; and Louis joining in, they cried in concert until eight o'clock, when we finally got off. What a din! Lilly looked perfectly exhausted; that look on her face made me heartsick. Miriam flew around everywhere; mother always had one more article to find, and the noise was dreadful, when white and black assembled in the hall ready at last. Charlie placed half of the trunks on the dray, leaving the rest for another trip; and we at last started off. Besides the inevitable running-bag, tied to my waist, on this stifling night I had my sunbonnet, veil, comb, toothbrush, cabas filled with dozens of small articles, and dagger to carry; and then my heart failed me when I thought of my guitar, so I caught it up in the case; and remembering father's heavy inkstand, I seized that, too, with two fans. If I was asked what I did with all these things, I could not answer. Certain it is I had every one in my hands, and was not very ridiculous to behold.

Seventeen in number, counting white and black, our procession started off, each loaded in their own way. The soldiers did not scruple to laugh at us. Those who were still waiting in front of the churches to be removed laughed heartily, and cried, "Hello! Where are you going? Running? Good-bye!" Fortunately they could not see our faces, for it was very dark. One stopped us under a lamp-post and wanted us to go back. He said he knew we were to be attacked, for the Confederates were within five miles; but we were as safe at home as at the Asylum. He was a very handsome, respectable-looking man, though dirty, as Yankee soldiers always are, and in his shirt-sleeves besides. We thanked him for his kindness, and went on. All stopped at the Brunots', to see that they were ready to fly; but the two parties were so tremendous that we gladly divided, and Miriam and I remained with them until they could get ready, while our detachment went on.

Wagons, carts, every vehicle imaginable, passed on to places of safety, loaded with valuables, while women and children hurried on, on foot. It took the Brunots as long to prepare as it did us. I had to drag Sophie out of her bed, where she threw herself, vowing she would not run; and after an interminable length of time, we were at last ready and started, with the addition of Mrs. Loucks and her sons in our train. The volunteer, whose sole duty seems to be to watch the Brunots, met us as we got out. He stopped as he met the first, looked in silence until Sophie and I passed, and then burst out laughing. No wonder! What a walk it was! Nobody hesitated to laugh, even though they meant to run themselves, and we made fun of each other, too, so our walk was merry enough.

When we reached there, the Asylum was already crowded - at least, it would have been a crowd in any other place, though a mere handful in such a building. The whole house was illuminated, up to the fifth story, and we were most graciously received by the director, who had thrown the whole house open to whoever chose to come, and exerted himself to be accommodating. It looked like a tremendous hotel where every one is at home; not a servant or one of the deaf and dumb children was to be seen; we had all the lower story to ourselves. Was n't it pleasant to unload, and deposit all things in a place of safety! It was a great relief. Then we five girls walked on the splendid balcony which goes around the house until we could no longer walk, when I amused myself by keeping poor Sophie standing, since she would not sit down like a Christian, but insisted on going to bed like a lazy girl, as she is. When I finally let her go, it did not take her many minutes to undress, and soon we were all ready for bed. The Brunots had beds on the parlor floor; across the wide hall, we had a room opposite; and next to ours, Lilly and the children were all sleeping soundly. I ran the blockade of the hall in my nightgown, and had a splendid romp with the girls after rolling Sophie out of bed, and jerking Nettie up. Mother and Mrs. Brunot cried, "Order," laughing, but they came in for their share of the sport, until an admiring crowd of females at the door told us by their amused faces they were enjoying it, too; so I ran the gauntlet again, and got safely through the hall, and after a few more inroads, in one of which Miriam accompanied e, and on which occasion I am sure we were seen in our nightgowns, we finally went to bed. I won't say went to sleep, for I did not pretend to doze. All our side of the house had bars, except me; and the mosquitoes were unendurable; so I watched mother and Miriam in their downy slumbers and lay on my hard bed for hours, fighting the torments with bare arms.

Every now and then I heard a stir among the females above, indicating that some few were anticipating a panic. Once they took a rush from the fourth story, and cried they heard the cannon; twenty guns had been fired, etc. I lay still, determined not to believe it; and presently all subsided. I lay there for hours longer, it seemed, when Nettie at last wandered in disconsolate to find if we were asleep; for with the exception of Sophie, they, too, had been awake all night. I went to the parlor with her, when she, Dena, and I, decided to dress at once and sit on the balcony, since sleep was hopeless. Behold me in a blue muslin flounced to the waist, with a cape, too! What a running costume! Miriam only had time to take off her white dress before starting. All dressed, we went to the northwest corner, as far as possible from the rest of the household, and sat in a splendid breeze for hours. It was better than fighting insatiable mosquitoes; so there we sat talking through the greater part of a night which seemed to have borrowed a few additional hours for our benefit. We'll have no Leap Year in '64; the twenty-four extra hours were crowded in on that occasion, I think.

We discussed our favorite books, characters, authors, repeated scraps here and there of the mock sentimental, talked of how we would one day like to travel, and where we would go; discussed love and marriage, and came to the conclusion neither was the jest it was thought to be. (O wise young women!) Poor Nettie retired in despair, and we two watched alone for hours longer. The sun must have been arrested by some Joshua on the road; could n't make me believe it was doing its duty as usual. We wandered around the balconies, through the grounds in the dim starlight (for it was cloudy), and finally, beholding a faint promise of morning, sat still and waited for the coming of the lazy sun. What was still more aggravating was that every time we looked in at the others showed them sleeping peacefully. Miriam lay her full length with outstretched arms, the picture of repose, looking so comfortable! When the sun finally made his appearance (he was out on a spree, I found, for his eyes were not half opened, and he looked dull and heavy as he peeped from behind his bed curtains), others began to stir, and in an hour more, we were ready to leave. Those who had slept, came out with swelled eyes and drowsy looks; while we three, who had been up all night, were perfectly calm, though rather pale; but I am seldom otherwise.

Were we not thankful to see home still standing! I did not feel tired much, but somehow, when it struck half-past six, and I found myself alone here (Miriam having stopped at Mrs. Day's), I suddenly found myself divested of my flounces, and most other articles, and involuntarily going towards the bed. I could not sleep, was n't thinking of such a thing; meant to - there was an end of my soliloquy! Where I went, I don't know. As the clock struck eight, I got up as unaccountably, and discovered I had lost all idea of time in sleep. If it had not been for the clock, I should have said I had slept a day and a night, and it was now Thursday morning. A giant refreshed, I rose from my slumbers, took a hasty cup of coffee, and set to work packing Lilly's trunk, for I was crazy to see the children off as soon as possible.

It was no short work, but we all hurried, said good-bye, and saw them go with a feeling of relief. By the experience of the night before, we knew that when the real moment came it would be impossible to get them off in time to escape danger. Poor Lilly! we miss her sadly; but are thankful to know that she is out of danger with her poor little children. She looked heartbroken at the idea of leaving us alone; but then, when one weak woman has five small babies to take care of, is it fair to impose three big ones on her? I'd never stay here, if she sacrificed her children to take care of us who need no protection. I was very lazy after they left; and sat reading until a note was brought from Charlie saying they were safe beyond the lines.

Last night came another alarm. Some fifty cannon were fired somewhere above, reports came that a body of our troops were a few miles out, so a thousand of these men took courage and went out to reconnoitre. Mrs. Brunot and mother insisted on going again to the Asylum for protection against the coming attack, though we at first begged and pleaded to stay at home. But we had to follow, and I don't think any of us were in the best of humors, as we were all conscious of doing a foolish thing.

We were cordially received again, and got quite gay. Sleeping accommodations no better than before, as far as I was concerned. Sophie, Miriam, and I had but one bar between us, so we placed two mattresses side by side, and by dint of chairs and strings, stretched the net as far as possible over them. Those two were well enough; but to my share fell a baby's mattress two feet by four, placed between the wall and the other great bed, with the end of the bar a foot above my face, and one sheet to do the duty of two - however, they had only one, also. Well! I believe I am tall, so my bed did not fit me. As it was two inches higher than theirs, there was no sharing. In spite of a heavy rain that was now pouring, my warm place was intolerable, and the perspiration streamed from my face so as to be disagreeable, to say the least. It drove me to walk in my sleep, I am afraid, for I have an indistinct recollection of finding myself standing at the window trying to breathe. It was a very, very little piece of sleep I got after all, and that little by no means refreshing.

Up at sunrise again, but it took some time to get ready, for I had to get some clothes out of the trunk, to send home. Well, ever since I reached here I have been writing, and I am ashamed to say how long it is. As the time grows more exciting, my book grows shorter, to my great distress. What will I do?

We all vowed that would be the last time we would run until we heard the cannon, or had some better reason than a Yankee panic to believe the Confederates were coming; though if we listened to mother, she would go there every night if this lasted for a whole year. Kind Phillie Nolan wrote insisting on our staying with them on the plantation until it was over, but we cannot do it; the time is too uncertain; if we knew it was to come this week, we might stay that long with her; but to go for an indefinite period, Miriam and I would not hear of.

I have kept for the last a piece of news I received with thankfulness, when I finally heard it; for, though known to the whole family and all the town on Tuesday night, no one thought it worth while to tell me until I heard it by accident last evening. It was that a Mr. Bell, writing to his wife, says Gibbes asked him to send word to mother that he, George, and Jimmy were in the fight of the 10th and 11th, and all safe. God be praised!

July 25th.

An old gentleman stopped here just now in a carriage and asked to see me. Such a sad, sick old man! He said his name was Caldwell, and that passing through East Feliciana, Mrs. Flynn had asked him to deliver a message to us. Had we heard from our brothers? I told him the message from Mr. Bell. He commenced crying. There was one of them, he said, who got hurt. I held my breath and looked at him. He cried more still, and said yes, it was Gibbes - in the hand - not dangerous - but - Here I thought he meant to tell me worse; perhaps he was dead; but I could not speak, so he went on saying Lydia and the General had gone on to Richmond instantly, and had probably reached there before today. He took so long to tell it, and he cried so, that I was alarmed, until I thought perhaps he had lost one of his own sons; but I dared not ask him. Just then one of the horses fell down with sunstroke, and I begged the old gentleman to come in and rest until they could raise the horse; but he said no, he must go on to the river. He looked so sick that I could not help saying he looked too unwell to go beyond, and I wished he would come in. But he burst into tears, saying, "Yes, my child, I am very, very sick, but I must go on." Poor old man, with his snowwhite beard!

Benjamin F. Butler, Maj. Gen.

July 27th.

I have my bird back! As I waked this morning, I heard a well-known chirp in the streets, and called to mother I knew it was Jimmy. Sure enough it is my bird. Lucy Daigre has had him ever since the shelling, as a negro caught it that day and gave it to her.

July 29th.

This town, with its ten thousand soldiers, is more quiet than it was with the old population of seven thousand citizens. With this tremendous addition, it is like a graveyard in its quiet, at times. These poor soldiers are dying awfully. Thirteen went yesterday. On Sunday the boats discharged hundreds of sick at our landing. Some lay there all the afternoon in the hot sun, waiting for the wagon to carry them to the hospital, which task occupied the whole evening. In the mean time these poor wretches lay uncovered on the ground, in every stage of sickness. Cousin Will saw one lying dead without a creature by to notice when he died. Another was dying, and muttering to himself as he lay too far gone to brush the flies out of his eyes and mouth, while no one was able to do it for him. Cousin Will helped him, though. Another, a mere skeleton, lay in the agonies of death, too; but he evidently had kind friends, for several were gathered around holding him up, and fanning him, while his son leaned over him crying aloud. Tiche says it was dreadful to hear the poor boy's sobs. All day our vis-à-vis, Baumstark, with his several aids, plies his hammer; all day Sunday he made coffins, and says he can't make them fast enough. Think, too, he is by no means the only undertaker here! Oh, I wish these poor men were safe in their own land! It is heartbreaking to see them die here like dogs, with no one to say Godspeed. The Catholic priest went to see some, sometime ago, and going near one who lay in bed, said some kind thing, when the man burst into tears and cried, "Thank God, I have heard one kind word before I die!" In a few minutes the poor wretch was dead.

July 31st.

I believe I forgot to mention one little circumstance in my account of that first night at the Deaf and Dumb Asylum, which at the time struck me with extreme disgust. That was seeing more than one man who had no females or babies to look after, who sought there a refuge from the coming attack. At daylight, one dapper young man, in fashionable array, came stepping lightly on the gallery, carrying a neat carpet-bag in his hand. I hardly think he expected to meet two young ladies at that hour; I shall always believe he meant to creep away before any one was up; for he certainly looked embarrassed when we looked up, though he assumed an air of indifference, and passed by bravely swinging his sack - but I think he wanted us to believe he was not ashamed. I dare say it was some little clerk in his holiday attire; but I can't say what contempt I felt for the creature.

Honestly, I believe the women of the South are as brave as the men who are fighting, and certainly braver than the "Home Guard." I have not yet been able to coax myself into being as alarmed as many I could name are. They say it is because I do not know the danger. Soit. I prefer being brave through ignorance, to being afraid in consequence of my knowledge of coming events. Thank Heaven, my brothers are the bravest of the brave! I would despise them if they shrunk back, though Lucifer should dispute the path with them. Well! All men are not Morgan boys! They tell me cowards actually exist, though I hope I never met one. The poor men that went to the Asylum for safety might not have what Lavinia calls "a moral backbone." No wonder, then, they tumbled in there! Besides, I am told half the town spent the night on the banks of the river, on that occasion; and perhaps these unfortunates were subject to colds, and preferred the shelter of a good roof. Poor little fellows! How I longed to give them my hoops, corsets, and pretty blue organdie in exchange for their boots and breeches! Only I thought it was dangerous; for suppose the boots had been so used to running that they should prance off with me, too? Why, it would ruin my reputation! Miss Morgan in petticoats is thought to be "as brave as any other man"; but these borrowed articles might make her fly as fast "as any other man," too, if panic is contagious, as the Yankees here have proved. One consolation is, that all who could go with any propriety, and all who were worthy of fighting, among those who believed in the South, are off at the seat of war; it is only trash, and those who are obliged to remain for private reasons, who still remain. Let us count those young individuals as trash, and step over them. Only ask Heaven why you were made with a man's heart, and a female form, and those creatures with beards were made as bewitchingly nervous?

August 2d, Saturday.

I had thought my running days were over; so little did I anticipate another stampede that I did not notice the report of the attack that was prophesied for night before last, and went to bed without gathering my clothes. But to-day comes a hasty note from Charlie, telling us to leave instantly as General Breckinridge is advancing with ten thousand men to attack us, and at 12 M. yesterday was within thirty-four miles. He begged us to leave to-day; there would be trouble before to-morrow night. It was so earnest, and he asserted all so positively, that we are going to Phillie's this evening to stay a week, as they say eight days will decide. Ah, me! our beautiful town! Still I am skeptical. If it must be, pray Heaven that the blow comes now! Nothing can be equal to suspense. These poor men! Are they not dying fast enough? Will Baumstark have orders for an unlimited supply of coffins next week? Only Charlie's family, ours, and the Brunots know it. He enjoined the strictest secrecy, though the Brunots sent to swear Mrs. Loucks in, as she, like ourselves, has no protector. I would like to tell everybody; but it will warn the Federals. I almost wish we, too, had been left in ignorance; it is cruel to keep it to urselves. I believe the Yankees expect something; "they say" they have armed fifteen hundred negroes. Foes and insurrection in town, assailing friends outside. - Nice time!

Our cavalry has passed the Amite. Poor Charlie has come all the way to the ferry landing on the other side to warn us. If we do not take advantage, it will not be for want of knowing what is to come. How considerate it was in him to come such a long way! I am charmingly excited! If I only had a pair of breeches, my happiness would be complete. Let it come! I lose all, but in Heaven's name let us have it over at once! My heart fails when I look around, but "Spit fire!" and have an end to this at once! Liberty forever, though death be the penalty.

Treason! Here lies my pass at my elbow, in which has been gratuitously inserted that "Parties holding it are considered to give their parole not to give information, countenance, aid, or support to the so-called Confed. S." As I did not apply for it, agree to the stipulation, or think it by any means proper, I don't consider it binding. I could not give my word for doing what my conscience tells me is Right. I cross with this book full of treason. It "countenances" the C. S.; shall I burn it? That is a stupid ruse; they are too wise to ask you to subscribe to it, they just append it.

August 3d, Westover.

Enfin nous sommes arrivées! And after what a trip! As we reached the ferry, I discovered I had lost the pass, and had to walk back and search for it, aided by Mr. Tunnard, who met me in my distress, as it has always been his luck to do. But somebody had already adopted the valuable trifle, so I had to rejoin mother and Miriam without it. The guard resolutely refused to let us pass until we got another, so off flew Mr. Tunnard to procure a second - which was vastly agreeable, as I knew he would have to pay twenty-five cents for it, Yankees having come down as low as that, to procure money. But he had gone before we could say anything, and soon returned with the two-bits' worth of leave of absence. Then we crossed the river in a little skiff after sundown, in a most unpleasant state of uncertainty as to whether the carriage was waiting at the landing for us, for I did not know if Phillie had received my note, and there was no place to go if she had not sent for us. However, we found it waiting, and leaving mother and Miriam to pay the ferry, I walked on to put our bundles in the carriage. A man stepped forward, calling me by name and giving me a note from Charlie before I reached it; and as I placed my foot on the step, another came up and told me he had left a letter at home for me at one o'clock. I bowed Yes (it was from Howell; must answer to-morrow). He asked me not to mention it was "him"; a little servant had asked his name, but he told her it was none of her business. I laughed at the refined remark, and said I had not known who it was - he would hardly have been flattered to hear I had not even inquired. He modestly said that he was afraid I had seen him through the window. Oh, no! I assured him. "Well, please, anyhow, don't say it's me!" he pleaded most grammatically. I answered, smiling, "I did not know who it was then, I know no more now, and if you choose, I shall always remain in ignorance of your identity." He burst out laughing, and went off with, "Oh, do, Miss Morgan, forget all about me!" as though it was a difficult matter! Who can he be?

We had a delightful drive in the moonlight, though it was rather long; and it was quite late when we drove up to the house, and were most cordially welcomed by the family. We sat up late on the balcony listening for the report of cannon, which, however, did not come. Baton Rouge is to be attacked to-morrow, "they say." Pray Heaven it will all be over by that time! Nobody seems to doubt it, over here. A while ago a long procession of guerrillas passed a short distance from the house, looking for a party of Yankees they heard of in the neighborhood, and waved their hats, for lack of handkerchiefs, to us as we stood on the balcony.

I call this writing under difficulties! Here I am employing my knee as a desk, a position that is not very natural to me, and by no means comfortable. I feel so stupid, from want of sleep last night, that no wonder I am not even respectably bright. I think I shall lay aside this diary with my pen. I have procured a nicer one, so I no longer regret its close. What a stupid thing it is! As I look back, how faintly have I expressed things that produced the greatest impression on me at the time, and how completely have I omitted the very things I should have recorded! Bah! it is all the same trash! And here is an end of it - for this volume, whose stupidity can only be equaled by the one that precedes, and the one that is to follow it. But who expects to be interesting in war times? If I kept a diary of events, it would be one tissue of lies. Think! There was no battle on the 10th or 11th, McClellan is not dead, and Gibbes was never wounded! After that, who believes in reliable information? Not I!

Letter from Richard P. Watters, 8th Infantry, Georgia

Dear Brother:

Once more settled, in Camp near Winchester, I take the present opportunity to write you a few lines to let you know that I am well and unhurt after going through the hard fight that is reported we got into at Harper's Ferry, I learn it has been reported in home that we had a fight and only twenty four of our company survived. Nothing surprised me more. Not one of us has seen a Yankee since we left home. If we did, we did not know it. We left Harper's Ferry last Saturday, was a week (ago). There was a large force of the enemy marching on this place. Hence (they) would have cut off our supplies, and left us in a box from which there would have been no getting out--except cutting our way through. To prevent this, we blew the rail-road bridge and destroyed other public property--and went to meet them. But instead of meeting them, they heard of our coming and fled to their own side of the river. I see the Rome Courier has denominated us the Georgia Hunters. I think the name very appropriate. We have done nothing else since we came here. As soon as we left Harper's Ferry, several Federal flags were hoisted. The 11th Miss. Regiment went back there night before last--consisting of not more than a thousand men--and pitched into the enemy numbering fifteen hundred. (They) were engaged in rebuilding the bridges. They killed one hundred and thirty one and lost only 27. The enemy fled leaving the ferry in possession of the Mississippians. I hope we have got to a place where (we) will stay until we can make some decided move--either in the direction of Georgia, or where we will have to do our fighting, I am tired of toting my knapsack over this country--though I never saw finer country. The wheat crops here are as fine as I ever saw. The people have just commenced harvesting. There is very little corn (here), principally wheat and clover. I think if I ever get home and farm, I will be certain to grow clover instead of cotton. I never could before account for such fine stock, coming from this country and Tennessee. It is the clover fields that make them. The common old dray horse of Linchburg is finer looking than the best buggy and carriage horses of Floyd.

These lines leave the Rome light Guards--with the exception of two--in good health and spirits. John Pinson with several others arrived here a few days since--all safe and sound. Write to me soon and as often as convenient. I have not received any letters from home except the one by Pinson. Nothing more.

Your brother,
Richard P. Watters

View of Harper's Ferry

Reminiscences Of A Rebel

By The Rev. Wayland Fuller Dunaway, D.D.

Formerly Captain of Co. I, 40th Va. Regt.,Army of Northern Virginia

"Omnibus hostes Reddite nos populis—civile avertite bellum." —Lucan.

Preface

Notwithstanding the title of this volume, I do not admit that I was ever in any true sense a rebel, neither do I intend any disrespect when I call the Northern soldiers Yankees. The use of these terms is only a concession to the appellations that were customary during the war.

It is my purpose to record some recollections of the Civil War, and incidentally to furnish some historical notices of the brigade to which I was attached. Here and there I have expressed, also, some opinions concerning the great events of that dreadful period, some criticisms of the conduct of battles and retreats, and some estimates of the abilities of prominent generals.

The incentive to write is of a complex nature. There is a pleasure, especially to the aged, in reviving the memories of the past[Pg 6] and narrating them to attentive hearers. Moreover, I hope that this book will furnish instruction to those who have grown up since the war, and entertainment to older persons who participated in its struggles, privations, and sorrows. And besides, the future historian of that gigantic conflict may perhaps find here some original contribution to the accumulating material upon which he must draw. He will need the humble narratives of inconspicuous participants as well as the pretentious attempts of the partial historians who have preceded him. The river flows into the sea, but the river itself is supplied by creeks and rivulets and springs.

W. F. D.

Chapter I

"Lay down the axe; fling by the spade;
Leave in its track the toiling plow;
The rifle and the bayonet-blade
For arms like yours were fitter now;
And let the hands that ply the pen
Quit the light task, and learn to wield
The horseman's crooked brand, and rein
The charger on the battle field."—Bryant.

In the fall of the year 1860, when I was in my nineteenth year, I boarded the steamboat Virginia,—the only one then running on the Rappahannock river,—and went to Fredericksburg on my way to the University of Virginia. It was my expectation to spend two sessions in the classes of the professors of law, John B. Minor and James P. Holcombe, and then, having been graduated, to follow that profession in Lancaster, my native county.

The political sky had assumed a threatening aspect. The minds of the Southern people had been inflamed by the insurrectionary raid of John Brown upon Harper's Ferry, especially because it had been approved by some Northern officials, and because the surrender of some fugitives from justice, who had taken part in that murderous adventure, had been refused by Ohio and Iowa. The election of Abraham Lincoln added fuel to the flame. Having been nominated by the Republican party, he was constitutionally chosen President of the United States, although he had not received a majority of the popular vote. The election was ominous, because it was sectional, Mr. Lincoln having carried all the Northern states but not one of the Southern. The intensest excitement prevailed, while passion blew the gale and held the rudder too.

While I believed in the right of secession I deprecated the exercise of that right, because I loved the Union and the flag under which my ancestors had enjoyed the blessings of civil and religious liberty. I did not think that Lincoln's election was a sufficient cause for dissolving the Union, for he had announced no evil designs concerning Southern institutions; and, even if he had, he was powerless to put them into execution. He could have done nothing without the consent of Congress, and his party was in a minority both in the Senate and in the House of Representatives.

Before Christmas South Carolina, not caring for consequences and blind to the horrible future, passed an ordinance of secession; and her example was followed in quick succession by Mississippi, Florida, Alabama, Georgia, Louisiana, and Texas. These seven states organized the Southern Confederacy, of which Jefferson Davis was inaugurated President, February 18, 1861. In April Fort Sumter was captured, and on the 15th of that month President Lincoln issued a proclamation calling on the remaining states to furnish their quotas of an army of seventy-five thousand soldiers for the purpose of destroying the Confederate government. Two days later the Virginia convention passed an ordinance of secession. Being compelled to take sides, the Old Dominion naturally cast her lot with her Southern sisters. War had begun,—intestine war, of whose magnitude and duration no living man had any adequate conception.

These events conspired with other causes to infuse in me a martial spirit. The conviction was growing in me that, as my native state was about to be invaded, I must have a place in the ranks of her defenders. I was influenced by speeches delivered by Governor Floyd, Professor Holcombe, and Dr. Bledsoe, and still more by the contagious example of my roommate, William H. Chapman, who had gone with a company of students to Harper's Ferry, and had returned. What brought the conviction to a head was a flag. One morning in the latter part of April, as I was walking from my boarding-house to the University I saw a Confederate banner floating above the rotunda. Some of the students during the night, surmounting difficulty and braving danger, had clambered to the summit and erected there the symbol of a new nation. I was thrilled by the sight of it as if by an electric shock. There it was, outstretched by a bracing northwest wind, flapping defiantly, arousing patriotic emotion. Unable longer to refrain, I went as soon as the lecture was concluded to Professor Minor's residence and told him I was going to enter the military service of Virginia. He sought to dissuade me, but, perceiving that he could not alter my rash decision, he gave at my request a written permission to leave his classes.

But how to get home?—that had become a perplexing question. I could not go the way I had come, because the Virginia fearful of capture had ceased to make trips from Fredericksburg to Lancaster, and there was no railroad to that part of the state. Knowing that my uncle, Addison Hall, was a member of the Convention, I determined to take a train to Richmond and seek his advice. I felt relieved when he informed me that he was going the next morning, and that I could go along with him. We took an early train to West Point, and being ferried across the Mattaponi river, obtained from one of his friends a conveyance to Urbanna. We hired a sloop to take us to Carter's creek, and thence we proceeded in a farm wagon to his home in the village of Kilmarnock. The next morning he sent me to the home of the Rev. Dr. Thomas S. Dunaway, my brother, and my guardian.

In a few days I enlisted in a company that was being raised by Captain Samuel P. Gresham, who had been a student at the Virginia Military Institute. And thus the student's gown was exchanged for the soldier's uniform.

Before we were regularly mustered into service an expedition was undertaken that indicated at once the forwardness of our people to engage the enemy and their ignorance of military affairs. The report having been circulated that a Federal gunboat was lying[Pg 13] in Mill Creek in Northumberland county, its capture, or destruction, was resolved upon by about a hundred men, who had assembled at the county seat of Lancaster. With no weapons except an old smooth-bore six-pound cannon, and that loaded with scrap iron gathered from a blacksmith's shop, we proceeded to Mill Creek and unlimbered on the bank in plain view of the boat, and distant from it some two or three hundred yards. I have always been glad that we had sense enough to refrain from shooting, for otherwise most of us would have been killed then and there. Seeing the hopelessness of an unequal combat, we retired from the scene somewhat wiser than when we went. In that instance was not "discretion the better part of valor"?

Jefferson Davis and his staff

Chapter II

War, war is still the cry, "War to the knife."—Byron.

There was in the central part of the county a beautiful grove in which the Methodists were accustomed to hold their annual camp-meetings. On account of its location and the shelter afforded by its tents it was in 1861 transformed into a rendezvous of a radically different nature, the military companies that had been raised in the county assembling there preparatory to going into the army. It was there that Captain Gresham's company, known as the Lacy Rifles, was formally enrolled by Col. R. A. Claybrook and Dr. James Simmonds. When they came to where I stood in the line of men they declined to enlist me because I appeared pale and weak on account of recent sickness. I said, "Do as you like, gentlemen, but I am going with the boys anyhow." "If you talk like that," they replied, "we will insert your name."

Not many days afterward the company assembled at the court-house, and, having sworn allegiance to the Southern Confederacy, was duly mustered into its service. In vehicles of all sorts we drove to Monaskon wharf, where the schooner Extra was moored to receive us and to convey us up the Rappahannock river. As the vessel glided along what a jolly set we were!—gay as larks, merry as crickets, playful as kittens. There was singing, dancing, feasting on the palatable provisions supplied by the loving friends we were leaving, with no thought of captivity, wounds, nor death. Ignorant of war, we were advancing toward its devouring jaws with such conduct as became an excursion of pleasure. The only arms we then possessed were two-edged daggers made of rasps in blacksmith shops, and with these we were going to hew our way to victory through the serried ranks of the invading army! Ah, well! we knew better what war was after we had become the seasoned veterans of many campaigns.

When the vessel had proceeded up the river as far as Fort Lowry it rounded to, because a solid shot ricochetted before the bow, and we were transferred to the steamboat Virginia, which carried us to Fredericksburg. Passing along the streets, attracting attention by our neat gray uniforms, we marched out to the fair-grounds, and rejoiced to obtain the friendly shelter of the cattle stalls. They were not as comfortable as the chambers of our homes—but what of it? Were we not soldiers now? It is wonderful and blessed how human nature can accommodate itself to altered environments.

We were supplied with smoothbore, muzzle-loading, Springfield muskets, small leather boxes for percussion caps, and larger ones for cartridges. For the information of the present generation let it be explained that the cartridge was made of tough paper containing powder in one end and the ounce ball of lead in the other; and the manner of loading was this: the soldier tore off with his teeth the end, poured the powder into the muzzle, and then rammed down the ball; this being done, a cap was placed on the nipple of the breech, and the gun was ready to be fired. That musket is antiquated now, but it did much execution in former days.

Maj. J. H. Lacy, for whom the company was named, presented an elegant silk banner, which at Captain Gresham's request I received in the best language at my command. It was never borne in battle, for it was not companies but regiments that carried banners. There was but one flag to a regiment, and that was always carried in the center. Twice a day there was a course of drilling in tactical evolutions and in the handling of the muskets. At first I was hardly strong enough to sustain the fatigue, but I rapidly grew stronger under the combined influence of exercise, sleeping in the open air, and the excitement of a military life. The war did me harm in many ways, but it was the means of increasing my capacity for bodily exertion. During the encampment at Fredericksburg many of my spare moments were spent in reading the New Testament and Pollok's "Course of Time."

We did not long remain in Fredericksburg; but being transported on cars to Brooke Station we marched up to camp Chappawamsic, near a Baptist church of that name. There the Lacy Rifles became Company F in the 47th regiment of Virginia Volunteers, commanded by Col. G. W. Richardson of Henrico county, who had been a member of the Virginia Convention that passed the ordinance of secession. He was a brave and patriotic gentleman, but unskilled in military affairs; and he did not long retain the command.

From the summer of 1861 until the spring of 1862 we spent the time in company and regimental drill, and in picketing the shore of the Potomac river day and night, lest the enemy should effect a landing and take us unaware. During that time no shots were exchanged with the enemy, because no landing was attempted. The only fighting that we saw was at Dumfries where there was a Confederate fort, to which we marched to act as a support in case the Yankees came ashore. Three vessels of the Federal navy passed slowly down the river, between which and the fort there was a brief but lively cannonade; but so far as I know there was no resulting damage to either side.

On Sunday, July 21, we heard the booming of the cannon at Bull Run, lamenting that we had no part in the battle. When we afterward heard how McDowell's army skedaddled back to Washington more rapidly than they came, we thought that the war would end without our firing a gun. So little did we understand the firmness of President Lincoln's mind and the settled purpose of the North!

The winter was spent in comparative comfort, for we moved out of tents into cabins built of pine logs, each one having a wide arch and a chimney. At Christmas some good things were sent to me, among which was a dressed turkey, which I did not know how to prepare for the table, for even if I had possessed some knowledge of the culinary art there was no suitable oven. Fortunately a comrade by the name of John Cook,—an appropriate name for that occasion,—came to my relief and solved the problem in a most satisfactory manner. The bird was suspended by a string before the open fire, and being continually turned right and left, and basted with grease from a plate beneath, it was beautifully browned and cooked to a turn.

Glouchesterr Point

Chapter III

Drummer, strike up, and let us march away.—Shakespeare's Henry VI.

In the spring of 1862 Gen. George B. McClellan with an army of 120,000 men, thoroughly drilled and lavishly equipped, set out from Washington to capture Richmond from the north; but he had not proceeded far before he changed his mind about the line of advance. His forces were transported to Fortress Monroe with the design of approaching the city by the way of the peninsula that lies between the York and the James rivers. The correctness of his judgment was justified by subsequent campaigns; for the successive attempts of Pope, Burnside, Hooker, and Grant to take the Confederate capital from the north were all disastrous failures.

In order to check the upward progress of McClellan's army, Gen. Joseph E. Johnston withdrew his forces from Manassas and the shore of the Potomac and concentrated them on the Peninsula. The 47th regiment marched from its winter quarters to Richmond, and was thence transported down the James to a wharf not far from Yorktown. During our brief stay in that vicinity, the companies were authorized to elect their officers; and I, who had been acting as Orderly Sergeant, was chosen Third Lieutenant.

As the National army advanced, the Confederates fell back toward Richmond. Our regiment was not in the engagement that took place near Williamsburg on the 5th of May, but I saw then for the first time some wounded men and prisoners. The retreat was conducted somewhat rapidly, but in an orderly and skilful manner. I do not remember that we marched in darkness but once, and then we trudged all night long through shoe-deep mud. At times when the men in front encountered an unusually bad place those who were behind were compelled to come to a temporary halt. If I did not sleep while walking along I came as near to it as weary mortal ever did, and I am sure that I dozed while standing still.

General Johnston posted his army between Richmond and the Chickahominy river, the 47th regiment being on the left, not far from Meadow bridge, and in the pestilential low-grounds of that sluggish stream. Swarms of mosquitoes attacked us at night and with their hypodermic proboscides injected poisonous malaria in our veins, to avoid which the sleeping soldier covered his head with a blanket. The complexion of the men became sallow, and every day numbers of them were put on the sick-list by the surgeons.

The 47th regiment, commanded by Col. Robert M. Mayo, and having brigade connection with some regiments from North Carolina, had its first experience of real war in the battle of Seven Pines (or Fair Oaks), which was fought on the 31st of May. On that day General Johnston attacked the left wing of the Federal army, which had been thrown across to the southern side of the Chickahominy. To some persons the declaration may seem surprising, but it was with real pleasure that I went into the battle. It was the novelty of it, I suppose, that prevented me from being frightened by exploding shells and rattling musketry. The dread of these things came afterward when I saw fields scattered over with the wounded, the dying, and the dead, and among them some of my dearest friends. In that affair our Lieutenant-Colonel, John M. Lyell, was seriously wounded, and the regiment sustained a loss of about fifty men. Our chaplain, Mr. Meredith, of Stafford county, went into action with us, but while he did not do the like again, it is no impeachment of his courage. His duty lay in other directions; and it ought to be recorded in his praise that after every battle he might be found doing all he could to relieve and comfort the wounded.

Chapter IV

In peace there's nothing so becomes a man

As modest stillness, and humility;

But when the blast of war blows in our ears,

Then imitate the action of the tiger;

Stiffen the sinews, summon up the blood.—Shakespeare's Henry V.

After the undecisive battle of Seven Pines the 47th regiment together with the 40th and the 55th Virginia regiments and the 22nd Virginia battalion was formed into a brigade, and this combination continued until the close of the war. It was known as the First Brigade of the Light Division, which was composed of six brigades, and commanded by Maj.-Gen. A. P. Hill. Why it was called the Light division I did not learn; but I know that the name was applicable, for we often marched without coats, blankets, knapsacks, or any other burdens except our arms and haversacks, which were never heavy and sometimes empty.

On Thursday, June 26, the memorable but miss-called "battles around Richmond" began. Being on the left of the army, the First Brigade had the honor and the danger of being the first to cross the Chickahominy. Passing over Meadow bridge, we dispersed the enemy's outpost, only one man being wounded in the passage, and hurried on towards Mechanicsville and Beaver Dam, where was posted the extreme right of the Federal army. The contest raged for six hours. We failed to dislodge the enemy from its naturally strong and well-fortified position across Beaver Dam creek, and our loss was heavy,—heavier in some other brigades than in ours. The following morning, discovering that our antagonists had withdrawn, we crossed over Beaver Dam in pursuit.

McClellan had decided to retreat! He called it a change of base; but if a change of base from the York to the James river was good strategy, why did he not do it before he was attacked? It looks very much as if he gave "a reason upon compulsion." It must be conceded that he managed the retreat with admirable ability, although, while inflicting severe punishment upon Lee's army, it involved the loss of 10,000 prisoners, 52 pieces of artillery and 35,000 stand of small arms, besides immense stores of ammunition and provisions. But why retreat? Was it for this that he had led to the gates of Richmond a grand army of brave and disciplined men, at an enormous cost to his government? Having many qualities of a great commander, he lacked the gaudium certaminis and the daring that assumes the hazard of defeat. In war the adage holds good with emphasis: "Nothing venture, nothing gain." The celebrated generals of all times, confiding in their own skill and the bravery of their soldiers, have been bold even to the degree of seeming rashness. Such was the spirit and conduct of Lee when with half the numbers he assaulted Hooker, and afterward Grant, in the Wilderness.

McClellan's army being astraddle the Chickahominy, two courses of action were open to him when he was attacked.

He might have concentrated on the north side of the river, leaving a sufficient force to guard the bridges in his rear, and then assumed a strong defensive position. Having abandoned Beaver Dam he withdrew to Gaines' Mill,—a place most favorable for defense,—still having 60,000 men in striking distance across the river. If instead of vacating that position, or suffering a portion of his army to be driven from it, he had reënforced it by a half of those unoccupied 60,000 men, I do not believe he could have been dislodged by all the valor and dash of the Confederate army.

The other line of action that he might have chosen was to concentrate on the southern side of the river, destroy the bridges, and then crushing the small army of Magruder, make a quick attack upon Richmond, while the forces of Lee and Jackson were on the other side. It seems to me that either course would have been better and nobler than the inglorious retreat to Harrison's Landing. It appeared that Lee was gaining victory after victory; but until the battle of Malvern Hill he was fighting only portions of McClellan's forces. In that engagement alone did the Union army contend with its undivided strength, and there it gained a victory. If it could hold its ground there after having suffered many losses, could it not much better have repulsed the Confederates at Gaines' Mill?

When the First Brigade advanced to the charge at Gaines' Mill, on the 27th of June, it emerged out of a wood into a large field, which declined toward a ravine through which a stream of water ran, and on the other side of which the ground rose somewhat precipitously to a considerable altitude. It had been wisely chosen for defense, and the opposite high ground was lined with infantry and crowned with batteries. As it was impossible to dislodge the enemy until some diversion should be created on one of his flanks, our men lay prone upon the ground, while bullets and shells hurtled among us and above us. At length seeing a brigade on our left rapidly advancing where the enemy's position was less formidable, we rose up and, with the inspiring "rebel yell," ran down the slope, crossed the little creek, clambered up the hill, and poured a volley into the retiring Yankees, some of whom were Duryea's Zouaves with their flaming uniforms. It was then that we more than repaid them for the loss they had inflicted upon us. On that day there fell some of my dearest friends, among whom was St. John F. Moody, who for three years had been my teacher, and afterward became my beloved companion. So patriotic and brave was he that if "Dulce et decorum est pro patria mori" ever was true of any hero it was of him.

The next battle in which the brigade took part was that of Frazier's Farm, three days later. As we entered a field we saw before us a battery (which I believe was Randell's) supported by a firm line of infantry. In Wilson's history of the war he says: "One of the most brilliant charges of the day was made by the 55th and the 60th Virginia." The correct statement is that it was made by our brigade composed, as has been said, of the 40th, the 47th, the 55th, and the 22d Virginia. We rushed across the field, drove away the opposing infantry, and captured the battery. One of the gunners lying on the ground badly wounded jerked the lanyard of a loaded cannon just as we had almost reached the battery. Happily for us the discharge flew over our heads. He knew that he was in our power, for all his comrades were fleeing away, and he had no right to fire upon us. The deed was more like vengeful murder than honorable war; however, we did him no harm, for though his spirit was spiteful his pluck was commendable.

It was late in the afternoon; and as we stood in line by the captured guns, ready to receive an expected countercharge, a lone horseman approached who proved to be Major-General McCall, who in the fading twilight had mistaken us for his own men. Hearing numerous cries to halt and seeing many muskets leveled at him, he dismounted and led his horse to where we stood. Being conducted before Colonel Mayo, he said, "For God's sake, Colonel, don't let your men do me any harm." Colonel Mayo was so indignant at the implied accusation that he used some cuss words, and asked him whether he thought we were a set of barbarians. If he had been captured in battle, I should have been glad; but, as it was, I felt sorry for him, and if I could have had the disposal of him I would have paroled him and turned him loose.

The First Brigade did not again come under fire until we reached Malvern Hill, the 1st of July. There McClellan had skilfully stationed his entire army, and all the valorous efforts of Lee's army to storm the position were unavailing. One of our men addressed a North Carolina regiment as "Tarheels" and received for answer, "If you had had some tar on your heels, you would have stuck to that battery better than you did."

McClellan, having for six days acted on the defensive, and in the last engagement having been virtually victorious, had an opportunity to assume the offensive; for in war as in the game of chess an unsuccessful attack invites defeat. On the 2d of July, if he had inspirited his regiments with the cry of "On to Richmond" and attacked the Confederates unprepared for so surprising a reversal, who can tell what might have been the result? Was it not worth the trial? And if he had failed, could he not then have fallen back to the cover of the gunboats? But he was bent on going to Harrison's Landing, and thither his army retreated all night over a muddy road. Thus ended the second attempt to capture the Confederate capital.

Chapter V

When Greeks joined Greeks, then was the tug of war.—Nathaniel Lee.

After the battle of Malvern Hill the First Brigade had a brief and enjoyable respite from marching and fighting, while it bivouacked in the pine forest near Savage Station.

Gen. John Pope, with his "headquarters in the saddle," set out from Washington with a numerous force to capture Richmond, and was reënforced by the remains of McClellan's army that had been transported from Harrison's Landing to Acquia creek. Jackson's corps, of which Hill's Light Division was an important part, was dispatched to watch his movements and to check his progress. From the flat lands of the James and the Chickahominy we marched to the hill country, and for a few days remained near Orange Court House. On the 9th of August we forded the Rapidan in search of the enemy. A suffocating cloud of dust enveloped our toiling host, and so intense was the heat that a few of the men fell sunstruck in the road. During this march, as also on similar occasions, I saw packs of cards scattered along the highway; for though the soldier might play them for money or amusement when there was no prospect of an engagement, he did not relish the thought of their being found upon him if he should be killed. In the afternoon we encountered a portion of the National army under the command of General Banks and fought the battle of Cedar Run, in which our people were victorious. That night the hostile lines were so close that we could hear the Yankees talking, but could not distinguish the words. When daylight came they were far away.

Toward the latter part of the month Pope's army occupied a position near Warrenton in Fauquier county, while across the North For of the Rappahannock river he was confronted by Lee's united army in Culpeper.

To cross the river and force the Federal position by a front attack was plainly impracticable; but in some way the Yankees must be removed and compelled to fight on something like equal terms. The plan was formed that Jackson with his corps should by a forced circuitous march obtain the enemy's rear and thus, cutting the line of his communication, compel him to retire from his advantageous location, and that Lee with Longstreet's corp should rejoin Jackson and bring on an engagement with his entire army. To some military critics this division of the army in the face of an unchastised antagonist might seem to contradict the rules of sound strategy, but in the fertile minds of Lee and Jackson it was the dictate of consummate genius. Such a division occurred in Maryland, just before the battle of Sharpsburg, and again at Chancellorsville the following year, and each time it was advantageous to the Confederate arms. These two men had the utmost confidence in each other, and either felt safe while the other was making an independent movement. In the course of the years that have elapsed since the termination of the war I have frequently been asked, "Which was the greater general, Lee or Jackson?" After pondering this question for forty-five years I am yet unable to decide; and that reminds me of Abe Lincoln and the hats. When he became President, two enterprising merchants in Washington, desiring to secure his custom, each presented him with an elegant silk hat, and it so happened that they called at the same time to learn his opinion of their gifts. "Gentlemen," said Mr. Lincoln, "these hats mutually excel each other."

On Tuesday, the 26th of August, the march of Jackson's corps began, every step of the onward way bringing us nearer to the Blue Ridge where it borders the county of Rappahannock, and causing us to guess that through some gap of the mountain we were going into the valley. We did not know what Old Jack, (as he was familiarly and [Pg 38]affectionately called,) was up to, but it did not matter what was the objective,—so implicit was the confidence reposed in his military judgment. Passing out of Rappahannock and skirting the base of the Blue Ridge, we rested for the night at Salem, in Fauquier, a station of the Manassas Gap Railroad, the name of which has since been changed to Marshall. Betimes the next morning we were hurrying eastward through Thoroughfare Gap of Bull Run Mountain, and late in the evening we arrived at Manassas Junction,—between Pope's army and Washington. I had read that walking was an excellent form of exercise because it brought into play every muscle of the body, and having walked nearly sixty miles in two days I was convinced that the reason assigned was valid, for the muscles of my arms and neck were almost as sore as were those of my legs. The making of long marches unexpectedly and quickly was one of the secrets of Jackson's success. It may be supposed by the uninitiated that after such fatigue the soldier is not in good condition for fighting; but the sense of weariness is lost when the excitement of battle begins.

The few Federal regiments on guard at the Junction were quickly dispersed, and trains of cars loaded with all sorts of army supplies were burned. A large building filled with commissary stores was also burned, but not before our empty haversacks had been replenished. By the light of the fires we supped plentifully on potatoes and beef and then lay down upon the ground, not to pleasant dreams, but to dreamless sleep.

On the 28th our brigade with some others went toward Centerville, in Fairfax county, and thence turning away came back into Prince William and took position on a part of the ground whereon the first battle of Manassas had been fought. Ewell's division, which had been left behind to befog Pope's mind and retard his movements, joined us and completed the defensive line of Jackson's entire corps.

The next day the Federal army began to press us vigorously, but the numerous attacks made upon us were repelled and followed by counter charges. Our Brigadier-General, Field, was wounded badly, and Company F lost some men, among whom was Lieutenant James Ball, who in the absence of Capt. William Brown was in command. By his death the control of the company was devolved upon me.

Let me here relate an incident to show that between individuals of the opposing hosts there was no animosity. During a lull in the battle I left the regiment and circumspectly proceeded forward to reconnoiter. I found in a wood a Yankee captain dangerously wounded, a fine-looking man and handsomely dressed. In reply to the question whether I could do anything for him he asked for water, and I, kneeling down, held my canteen to his lips, for which kindness he made grateful acknowledgments. "And now," said I, "there is something you can do for me: you can give me your sword, but I will not take it unless you part with it freely." He replied that I was welcome to it, for he would never need it again. After I had taken it he said: "You had better retire, because our men will soon be here again." He was thirsty, and I gave him drink; I was in danger, and he gave me friendly warning.

That sword had an unfortunate history: its beautiful scabbard, belt, and shoulder strap were ruined when my tent was burned the next winter; its hilt was shot off at Chancellorsville, and the naked blade was thrown away on that ensanguined field.

I returned to where the regiment was standing prepared to receive another attack, which, however, was not made that day. When we were ordered to fall back to our first position, I caused to be brought with us the bodies of Lieutenant Ball and his most intimate friend, Mordecai Lawson, who, like him, had been shot in the forehead. With bayonets and hands a grave was dug, in which we laid them side by side, and spreading over them a soldier's blanket, we heaped above them the turf and clods. In neither army could there have been found two braver men. Boon companions in life, in death they were not divided.

The next day, Saturday the 30th, witnessed the grand struggle that has become famous in history as the Second Battle of Manassas. After a separation of four days Longstreet's corps had come up and formed on Jackson's right, and General Pope was compelled either to retreat or fight on ground so skilfully selected by General Lee. The line of battle was nearly parallel with Bull Run, whereas in the first battle it was perpendicular to it.

There was between the two armies a bed that had been graded for a railroad, but upon which no rails have ever been laid. It was the fortune of the First Brigade to fight on Friday over a shallow cut, and on Saturday over the deepest of all. Our line being formed in an oak forest and ordered to charge, we rushed from the wood into a large field across which the cut had been dug, not knowing it was there until we came close to it. The Federal soldiers on the other side made but feeble resistance, because they had already been hotly engaged with a brigade composed of the 60th Virginia and some regiments from Louisiana. That brigade was down in the cut, having exhausted their ammunition, and it would have been captured but for our timely arrival, which filled them with rejoicing. In that charge the saber was knocked from my uplifted hand, and falling it stuck in the ground some paces behind me.

The brigade did not cross the cut, but a few of the men clambered over and I among them. There was a cannon over there which they pulled back with all the hilarity of college students, some riding astraddle the piece, cheering, and waving their caps.

We had no sooner recrossed the cut and regained our places in the line than the grand spectacle of dense columns of Pope's army coming to the assault was witnessed. In perfect array, they kept step as if on dress parade, and bore their banners proudly. I looked for a terrific shock, but before they came to close quarters with us, the Confederate artillery, massed on high ground behind us, opened upon their closed ranks, and wrought such fearful destruction as, I believe, was not dealt in any other battle of the entire war. Shells burst among them so thick and fast that in a few minutes the field was literally strewn with the killed and wounded. They halted, they turned, they fled; and Lee's whole army assuming the offensive, rushed forward and won the battle.

General Pope was going to hoist the Stars and Stripes above the capitol in Richmond, but he came no nearer to the city than Cedar Run. His men were brave, but from first to last he was mystified by Lee's superior strategy. A prisoner said to me, "If we had your Jackson, we would soon whip you." And I will express the opinion that if the Army of the Potomac had been commanded by generals who were the equals of Lee and Jackson the Southern Confederacy would have collapsed before April, 1865; and sooner still if Lee and Jackson had led the Northern armies, while the Confederates were marshaled by leaders of Pope's caliber.

Chapter VI

'Tis the soldiers' life

To have their balmy slumbers waked with strife.—Shakespeare's Othello.

Our next encounter with the Yankees occurred on the first day of September at a place called Ox Hill, near Chantilly on the Little River turnpike, in which they sustained a heavy loss in the death of General Philip Kearney, one of their best and bravest commanders. Inasmuch as the action took place during a thunderstorm its awful impressiveness was increased, and it was difficult to distinguish between the reverberations of the heavens and the detonations of the mimicking artillery, sometimes alternating and sometimes simultaneous.

That night, when all was still and darkness had settled upon the field where lay the victims of war, a soldier of the 40th regiment, an intrepid Irishman, George Cornwell by name, went out prowling for food and plunder, taking his musket with him. Unexpectedly meeting a Federal lieutenant and four men bearing a stretcher and searching for their wounded captain, he was asked to what regiment he belonged. With ready wit he named a New York regiment, and then learning their business and finding that they were unarmed, he leveled his musket, demanded their surrender, and brought them as prisoners within our lines. I myself did a little searching until I found a full haversack strapped to a man who would never use his teeth again. I was hungry, and chilled by the recent rain. I found in the haversack crackers and ground coffee mixed with sugar; and bringing into requisition my matches, tin cup, and canteen of water (which three things I was always careful to have about me), I soon had a pint of steaming beverage. I ate my supper, and then laid down to sleep. This was only one of many times that I slept in wet garments on the rain-soaked lap of earth without injury to my health; and the only reason I can give for the immunity is, that those were "War times."

The National army returned to Washington, and together with all the forces in and around that city was again put under the command of General McClellan.

From Chantilly we marched to the vicinity of Leesburg and went into camp near a beautiful spring, several feet deep, which was in a large square walled up with brick. The next day we came to the Potomac river, which was then about four feet deep, with its bottom covered with rounded stones of many sizes. We were not so favored as Joshua's host at the Jordan, but we just walked from shore to shore as if there were no water there. Beautiful was the scene. As I approached the river I beheld those who had crossed ascending the hill on the farther shore; in the water a double line of soldiers stretching from side to side, their guns held high above the current and gilded by the beams of the westering sun; and others behind them going down the declivity of the Virginia shore. There came unbidden to my mind some lines of one of Charles Wesley's hymns:

One army of the living God,
To his command we bow;
Part of the host have crossed the flood,
And part are crossing now.
E'en now to their eternal home
Some happy spirits fly;
And we are to the margin come,
And soon expect to die.

From Bunyan's time onward, and I know not how long before, a river has been the Christian symbol of death.

There was some expectation that when we came into Maryland many of her sons would rally to our banners, according to the prediction of a well-known song:

"She breathes, she burns, she'll come, she'll come,

Maryland, my Maryland;"

but the cold fact is, she did not come; and in the light of subsequent events, it is well that she did not.

From the Potomac the march was continued to the Monocacy river, near Frederick City. During our brief sojourn there we bought goods in the stores and paid for them in Confederate money, although, no doubt, the merchants would have preferred greenbacks or specie; and so far as I know nothing was taken without that remuneration.

Again Lee's army was divided, Jackson's corps being detached and sent forward for the purpose of capturing Harper's Ferry. For three days during the westward march in Maryland no rations were issued, and our only food was ears of green corn roasted or boiled without salt. These served for supper and breakfast, but we had nothing for dinner, for if when we started in the morning we put the cooked corn in the haversacks it soured under the hot rays of the sun, and time was too precious to allow a halt for cooking a fresh supply at noon.

Fording the Potomac again, we passed out of Maryland into Virginia at Williamsport and proceeded rapidly to Harper's Ferry. The Federal force occupying a very high hill which had been fortified by abattis and entrenchments, any attempt to storm it would have inflicted terrible loss upon the attacking party. With much difficulty our cannon had been placed on the Maryland Heights, on the Loudoun Heights, and on other eminences that overlooked the enemy's position; and when all was ready the order was given to the infantry to begin the assault. When we came to the foot of the little mountain occupied by the Yankees we discovered that trees had been cut so as to fall downward, and that their interlacing limbs had been trimmed and sharpened to a point. To advance upward through these innumerable spikes appeared impossible; nevertheless we began the ascent at the same time that our artillery on the mountains opened fire. The enemy, seeing our advance and being torn by plunging shots and shells from so many enfilading directions, were persuaded to surrender. As we were slowly struggling upward I looked and with a joyful feeling of relief saw the white flag flying, and a large one it was. This was on Monday, the 15th of September. So well was this affair planned by Jackson that without the loss of a man we captured 11,000 prisoners, 13,000 stand of small arms, and 73 pieces of artillery.

Having performed what was necessary to secure the fruits of this remarkable achievement, it was of the utmost importance that we should hurry away to reënforce Longstreet's corps, which was confronted by the northern army at Sharpsburg. Passing through Shepherdstown we waded the Potomac the third time. Our brigade did not reach the battle field until the evening of the 17th, when the most of the severe fighting of the day had ended. It was a drawn battle with very heavy losses on both sides. On the 18th the opposing hosts confronted each other without coming to blows. Did not McClellan blunder again? Having a much greater army, a part of which had not been engaged, ought he not to have renewed the battle in the attempt to crush the Confederates and drive them into the river? When he awoke on the 19th Lee's army was on the Virginia side.

Chapter VII

The midnight brought the signal-sound of strife,

The morn the marshalling in arms, the day

Battle's magnificently-stern array.—Byron.

On the 20th of September McClellan sent one of his divisions over into Virginia, with the purpose, I suppose, of making a reconnoissance in force. It was attacked by the Light Division and driven back to the Maryland side of the river, not a few of the men perishing in the water. On that occasion the 47th passed within a few paces of a Yankee regiment standing in line in a field and displaying their national banner. Not a musket was fired by either party; for they, being cut off from the river, were doomed to captivity, and we were going at double-quick against another force. When the engagement had ended and we were marching away, a solid shot from beyond the river ricochetted along our line and in unpleasant proximity to it. Though much of its force was spent, yet if it had struck our line it had sufficient momentum to have destroyed many lives. Here was a close call, which differed from many another in that the bounding ball was visible.

The Maryland campaign being over, Jackson's corps retired to Bunker Hill between Winchester and Martinsburg, and there we had for more than two months an unusual season of rest and recuperation. I remember one day of special enjoyment. Obeying an order, I took a squad of men some seven or eight miles along the turnpike in the direction of Martinsburg to keep a lookout for the approach of the enemy. We halted where there was a grove on one side of the road and a dwelling-house on the other. We purchased a shoat from the matron of that domicile, who made us a stew that would have done credit to the Maypole Inn. After dinner,—the only meal worthy of that name that I had enjoyed for many months,—I took a musket, and leaving the men a short distance behind, took a stand in the middle of the road. No Yankee came in sight, but while I was there silently waiting and watching two large, beautiful wild turkeys walked with stately step across the road in easy range. Was I tempted to shoot? Yes. Did I do it? No; for I was particularly instructed that on no account must a gun be fired except on the enemy's approach. The report would have been repeated by squads in my rear, the camp would have been falsely alarmed, and I would have been justly court-martialed.

The Army of the Potomac, 100,000 strong and commanded by General Burnside, once more took up the slogan,—"On to Richmond,"—but that was more easily said than done. Before it reached the northern bank of the Rappahannock river, opposite Fredericksburg, the ever-watchful Lee, having left the valley, had occupied the heights on the other side. Jackson's corps by rapid marches arrived at Fredericksburg on the 11th of December, none too soon for the impending conflict, and took position on Longstreet's right. Nearly five miles from the town our brigade formed the extreme right of the Southern Army, which was an assignment of honor; and the 47th held the right of the brigade. The other brigades of Hill's Light Division formed on our left, Gregg's next to ours, and between the two on higher ground twenty pieces of artillery looked out across the field. Lee's army had the advantage of position, and had the rare pleasure of fighting on the defensive. It occupied the high ground that borders the river flat, and which is close to the town, but, as it continues, recedes from the river, leaving an ever widening plain. On the morning of the memorable 13th that plain resounded to the martial tread of Burnside's army.

Before the battle began General Lee, inspecting the disposition of his forces all along the line, rode up to where we stood, and dismounting from Traveller, handed the bridle-rein to an orderly. This was the first time that I saw him, and his appearance made an indelible impression upon my mind. What a noble man he was in form and face as well as in moral character! While he was examining the outlying field I had a conversation with the orderly, who spoke of the General's fondness for his horse.

Having observed that a few men of the Confederate cavalry had brought up a piece of artillery in front of our right, I obtained permission of Colonel Mayo and ran forward to join them. Two Federal batteries came forward in a gallop and in a minute's time unlimbered and began firing against Hill's division, the twenty guns of which I have spoken giving them as good as they sent and a little better. The Yankees were so hotly engaged by the firing in front of them that they paid no attention to the little cavalry gun upon the flank. The first shot did no execution, but the next struck a caisson and exploded its contents.

What more was done there I cannot say; for seeing that the Federal infantry were advancing to the charge, I hastily returned to my position in the regiment. Our men, lying in a railroad cut about two feet deep, waited until the Yankees were close upon them, and then rising up poured such volleys upon them as caused them to retire in confusion; but on our left Gregg's South Carolina brigade was broken through and he was killed. Being thereby severed from the rest of the army, we changed front and took the victorious Yankees in flank, causing them to lose their advantage and fall back to the railroad which they had crossed. Then occurred a pretty duel. The blue and the grey lines were about sixty yards apart and each was loading and firing as rapidly as possible. The Federal general and his two aides on horseback were urging their men to charge, as was evident from their gestures; but their men would not respond.

Being an officer I had no weapons but sword and pistol, but I picked up the musket of one of our men, who had loaded it but was killed before he could discharge it, and called on some of our company to shoot down the horsemen. We took deliberate aim and fired; and down went horses and riders. "Now," said I, "shoot down the colors." Four times they fell, only to be quickly raised again. I would not affirm that the little group about me shot down the horsemen and the flag, for many others were shooting at the same time; I only know that we calmly did our best in that direction. After a while the enemy turned and fled; and I was glad, for they had inflicted on the 47th a loss of fifty men in killed and wounded. However, their loss greatly exceeded ours. The next day, when a truce prevailed for burying the dead and caring for the wounded, I was informed by some of the Union soldiers that the name of that general was Jackson. He was a brave man, deserving a better fate, and he fell while nobly performing what he believed was his duty to his country.

It was the general and confident expectation that the battle would be renewed, and we were, therefore, surprised to discover on the morning of the 15th that the enemy had during the night recrossed to the northern side of the river. Their loss in the engagement was three times greater than ours. Burnside made the mistake of putting forth his greatest strength where the Confederates were strongest. If he had assailed our right as fiercely as he did our left, perhaps there might have been a different result.

In a few days after the battle I was informed by Colonel Mayo that I was "for gallant and meritorious conduct promoted to be First Lieutenant and Adjutant of the 47th regiment." I had not thought of trying to make an exhibition of unusual gallantry among so many intrepid men, but, of course, the commendation and promotion were highly gratifying.

"The love of praise, howe'er concealed by art,

Reigns more or less, and glows in ev'ry heart."

The campaign having come to an end, Lee's army went into winter quarters at camp Gregg, so named in honor of Brigadier-General Maxcy Gregg who was killed in the battle of Fredericksburg. It was near Moss Neck, the large and fertile farm of Mr. Richard Corbin. The Rappahannock river flowed between the Yankee and the Rebel armies, each picketing its own side of the stream. By common consent there was no shooting across the river, but on the other hand there was an occasional exchange of tobacco and coffee by means of little boats. We could hear them impudently singing: "O soldiers, won't you meet us." We had met them on fields of carnage, and expected to meet them again on the return of spring; but whether we should meet them "On Canaan's happy shore," or in some less pleasing locality in the eternal world, who could say?

I distinctly remember one night when my turn came to go to the river on picket duty, and the earth was covered with snow several inches deep. When my watch was off and the opportunity to sleep was afforded the question was, where to lie down. I spread on the snow some boughs that I had cut from a cedar tree and laid a gum cloth upon them. Upon this pallet I lay down and covering myself head and all with a blanket enjoyed sweet, refreshing, and healthful sleep. The next morning the blanket above my head was stiff-frozen with the moisture from my breath.

There was one man that should have been mentioned before this time,—a negro of my own age, whose name was Charles Wesley. We had grown up on the farm together, and had played, and boxed, and wrestled without respect to color. Not as a slave but as a friend he followed me to the war,—my launderer, my cook, and when I was sick, my nurse. Having orders to keep himself out of danger, he very willingly remained far in the rear when a battle was in progress, but when the firing ceased he faithfully sought me and reported for duty. While writing about Charles, I may anticipate a little and say that when we were in Pennsylvania I told him that we were on Yankee soil, and that he had the opportunity of deserting me and of remaining there as a free man. He replied that he already knew that, but that he was going to abide with me. And when I was captured at Falling Waters he had the intelligence and fidelity to ride my horse home and deliver him to my brother.

It was while we were encamped at Moss Neck that I witnessed a military execution for the offense of desertion from the 47th regiment. The criminal was on his knees, blindfolded, with his hands tied behind him to a stake. A short distance in front of him was the line of twenty men detailed to do the shooting, and commanded by an officer especially appointed. No man could tell who did the killing, for the twenty muskets were handed to them, one-half of them being loaded with blank cartridges. The rest of the regiment was drawn up, one-half on the right, and the other on the left. At the word "Fire!" the report of the guns rang out and the deserter fell forward pierced by balls. Death was instantaneous. Although the crime was mortal, the scene was painfully sad.

Chapter VIII

Nothing except a battle lost can be half so melancholy as a battle won.—Wellington.

I did not serve long as the adjutant of the 47th regiment. In March, 1863, Company I of the 40th regiment, having from one cause or another lost all its officers, unanimously desired that I should become their captain, and this desire was approved by Colonel Brockenbrough, who commanded that regiment, as well as by General Heth, who commanded the brigade. I was loath to sever connection from the regiment to which I had been attached since the beginning of the war, but I accepted the new position, because it was in the line of promotion, and the men of the company were from my native county and well known to me; moreover, I would still be in the same brigade with my old comrades of the 47th. My captain's commission was dated April 30, and was signed by James A. Seddon, Secretary of War.

When the spring had come General Joseph Hooker, the successor of unfortunate Burnside, having crossed the Rappahannock river, took up a strong position at Chancellorsville, with an army numerically twice as strong as the available Confederate forces, and declared by him to be "the finest army on the planet." At the same time a powerful detachment under General Sedgwick crossed the river below Fredericksburg and made demonstrations of attack upon the Confederate lines. Never was General Lee confronted by a more perilous situation, and never did his military genius more brilliantly appear.

In war so much depends upon the commander, that I advance the confident opinion that if the Confederates had been under the charge of Hooker and Sedgwick, and Lee and Jackson had had command of the Federal soldiers above and below Fredericksburg, the Confederate army would have been destroyed; and the Army of the Potomac would have walked straight into Richmond. That army would indeed have been "the finest on the planet," if the skill and the courage of its commander had equaled its numbers, its aggressive power, and its opulent equipment.

Hooker had a grand opportunity, but ingloriously failed to use it. He had conceived a good plan of action, and he successfully executed its initial movement; but when the decisive hour arrived his resolution failed. Instead of advancing aggressively on to Fredericksburg, as he had begun to do, he turned back and fortified his army with intrenchments. Did he mistrust himself, or his army, or both? His original scheme contemplated offensive tactics, and all its merit was sacrificed when he began to erect defensive fortifications.

Let me here briefly describe Chancellorsville and its environments as I saw them during the battle. There was no village there, but only a large brick tavern with a few outbuildings, located immediately on the north side of the road that connects Fredericksburg and Orange. In the rear it was separated from the forest by a narrow field, while in front and across the road there was a large space of open land. In the direction of Orange the road and fields declined to a wooded ravine. On the slightly elevated land in front of the tavern the Yankees had unlimbered twenty Napoleon cannon, and along the side of the ravine they had erected breastworks of logs and earth.

Late in the afternoon of Friday, May 1, our brigade had marched up from Fredericksburg and halted in striking distance of the Federal army. What could we expect but that in the morning we should be waging an assault upon its fortified position? Instead of that Jackson led us with the rest of his corps around the front of that position until we struck the road on the Orange side of Chancellorsville. We were now on Hooker's right flank, having marched quickly and silently fifteen miles over a rough and unfrequented road. The sun was sinking toward the western horizon when our lines of attack were formed on both sides of the road and at right angles to it. Immediately the onslaught began, silent, rapid, resolute, Heth's brigade being on the north or left side of the road. We had not proceeded far before we struck Howard's corps all unsuspecting and unprepared. Their fires were kindled for cooking supper, and dressed beeves were ready for distribution among the companies. They fled before us, strewing the ground with muskets, knapsacks, and other accouterments. Whoever censures them for running would probably have acted as they did, for our charge was as lightning from a cloudless sky. On the way we crossed a little farm, and as I passed the dwelling I saw several ladies who were wildly rejoicing.

When we had come within half a mile of Chancellorsville daylight had faded into night. The moon had risen, but her rays were rendered intermittent by scudding clouds. The darkness, the tangled undergrowth of the forest, and the entrenchments and artillery of the enemy combined to arrest our progress. Those cannon of which I have spoken shelled the woods in which we lay, and what a cannonade it was! The trees and bushes trembled, the air was laden with sulphurous fumes, the very earth seemed to quake under the impulse of exploding shells. There was, however, more noise than execution; only one man of my company was struck, and his broken jaw was bound up by my handkerchief.

From my position on the roadside I saw a few riderless horses running terror-stricken to the rear. These were, I believe, the animals that Jackson and his aides had ridden to the front. It is recorded that he was wounded by some soldiers of the 18th North Carolina regiment who were in the brigade of General James H. Lane. If this statement were made on less reliable authority it might be questioned; for I know that the Yankees were close to our front and that Jackson could not have ridden far beyond our line without encountering their volley. We did not hear until next morning that our peerless leader had been shot. Alas! As when Hector fell the doom of Troy was sealed, so with the death of Jackson the star of the Southern Confederacy declined.

Late in the night the firing ceased, and the Gray and the Blue lay on their arms, catching brief snatches of troubled sleep, and abiding the renewal of hostilities with the coming morning.

On the bright and pleasant Sunday that ensued no chiming bells nor melodies of sacred music were heard upon that famous field, but only the cries of antagonistic men and the horrid din of batteries and muskets. Our brigade being transferred to the right side of the road and drawn up in line of battle in the forest, it was not long before the renowned Stonewall brigade passed by us and charged upon the breastworks of the enemy. It was repulsed with heavy loss, the Yankees having preponderating advantage of position. Then Pender's intrepid brigade of North Carolinians had a similar experience. There were no braver soldiers in the army than the men composing these two defeated brigades. When, therefore, the command to charge was given to us, could we hope for a better result? As we advanced a shell struck the ground immediately before me, exploded and covered me with dirt, but providentially inflicted no wounds. Onward we rushed with the usual inspiriting Rebel yell. When we came in sight of those formidable rifle pits we were delighted to find them abandoned by our foes; and when we climbed over them and entered the field just beyond them we were no less glad to discover that those batteries that had so noisily shelled us the night before had been withdrawn.

There in full view toward our left stood Chancellor's tavern, and the large field in front was literally filled with Federal soldiers in perfect array marching northward,—that is, to the rear. The retreat of Hooker's army had begun; they were not whipped but out-generaled. Passing across the road by the tavern and entering the forest behind it, they left not in sight a single blue coat, save that a battery in the tavern yard was firing upon us. Two Confederate batteries galloped up to our line, and, unlimbering, opened upon the battery in the yard at close range. There were in the Southern armies many soldiers in their teens, but here at one of the guns labored a boy who was, as I guessed from his size, not more than twelve years old. It was his part to fire the gun by pulling the lanyard, and as often as he did it he playfully rolled over backward. "Boys will be boys" even in the peril of battle. In the meantime Jeb Stuart, temporarily assigned to the command of Jackson's corps, came riding into the field, and in a spirit not unlike that of the boy was singing, "Old Joe Hooker, won't you get out the wilderness?" The Yankee battery withdrew; the battle was ended. The tavern was all ablaze, having been ignited by one of our shells,—the house that an hour before had been the headquarters of General Hooker. Our army was resting along the road in front of the burning building. As General Lee rode by, a waggish fellow of the 47th said, "General, we are too tired to cheer you this morning," and he pleasantly replied, "Well, boys, you have gotten glory enough for one day."

Chapter IX

He that fights and runs away

May turn and fight another day.—Ray.

After the lamented death of General Jackson the divisions of the Army of Northern Virginia were organized into three corps, commanded, respectively, by Longstreet, Ewell, and A. P. Hill. General Heth was assigned to the command of the Light Division, and the senior colonel of the first brigade, John M. Brockenbrough took the command made vacant by Heth's promotion.

In forming his staff Colonel Brockenbrough selected me to be his acting assistant adjutant-general. As this new sphere of duty required that I should have a horse, and as it was useless to search for one in the neighborhood of Fredericksburg, I sought and obtained a furlough in order that I might seek one in my native county. The time was limited to five days,—not long enough, as Colonel Brockenbrough knew; but there was an understanding between us that if I overstayed the limit nothing would be said about it.

A tramp of a hundred miles was before me, but that was a matter of indifference to my buoyant body and practiced feet. It was my intention to cross the river at Tappahannock, and proceed down the Neck to my brother's home, but the southern bank was picketed by the 15th Virginia cavalry, which prohibited my passage. Walking back into the town and finding Colonel John Critcher, who was in command of the regiment, I explained my mission and requested the liberty of passing through his line. He informed me that on the other side the 8th Illinois cavalry were making a raid, and urged that I should not cross and run the risk of being captured. Telling him that I was familiar with the country and that I would avoid the enemy, I persisted in the request, being as desirous of a horse as was Richard III in his final battle. Having obtained his reluctant written permission I decided that instead of crossing at Tappahannock I would walk down as far as Owen Hill in Middlesex county and thence seek a passage over into Lancaster. A negro, whose service I secured in return for Confederate money, transported me in a canoe, and landed me at Morattico. During the passage I kept a sharp lookout up and down the wide river for Yankee gunboats, fearing that even if I should escape Scylla I might fall into Charybdis; and indeed some of the marauding bluecoats had but recently departed from the farm.

Having dined with the hospitable family, I set out for my brother's home fifteen miles away, not knowing that one part of the enemy was encamped on his farm and another part in the yard. Being informed that the hostile invaders were traversing all parts of the county in search of booty, I sought to evade them by walking not upon the familiar roads but in the woods parallel with them. When I drew near the county-seat, instead of crossing the road as prudence suggested I thought I would walk the road a short distance and then pass over, for my shoes had become uncomfortably smooth by treading on the fallen foliage of the pines. Rash procedure!

I had come into the road near what is called "the court-house mill hill," intending to go down, cross the bridge, and turn again into the woods in the rear of the village, scouting as I proceeded. When I had come nearly to the brow of the hill, I met a squadron of ascending Federal horsemen. If I had been two minutes earlier and they as much later we would have met as I was descending the hill; and then my capture would have been inevitable, because the steep banks on either side would have precluded all hope of escape. I heard the foremost riders say, "Here're the Rebels, boys; come on." I did not wait to see more than their heads and breasts as they were coming up the hill. I was in my full uniform, having a gray overcoat on my shoulder and a felt hat on my head. In the twinkling of an eye the coat was dropped, and the hat flew off as I made such a leap into the friendly forest as perhaps was never equaled by any athlete in the Olympic games. I had no time to become frightened, but I was angered by being pursued on my native soil by men who had no right to invade it. It is a wonder that they did not catch me. I heard them swearing, crying "Halt," and firing pistols. Three things favored me: the trees and undergrowth were coming into leaf, I was fleet of foot, and I took an unsuspected direction. Instead of running at right angles to the road, or obliquely backward, I ran obliquely forward, in the direction from which they had come. When I was nearly out of breath, I stopped to listen, and was glad to hear no sounds save those that were made by my thumping heart. The pursuit had ended, and I lay down to rest and to recover my wind,—not unlike the stag that had been chased by Fitz James' hounds.

In a little while rising refreshed from my rest, I went onward and crossing the mill stream higher up than I had purposed, I arrived at the residence of my cousin Robert. I had been there but a few minutes when his wife, who had glanced up the lane, cried out, "Run, run; the Yankees are coming!" At the first utterance of the word "run," I was making rapid tracks for the forest in the rear of the house; but before I reached it she called me back. Two of the Yankees had been there before, and her excited imagination had mistaken a Rebel officer for two more. It was her brother-in-law, Ned Stakes, major of the 40th Virginia. He and I then set out for a place near Wicomico church, where, as he told me, a few Confederates were in hiding. Having spent the night with them in the forest, we were in the morning informed by a faithful negro, who had been acting as commissary, that the Yankees had all gone. Although I trusted his report, it was with circumspection that I traveled homeward.

The departed Yankees had carried away teams and wagons loaded with plunder from meat-houses, barns, and cabins, and as many of the negroes as desired to take advantage of "the year of jubile?" which old Spencer said "had come." One girl, who refused to depart, was thus upbraided by her father: "You's a fool, gal, not to go where there's a plenty to eat and nothing to do." That regiment of cavalry had robbed my brother, and had treated many other peaceable citizens in the same way. Large was the booty they carried away, and long was the train of negroes, horses, and loaded wagons. It is said that "all things are lawful in war"; but this adage, like many others, sails under false colors. War is lawless, as Cicero observed: "Silent leges inter arma." There was neither constitutional nor statute law that justified the invasion of the South by armies from the North; none for the emancipation proclamation; none for the cruel and destructive deeds that were perpetrated by the Federal armies.

My furlough had run out, and my object was yet ungained. The next day I found a bay horse to my liking, five years old, large, tall, and strong, named John. The owner sold him to me for Confederate money, knowing that the sale bore close resemblance to a gift. After a night's rest I set out for the army. Riding in the wake of the retiring sons of Illinois, I recrossed the river at Bowler's, and on the second day rejoined the brigade near Fredericksburg. After having been chased by the Yankees, a feeling of safety came over me as I mingled again with my veteran companions.

That was not to be my last experience with the 8th Illinois. It was they who in less than two months afterward took me prisoner in Maryland. Some of them were riding horses that they had stolen,—no; impressed,—from my county. They showed me their repeating Spencer carbines, and asked that if I should be exchanged I would tell the 9th Virginia cavalry that they would be glad to meet them. The lapse of fifty years has made old men of them and me. I have forgiven the wrongs those brave fellows inflicted on my country, and I would be glad to meet them to talk over the stirring events of the past.

Pontoon bridges across the Potomac

Chapter X

Hand to hand, and foot to foot;

Nothing there, save death, was mute;

Stroke, and thrust, and flash, and cry

For quarter, or for victory,

Mingled with the volleying thunder.—Byron.

I come now to relate my experience of the disastrous invasion of Pennsylvania.

The first week in June the commands of Longstreet and Ewell began the northward movement, but Hill's corps remained at Fredericksburg to deceive the Federal commander and watch his movements. It was not until the middle of the month that Hooker divined Lee's purpose and withdrew his army from our front, leaving us free to follow the rest of the army. Marching through Culpeper, we crossed the mountains through Chester's Gap and struck out for the ford of the Potomac at Williamsport. I had four times waded the river, but this time, being on horseback, I escaped a wetting by holding my feet high on the saddle. My spirits would not have been so light and gay, if I could have foreknown that I should not lay eyes on the river again until the war should be over. Nothing of moment occurred while we passed across Maryland into Pennsylvania.

Tuesday night, June 30, our division bivouacked near Cashtown, about eight miles northwest of Gettysburg. The next morning Colonel Brockenbrough was informed that Pettigrew's brigade was on the way to Gettysburg to obtain shoes for the men, and was ordered to follow as a support in the contingency of need, none of us knowing that the advance of Meade's army occupied a strong position between us and the town. I was riding with Colonel Brockenbrough at the head of the column when we met Pettigrew and his men returning. He informed us that the enemy was ahead and that as he had not received orders to bring on an engagement he was coming back, to report. As to the source of his information I had no doubt, for by his side was a man on horseback, bearing an umbrella, and dressed in a suit of civil clothes. After a brief consultation between the commanders of the two brigades I was ordered to ride back quickly to Heth's headquarters, report the condition of affairs, and bring back his instructions. With a brusque manner, he said, "Tell General Pettigrew not to butt too hard, or he'll butt his brains out." I translated his command into politer terms, and we started again toward Gettysburg, knowing that Heth would follow with the other four brigades of the division.

We found the enemy posted on a ridge just beyond Willoughby's Run, and deploying on both sides of the road we went into the engagement. We had the honor,—if honor it may be called,—of losing and shedding the first blood in one of the most famous battles of the world. In war things sometimes just happen: the Army of the Potomac and the Army of Northern Virginia came into collision at a place where neither commander designed a general engagement. Pender's division formed on the right of Heth's and both pressed forward in the face of volleying musketry and thundering cannon. We found out afterward that the opposing force consisted of the three divisions of the First Corps under the command of General Reynolds. Right bravely did they fight, and being driven from the ridge they formed again on Seminary Ridge, determined to hold it. As our men, on the other hand, were no less determined to take it, the contest became furious and slaughterous. Our loss was heavy, but did not equal that which we inflicted. At last they gave way, and we pursued them to the edge of the town, through the streets of which they hastened until they lodged among the rocky fastness of Cemetery Ridge. I was in all the great battles, from Seven Pines to Chancellorsville, but never had I witnessed a fight so hot and stubborn. On a field of battle the dead and mortally wounded are usually scattered promiscuously on the ground, but here I counted more than fifty fallen heroes lying in a straight line. They belonged, as well as I now remember, to the 150th Pennsylvania. When a regiment stands its ground until it suffers so great a loss, it deserves honor for its courage, for the wounded must have numbered as many as two hundred and fifty. It is a rare thing that a regiment loses so many men in one engagement.

At the same time that we were struggling with the First Corps of Meade's army the divisions of Rhodes and Early on our left were driving the Eleventh Corps before them. But of the gallant part they bore in the battle I make no mention, inasmuch as I am not writing a general history, but only jotting down the things I saw, a small part of which I was.

When the battle had ended and the brigade was standing in line close to the town, Colonel Brockenbrough and I occupied positions in rear of the line; and near us were Capt. Austin Brockenbrough and Lt. Addison Hall Crittenden. First one and then the other of these two gallant officers fell mortally wounded, although no Yankee was in sight. It was the work of sharpshooters concealed in a large wooden building on our left. I took the liberty of causing a company to fire a volley into the house and that put a stop to the murderous villainy.

It was nearly midnight when the brigade fell back a short distance to seek some rest after the severe toils of the day; but notwithstanding the lateness of the hour and our tired condition I proposed to Colonel Brockenbrough that we should look up these two men who were especially dear to us, for Austin was his cousin and Addison was mine. We knew that they had been carried on stretchers from the place where they had been wounded. Our only guides as we slowly rode along in the dark were the fires that indicated the location of the improvised hospitals of the numerous brigades. Inquiring our way, we at last came to the hospital of our brigade where Mr. Meredith, chaplain of the 47th, conducted us to our friends who were lying upon pallets of straw. They knew that their wounds were mortal, but they faced "the last enemy" with the same intrepidity they had manifested on many a sanguinary field. If I had yielded to my emotions, I would have wept over Addison even as a woman weeps. He was named for my mother's only brother; he was pure in heart; and while he was gentle and sweet in manners and disposition, he was as brave as any man who followed Lee across the Potomac.

By some critics General Lee has been censured because he did not continue the battle and attempt to capture Cemetery Ridge on the evening of the first day. I think that the criticism is unjust; for, in the first place, the attempt would have been of doubtful issue, and then if he had tried and succeeded, what advantage would have been gained? It was clearly Meade's rôle to act on the defensive and select the arena upon which the decisive contest must be waged. If Cemetery Ridge had been taken, instead of hurrying his other[Pg 89] corps to that position to form a junction with the First and Eleventh, he would have retired behind Pipe Creek, or chosen some other ground as easily tenable as Cemetery Ridge. The state of things was such that Lee could not retreat without a general engagement, and he could not enter upon it except upon disadvantageous conditions. The tables were turned: as the Yankees had fought at Fredericksburg, so the Rebels had to fight in Pennsylvania.

On the second day Heth's division was not engaged, but occupied the ground near that on which it had fought the day before, close by the seminary in which General Lee had his headquarters. In the afternoon while Longstreet's corps was furiously fighting to wrest Little Round Top from the enemy, he came unattended to where I was standing. Looking down the valley of Plum Run, which separated the armies, there could be seen the flashing of the guns under the pall of smoke that covered the combatants. Now and then making a slight change of position he viewed the scene through his field-glass. His noble face was not lit up with a smile as it was when I saw it after the victory at Chancellorsville, but bore the expression of painful anxiety. Ah, if only his men could seize and hold that coveted elevation! It was the key to the situation, and victory would have been assured.

But that battle was lost, although the divisions of Longstreet performed prodigies of valor. Then and there the issue was decided.

That night Heth's division moved farther to the right. Being directed by Colonel Brockenbrough to ride ahead and pick out a place for his brigade, I went forward in the darkness, ignorant of the lay of the land, until the command to halt was given to me in an undertone. I did not see the man, but was informed that I was just about to ride through the line of Confederate skirmishers, and was cautioned to ride back as quietly as I could, because the Yankee skirmishers were not far in front.

On the morning of the 3d of July, although Ewell's corps on the left had waged a bloody but unsuccessful battle, not a shot was fired by Hill's corps in the center, nor by Longstreet's on the right; but the final struggle was yet to be made. More than a hundred cannon were placed in position, along the line of which lay the eighteen thousand men, who had been selected to make the assault upon Cemetery Ridge. Before the firing began Colonel Brockenbrough told me that when the cannonading should cease we should make the charge.

About one o'clock the guns opened, and for two dreadful hours pounded the adversary's position, being answered by almost as many of his guns. There has never been such a war of artillery on the American continent. Surely this was an exhibition of the "Pride, pomp, and circumstance of glorious War." It was hoped that so terrible a bombardment would demoralize the enemy and thus prepare the way for a successful onslaught of the infantry. During its continuance we lay among the guns, and as soon as their clamor hushed sprang to our feet and began rushing toward the enemy. We had to descend the slope of Seminary Ridge, cross a valley, and ascend the steep slope of Cemetery Ridge, a distance of nearly a mile. If while we were crossing the valley the artillery behind us had been firing at the enemy over our heads, our task would have been less dangerous and more hopeful, but unwisely and unfortunately the caissons had become almost exhausted. As we were ascending the eminence, where cannon thundered in our faces and infantry four lines deep stood ready to deliver their volleys, I noticed that the line of the Confederates resembled the arc of a circle; in other words, the right and the left were more advanced than the center, and were, therefore, the first to become engaged. Brockenbrough's brigade formed the extreme left of the attacking column.

The fame of Pickett's charge on the right has resounded through the world. The Virginians on the left achieved less glory, but they did their best. We came so close to the serried ranks of the Yankees that I emptied my revolver upon them, and we were still advancing when they threw forward a column to attack our unprotected left flank. I feel no shame in recording that out of this corner the men without waiting for orders turned and fled, for the bravest soldiers cannot endure to be shot at simultaneously from the front and side. They knew that to remain, or to advance, meant wholesale death or captivity. The Yankees had a fair opportunity to kill us all, and why they did not do it I cannot tell. Our loss was less than it was in the first day's battle. As in our orderly and sullen retreat we were ascending the ridge from which we had set out, I heard the men saying mournfully, "If Old Jack had been here, it wouldn't have been like this"; and though I said nothing I entertained the same opinion.

Suppose he had been there to turn the enemy's left flank as he did at Gaines' Mill, and again at Chancellorsville!

As I look back upon that final assault at Gettysburg, it seems strange to me that General Lee should have sent eighteen thousand men to dislodge a hundred thousand from a position much stronger than that which Wellington occupied at Waterloo. Perhaps he miscalculated the effect of the cannonade; perhaps he reposed too much confidence in his soldiers. When all was over he found no fault with them, but most magnanimously took the blame of defeat upon himself and endured great mental suffering. Adverse criticism is swallowed up in sympathy for that peerless man.

It was a drawn battle. The Army of Northern Virginia had not been beaten, but it had failed in the attempt to beat the Army of the Potomac. All day long on the 4th of July it remained in view of Meade's army, but he dared not assail it.

There was nothing left but to return to Virginia. On the night of the 4th of July the army began to retreat, and on the 7th it halted near Hagerstown and offered battle, which Meade refused. It seems to me that[Pg 95] he did not press the pursuit as closely and fiercely as he might have done; perhaps he was respecting the valor that he had lately witnessed.

Chapter XI

A prison is a house of care,

A place where none can thrive,

A touchstone true to try a friend,

A grave for men alive.

—Inscription on the Old Prison of Edinburg.

After falling back from Hagerstown the army took up a strong position near the Potomac, extending from Williamsport to Falling Waters. On the night of the 13th of July the retreat to Virginia began. The division of Heth and that of Pender, now commanded by Pettigrew, marched all night long in a drenching rain and over a very muddy road toward Falling Waters, where the engineers had constructed a pontoon bridge across the river. When the morning dawned we were about two miles from the river, and, so far as I know, there was no reason why we should not have kept on and followed the rest of the army over the bridge. Instead of that we halted and formed in line of battle across the road, facing northward, Heth on the right and Pettigrew on the left, well located for defense, being on rising ground and having a valley in front. It was supposed that our cavalry were between us and the enemy, (which was a false supposition,) and, contrary to well-established military rules, no skirmishers were sent to the front. The command was given to stack arms and rest, and the men exhausted by fatigue lay down on the wet ground behind the line of muskets and soon went to sleep. The guns were wet and muddy and many of them were either unloaded or unfit for action. Giving my horse to Charles to be held in the rear until called for, I too fell asleep. We were in no condition for anything except the surprise that startled us from our transitory slumbers.

We were awakened by the firing of the enemy. By the time that the muskets could be retaken from the stack, squadrons of cavalry were upon us. These were easily [Pg 98] repulsed, not, however, until riding down in front of our line they had mortally wounded General Pettigrew at the head of his division. General Heth, riding rapidly along behind our line, was crying out, "Keep cool, men, keep cool!" But judging from the tone of his voice and his manner of riding, he seemed to me to be the only hot man on the field.

The color-bearer of the 47th exclaimed, "Come on, boys; it's nothing but cavalry," and ran forward into the valley, showing more bravery than intelligence or discipline, for infantry does not charge cavalry, and he had no right to advance without an order. The color-bearers of the other regiments of the brigades, not to be outdone, likewise advanced, and some of the bolder spirits followed their respective flags. This action was so unwise that I requested Colonel Brockenbrough to authorize me to recall these brave fellows to their original and better position; but, to my surprise, he directed me to order all the men to join their colors; and this I tried to do, but the men would not obey, saying that their muskets were unfit for action. However, I went myself, though Colonel Brockenbrough and many men of the brigade remained behind. I never saw him again.

A spirited contest ensued, which I shall dignify with the name of the battle of Falling Waters, for a real battle it was, although it is not mentioned in the histories that I have read, and the number engaged was small. On one side were portions of the four regiments of Brockenbrough's brigade, with their bullet-pierced battle flags, and on the other side were dismounted men of the 8th Illinois cavalry regiment armed with their seven-shooting carbines. There were officers present who held higher rank than mine, but, as they knew me to be of the brigade staff, they permitted me to exercise authority over the entire force. For an hour we held the Yankees in check at close quarters.

While the action was in progress I observed that one of our enemies was protected by a large tree in the field, from behind which he stepped frequently and quickly to fire upon us. As he seemed to be taking special aim at me, I requested one of our men, who had a beautiful Colt's rifle, to give me his gun, and I shot at the man the next time he emerged from behind his natural protection. He was not killed, but he darted back without shooting. I handed back the gun. Then, with my right arm around the man, I was with my left arm pointing out the enemy when he fired at us and broke the arm of my comrade that was pressed between us.

Seeing another regiment of cavalry in front, hearing their bugle sound the charge, and knowing that our ammunition was nearly exhausted, I directed all the men to retire as quickly as possible to their former position. I had not once looked back, and I supposed that the two divisions were where we had left them; but they, taking advantage of our defense, had gone across the river. All of a sudden it flashed through my mind that we could neither fight nor run. Further resistance was vain; escape, impossible. I felt angry because we had been sacrificed, and chagrined because we were about to be captured. I had known all along that I might be killed or wounded, but it had never entered my mind that I might be made a prisoner. As we were scattered upon the field and the squadrons came charging among us, a group of men gathered about me were asking, "Captain, what shall we do?" "Stand still," I replied, "and cast your muskets upon the ground." At the same time I unbuckled my useless pistol and sword and cast them from me. After we had surrendered, I regretfully record that a cavalryman discharged his pistol in our midst, but fortunately no one of us was struck. An officer, indignant at an act so cowardly and barbarous, threatened him with death if he should do the like again. That day the Yankees captured on this field and in other places about thirty-five officers and seven hundred men.

The prisoners were escorted to the rear, huddled together, and surrounded by a cordon of armed men. That night I slept with Lt. W. Peyton Moncure on the blanket of one prisoner and covered by that of the other. In the afternoon of the next day, as I was standing near the living wall that surrounded us engaged in conversation with Col. William S. Christian, of the 55th Virginia, and Capt. Lee Russell, of North Carolina, some Federal officers approached and began to talk with us. One of them was the colonel of a New York regiment, (I think it was the 122d); another was the captain of one of his companies, and another was an officer on the staff of General Meade. The Colonel invited us to take supper with him and some of his friends, and the kind and unexpected proposal was gladly accepted, for recently we had had nothing but hard-tack to satiate our hunger.

At sunset he sent a guard to conduct us to his tent, which was large and comfortable. We found the table well supplied with a variety of savory eatables, and we were struck by the contrast of the tent and the table with those of the Rebels.

The Blue and the Gray gathered around that hospitable board as gleeful as boys, and as friendly as men who had been companions from childhood. The supper being ended, a polite negro who looked like an Old Virginia darky, and who acted in the two-fold capacity of cook and butler, cleared away the dishes and supplied their place with cigars and bottles of liquor of several varieties. More than once or twice the bottles passed from hand to hand, and in order to prevent drunkenness I was cautious to pour very sparingly into my tumbler. In the midst of this hilarious scene our Yankee host proposed a health to President Lincoln, which we of the Gray declined to drink; whereupon I offered to substitute a joint health to Abe Lincoln and Jeff. Davis, which they of the Blue rejected. I then proposed the toast, "The early termination of the war to the satisfaction of all concerned," and that was cordially drunk by all. It was nearly midnight when the Colonel told us that if we would promise to go back and deliver ourselves up, he would not call a guard to escort us; and we gave him our word, and bade him good night. There we were in the darkness, our limbs unfettered, our hearts longing for freedom, no Yankee eye upon us; and it is not strange that there flitted across our minds the temptation to steal away and strike out for Virginia; but though our bodies were for the moment free, our souls were bound by something stronger than manacles of steel,—our word of honor. We groped our way back, entered the circle of soldiers who were guarding our fellow-prisoners, and went to sleep on the ground, while our late entertainers reposed upon comfortable cots.

The next morning, July 16, we were hurried along by an unfeeling cavalry escort to a station near Harper's Ferry, and there put into box cars strongly guarded. On our arrival in Washington we were conducted along the streets to the Old Capitol prison. "To what vile uses" had that building come! It was superintended by a renegade Virginian, whose name I am not sorry that I have forgotten; but let me do him the justice to say that he behaved courteously and gave us a plenty to eat. The guard of the prison was the 178th New York regiment, composed of insolent Germans, some of whom could not speak the English language. I came near losing my life by the bayonet of one of them, because he could not understand a request that I made of him. The house was infested by insects whose name I will not call; but the reader will recognize their nature when I characterize them as malodorous, and blood-sucking. We could expel them from our bunks, but not from the walls and the ceiling, from the holes and the cracks of which they swarmed at night, rendering sound sleep impossible.

In a few days after having taken involuntary quarters in the Old Capitol I read with surprise and grief an article in the Baltimore American, headed "Meade versus Lee." General Lee, misinformed by somebody, had reported that there had been no battle at Falling Waters, and that none of his soldiers had been captured except those who had straggled during the night or fallen asleep in barns by the roadside. When he published that statement he knew that there had been no engagement of his ordering, but he did not know that the gallant and accomplished Pettigrew had been wounded on the field, nor that some of his men had kept the enemy in check, while others were thereby afforded the opportunity of safely crossing the river. No; the men who were captured with me were not stragglers: they were taken on the field of battle, and they were as brave and dutiful as any that ever wore the gray. Neither was General Meade's report strictly correct, but it corresponded more closely with the facts. He did not capture a brigade, as he said, but he did take the flags of Brockenbrough's brigade, and enough men of other commands to form one.

During the whole term of my imprisonment I anxiously longed to be exchanged, being willing any day to swap incarceration for the toils and dangers of active military service. In the early part of the war there were some partial exchanges, but as it was prolonged the government at Washington rejected all overtures for a cartel. Throughout the North there were raised loud and false reports that Federal soldiers in Southern prisons were being wantonly maltreated, while the National Government might have restored them to freedom and plenty by agreeing to the exchange of prisoners that was urged repeatedly by the Confederate Government. The refusal was an evidence of the straits to which the Union was pushed, and an act of injustice and cruelty to the prisoners of both sides. It was, moreover, an undesigned but exalted testimony to the valor of Southern soldiers, for it was as if Mr. Stanton, the secretary of war, had said to every man in the Federal armies: "If in the fortunes of war you should be captured, you must run the risk of death in a rebel prison. I will not give a Southern soldier for you,—you are not worth the exchange." Gen. Grant said: "Our men must suffer for the good of those who are contending with the terrible Lee;" and ignoring the claims of humanity and the usages of honorable warfare, he lowered the question to a cold commercial level when he declared that it was "cheaper to feed rebel prisoners than to fight them."

Chapter XII

But now we are in prison and likely long to stay,

The Yankees they are guarding us, no hope to get away;

Our rations they are scanty, 'tis cold enough to freeze,—

I wish I was in Georgia, eating goober peas.

Peas, peas, peas, peas,

Eating goober peas;

I wish I was in Georgia, eating goober peas.

—Stanza of a Prison Song.

Only about two weeks did we abide in the Old Capitol, the officers being transported to Johnson's Island, and the privates to other prisons. Our route was by Harrisburg, and as the train was leaving the city it jumped the track, jolting horribly on the cross-ties, but inflicting no serious injury.

The Sandusky river before it passes through its narrow mouth into Lake Erie widens into a beautiful bay about four miles wide. In this bay is situated Johnson's Island, low and level, and containing three hundred acres. It is not in the middle of the bay, but is on the north side, half a mile from the main land, while on the other side it is three or more miles from the city of Sandusky across the water.

The prison walls enclosed a quadrangular space of several acres, the southern wall running along the margin of the bay and facing Sandusky. They were framed of wooden beams, on the outer side of which, three feet from the top, there was a narrow platform on which the guard kept continual watch. Thirty feet from the wall all around on the inside there was driven a row of whitewashed stobs, beyond which no prisoner was allowed to go on pain of being shot by the sentinels. At night the entire space within was illuminated by lamps and reflectors fixed against the walls.

Within the walls there were eleven large wooden buildings of uniform size, two stories high. The first four were partitioned into small rooms, and were sheathed; the remaining seven had two rooms on each floor, and they afforded no protection against the weather except the undressed clapboards that covered them. In each house the upper story was reached by an outside flight of steps. In the larger rooms some sixty or seventy men were huddled together. Around the sides bunks were framed on pieces of scantling that extended from floor to ceiling, arranged in three tiers, so that a floor space of six feet by four sufficed for six men. My cotton tick was never refilled, and after doing service for many months it became flat and hard. Our quarters and accommodations were such as the Yankees thought good enough for rebels and traitors, but in summer we were uncomfortably and unhealthily crowded, and in winter we suffered from the cold, because one stove could not warm so large and windy an apartment. Many a winter night, instead of undressing, I put an old worn overcoat over the clothes I had worn during the day.

At first I "put up" in block No. 9, afterward in No. 8, and toward the end of my imprisonment in No. 3, which was much more comfortable.

In summer, water was obtained from a shallow well, but in winter, when the bay was frozen, a few men from each mess were permitted to go out of the gate in the afternoon and dip up better water from holes cut through the ice. On these occasions a strong guard extended around the prisoners from one side of the gate to the other.

From the time of my capture until the fall of the year the rations were fairly good and sufficient, but then they were mercilessly reduced, upon the pretext of retaliation for the improper treatment of Union prisoners in the South. The bread and meat rations were diminished by a half, while coffee, sugar, candles, and other things were no longer supplied. We did our own cooking, the men of each mess taking it by turns, but the bread was baked in ovens outside and was brought in a wagon every morning. A pan of four loaves was the daily allowance for sixteen men. When I got my fourth of a loaf in the morning I usually divided it into three slices, of which one was immediately eaten and the others reserved for dinner and supper; but when the time came for the closing meal I had no bread, for hunger had previously claimed it all. But for some clothes, provisions, and money that were sent to me by kind friends residing in Kentucky and Maryland I think that I could not have lived to witness the end of the war. There was not enough nutriment in the daily ration to support vigorous health, and it was barely sufficient to sustain life. I believe that a few of the prisoners succumbed to disease and died because they had an insufficiency of nourishing food. Bones were picked from ditches, if perchance there might be upon them a morsel of meat. I was begged for bread, when I was hungry for the want of it. All the rats were eaten that could be caught in traps ingeniously contrived. When prejudice is overcome by gnawing hunger, a fat rat makes good eating, as I know from actual and enjoyable mastication.

For a time we were permitted to obtain the news of the outside world through the New York World and the Baltimore Gazette, but these were suppressed; and then we had to depend upon a little Sandusky sheet and the Baltimore American, which vilified the South and claimed for every battle a Union victory.

How did we while the time away? Well, we organized a minstrel band, singing clubs, and debating societies; we had occasional lectures and exchanged books in a so-called reading room; we had two rival base-ball teams, and we played the indoor games of chess, checkers, cards, and dominoes. I spent much time in reading the Bible, besides some of Scott's novels and the charming story of Picciola.

On Sunday there were Bible classes, and sometimes sermons by men who had gone from the pulpit into the army. Among them were a Methodist colonel from Missouri, a Baptist colonel from Mississippi, and a Baptist captain from Virginia. At one time evangelistic services were held in a lower room of block No. 5, and a number of converts confessed Jesus Christ as Lord and Saviour, and declared their denominational preference. Those who decided to be Baptists were permitted, under guard, to go out to the shore and were baptized in the bay by Captain Littleberry Allen, of Caroline county, Virginia;

the rest could find within the walls as much water as they considered necessary for the ordinance.

Block No. 6 was set apart for a hospital, into which a prisoner might go in case of sickness. It was superintended by a Federal surgeon, but a large part of the prescribing was done by Confederate officers who had been practicing physicians. The nursing was performed by the patients' more intimate friends, who took it by turns day and night. I have a sorrowful recollection of sitting up one night to wait on Captain Scates of Westmoreland county, and to administer the medicines prescribed by the doctors. The ward was silent save for occasional groans, the lights were burning dimly, and there was no companion watching with me. About midnight the emaciated sufferer died, passing away as quietly as when one falls into healthy slumbers. I closed his eyes and remained near the body until the grateful dawn of morning. Guarded by soldiers we went to the cemetery without the walls, and committed the body to the ground, far away from his family and native land.

Nearly all the men confined on Johnson's Island were officers, of every rank from lieutenant to major-general, and numbering about twenty-six hundred. They represented all parts of the South and nearly every occupation, whether manual or professional. They were men of refinement,—ingenious, daring; and they were enclosed in this prison because it was secured no less by an armed guard than by the surrounding water.

Every man was trying to devise some method of escape, but only a few succeeded, not only because the difficulty was great, but also because there were spies among us. Three men tunneled out from Block No. 1, only to find themselves surrounded by Yankee soldiers. Captain Cole, a portly man, became jammed in the passage, and was somewhat like Abe Lincoln's ox that was caught and held on a fence, unable to kick one way or gore the other. The incident furnished the theme of another minstrel song, with the chorus, "If you belong to Gideon's band."

I had a secret agreement with Captain John Stakes, of the 40th Virginia, that if either saw a way of escape he would let the other know. Many a time with longing eyes we looked upon a sloop that used to tie up for the night at a wharf near the island. If we only could get to it! And so we began a tunnel under block No. 9, but finding that our labors were discovered by a spy, we were constrained to desist.

Two men filed saw teeth on the backs of case knives, and on a rainy, dark, and windy night they crawled down a ditch to the wall on the bay shore, and cut their way out; but they were captured and brought back.

There were a few successful escapes. One man, smarter than the rest of us, when we went to a vessel to fill our ticks with straw concealed himself under what remained in the hold and was carried back to Sandusky, whence he wended his stealthy flight. Colonel B. L. Farinholt, of Virginia, got away in a very artful manner, an account of which has been published. In January, 1865, when the thermometer registered 15° below zero and an arctic northwest wind was blowing furiously Captain Stakes took me aside and told me in whispers that he and five others were going out that night, and that they had agreed that I might go with them. I answered that if the Yankees were to throw open all the gates and grant permission, I would not in my feeble health and with clothes so insufficient, depart in such bitter weather. When the hour came those six men rushed to the wall, and setting up against it a bench, on which rungs had been nailed, climbed over. They were not shot at, perhaps because the sentries, not expecting such an attempt, had taken refuge from the cold in their boxes. On the thick ice that begirt the island they crossed over on the north side and gained the mainland. Captain Robinson, of Westmoreland, and three others with him, hiding in the daytime and traveling at night, after enduring many hardships arrived in Canada, where they were clothed and fed and supplied with money. Taking shipping at Halifax, they ran the blockade and landed in Wilmington, North Carolina. One of the six men was recaptured by a detective on a train in New York. My friend Stakes was overtaken the next morning and brought back so badly frostbitten that it became necessary to amputate parts of some of his fingers.

By some means, I know not how, information was received in the prison that certain agents of the Confederate government in Canada would come to the island in steamboats captured on Lake Erie to release the prisoners. It was agreed that when the approached and blew a horn the prisoners would storm the walls and overpower the guards. We, therefore, organized ourselves into companies and regiments and waited anxiously for the sight of the boats and the sound of the horn. Though we had no arms, except such as the rage of the moment might supply, and did not doubt that some of us would be killed, we were ready to fulfil our part of the desperate contract; and we felt no doubt of success, for the Hoffman Battalion that composed our guard had never been in battle nor heard the rebel yell. The expected rescuers never came. There must have been some real foundation for the proposed movement, for very soon the guard was reinforced by a veteran brigade, and the gunboat Michigan came and anchored near the island and showed her threatening portholes.

Chapter XIII

'Mid pleasures and palaces though we may roam,

Be it ever so humble, there's no place like home;

A charm from the skies seems to hallow us there,

Which seek through the world, is ne'er met with elsewhere.

—Payne.

If one longs for home while roaming amidst pleasures and palaces, how much more intense, suppose you, must be the nostalgia of the soldier confined in a far distant prison?

March 14, 1865, was one of the happiest days of my life. After a captivity of twenty months, I was led out of the prison with the three hundred others, conducted to a steamboat, and homeward bound transported to Sandusky. The thick ice that for three months had covered the bay was floating in broken pieces on the surface, through which the boat struggled with so much difficulty that I feared it would be necessary to put back to[Pg 122] the island; but the trip was made at the expense of some broken paddles. Why we were selected rather than our less fortunate compatriots I cannot guess, unless it was to save the annoyance and the expense of burial, for some of our party had been wounded, others as well as myself, had recently recovered from serious sickness, and all were adjudged to be unfit for military service; or perhaps there was the same number in Southern prisons that for special reasons the Federal War Office desired to have exchanged.

The train that was to convey us southward was made up of box-cars, upon the floors of which there was a thin covering of straw. We were so crowded that we all could not lie down at the same time. The sleepers lay with their heads at the sides of the cars, while their legs interlaced in the middle. We took the situation in good humor, and slept by turns, those who could not find room standing amidst entangled legs and feet. Thus we traveled several days and nights, our train being frequently switched for the passage of regular trains. Our route was by Bellaire to Baltimore, or rather to Locust Point, where we took passage on a steamboat for James river. Having landed the next day, we walked across a neck of land formed by a bend of the river to the wharf where a boat from Richmond was expected to meet us. A company of negroes made a show of conducting us across the neck, though a company of children armed with cornstalks would have been equally efficient.

We had not long to wait until the smokestack of the Confederate steamboat could be seen winding along as she tracked the serpentine course of the river. As she neared the wharf the band on board struck up that sweetest of tunes,—"Home, Sweet Home." Some of my companions laughed, some threw their caps into the air, others hurrahed, while my own emotions were expressed only by tears of joy that coursed down my cheeks. When, however, the music glided into the exhilarating notes of "Dixie" I joined in the cheering that mingled with the strain.

We arrived in Richmond on the 22d of March, the eighth day after we had started. I was pained to notice in the city so many signs of delapidation and poverty, and to learn that Confederate money had depreciated to the point of sixty for one. The captain's salary that the government owed me for two years was worth only about fifty dollars in specie, which a friend in the treasury department advised me to collect at once, inasmuch as he thought that the capital would be soon evacuated. I took him for a timorous prophet, and told him I would wait until I rejoined the army, when I should need it. I did not know, as he did, the impoverished and critical condition of the Confederacy.

I was not exchanged, but "paroled for thirty days unless sooner exchanged." I set out for the Northern Neck in company with Lieutenant Purcell, of Richmond county, and Captain Stakes, of Northumberland. We rode on a train as far as Hanover and then struck out afoot across the country. Notwithstanding the fact that one of my companions limped on a leg that had been wounded at Gettysburg and the other was a little lame from frosted toes, it taxed all my powers to keep up with them. If I had rejoiced to see the James, I was happier still to set foot once more upon the bank of the Rappahannock. When we had crossed over we went to the home of Lieutenant Purcell, where we spent the night, and the next day, Monday, March 27, I arrived at home. I supposed that I should take them by surprise, but somehow they had received intelligence of my coming; and as I approached the house I found them all lined up in the yard, white and black. "And they began to be merry."

I found John in the stable, having been ridden home by my faithful man, Charles Wesley, who supposed that he had left me dead at Falling Waters.

On the 14th of April, Good Friday, when I was thinking of returning to Richmond to inquire whether I had been exchanged and was still hoping for the independence of the Southern Confederacy, I attended religious services at a church in the neighborhood. When these had been concluded and the congregation were talking as usual in the yard a messenger arrived with a newspaper, which the Yankees had sent ashore from one of their gunboats, and which contained the details of General Lee's surrender of his army five days previously at Appomattox. My heart sank within me. My fondest hopes were crushed. The cause for which I had so often exposed my life, and for which so many of my friends had died, had sunk into the gloomy night of defeat.

I was thankful that out of the horrid conflict I had escaped with my life, a gray coat, and a silver quarter of a dollar. Although I had participated in all the battles that were fought by the Army of Northern Virginia, I was never seriously hurt. At Manassas one bullet struck my leg, and another forcibly wrenched my sword from my hand. At Chancellorsville a bomb exploded just in front of me, making a hole in the ground and covering me with dirt, the pieces flying away with discordant noises. Countless balls whizzed by my ears, and men fell all around me, some of them while touching my side. Am I not justified in appropriating the words of David addressed to Jehovah, "Thou hast covered my head in the day of battle?"

Withdrawal from the Union was the right of the Southern States, as appears from the history of the making and adoption of the federal constitution; and great was the provocation to use it. It is not, however, always wise,—either for persons or communities,—to exercise their rights. Secession in the year 1860 was a hot headed and stupendous political blunder,—a blunder recognized by the majority of the people of Virginia, who refused to follow the example of her southern sisters until there was forced upon her the cruel alternative of waging war either against them or against the States of the North.

Though secession was a grievous error, nevertheless the war that was waged by the Federal Government was a crime against the constitution, humanity, and God. But now, as we view the present and retrospect the past, who may say that all has not turned out for the best? We find consolation in the belief that the Lord's hand has shaped our destiny, and we meekly submit to his overruling providence.

"If it were done, when 'tis done, then 'twere well

It were done quickly."

But the war, like Duncan's murder, was not done after it was done. There supervened the unnecessary, vindictive, and malignant reconstruction acts of the Federal Congress.

On the 14th of April, only nine days after Lee had surrendered, a great calamity befell the South in the foolish and infamous assassination of President Lincoln, who was the only man who could have restrained the rage of such men as Sumner in the Senate and Stephens in the House of Representatives. The hatred of the Northern politicians was intensified by the supposition that his death was instigated by Southern men, and it did not abate even after they were convinced that the supposition was unfounded.

It is a singular fact that while the war was in progress the acts of secession were considered null and void, and the Southern States were declared to be parts of an indissoluble union, but when the war had ended they were dealt with as alien commonwealths and conquered territories. For four years Virginia was not a co-equal State in the Union but "Military District No. 1," governed by a Federal general, who appointed the local officers in the several counties. The affairs of the State were managed by carpetbaggers in close agreement with despicable scalawags and ignorant negroes. The elective franchise was granted to the emancipated slaves regardless of character or intelligence, while it was denied to many white men. In Lancaster county the negroes had a registered majority of a hundred voters; it was represented in a constitutional convention by a carpetbagger, and after the adoption of the constitution it was represented in the Legislature by a negro. To injury were added hatred and insult. It was not enough that the South was conquered, it must be humiliated by African domination!

The Southern people did not go to war—war came to them. Not to gain military glory did they fight, although this meed must be awarded to them. Nor was the perpetuation of African slavery the object for which they took up arms, for in Virginia nineteen-twentieths of the citizens owned no slaves, and there was perhaps the same proportion in the other States of the Confederacy. Neither was it for conquest that they so long waged the unequal contest; for though they twice crossed the Potomac it was not to gain an acre of territory, but only to relieve their own beleaguered capital. From first to last it was a purely defensive struggle to maintain for themselves the freedom they cheerfully accorded to other communities, and to make good the inherited belief that "all just government derives its power from the consent of the governed." They simply resisted subjugation by a hostile government whose right to rule them they denied.

As we review the history of that gigantic struggle we are not surprised that the South was subdued, the only wonder being that it was not sooner done. It required two and a quarter millions of soldiers four years to overcome one-third of that number. The South had no navy to open her ports, no commerce for her products, no foundries for the manufacture of arms. During the first year there were not muskets enough to supply her volunteers, though later on sufficient numbers were taken on the fields of battles, fifty-two cannon and thirty thousand small arms being captured in the battles around Richmond, besides the many thousands that were taken in subsequent engagements.

That the South for so long a time resisted the attempts of her powerful enemy, and during that period gained so many remarkable victories, is attributable to the skill of her generals and the valor of her soldiers. In these respects only was the advantage on her side.

The fame of her generals has spread throughout the world, and their campaigns enrich the text-books of the military students of Europe and Asia. They rank with the most famous commanders that ever led armies to victory. Their names are immortal, and their memory is enshrined not only in poetry and history, in marble and bronze, but also in the admiration of mankind and in the affections of the Southern people.

But what could strategy have achieved unless there had been soldiers to make it effective? The men had confidence in their commanders and were responsive to their genius. In attack they exhibited impulsive courage, and in defense possessed unyielding firmness. They made days and places forever historic, when their pay was money in little more than name, their garments torn, their rations coarse and scant. Footsore they charged against the dense Blue lines, or made those rapid marches that bewildered opposing forces.

When the end had come both officers and men surrendered as they had fought,—without mental reservation. Sadly they furled and yielded up the bullet-riddled battleflags they had carried so proudly. Now while they manfully accept the hard arbitrament of war, and yield unaffected loyalty to the United States, they make no confession of criminality. While the war continued they were asserting what they believed was a God-given right, and now they recall with pride the valor and victories of the Southern armies.

Those armies are rapidly disappearing from the land they loved so well. Many of the men fell in battle, and many died in prisons and hospitals, and since the close of the war more of them have fallen asleep in peaceful homes. Those who have departed and those who survive will not want a eulogist while one remains; and when the last of the men who wore the gray shall have joined his comrades beyond the river of death, coming generations will celebrate their heroism and scatter flowers upon the mounds that mark the places where their ashes repose.

Confederate Dead: W.O.B. Branch, Earl Van Dorn, J.H. Morgan, W. Barksdale, A.S. Johnston, J.E.B. Stuart, "Stonewall" Jackson, J.S. Bowen, Zollicoffer, L. Tilghman, A.J. Jenkins, Ben McCollough, Leonidas Polk, and G.J. Rains

References and Resources

These resources were valuable in preparing this edition. We urge anyone in possession of letters, diaries and memoirs from the Civil War era to share these with others through these websites and libraries.

Soldier Studies. http://www.soldierstudies.org/index.php
Civil War Gazette. http://www.civilwargazette.faithsite.com/content.asp?ListSG=5976
Dakota State University. http://www.homepages.dsu.edu/jankej/civilwar/diaries.htm
Civil War Letters. http://civil.war-letters.com/
Project Gutenberg. http://www.gutenberg.org/catalog/
Library of Congress. "Civil War Photographs". http://www.loc.gov/pictures/collection/cwp/
Library of Congress. "Prints and Photographs". http://www.loc.gov/rr/print/
Virginia Military Archives. http://www.vmi.edu/archives.aspx?id=3719

Photo credits:

"Confederate capitol" surrounded by portraits of confederate governing officials, LC-USZ62-14625
Confederate battery with Federal transports in the background, LC-DIG-cwpb-01019
Gabriel J. Rains, C.S.A., LC-DIG-cwpb-07529
Rappahannock River, Virginia. Bridge across the Rappahannock, LC-DIG-cwpb-00225
Sunken ship near Jamestown, LC-DIG-cwpb-02870
Famous Confederate commanders of the Civil War, LC-DIG-pga-02748
Robert E. Lee's home in Richmond, Va., LC-DIG-cwpb-02764
Lieut. General Thomas J. Jackson, LC-USZ62-1625
Fort Burnham (previously Confederate Fort Harrison), Va., Confederate Picket Line and Fort in background, LC-USZ62-61354
General Buell's map of the battle-field of Shiloh. [April 6-7, 1862], Library of Congress
Fort Burnham (previously Confederate Fort Harrison), Va., Confederate Picket Line and Fort in background, LC-USZ62-61354
Battle of Franklin, LC-DIG-pga-01852
Gen. J.E. Johnston, C.S.A., LC-DIG-cwpb-06281
William Hugh McDowell and Letter from Robert McDowell, May 30, 1964,, Virginia Military Archives. http://www.vmi.edu/archives.aspx?id=3719
Robert E. Lee, LC-B8175- 1
General Lee's Headquarters, LC-USZ62-11317
G.W.C. Lee, Robert E. Lee, Walter Taylor, LC-DIG-cwpb-06234
The naval engagement between the Merrimac and the Monitor at Hampton Roads - on the 9th of March 1862, LC-USZ62-150
Deck and turret of U.S.S. Monitor, LC-DIG-cwpb-01058
Railroad with supplies at Atlanta, LC-DIG-stereo-2s01399
Tredegar Iron Works, LC-USZC4-7968
Charleston, S.C. Confederate torpedoes, shot, and shell in the Arsenal yard, LC-DIG-cwpb-02382
U.S. iron clad gunboat Essex, LC-DIG-stereo-1s0282
Com. Farragut's fleet, LC-USZC2-2125
Benjamin F. Butler, Maj. Gen., LC-DIG-cwpb-04895
View of Harper's Ferry, LC-DIG-cwpb-0387
Jefferson Davis and his staff, LOC

Pontoon bridges across the Potomac, LC-B8171-7484
Confederate Dead, LC-DIG-cwpb-07607

Insert credits:
Death of Colonel Ellsworth, LC-USZ62-79796
Seal of the Confederate States, http://www.loc.gov/pictures/item/2003688757/
Jefferson Davis, first president of the new Southern Confederacy, LC-USZ62-129742
Mrs. Jefferson Davis, full-length studio portrait, standing, facing slightly right with left hand resting on the back of a chair, LC-DIG-ppmsca-07786
Confederate White House, home of Jefferson Davis in Richmond, LC-D4-43165
Confederate money, LOC, LOT 4421-D
The ordnance armory, Charleston, South Carolina, the volunteer troops trying the arms, LC-USZ6-1909
Deck of iron-clad gunboat Galena, showing stack damaged by fire from Fort Darling, LC-B8171-0652
Thomas Jonathan Jackson, full-length portrait, on horseback, facing left, holding up hat in his right hand, LC-USZC4-4990
General Robert E. Lee on horseback flanked by Stonewall Jackson and Jeb Stuart, riding in review before a crowd of cheering soldiers., LC-DIG-ppmsca-22750
Great Battle of Murfreesboro, Tennessee between the Union Forces, under General Rosecrans and the Rebel Army under General Bragg, LC-USZC2-2510
Atlanta, before being burnt, taken by order of General Sherman, LC-USZC4-5757
The Rebel forces under General Jackson advancing upon the Rappahannock Station at the river, LC-USZ62-93011
Mrs. Robert E. Lee, LC-USZ62-100483
General Robert E. Lee, C.S.A., LC-DIG-cwpbh-03115
Unidentified soldier in Confederate frock coat with gold trim, The Liljenquist Collection, Library of Congress, LC-DIG-ppmsca-40604
Unidentified soldier in Confederate uniform, The Liljenquist Collection, Library of Congress, LC-DIG-ppmsca-37159
Struggle on a bridge during the retreat from Manassas, LC-DIG-ppmsca-1992
Battle of Corinth, LC-DIG-pga-01847